THE AFGHAN ECONOMY

SOCIAL, ECONOMIC AND POLITICAL STUDIES OF THE MIDDLE EAST
ÉTUDES SOCIALES, ÉCONOMIQUES ET POLITIQUES DU MOYEN ORIENT

VOLUME XV

MAXWELL J. FRY

THE AFGHAN ECONOMY

LEIDEN
E. J. BRILL
1974

THE AFGHAN ECONOMY

MONEY, FINANCE, AND THE CRITICAL CONSTRAINTS TO ECONOMIC DEVELOPMENT

BY

MAXWELL J. FRY

LEIDEN

E. J. BRILL

1974

330.9581
F9472

Le but de la collection est de faciliter la communication entre le grand public international et les spécialistes des sciences sociales étudiant le Moyen-Orient, et notamment ceux qui y résident. Les ouvrages sélectionnés porteront sur les phénomènes et problèmes contemporains: sociaux, culturels, économiques et administratifs. Leurs principales orientations relèveront de la théorie générale, de problématiques plus précises, et de la politologie: aménagement des institutions et administration des affaires publiques.

The series is designed to serve as a link between the international reading public and social scientists studying the contemporary Middle East, notably those living in the area. Works to be included will be characterized by their relevance to actual phenomena and problems: whether social, cultural, economic, political or administrative. They will be theory-oriented, problem-oriented or policy-oriented.

78-1855
ISBN 90 04 03986 4

CONTENTS

TABLES

FIGURES

PREFACE

At the end of an eventful eighteen months in Afghanistan, many pleasant memories vie for predominance: a mountain view from every window; walking holidays in Bamian and Nuristan; skiing in the Hindu Kush; field trips to all the major towns in the country; colourful nomads on the move; the variety of people in the bazaars; and the friendly social and working relations with many individuals both in and outside the Government. During this period the structure and contents of this book took shape. It started with work on the financial system, much of which was presented as working papers to the Financial Development Committee for which the Minister of Finance asked me to act as Secretary at the beginning of 1973. The first six months of this year were spent in this capacity preparing background reports, etc., for the Committee. Regretfully, it was one of the casualties of the July coup. The last six months have, therefore, been devoted exclusively to writing this book.

There are many people whom I wish to thank for their help in this endeavour. Numerous bankers and civil servants have been most kind in supplying information. For help on the analytical side, I would like to thank Raymond Hooker of the United States Agency for International Development, Stig von Post, Resident Representative of the International Monetary Fund, and Edward Shaw of Stanford University. For conscientious research assistance throughout the past eighteen months, I am very grateful to Mir Aqa Kabiri. Acknowledgement is due to the British Social Science Research Council, the City University, London, and the United States Agency for International Development Mission to Afghanistan for their financial support, without which this study could not have been undertaken. Finally, my heartfelt thanks go to my wife, Celia, for typing every word of several provisional drafts as well as the final manuscript.

Kabul   *Maxwell Fry*
December 1973

NOTE

In transliteration, the spellings at present in most common use in Afghanistan have been adopted. This may frustrate Persian scholars but is hopefully more convenient for readers familiar with Afghanistan. However, there is still considerable scope for choice in using this criterion. For example, at present Bank Millie, the oldest commercial bank in the country, itself uses three spellings, namely Bank Millie, Banke Millie and Bank Melli, interchangeably. In the past, the Bank has used a variety of alternative spellings, as have other authors, one of the most popular being Bank-i-Milli. Although the form Bank-e-Melli is probably the closest phonetic transliteration, the spelling Bank Millie has been adopted here since it is used on the Bank's most recent balance sheets and appears on a set of blue signs, one of which is displayed outside each of its domestic branches. The forerunner of Bank Millie was the Shirkat-i-Sahami-i-Afghan or the Afghan Joint Stock Company. For some unknown reason, it has frequently been spelt in the plural, Shirkat-i-Ashami-i-Afghan. There is a particular problem over the choice of K and Q in certain cases. Thus, earlier reports mention Qandahar while contemporary writings refer to Kandahar. Karakul, similar to and sometimes known as astrakhan or Persian lamb, the skin of very young or unborn lambs from an Asiatic breed of sheep, is perhaps more correctly, though rarely, spelt qarakul.

Where dates appear, the Afghan *Shamsi* (solar) date is given first followed by the Gregorian date in brackets. Since the *Shamsi* calendar is based on the solar year, i.e. 21 March to 20 March, corresponding Gregorian dates can be either 621 or 622 years greater than the *Shamsi* date. End of year figures will show 622 years' difference, while mid-year estimates only 621. Where an entire year is referred to the 621 year difference is shown.

The alphanumeric code in square brackets relates to the list of materials in the bibliography at the end of the book. Afs 1 million = Afs 1,000,000; Afs 1 billion = Afs 1,000,000,000. Afs is the abbreviation of Afghanis, the monetary unit of Afghanistan. It is subdivided into 100 Puls. A common unit of weight is the seer; one seer equals 7.1 kilograms. All logarithms used in the text are natural logarithms unless otherwise stated.

CHAPTER ONE

INTRODUCTION

i. *Development Potential and Five Critical Constraints*

This book analyses some of the factors which have prevented rapid economic growth in Afghanistan. In particular, it is concerned with five determinants of Afghanistan's development potential. Because this potential is low, these are the critical constraints to development. Unless attention is focused first on them, development effort and expenditure in other directions cannot be expected to produce significant results or accelerate the rate of growth.

Much that is written below is critical. The purpose of this book, however, is to reconstruct the economic history of Afghanistan during the Musahiban period, 1308-1352 (1929-1973), and so illuminate past mistakes to be avoided in the future. Hopefully, the new Republican Government established on 26 Saratan 1352 (17 July 1973) may find such analysis of some use in its attempts to remove the constraints to economic development. The findings of the analysis can be interpreted optimistically. The critical constraints are, in the main, policy variables; they can be overcome. Indeed, their removal is not a question of vast financial outlay but of determination on the part of the nation's leaders.

This book has been written in the hope that the analysis will be useful to those planning Afghanistan's development in the future. Therefore, an attempt has been made to produce constructive rather than destructive criticism. Positive recommendations have, however, largely been deferred to the final chapter since the body of the book is designed to elucidate in detail the factors which have constrained economic development to date. This follows the tenet that too many recommendations in the past based on misleading assumptions and insufficient data have been presented to the Government by the army of foreign advisors in Afghanistan. Given the dearth of hard facts, the analysis and conclusions put forward below must still be used with caution. It is hoped, however, that the documentation of data sources throughout will be of value in this regard.

In 1968, Adelman and Morris published the results of a comparative study of 73 countries designed to measure development potential [A2]. Using discriminant analysis, the study finds five indicators of development potential:

A. The degree of improvement in financial institutions as measured by the growth in private savings flowing through the banking system and the growth in bank lending on medium and long term to the private sector;

B. The degree of improvement in physical overhead capital as measured by the improvement in transport systems;

C. The degree of improvement in agricultural productivity achieved through the application of "modern" inputs and techniques;

D. The degree of modernisation of outlook measured in part by the extent to which development programmes have gained support of both the rural and urban population;

E. The degree of commitment by the leadership to promoting economic development as measured by the existence of concerted efforts by heads of agencies involved in central guidance of the economy to promote economic growth, by whether the planning effort included serious attempts to alter institutional arrangements which clearly blocked the achievement of planning goals, and by the existence of a national plan or planning agency.

The absence of any improvement in financial institutions, i.e. financial development, is briefly mentioned in the next chapter and is discussed at length in Chapter V. There it is shown that financial development has not occurred partly because Government activities and policies have impeded it, partly because the banks themselves have not been interested in change and partly because the external environment has not been conducive to the expansion of banking. It is also shown that the private sector has been squeezed as the Government acquired an increasing share of domestic credit to finance development expenditure.

There is no railway system in Afghanistan. The improvements in the road system, however, are analysed in Chapter III. Despite a sizable investment in roads over the past two decades, the total length of motorable roads in 1351 (1972) was only 29 miles per 1,000 square miles [U19, p. 9]. The rate of improvement has been greatly reduced since the early 1340s (1960s) when the foreign aid input into road building reached a peak.

The negligible improvement in agricultural productivity is discussed in Chapters III and IV. The development expenditure in the agricultural sector has been predominantly on large scale infrastructure projects rather than on small scale on-farm investment which might have rapidly increased output. Furthermore, the very limited institutional credit facilities have prevented farmers from realising modest but highly productive investment opportunities. Following two years of drought, the Government realised that priority had to be given to raising agricultural productivity. To this end, fertiliser imports were substantially increased in 1351 (1972). The Afghan Fertiliser Company, able to obtain fertiliser using a loan from the United States Agency for International Development, was established and the Agricultural Development Bank agreed to extend credit for fertiliser purchases in 1352 (1973). Unfortunately, these last two developments took place during a year of exceptional precipitation. This resulted in wheat prices so low that many farmers were deterred from obtaining fertiliser for the next year's crop. In addition, fertiliser prices exploded in the same year. The combination of low wheat and high fertiliser prices has produced serious problems for the Afghan Fertiliser Company, as yet unresolved. Projections for future fertiliser demand have had to be revised downwards.

As shown in Chapters IV and VI, there has been little support for Afghanistan's development programmes and the commitment on the part of the country's leaders to economic development appears to have decreased over the past decade. The lack of support has been due to the absence of any clear benefits to the majority of the population from development projects. The lack of commitment to economic development was seen in the unwillingness of Zahir Shah or his Government to make institutional changes repeatedly shown to be prerequisites for successful development, the demise of the economic plans and the low fiscal effort resulting in 80 per cent of the development expenditure being financed by foreign aid. The necessity on the donor's part to hold out only extremely limited expectations of results under such circumstances has been expressed as follows:

> .... achievement of a substantial and cumulative process of development depends essentially on efforts and conditions in the less-developed country itself. If local conditions are unfavourable and local efforts are insufficient or misapplied, assistance can make only limited contributions to economic and social advance, if any. [D6, p. 3]

It is not, therefore, surprising to find Afghanistan classified in the Low Prospect Group in the Adelman and Morris study [A2, p. 262].

A real commitment to planned economic development in Afghanistan cannot be said to exist until several decisive institutional changes have been made. The most important of these must consist of measures to improve administration. These are also critical in any programme of financial development. Middle and lower level executives need rigorous training in simple office procedures and many more Afghans who have received higher education abroad have to be enticed to return home. This requires not only a realistic look at remuneration, e.g. following the Iranian example of the 1950s, in which a special cadre of Iranians were recruited to form the Plan Organisation at higher salaries than other civil servants [B3, Chapter 2], but also the prospect of rewarding job content in the form of reasonable independence and responsibility. A successful start on systematic project preparation and evaluation will be the indication that the necessary changes are being made at the higher levels. An overhaul of civil service personnel policies and the introduction of training will indicate efforts to improve middle and lower levels. The latter measures applied within the financial institutions together with the granting of autonomy in personnel policies to the Government banks will be a major step in the direction of financial development. Further, legal reform is a *sine qua non* for rapid expansion of bank lending to the private sector. Such measures can all be regarded as indicators of a real commitment to development. They do not form a comprehensive list of all that needs to be done. They do, however, comprise those for which high priority must be given.

Recent research conducted by the Development Assistance Directorate of the Organisation for Economic Co-operation and Development has attempted to measure the stage of development in 82 underdeveloped countries [D6]. The index which is produced places Afghanistan at the sixty-eighth position with a per capita GNP equivalent of $100, compared to seventy-third position with a World Bank estimated figure of $70. Of most interest in the Development Assistance Directorate's study is the finding that the volume of investment is not strongly correlated with the stage of development [D6, p. 113]. Furthermore, other cross-country comparisons also show that the relationship between the volume of investment and growth, although positive, is weak [D6, p. 28]. The implication is important in that it suggests that Afghanistan's low stage of development *per se* is no impediment to rapid economic growth. In other words, should the factors identified by Adelman and Morris [A2] as critical determinants of development potential be altered in appropriate respects, a high growth rate could be achieved despite the low stage of Afghanistan's development at the outset. Given that the efficiency of resource utilisation is considerably more important than the amount of investment, as shown in Chapter IV, this conclusion is not surprising. Only the volume of investment, not its efficiency, is determined by the stage of development.

In sum, therefore, without precedent changes in the five Adelman-Morris indicators, no amount of development expenditure is likely to be effective in producing rapid economic growth. Hence, the reason for stress throughout this book on these five critical constraints to development. With appropriate action to remove these constraints, rapid growth seems possible despite Afghanistan's low starting position.

ii. *Summary of Subsequent Chapters*

The next chapter contains a selective economic history of Afghanistan over the past forty years. In it, an attempt is made to trace long run and cyclical movements in economic activity over this period. The final section presents estimates of Gross National Product for 1314-1352 (1935-1973). The important points which emerge include indicators of the damage to the embryonic modern sector suffered as a result of the Second World War in which Afghanistan played no part, the protracted period of recovery, and the decelerating rate of growth despite large inflows of foreign aid from the second half of the 1330s (1950s) to the second half of the 1340s (1960s).

Chapter III looks at the economy as a heterogeneous system with only weak links between its separate sectors. This approach is pursued at three levels. First, the Government, the modern private sector led by the Bank Millie Group and the bazaar or traditional economy are viewed as separate parts within the economy as a whole. Where there has been interaction it is shown to have been one of antagonism. The ground rules in this struggle have promoted destructive rather than productive competition. Second, the subsistence agricultural economy and industry are analysed, the former because at least 50 per cent of Gross Domestic Product arises in this sector, the latter because it illustrates the problems of modernising the economy. The third view is of geographic fragmentation. Here the critical transport constraint is examined. The final section of this chapter presents a generalisation and explanation of the phenomenon of economic fragmentation.

Development planning has existed in one form or other throughout the past four decades. It is, however, only with the plans starting in 1335 (1956) that Chapter IV is concerned. The important issue taken up here is Afghanistan's commitment to economic development through planning. The conclusion is reached that on this critical determinant of development potential a low score must be recorded.

The financial system is described in detail in Chapter V. A survey of the financial institutions and central banking is followed by an analysis of the problems of bank lending. The findings show that financial development has not taken place and that the financial sector is a lagging part of the economy. Private financial savings have been small and domestic credit allocated to the private sector has declined in real terms. Thus, the contribution to Afghanistan's low development potential by the total absence of financial development has been strong.

Chapter VI examines public finance. After a description of the fiscal system and domestic revenue sources, the fiscal effort is measured. That only a very low effort appears to have been forthcoming suggests not only a lack of commitment to economic development on the part of the country's leaders (the conclusion also reached in Chapter IV) but also the rejection of Government promoted development activities on the part of a large section of the population. The reason for this is discussed after an analysis of the incidence of the benefits from development expenditures. These appear to have been negligible or even negative to the vast majority of the community.

Afghanistan's foreign trade and the role played by the money bazaars is the subject of Chapter VII. Because future development efforts must concentrate on export promotion activities, the importance of foreign trade cannot be overestimated. After a description of foreign trade developments and of Afghanistan's foreign trade and exchange system, the role of the money bazaars in foreign trade is discussed. The conclusion is reached that not only have the Kabul and Kandahar money bazaars financed the major part of foreign trade but that their foreign exchange operations produced a highly efficient market in sharp contrast to inefficiencies observed in Government and modern sector operations. This chapter ends with an analysis of the determinants of both seasonal and year-to-year fluctuations in the free market Afghani/Dollar exchange rate.

The final chapter presents an outline of a programme of financial and fiscal reform which would need to be pursued concomitantly with an increased commitment to economic development, a greatly expanded road building programme and much more effort to raise agricultural productivity, all of which should be designed to raise Afghanistan's development potential. More attention is focused on financial development than on fiscal reform since prescription for the latter is considerably simpler. The penultimate section indicates the possible direct benefits which might be obtained from reform along the lines suggested in these areas.

Afghanistan in the Adelman-Morris Study

Adelman and Morris examined data from 73 non-communist under-developed countries having first classified these countries into three groups according to their past records of economic growth. Through discriminant analysis, four out of 29 indicators were selected which together accounted for 97 per cent of the discriminable variance between the three groups of countries [A2, p. 268]. After normalising the estimated equation so that its variance in each group is unity, the following result is obtained:

$$D'_1 = 127F + 65K + 108M + 72L \qquad (1.1)$$

where F is financial development, K transport improvement, M modernisation in outlook and acceptance of economic development on the part of the population at large, and L the commitment of leadership to development [A2, p. 269]. In terms of the overall contribution to the discriminating power of the function, the order of importance of the variables is given by ranking the magnitudes of their coefficients.

Adelman and Morris then omitted all countries which had originally been misclassified on the basis of their past economic growth record according to the results of Equation 1.1, and re-ran the discriminant analysis. This produced the following result:

$$D'_2 = 95F + 139M + 88L + 70A \qquad (1.2)$$

where A is improvement in agricultural productivity [A2, p. 277]. This equation also accounts for over 97 per cent of the overall variance [A2, p. 278]. Furthermore, the separation between the groups is much better and the dispersion within the groups reduced. The probability of Afghanistan's membership in the Low Potential Group is 1.00 with a score of 62 [A2, Table V, p. 279]. The mean scores for the three groups are 174, 113 and 53 for high, intermediate and low potential groups, respectively [A2, pp. 278-80].

An important point to note is that the data used in this study refer in general to the period 1336-1341 (1957-1962) when all indicators for Afghanistan must have been near their peaks. There had been rapid development in the fields of banking and road building, commitment to development was relatively strong among the country's leaders and the population had not become disillusioned with the development programme as it had only just started. Nevertheless, Afghanistan is classified among

.... countries that have shown no significant improvement in the effectiveness of their financial institutions as indicated by qualitative information on saving and lending activities and, for countries for which the relevant data are available, by either (1) a negligible increase or a decrease in the ratio of the sum of demand and time deposits to GNP [Gross National Product] or (2) a negligible increase or a decrease in the real value of private domestic liabilities to the banking system. [A1, p. 123]

On the degree of improvement in physical overhead capital, Afghanistan receives an A+ because the annual percentage increase in paved roads between 1336 (1957) and 1343 (1964) exceeded 15 per cent. Since there were no such roads in 1335 (1956) and the road-building boom took place between 1335-1345 (1956-1966) this result is not surprising even if it is misleading.

With respect to agricultural productivity, Afghanistan is classified as a country

.... in which there has been no significant improvement in agricultural productivity since 1950. Included in this category are some countries in which substantial increases in total agricultural output have occurred but in which the increases in output are largely due to additional inputs of the same quality as those generally prevailing in 1950. [A1, p. 108]

On the degree of modernisation in outlook Afghanistan is mentioned together with other countries

.... in which the outlook of the educated urban sector was partially but not significantly modernized and in which programs of modernization, if they existed, had gained relatively little support among either the urban or rural population. [A1, p. 51]

Finally, Afghanistan appears as one of a number of countries

.... in which some government leaders evidenced a definite commitment to economic development (during the period 1957-62) as indicated by the practice of some form of national development planning. However, it was typical of the countries in this category that the activities of agencies involved in central guidance of the economy were poorly co-ordinated and that government attempts to alter institutional arrangements unfavourable to economic growth were infrequent or poorly sustained. [A1, p. 80]

One might simply add that had the data referred to the late 1340s (1960s) instead of the early years of that decade, Afghanistan's score would have been considerably lower than the 62 achieved in the Adelman-Morris study.

CHAPTER TWO

THE ECONOMY

i. *Introduction*

The paucity of quantitative data on Afghanistan makes any attempt to survey economic developments over a forty year period difficult and conclusions tenuous. Nevertheless, an attempt appears warranted if only to dispel a commonly held belief, reinforced by the recent classification of Afghanistan as a Least Developed Country, that change has been negligible. On several fronts, changes over the past forty years have taken place at a pace many times faster than that with which comparable changes took place in medieval Europe. Indeed, considerable change had already occurred during the 1300s (1920s). It is interesting to note a passage in a report written in 1306 (1928) in which Afghanistan is described as follows:

> It is becoming a modern state. Its road communications have been transformed. There is a well-trained army. There are excellent schools. The metric system was recently adopted. In the centre of Asia what is almost a new country is in process of birth—or, at least, the old country is being metamorphosed. [H10, p. 486]

The improvements recorded must, of course, be interpreted in relative terms. Nevertheless, it behoves planners, technical advisors and donor agencies frustrated by resistance to new projects, procedures and programmes to compare the present situation in an economy so often labelled stagnant with that of a mere forty years ago.

The Afghan economy at the start of 1311 (1932) was still recovering from the holocaust of 1307 (1929) and the reign of the bandit, Bacha Saqao, 1307-1308 (1929), during which severe economic disruption, cessation of foreign trade, the closure of schools and hospitals and a flight of capital took place [G15, pp. 263-75; G21, p. 424; M21, p. 182]. Conditions during and immediately after Saqao's rule were described as follows in a contemporary report:

> During the short space of nine months the terrible Saqaoists had spread devastation and ruin all over the country; from the confines of Herat in the west right up to the Indian border in the east, pestilence and famines, robbery and dacoity were the order of the day. There was no order, no law, save that might was right. When the present king took Kabul, he found the whole country in a chaos, tribal wars raging on all sides, trade

and agriculture badly crippled, people half starving and diseased, and many
dressed in rags with their skin showing through the rents and imploring for
food, villages deserted, houses burnt, thousands of people rendered home-
less, schools and colleges entirely closed, some of them burnt and
demolished, the students having taken shelter in far off and remote places
to avoid the wrath of this ignorant tyrant, who regarded them as renegades
.... The granaries were empty, and the grainfields had been neglected for
reaping the gruesome harvest of human lives. [A15, pp. 177-78]

On the accession of Nadir Shah, the country was

.... without an army, police or money in the treasury. The southern
tribes were in ferment, the northern provinces had virtually seceded. It
took almost two years and an army of 40,000 to pull the country together
again. [K12, p. 245]

To be sure, the economy was then as now predominantly an agricultural, subsistence economy:

.... there was literally no industry, only fragmentary handicraft, and
scanty trade. While the majority of Afghans tilled the soil or kept their
flocks, nearly all the commerce of the country, with the exception of that
carried on by the Kuchis or camel nomads, was in the hands of Sikh and
Hindu merchants. [F9, p. 229]

There were, in fact, a few Government munitions factories in Kabul
[S16, pp. 642-43] but no electricity. Transport and communications were
rudimentary and unreliable. A contemporary report states:

The following roads are fit for motor traffic, except after snow or heavy
rain, but are badly constructed and mostly unmetalled: Khaibar-Kabul,
Kabul-Kandahar, Kabul-Gardez, Kandahar-Chaman, and Kabul-Bamian.
In addition there are some 200 miles of minor roads fit for motor traffic,
mostly in the vicinity of Kabul. Merchandise, however, is still transported
chiefly on camel or pony back. [S16, p. 643]

It did not add that travellers were likely to be robbed. The Governor of
Kandahar, for example, had had to deal summarily with highway
robbery at this time:

When he arrived at Kandahar the tribesmen were playing tricks on the
road of a rather old-fashioned kind, shooting drivers and robbing motors.
The Governor had the criminals hanged in public at the gates of Kandahar.
[F20, p. 11]

Difficulty in obtaining petrol was another problem of motorised transport
[E3, p. 204]. The poor road conditions impeded foreign trade. It took, for
example, two full days for the British Legation's mail lorry to reach
Peshawar [B33, pp. 34-39], nevertheless a substantial reduction from the
45 days previously taken by caravans [M1, p. 225].

Government revenue raised mainly from tariffs on foreign trade was "subject to considerable fluctuations" [S16, p. 642]. In 1311 (1932), total Government revenue was Afs 140 million. There were no banks or paper money. Two currencies, the Afghani and Kabuli, circulated side by side in the form of silver coins [S16, p. 643]. In the field of commercial transactions, another contemporary report states:

> Afghanistan has not responded to the invitation of the League of Nations to accede to various recent conventions concerning cheques and negotiable instruments; innumerable transactions are carried on through mysterious *hundis* and by word of mouth, and credit is based on personal note of hand rather than on documents which represent specific goods. [S19, p. 722]

Primary schools had been re-opened by the beginning of 1311 (1932) but the quality of the education provided was generally low and compulsory elementary education was an unrealistic ideal included in the Constitution of 1310 (1931) [G15, pp. 307-308]. There were only 22 schools, 1,350 pupils, and 105 teachers in the country [M13, p. 88]. Eventually, the four secondary schools in Kabul were re-opened but had to be staffed by French, Germans and Indians since no qualified Afghans could be found [F9, p. 231]. There were no facilities at all for vocational training [K12, p. 257].

Trade took place between Afghanistan and India as well as between Afghanistan and the U.S.S.R. The total value of Afghanistan's foreign trade in 1311 (1932), of which one-third was with the U.S.S.R., was Afs 209 million [M12, pp. 101-103]. It is of interest, however, that contemporary economic reports make little reference to either the U.S.S.R. or to the northern part of Afghanistan. It was not until the Great North Road joined the two halves of the country that the towns of the north are mentioned. Even then malaria deterred visitors until its irradication with the help of the United Nations in the 1330s (1950s).

The Afghan economy of 1352 (1973) is still basically agricultural. However, assuming on the scantiest of evidence that population was 6.85 million in 1310 (1931) and 10 million in 1352 (1973), wheat production, the staple food in Afghanistan, which has increased from 2.0 million tons in 1332 (1953), the earliest year for which a consistent estimate exists, to 2.4 million tons in 1351 (1972), shows a small decrease in per capita terms for this period. The production of other grains has increased at a somewhat faster rate. Fertiliser use in 1351 (1972) was estimated at 48,000 tons [K11, p. 14] compared to nil in 1311 (1932). If fertiliser use increases as predicted, Afghanistan may become self-sufficient in food production during the 1350s (1970s).

There is now some industry in Afghanistan. A total equity capital of
Afs 15 billion with a labour force of 30,000 has been estimated for public
sector enterprise and capital of Afs 3 billion with a labour force of 15,000
for the private sector [G6, p. 2]. Of the latter Afs 1.2 billion, creating
6,000 jobs, has been invested under the terms of the 1345 (1967) Foreign
and Domestic Private Investment Law.

Two thousand five hundred kilometres of paved road now links north
and south and east and west and there is a total of 17,300 kilometres of
motorable roads [M31, p. 89] compared to 2,880 kilometres of barely
passable tracks in 1311 (1932) [A15, pp. 221-22].

Government revenue has not increased rapidly if measured at constant
prices. In 1340 (1961) prices, domestic revenue was Afs 1,428 million in
1311 (1932) and Afs 2,683 million in 1351 (1972), giving a per capita
increase of only 30 per cent over the entire period, or an average annual
per capita increase of 0.6 per cent. This unsatisfactory development is
considered in detail in Chapter VI.

There are now three commercial banks, one of which is also the central
bank, and three specialised banks. Although considerable attention is
devoted later to the inadequacies of the financial system, transfers can
be effected and accounts maintained. There is a generally acceptable
paper currency in wide circulation, although problems of making commercial transactions have changed little from those existing in 1311 (1932)
described above. In real terms, the money stock has increased only slightly
faster than the Government's domestic revenue. Subsequently, it will be
argued that both the fiscal system and the financial sector are in fact
underdeveloped even in relation to other sectors of the economy. Nevertheless, the widespread acceptance and use of paper currency is a major
change from the bi-metallic specie system existing in 1311 (1932).

In 1311 (1932) there were only 22 schools in the whole country, but
by 1351 (1972) there were 3,972 schools, 21,920 teachers and 760,469
students. In relation to total population, however, education still reaches
only a small minority and literacy is very low.

In 1340 (1961) prices, the total value of foreign trade in 1311 (1932) of
Afs 2,133 million can be compared to a figure of Afs 7,015 million for
1351 (1972), showing an increase of over 200 per cent or 3 per cent
annually. Foreign trade has been a beneficiary of road improvements.

This brief comparison of a few key variables for the years 1311 (1932)
and 1351 (1972) indicates that changes have occurred, some quite rapid,
others relatively slow. That Afghanistan still lacks almost all signs of a
rapidly expanding modern economy suggests that changes have taken

place from an exceedingly low initial position. There is no dispute with the assertion that the country is poor. The lack of main drains and a main water supply even in the capital, the prevalence of disease, the absence of modern skills generally and of administrative ability within the civil service in particular, and the subsistence standards of living of all but a small minority amply attest to the poverty of the nation. Yet, if only because banditry has been suppressed, violence and cholera, malaria and smallpox epidemics reduced, life expectancy has increased.

ii. *Economic and Social Indicators of Change*

A. Non-Monetary Indicators

Lack of reliable data is perhaps no better illustrated than in the demographic field. In 1311 (1932), population estimates ranged from six to 15 million, of which nomads comprised one-third [S19, p. 716]. In

Table 2.1

Population 1310-1352
(Millions)

Date	Population	Date	Population
1310	6.85	1333	7.80
1311	6.89	1334	7.88
1312	6.92	1335	7.96
1313	6.96	1336	8.04
1314	6.99	1337	8.12
1315	7.03	1338	8.20
1316	7.06	1339	8.28
1317	7.10	1340	8.36
1318	7.13	1341	8.49
1319	7.17	1342	8.62
1320	7.20	1343	8.75
1321	7.24	1344	8.88
1322	7.28	1345	9.01
1323	7.31	1346	9.15
1324	7.35	1347	9.28
1325	7.39	1348	9.42
1326	7.42	1349	9.56
1327	7.46	1350	9.71
1328	7.50	1351	9.85
1329	7.53	1352	10.00
1330	7.57		
1331	7.65	Average Annual	
1332	7.72	Percentage Increase	0.905

Note: Population in 1352 (1973) is assumed to be 10 million. Annual growth rates assumed are 0.5 per cent for the 1310s (1930s) and 1320s (1940s), 1.0 per cent for the 1330s (1950s) and 1.5 per cent for the remaining years.

THE ECONOMY

1351 (1972), estimates ranged from eight to 17.88 million, the latter being
the official estimate [I 2, p. 40]. Thus, no direct estimates of the rate of
change in the population can be derived. The range in the estimates
allows for increasing, decreasing or stable population, although the
official series shows an annual increase over the 1340s (1960s) of 2 per cent
[I 3, pp. 228-29].

Table 2.2

Education and Health Statistics 1311-1351

Date	Number of Schools	Number of Pupils	Number of Teachers	Number of Hospitals	Number of Medical Doctors	Number of Hospital Beds
1311	22	1,350	105			600
1315	92	9,275	309			650
1320	331	64,000	2,190		38	730
1325	359	93,544	2,677		88	770
1330	378	98,743	3,128	50	137	
1335	804	126,092	4,007	52	149	1,380
1340	1,436	235,301	5,983	59	250	1,759
1345	2,298	443,459	9,824	63	527	2,197
1351	3,972	760,469	21,920	67	827	3,504
Average Annual Percentage Increase	13.9	17.2	14.3			4.5

Source: Education—Ministry of Education, *Education in Afghanistan* (Kabul:
Ministry of Education, 1956), p. 88; Ministry of Planning, *Survey of Progress 1962-
64* (Kabul: Ministry of Planning, 1964), Table A-50, pp. 150-51; Ministry of Planning,
Survey of Progress 1971-1972 (Kabul: Ministry of Planning, 1972), Table S-32; and
Ministry of Planning.
    Health—Ministry of Planning, *Survey of Progress 1961-62* (Kabul: Ministry of
Planning, 1963), Part II, Table Health (1), p. 21; Ministry of Planning, *Survey of
Progress 1971-1972* (Kabul: Ministry of Planning, 1972), Table S-41; and Ministries
of Planning and Public Health.

Population estimates should be forthcoming from the Afghan Demographic Survey towards the end of 1352 (1974). At the present, however,
there is virtually no foundation on which any estimate can be based.
Here, it has been assumed for convenience that the population in 1352
(1973) is 10 million and that annual growth rates have been 0.5 per cent
for the 1310s (1930s) and 1320s (1940s), 1.0 per cent for the 1330s (1950s)
and 1.5 per cent thereafter. Annual estimates are presented in Table 2.1.
By 1352 (1973), the population growth rate might have reached 2.0
per cent.

Table 2.3

Transport and Communications Statistics 1311-1351

| Date | Number of Kilometres of Motorable Road | | | Number of Motor Vehicles | Number of Telephones | Number of Letters (in 000s) |
	Asphalt and Concrete	Other	Total			
1311	0	2,880	2,880	350	50	
1315	0				120	
1320	0					
1325	0					
1330	0					
1335	0	6,200	6,200	5,350	3,136	2,429
1340	494			13,802	6,238	3,034
1345	1,886	11,434	13,320	45,102	9,866	4,824
1351	2,500	14,800	17,300	55,076	19,939	4,907
Average Annual Percentage Increase		4.2	4.6	13.5	16.1	

Note: The number of motor vehicles given are only those registered in Kabul. In 1349 (1970), this accounted for 87 per cent of the total. The numbers of letters recorded for 1351 (1972) are 1350 (1971) figures.

Source: Roads—M. Ali, *Progressive Afghanistan* (Lahore: Punjab Educational Electric Press, 1933), pp. 221-22; Ministry of Planning, *Survey of Progress 1960* (Kabul: Ministry of Planning, 1960), p. 119; Ministry of Planning, *Survey of Progress 1961-62* (Kabul: Ministry of Planning, 1963), p. 24; Ministry of Planning, *Survey of Progress 1966-1967* (Kabul: Ministry of Planning, 1967), p. 73; Ministry of Planning, *Survey of Progress 1971-1972* (Kabul: Ministry of Planning, 1972), p. 89.

Vehicles—A. Guha, "The Economy of Afghanistan during Amanullah's Reign, 1919-1929," *Journal of International Studies*, 9 (2), October 1967, p. 180; D. N. Wilber (Ed.), *Afghanistan* (New Haven: Human Relations Area Files, 1956), p. 251; Ministry of Planning, *Survey of Progress 1961-62* (Kabul: Ministry of Planning, 1963), p. 25; Ministry of Planning, *Survey of Progress 1971-1972* (Kabul: Ministry of Planning, 1972), Table S-44; Ministry of Planning, *Statistical Pocket-Book of Afghanistan, 1350* (Kabul: Ministry of Planning, 1351), Tables 54 and 55, pp. 104-105; and Ministry of Planning.

Telephones and Letters—Ministry of Planning, *Survey of Progress 1960* (Kabul: Ministry of Planning, 1960), pp. 132, 134 and 136; Ministry of Planning, *Survey of Progress 1961-62* (Kabul: Ministry of Planning, 1963), pp. 21-22; Ministry of Planning, *Survey of Progress 1962-64* (Kabul: Ministry of Planning, 1964), Table A-37, p. 141 and Table A-40, p. 143; Ministry of Planning, *Survey of Progress 1971-1972* (Kabul: Ministry of Planning, 1972), Tables S-43 and S-44; and Ministry of Planning.

A number of indicators can be used to provide some information on changes which have occurred in Afghanistan over the past forty years. However, given that most of them start at negligible levels, rapid growth does not necessarily suggest significant impact on the bulk of the population. Educational statistics, for example, indicate rapid development, as can be seen in Table 2.2. Nevertheless, the literacy rate was estimated at only 8 per cent of the population in 1347 (1968) [M5, Table V-1, p. 104].

In the field of health and medicine, changes have also taken place. Figures in Table 2.2 show rapid expansion but again still left much room for further advances by 1351 (1972), as illustrated for example in the high patient/doctor ratio, whatever population estimate is used. However, in public health, effects have been more wide-reaching with the elimination of cholera, malaria and smallpox epidemics.

Transport and communications have shown similar rapid expansion as is shown in Table 2.3. Again, the numbers of telephones and letters

Table 2.4

Various Economic Indicators Specified in Non-Monetary Units 1311-1351

Date	Cement (Thousands of Tons)	Electricity (Millions of Kilowatt Hours)	Coal (Thousands of Tons)	Gas (Millions of Cubic Metres)	Wheat (Thousands of Tons)	Karakul Exports (Thousands of Skins)
1311	0			0		906
1315	0			0		1,715
1320	0	6		0		1,839
1325	0	7		0		1,537
1330	0	9	14	0		1,423
1335	0	36	29	0	2,200	1,874
1340	41	126	69	0	2,279	2,089
1345	177	302	162	0	2,033	1,373
1351	91	487	71	2,849	2,401	1,313

Source: Bank Millie, *Report of the Board of Directors and Balance Sheet 1336* (Kabul: Bank Millie, mimeo, 1337), p. 19; *Da Afghanistan Breshna Muassessa* (Kabul: National Defence Press, Sunbula 1349); A. Guha, "The Economy of Afghanistan during Amanullah's Reign, 1919-1929," *Journal of International Studies*, 9 (2), October 1967, p. 168; N. Koenig and H. V. Hunter, *A Wheat Stabilization Program for Afghanistan* (Kabul: United States Agency for International Development, mimeo, September 1973), pp. 3-4; Ministry of Commerce, *Afghanistan's Foreign Trade, 1335 through 1342* (Kabul: Ministry of Commerce, mimeo, 1343), Table V, p. 26; Ministry of Commerce, *A Summary of Afghanistan's Foreign Trade from 1343 to 1348* (Kabul: Ministry of Commerce, mimeo, Qaus 1350); Ministry of Planning, *Survey of Progress 1960* (Kabul: Ministry of Planning, 1960), Table Agriculture (1); Ministry of Planning, *Survey of Progress 1961-62* (Kabul: Ministry of Planning, 1963), Table Agriculture (1); Ministry of Planning, *The Third Five Year Economic and Social Plan of Afghanistan* (Kabul: Ministry of Planning, 1967), p. 11; Ministry of Planning, *Survey of Progress 1969-1970* (Kabul: Ministry of Planning, 1970), Tables S-22 and S-24; E. Rhein and A. G. Ghaussy, *Die wirtschaftliche Entwicklung Afghanistans 1880-1965* (Bielefeld: C. W. Leske Verlag Opladen, 1966), Table 6, p. 201; Central Statistics Office and Ministries of Commerce and Planning.

delivered were not high in 1351 (1972), despite the rapid increase over the period. Transport developments, on the other hand, have had a significant effect on the majority of the population. Because transport developments may well have been the most important single factor causing change for both good and ill in Afghanistan over the past four decades, it is taken up again in more detail in the following chapter.

Other statistics used to compare living standards between countries or over time include cement and coal production, electricity and steel consumption, and cultivated land, protein and calories per capita. Data available on some of these indicators are provided in Table 2.4. Apart from agricultural statistics, magnitudes for 1351 (1972) are still so small as to imply insignificant impact on the majority of the population.

B. Price Indices

Before turning to indicators given in value terms, the first problem which must be examined is that of measuring price changes which have occurred over the period. Even the official price index for the past decade is poor. It was the first task of the Central Statistics Office (CSO), established in 1351 (1972), to prepare a new price index. Hansen and Tourk have also constructed an alternative price index for the 1340s (1960s) because they found the official index misleading [H2, Table 1-10, p. 16]. Given that indicators in value terms allow relatively short run comparisons and provide clues to cyclical movements, some attempt at producing a price index for the purpose of deflating value figures to a constant price base is necessary. The price of wheat, the consumer price index and the Hansen-Tourk index for the 1340s (1960s) are presented in Table 2.5. The consumer price index is a composite spliced together from five different series used in Wilber [W3, p. 197], the Tudor Report [T6, p. 157] and Surveys of Progress [M19; M22; M27; M28; M29; M30] and a revised series for the last three years produced by the Central Statistics Office as one of its first publications [C7]. Its accuracy has been improved since 1340 (1961) but the revisions for the last three years by the Central Statistics Office suggest that even the data for the 1340s (1960s) are rough.

Taking the criticisms of the official index, which centre around the over-weight given to food items (the Hansen-Tourk index simply uses different weights on the same price data used for the official index), and the impossibility of using wheat prices as a general deflator on a year-to-year basis, the alternatives appear to be either a backward extension of the CSO or the Hansen-Tourk index or a new approach. As price data do

THE ECONOMY

Table 2.5

Price Indicators, 1303, 1312-1351

Date	Wheat (Afghanis per Seer)	Consumer Price Index (1340 = 100)	Hansen-Tourk Price Index (1340 = 100)
1303	1.00	n.a.	—
1312	1.86	n.a.	—
1313	n.a.	n.a.	—
1314	n.a.	n.a.	—
1315	n.a.	n.a.	—
1316	n.a.	13.2	—
1317	n.a.	n.a.	—
1318	n.a.	n.a.	—
1319	n.a.	n.a.	—
1320	n.a.	n.a.	—
1321	n.a.	n.a.	—
1322	n.a.	n.a.	—
1323	5.01	n.a.	—
1324	8.38	50.5	—
1325	n.a.	58.6	—
1326	n.a.	61.6	—
1327	14.26	63.2	—
1328	n.a.	71.8	—
1329	n.a.	75.8	—
1330	11.90	76.8	—
1331	25.84	75.8	—
1332	19.71	74.8	—
1333	n.a.	70.3	—
1334	n.a.	79.4	—
1335	n.a.	84.2	—
1336	n.a.	102.4	—
1337	n.a.	93.3	—
1338	28.40	97.9	—
1339	22.31	106.7	—
1340	12.86	100.0	100.0
1341	15.72	98.1	98.7
1342	21.84	132.2	125.2
1343	31	156.1	144.5
1344	35	170.5	161.7
1345	45	214.1	195.3
1346	60	264.2	233.1
1347	42	208.3	189.5
1348	38	207.9	—
1349	55	264.6	—
1350	75	312.5	—
1351	56	267.0	—

Note: Simple averages of all wheat prices recorded during the year have been calculated.

Source: Wheat prices—A. Guha, "The Economy of Afghanistan during Amanullah's Reign, 1919-1929," *Journal of International Studies*, 9 (2), October 1967, p. 167;

Iqtisad Journal, 1312, 1323, 1324, 1327, 1330, 1338, 1339, 1340, 1341, 1342; N. Koenig and H. V. Hunter, *A Wheat Stabilization Program for Afghanistan* (Kabul: United States Agency for International Development, mimeo, September 1973), Table 6, p. 26.

Consumer Price Index—1316 from D. N. Wilber, (Ed.), *Afghanistan* (New Haven: Human Relations Area Files, 1956), p. 197; 1323-1328 from Tudor Engineering Company, *Report on Development of Helmand Valley, Afghanistan* (Washington, D.C.: Tudor Engineering Company, November 1956), p. 157; 1329-1335 from Ministry of Planning, *Survey of Progress 1958* (Kabul: Ministry of Planning, 1958), Volume I, Table 4, p. 5 of Money Section (Part III); 1332-1340 from Ministry of Planning, *Survey of Progress 1961-62* (Kabul: Ministry of Planning, 1963), Table 9, p. 78; 1340-1350 from Ministry of Planning, *Survey of Progress 1967-1968* (Kabul: Ministry of Planning, 1968), Table S-12; Ministry of Planning, *Survey of Progress 1968-1969* (Kabul: Ministry of Planning, 1969), Table S-13; Ministry of Planning, *Survey of Progress 1969-1970* (Kabul: Ministry of Planning, 1970), Table S-19; Ministry of Planning, *Survey of Progress 1970-1971* (Kabul: Ministry of Planning, 1971), Table S-19; Central Statistics Office, *Revised National Price Indexes for Afghanistan for the Years 1348-1350* (Kabul: Central Statistics Office, mimeo, 1972); 1351 from Ministry of Planning.

Hansen-Tourk Price Index—B. Hansen and K. Tourk, "Three Papers on Price and Trade Indices for Afghanistan," *Economic Bulletin for Asia and the Far East*, 22 (1-2), June/September 1971, Table 1-10, p. 16.

not exist to enable the former alternative to be used, a new approach, namely the construction of a purchasing power parity price index, has been adopted.

Recent work by Galliot [G1] shows that over relatively long periods the purchasing power parity theory is valid even under fixed exchange rate systems. Using it, the following relationship is found

$$\text{(Relative inflation in Afghanistan)} \cdot \frac{ER^o{}_{Afs/\$}}{ER^t{}_{Afs/\$}} = 1 \qquad (2.1)$$

where $ER_{Afs/\$}$ is the exchange rate in Afghanis (the monetary unit in Afghanistan) per United States Dollar. The superscripts denote the base year "o" and the current year "t". The relative inflation in Afghanistan is measured by

$$\frac{WPI^t_A}{WPI^t_{USA}} \bigg/ \frac{WPI^o_A}{WPI^o_{USA}} \qquad (2.2)$$

where WPI is the wholesale price index. Taking $WPI^o_A = 100$, it is possible to express the remaining unknown variable, WPI^t_A, as follows

$$WPI^t_A = \frac{ER^t{}_{Afs/\$}}{ER^o{}_{Afs/\$}} \cdot \frac{WPI^o_A}{WPI^o_{USA}} \cdot WPI^t_{USA} \qquad (2.3)$$

THE ECONOMY

Table 2.6

Exchange Rates, U.S. Wholesale Price Index and Purchasing
Power Parity Price Index 1310-1351

Date	Afghani/Dollar Exchange Rate	U.S. Wholesale Price Index	Purchasing Power Parity Price Index
1310	9.92	39.79	9.1
1311	12.06	35.34	9.8
1312	9.42	35.93	7.8
1313	10.04	40.88	9.4
1314	9.99	43.65	10.0
1315	9.73	44.07	9.9
1316	9.72	47.09	10.5
1317	11.24	42.89	11.1
1318	12.02	42.05	11.6
1319	13.05	42.89	12.9
1320	13.05	47.68	14.3
1321	13.05	53.89	16.2
1322	13.05	56.24	16.9
1323	13.05	56.74	17.0
1324	13.05	57.75	17.3
1325	13.7	66.06	20.8
1326	17.2	80.92	32.0
1327	27.0	87.6	54.4
1328	33.0	83.3	63.2
1329	39.0	86.5	77.6
1330	35.0	96.4	77.6
1331	37.0	93.7	79.7
1332	37.1	92.4	78.8
1333	42.1	92.6	89.6
1334	45.2	92.9	96.5
1335	53.8	95.9	118.6
1336	54.1	98.7	122.8
1337	54.7	100.1	125.9
1338	46.6	100.3	107.4
1339	40.8	100.4	94.2
1340	43.5	100.0	100.0
1341	52.8	100.3	121.7
1342	51.3	100.0	117.9
1343	63.6	100.2	146.5
1344	75.3	102.2	176.9
1345	76.4	105.6	185.5
1346	76.4	105.8	185.8
1347	74.8	108.4	186.4
1348	75.4	112.7	195.3
1349	84.8	116.8	227.7
1350	84.6	120.6	234.5
1351	79.4	126.0	230.0
Average Annual Percentage Increase	5.20	2.85	8.20

Note: The exchange rate is the average daily buying rate for drafts and cheques quoted by dealers in the Kabul money bazaar. This rate is normally referred to as the bazaar rate.

Source: Afghani/Dollar Exchange Rate—1310-1324 from *Iqtisad Journal*, 1310-1324; 1325-1327 from A. H. Kayoumy, "Monopoly Pricing of Afghan Karakul in International Markets," *Journal of Political Economy*, 77 (2), March/April 1969, Table 1, p. 221 and Ministry of Planning, *Survey of Progress 1960* (Kabul: Ministry of Planning, 1960), p. 184; 1328 is the average of the 1327 and 1329 rates; 1329-1351 from Research Department, Da Afghanistan Bank.

United States Wholesale Price Index—United States Bureau of the Census, *Historical Statistics of the United States, Colonial Times to 1957* (Washington, D.C.: United States Department of Commerce, 1960); *International Financial Statistics*, 26 (10), October 1973, pp. 370-71; *International Financial Statistics: 1972 Supplement*, pp. 4-5.

The United States wholesale price index and the free market Afghani/ Dollar exchange rate are combined in this way to produce a purchasing power parity price index for Afghanistan which is given in Table 2.6.

The purchasing power parity price index can give an indication of short run price movements in a country such as Afghanistan whose exchange rate floats. However, the disruption to international trade caused by the Second World War reduces the reliability of the index during the 1320s (1940s) to the point where an alternative has to be used. Scattered information on consumer prices which has been used for the consumer price index in Table 2.5 does exist. If the purchasing power parity index for the period 1321-1328 (1942-1949) has been distorted by wartime disruptions, an alternative can be provided in the following manner. It is assumed that the price level did increase from 13.2 in 1316 (1937) to 79.4 in 1334 (1955) as in Table 2.5. The price increase given by the consumer price index in Table 2.5 between 1316 (1937) and 1324 (1945) is 283 per cent. The purchasing power parity price index consistent with this increase is 39.66 for 1324 (1945). Assuming prices rose by equal percentage steps over the period 1321-1324 (1942-1945), the intermediate figures can be calculated. This gives annual percentage price increases of 29.05 per cent. From 1325-1328 (1946-1949) price increases are assumed to have taken place in proportion to those of the consumer price index recorded in Table 2.5. However, the total rise in prices between 1324 (1945) and 1329 (1950) using the revised purchasing power parity index is 95.54 per cent compared to 50 per cent shown in Table 2.5. Thus, each annual price increase shown in this table is appropriately inflated to obtain the 95.54 per cent price rise over the entire period. In this manner, the modified purchasing power parity price index which is used hereafter has been constructed and is presented in its entirety in Table 2.7.

THE ECONOMY

Table 2.7

Modified Purchasing Power Parity Price Index 1310-1351

(Base 1340 = 100)

Date	Index	Date	Index
1310	9.1	1333	89.6
1311	9.8	1334	96.5
1312	7.8	1335	118.6
1313	9.4	1336	122.8
1314	10.0	1337	125.9
1315	9.9	1338	107.4
1316	10.5	1339	94.2
1317	11.1	1340	100.0
1318	11.6	1341	121.7
1319	12.9	1342	117.9
1320	14.3	1343	146.5
1321	18.5	1344	176.9
1322	23.8	1345	185.5
1323	30.7	1346	185.8
1324	39.7	1347	186.4
1325	51.8	1348	195.3
1326	56.3	1349	227.7
1327	58.6	1350	234.5
1328	71.5	1351	230.0
1329	77.6		
1330	77.6	Average Annual	
1331	79.7	Percentage	
1332	78.8	Increase	8.20

Note: Figures for 1321-1328 derived as described in the text.
Source: Same as Tables 2.5 and 2.6.

The exchange rate data are accurate for the period 1329-1351 (1950-1972), the figures given being the averages of buying rates for drafts and cheques collected daily by Da Afghanistan Bank from Seray Shozda, the Kabul money bazaar. The data for 1310-1328 (1931-1949) are probably not as accurate as those for the later years. Furthermore, controls instituted by Bank Millie in 1315 (1936) and the disruptions created by the Second World War throw serious doubts on the utility of the index in this period for short run purposes. A few checks, however, can be made on the reliability of the index over the long run. The first springs from the fact that in 1310 (1931) the currency in Afghanistan was silver. A comparison can, therefore, be made between an exchange rate based on world silver prices combined with the silver content of the currency, on the one hand, and the recorded exchange rate, on the other. Assuming one silver Kabuli contained nine grams of silver in 1303 and 1304 (1924 and 1925) and thereafter one silver Afghani also contained nine grams, notwith-standing the official conversion of 11 Kabulis to 10 Afghanis, implicit exchange rates can be calculated using silver prices quoted on the New York Bullion Market [A21, Chart 77]. Two year moving average prices have been used, e.g. for the 1310 (1931) exchange rate the average silver price in New York for 1930 and 1931 is adopted. The results are presented in Table 2.8.

Table 2.8

Afghani/Dollar Exchange Rates Derived from the Silver Content of the Afghani and Silver Prices on the New York Bullion Market 1303-1320

Date	Afghani/Dollar Exchange Rate	Date	Afghani/Dollar Exchange Rate
1303	4.73	1312	11.04
1304	4.56	1313	8.36
1305	5.25	1314	6.16
1306	5.83	1315	6.32
1307	6.03	1316	7.68
1308	6.22	1317	7.85
1309	7.58	1318	8.40
1310	10.34	1319	9.36
1311	12.21	1320	9.94

Note: Exchange rates calculated by method described in the text.
Source: American International Investment Corporation, *World Currency Charts 1970* (San Francisco: American International Investment Corporation, 1970), Chart 77.

For the years 1304-1312 (1925-1933) the implicit exchange rates appear realistic, with the rates for 1310-1312 (1931-1933) very close to the recorded rates shown in Table 2.6. The fall in the implicit exchange rate after 1311 (1932) resulting from the upturn in world silver prices was not, in fact, reflected by a significant downturn in the recorded exchange rate for the simple reason that debasement of the currency occurred continu-ously from the introduction of the Afghani in 1305 (1926) [B29, p. 433; G22, p. 173].

The second check on the purchasing power parity price index for long run trends lies in a comparison with other prices and price indices. The consumer price index produces roughly the same picture as the index in Table 2.7. The wheat price data given in Table 2.5 also follow the same broad trends as the modified purchasing power parity price index. Furthermore, the change in both price indices, 2,911 per cent for wheat

THE ECONOMY

Table 2.9

Economic Indicators Specified in Monetary Units 1311-1351
(Millions of Afghanis)

Date	Gross National Product	Government Domestic Revenue	Exports	Money Stock (M2)
1311		140	69	171
1312		145	70	183
1313		150	84	196
1314		160	108	209
1315		175	110	224
1316		190	111	240
1317		210	87	257
1318		247	148	275
1319		250	165	292
1320		260	148	338
1321		270	61	420
1322		280	285	502
1323		290	391	582
1324		300	486	684
1325		310	388	797
1326		315	494	850
1327		319	482	855
1328		387	436	907
1329		473	739	1,040
1330		548	731	1,168
1331		614	806	1,274
1332	12,500	775	950	1,339
1333		964	1,440	1,593
1334		1,283	1,352	2,097
1335	21,000	1,149	2,775	2,473
1336		1,348	3,156	2,481
1337		1,533	2,486	2,417
1338		1,601	2,722	2,587
1339		2,099	1,950	2,728
1340		2,110	2,222	2,981
1341	28,104	2,123	2,968	3,565
1342	39,339	2,677	3,459	4,405
1343	47,888	3,061	4,152	5,393
1344	54,147	3,976	5,025	6,160
1345	60,934	4,285	4,835	6,355
1346	63,270	4,211	5,018	6,289
1347		4,465	5,348	6,538
1348		5,085	6,180	7,341
1349		5,702	7,160	8,181
1350		5,823	8,427	8,759
1351		6,172	7,162	9,954
Average Annual Percentage Increase		9.93	12.31	10.19

Note: To estimate the money stock series for the period 1311-1329, the following assumptions have been made: 1) Afs 165 million in specie was in circulation at the end of 1310 (1932); 2) The money stock increased steadily between 1310 (1932) and 1319 (1941). (By 1315 (1936) it consisted of specie, banknotes and bank deposits); 3) A constant currency/money ratio of 0.8 was maintained between the end of 1319 (1941) and 1329 (1951). (Currency notes in circulation have been recorded since 1315 (1937)); 4) All specie was withdrawn by 1318 (1940). The money stock data are the averages of beginning and end of year figures thus providing a mid-year estimate.

Source: Gross National Product—1332 from United Nations, *Economic Survey of Asia and the Far East 1954* (Bangkok: United Nations, 1955), Table 18, p. 57; 1335 estimate by A. Paul quoted in J. Bharier, *Vicious Circles of Poverty* (Durham: University of Durham, Department of Economics, typescript, 1972), Table 4-4; 1341-46 estimates by a World Bank team supplied by the Ministry of Planning.

Government Domestic Revenue—Same as Table 6.1 below.

Exports—1311-34 from *Da Afghanistan Bank Economic Bulletin*, (in Dari), 5 (1), August 1961, Table 18; 1335-42 from Ministry of Commerce, *Afghanistan's Foreign Trade, 1335 through 1342* (Kabul: Ministry of Commerce, 1343), Table 1-A, p. 75; 1343-48 from Ministry of Commerce, *A Summary of Afghanistan's Trade from 1343 to 1348* (Kabul: Ministry of Commerce, Qaus 1350); 1349 from Ministry of Commerce, *Exports of Merchandise from Afghanistan, 1349* (Kabul: Ministry of Commerce, 1352), Table 1; 1350 from Ministry of Commerce, *Exports of Merchandise from Afghanistan, 1350* (Kabul: Ministry of Commerce, 1352), Table 1; 1351 from *International Financial Statistics*, 26 (10), October 1973, p. 40.

Money Stock (M2)—1315-18 from M. H. K. Zia, "From Brokerage to National Bank," *Iqtisad Journal*, 220, Saratan 1319, pp. 321-28; 1319-39 from balance sheet data provided by Da Afghanistan Bank; 1330-36 from Ministry of Planning, *Survey of Progress 1958* (Kabul: Ministry of Planning, 1958), Volume II, Table Money 7-30; Ministry of Planning, *Survey of Progress 1959* (Kabul: Ministry of Planning, 1959), Volume IV, Table 47, p. 186; Ministry of Planning, *Survey of Progress 1962-64* (Kabul: Ministry of Planning, 1964), Table A-7, p. 106; 1337-51 from *International Financial Statistics*, 26 (10), October 1973, pp. 40-41 and *International Financial Statistics: 1972 Supplement*, pp. 228-29.

and 2,849 per cent for the modified purchasing power parity price index between 1312 (1933) and 1351 (1972) is virtually identical.

Wage rates also provide some indication of the long run movement in prices. In 1311 (1932), the British Legation paid between Afs 30 and Afs 45 per month to "Afghan inferior servants" [B33, Standing Order No. 14]. In 1334 (1955) domestic servants received about Afs 600 per month [P15, p. 41; W3, p. 207]. In 1351 (1972), wages for the same type of employment were around Afs 1,800 per month. The rise in wages of 1,233 to 1,900 per cent between 1311 (1932) and 1334 (1955) can be compared with a rise in prices of 885 per cent, the rise of 200 per cent between 1334 (1955) and 1351 (1972) with the 138 per cent increase in prices. Thus, real wages over the forty years have increased by between 70 and 156 per cent or 1.3 to 2.4 per cent annually, figures which appear reasonable in their own right and consistent with the rate of growth in the Gross National Product estimated below.

THE ECONOMY

Table 2.10

Economic Indicators Specified in Monetary Units at Constant Prices 1311-1351
(Millions of Afghanis, 1340 Prices)

Date	Gross National Product	Government Domestic Revenue	Exports	Money Stock (M2)
1311		1,428	704	1,745
1312		1,859	897	2,346
1313		1,596	894	2,085
1314		1,600	1,080	2,090
1315		1,768	1,111	2,263
1316		1,810	1,057	2,286
1317		1,892	784	2,315
1318		2,129	1,276	2,371
1319		1,938	1,279	2,264
1320		1,818	1,035	2,364
1321		1,459	330	2,270
1322		1,176	1,197	2,109
1323		945	1,274	1,896
1324		756	1,224	1,723
1325		598	749	1,539
1326		560	877	1,510
1327		544	823	1,459
1328		541	610	1,269
1329		610	952	1,340
1330		706	942	1,505
1331		770	1,011	1,598
1332	15,863	983	1,206	1,699
1333		1,076	1,607	1,778
1334		1,330	1,401	2,173
1335	17,707	969	2,340	2,085
1336		1,098	2,570	2,020
1337		1,218	1,975	1,920
1338		1,491	2,534	2,409
1339		2,228	2,070	2,896
1340		2,110	2,222	2,981
1341	23,093	1,744	2,439	2,929
1342	33,366	2,270	2,934	3,736
1343	32,688	2,089	2,834	3,681
1344	30,609	2,248	2,841	3,482
1345	32,849	2,310	2,606	3,426
1346	34,053	2,266	2,701	3,385
1347		2,395	2,869	3,508
1348		2,604	3,164	3,759
1349		2,504	3,144	3,593
1350		2,483	3,594	3,735
1351		2,683	3,114	4,328
Average Annual Percentage Increase		1.59	3.79	1.83

Source: Figures in Table 2.9 have been deflated by the modified purchasing power parity price index in Table 2.7.

C. Monetary Indicators

Having constructed a price index, it is now possible to examine the available economic statistics given in value terms and to deflate them for comparative purposes to a constant price base. The data now discussed include Gross National Product (GNP), Government revenue, exports and the money stock. Figures in current prices are presented in Table 2.9 and deflated by the modified purchasing power parity price index in Table 2.10.

The reliability of the data is low. The GNP estimates are considered so inaccurate that they are no longer referred to in official publications. Government revenue figures are more accurate for the last two decades than for the first two. In general, the public finance data together with the exchange rate and money stock figures are the only aggregate economic series unlikely to be misleading. Foreign trade statistics are known to seriously understate Afghanistan's foreign trade. Throughout the period, smuggling has probably accounted for at least one-third of actual foreign trade. Obviously, no reliable information on the extent of smuggling is available. Nevertheless, accounts for the earlier years estimate smuggling at about one-third, while for the later period a proportion of one-fifth has been quoted [R9, p. 95; S13, pp. 328-29]. In Chapter VII it is suggested that the latter figure is an underestimate. Despite these drawbacks, the trend in the recorded foreign trade statistics probably gives an accurate indication of overall trade movements. Considerable growth is recorded in all decades except the 1320s (1940s). In the 1310s (1930s) the Government actively encouraged exports:

> In spite of the great financial crisis due to the fall in the price of silver and general economic depression, statistics clearly show a steady increase in exports and imports. Government lends a helping hand to all the promising merchants and enterprisers by supplying them with large sums of money without interest. [A15, p. 220]

Such encouragement has not taken place in the last two decades.

Finally, the money stock series, defined to include private demand, savings and time deposits, are much less accurate for earlier years than for the 1340s (1960s). The availability of any monetary statistics at all is in large part due to assistance provided by the International Monetary Fund. A resident representative of the Fund has worked in Da Afghanistan Bank, the central bank, for a number of years providing assistance on statistical as well as other matters. For a time, the Fund also provided a statistician. Even now, however, inaccuracies exist. For example, deposits in the commercial banks' provincial branches are excluded from money stock calculations. An improved series will be appearing soon. Despite these *caveats*, the fact that the main component of the money stock is currency in circulation, a relatively easy statistic to measure, makes serious error unlikely. Thus, in order of reliability one might list exchange rate data first, followed by money stock and public finance figures. The foreign trade data consistently underestimate actual values and GNP estimates are of extremely doubtful utility.

The general picture presented by all the indicators so far discussed is of one decade of rapid recovery and expansion, the 1330s (1950s), one of recession, the 1320s (1940s), and two of moderate growth, the 1310s (1930s) and 1340s (1960s). Of interest in Table 2.10 is the fact that Government domestic revenue failed to increase as fast as the real values of exports and the money stock, primarily because of the much greater decrease in the real magnitude of the former during the 1320s (1940s).

The disruption caused by the Second World War was considerable and recovery slow. One contemporary report presents the following analysis:

> The capital accumulation process, well launched by 1939, was set back by the war and the attendant uncertainty in world markets, the cutting-off of capital equipment deliveries from Central Europe, and a severe business dislocation. Some *shirkats* fell apart, others became mere facades for proprietary business activities, promotion schemes, and outright profiteering. Government control over prices and essential supplies of food and cloth were not effective enough to curb black markets.
> To halt the growing disintegration of the country's business organization and the ensuing inflation, Banke Millie curtailed business newcomers, induced traders with idle funds to invest them in sound projects, and assumed more control over the remaining *shirkats* through amalgamation and joint management boards. By the end of 1947 the new policy had largely succeeded, and today most industrial, utility and service enterprises, as well as the bulk of foreign trade, are again in the hands of well-organized *shirkats*. [F15, p. 432]

The developments during the 1310s (1930s), mainly in the first half of the decade, were due to Nadir Shah's serious commitment to a rational programme of economic development. The latter was prepared by Abdul Majid Zabuli, the founder of the first bank, Bank Millie [B7]. Set against the backcloth of the Great Depression, developments in Afghanistan in the fields of education, health and industry were impressive during this decade [G15, Chapters 11 and 13]. Of significance is the fact that little external finance was solicited for them. The development programmes of the post-war period, on the other hand, relied heavily on the inflow of foreign aid. Before discussing the development strategy, however, an attempt is made to construct an alternative GNP series.

iii. *An Estimate of Gross National Product*

It is noteworthy that most economic reports on Afghanistan start with an analysis of public finance almost as if such analysis could stand in lieu of a study of developments in the economy as a whole. The explanation for this tendency to equate an analysis of public finance with a broader economic appraisal simply lies in the fact that data are easily available for the former but not for the latter. For certain economies, extrapolation from public sector developments to the economy as a whole for short run analysis may not lead to serious error, since movements in one sector are paralleled elsewhere. For the Afghan economy, this practice can and does mislead. Thus, the regressive changes in the fiscal accounts over the past ten years have led to the conclusion that the economy has been stagnant, while indicators from the private sector point to some economic growth over the same decade. The figures in Tables 2.9 and 2.10 also support this.

There are two basic reasons for the independence of movements in public finance from changes in other sectors of the economy. The first is the fact that the Afghan economy is highly fragmented; few links exist between one sector and the other. The second is that the public sector is small in relation to any GNP estimates. Therefore, it is neither a strong leading sector nor a large component in the total. Thus, extrapolation is impossible.

Having suggested that the commonly adopted approach to aggregative analysis of the Afghan economy is misleading, an alternative is now put forward, namely monetary estimates of GNP. Both Friedman and Duggar have suggested and tested such a procedure with good results [F21; D8]. The theoretical underpinning behind this method lies in a simple economic model from which a reduced form equation relating GNP to the money stock and the expected rate of inflation can be derived. The fundamental empirical prerequisite is a stable functional relationship between these three variables or, looked at in a slightly different way, a stable velocity function.

In fact, Park finds higher coefficients of variation for velocity in underdeveloped than in developed economies [P2]. However, Brunner and Meltzer find that the quantity theory, based on the assumption of a stable velocity function, as a short run theory performs significantly better in econometric tests than any of the alternative hypotheses tested [B36]. For an excellent discussion of alternative approaches to monetary model building, the interested reader is referred to Park's recent contribution [P3].

Velocity of circulation is customarily measured by dividing a country's GNP by the money stock. The figure so obtained is designed to indicate how many times, on average, money circulates during the course of a year for the purchase of final goods and services, i.e. for those transactions constituting GNP.

In an economy like Afghanistan's, a large proportion of GNP consists of goods and services for which money transactions are not made, e.g. agricultural products consumed by those who grow them, the value of owner occupied housing, etc. Provided that the proportion of such items, for which imputed values are given when GNP estimates are derived, in the total GNP remains constant over time, measured velocity will, *ceteris paribus*, remain constant. On the other hand, if the process commonly known as monetisation is taking place in the economy an increasing proportion of GNP will take the form of goods and services for which money payments are made. This process can be expected to occur in underdeveloped economies as they develop: farming gradually switches from subsistence to commercial agriculture, urbanisation increases and modern sectors of the economy expand. Under such circumstances, measured velocity will, *ceteris paribus*, decline. A numerical example may be useful in illustrating why this is so.

In the base year, it is assumed that GNP is composed of $100 million of final goods and services for which money transactions are made and $100 million of final goods and services for which there are no such transactions. Thus, 50 per cent of GNP is imputed. If it is further assumed that the money stock averaged $40 million over the year, the velocity of circulation can be calculated as 5. The $40 million has in fact been used to purchase only $100 million of final goods and services over the year and has therefore only circulated on average $2\frac{1}{2}$ times for the payment of such items.

Assuming everything else remains unchanged, e.g. the proportion of imputed value in GNP, institutional payments arrangements, per capita income, expected rates of inflation and interest, tastes and preferences, etc., a GNP in the following year of $400 million would only be possible if the money supply averaged $80 million over the year. Velocity would again be measured as 5. However, had the composition of the $400 million GNP not remained the same, but consisted of $300 million of final goods and services for which money payments were made and $100 million for which no money transactions took place, the money needed to finance the $300 million component would be $120 million on the original assumption that money circulates on average $2\frac{1}{2}$ times a year for the purchase of final goods and services. Calculated velocity now falls to 3.33.

Another reason for expecting velocity to fall as development takes place is that the income elasticity of demand for money is greater than one. In other words, as real per capita income increases, the demand for money increases more than proportionately. For example,

$$\left(\frac{M}{P}\right) = a \left(\frac{Y}{P}\right)^b \tag{2.4}$$

where b is the elasticity of demand, a is a constant, (M/P) is demand for money in real terms and (Y/P) is real income. With $a = 0.001$ and $b = 2$, an increase in real per capita income from $200 to $400 will increase real demand for money for $40 to $160. If, in the previous example the increase in GNP from $200 million to $400 million doubled per capita income, i.e. assuming no population growth, calculated velocity would *ceteris paribus* fall from 5 to $2\frac{1}{2}$.

From the above, it is evident that a relationship between velocity and demand for money exists. The higher demand for money at a given level of income, the lower velocity. It is therefore possible to analyse velocity by examining the demand for money function; this approach is now followed. The demand for money function chosen takes the form:

$$\left(\frac{M}{P}\right) = a_0 \left(\frac{Y}{P}\right)^{a_1} e^{a_2 i *} \tag{2.5}$$

in which (M/P) is per capita demand for real money balances, (Y/P) is per capita real income and i* is the expected rate of inflation expressed as a proportion rather than a percentage. If the constants a_0, a_1 and a_2 are known, a unique velocity consistent with given values for any two of the three variables (M/P), (Y/P) and i* can be derived. *A priori*, it can generally be assumed that $0 < a_0 < 1$, $a_1 > 1$ and $a_2 < 0$. Two predictions can be based on these assumptions, namely, that a rise in per capita income will cause a fall in velocity, and a rise in the expected rate of inflation will conversely increase it.

It is usual to include the interest rate in a demand for money function. Unfortunately, no data exist for either interest rates or per capita real income. However, the effect of rising per capita income, which can reasonably confidently be assumed to have occurred during the past two decades in Afghanistan, on velocity will have tended to offset the effect of the reported upward movement of interest rates. Income and interest elasticities of demand for money are usually found to be of the same order of magnitude with reverse signs [E7; P12]. For example, a 10 per cent increase in per capita income produces a 14 per cent increase in the demand for money. A 10 per cent increase in the rate of interest causes a 4 per cent decrease in demand for money. The net effect of the combined changes in income and interest rate is a 10 per cent increase in the demand for money which, of course, results in a constant velocity. It will therefore be assumed that the combination of changes in the level of per capita income and changes in the rate of interest will, over the 40 year span under analysis, cancel one another and thus produce no overall effect on velocity. In fact, both per capita income and interest rates are assumed to have risen on average annually by 0.4 per cent with elasticities of 1.4 and —0.4, respectively. The combined effects of these assumptions can be incorporated in Equation 2.5 by making $a_1 = 1$.

Table 2.11

Currency/Money Ratios and Velocities in Iran, Pakistan and Turkey 1962-1970

Date	Iran C/M	V	Pakistan C/M	V	Turkey C/M	V
1962	0.28	5.7	0.48	4.7	0.38	5.2
1963	0.27	5.1	0.45	4.4	0.37	5.4
1964	0.25	4.8	0.43	4.1	0.38	5.2
1965	0.24	4.7	0.40	4.0	0.36	4.7
1966	0.22	4.4	0.40	4.0	0.33	4.6
1967	0.21	4.2	0.37	3.9	0.32	4.3
1968	0.19	3.9	0.35	3.9	0.30	4.1
1969	0.18	3.8	0.35	3.8	0.27	4.0
1970	0.17	3.6	0.34	3.6	0.27	4.0

Note: C—Currency; M—Money Stock; V—Velocity.
Currency and money stock data are centred annual averages.
Source: Iran—Money stock data from *Bank Markazi Iran Bulletins*, 3-10, 1962-1971; GNP data from Bank Markazi Iran, *Annual Report and Balance Sheet, 1971* (Tehran: Bank Markazi Iran, 1971), Table 2, p. 116.
Pakistan—Money stock and GNP data from Central Statistical Office, Government of Pakistan, *Monthly Statistical Bulletins*, 1962-1971.
Turkey—Money stock data from *Türkiye Cumhuriyet Merkez Bankası Aylık Bülteni*, 1962-1971; GNP data from State Institute of Statistics, *National Income, Total Expenditure and Investment of Turkey, 1938, 1948-1970* (Ankara: State Institute of Statistics, 1971), Table 1, pp. 10-11.

Fortunately, there is a further independent indicator to support these somewhat heroic assumptions. A significant trend in velocity is usually accompanied by a trend in the same direction in currency/money ratios [G27; K10]. Table 2.11 provides examples of this phenomenon for Iran, Pakistan and Turkey. In Afghanistan, the currency/money ratio in 1331 (1952) was 0.753 and in 1351 (1972) 0.752 as is shown in Table 2.12. The absence of any change in this ratio over the long run would not normally be associated with any distinct trend in velocity.

Table 2.12

Currency/Money Ratios 1331-1351
(Millions of Afghanis)

Date	Currency in Circulation	Money Stock (M2)	Currency/ Money Ratio
1331	959	1,274	0.753
1332	984	1,339	0.734
1333	1,091	1,593	0.685
1334	1,334	2,097	0.636
1335	1,617	2,473	0.654
1336	1,825	2,481	0.736
1337	1,869	2,417	0.766
1338	1,865	2,587	0.721
1339	2,018	2,728	0.740
1340	2,381	2,981	0.799
1341	2,883	3,565	0.809
1342	3,521	4,405	0.799
1343	4,303	5,393	0.798
1344	4,683	6,160	0.760
1345	4,634	6,355	0.729
1346	4,714	6,289	0.749
1347	5,021	6,538	0.768
1348	5,691	7,341	0.775
1349	6,338	8,181	0.775
1350	6,659	8,759	0.760
1351	7,483	9,954	0.752
			Average 0.748

Source: Same as Table 2.9.

The effect of changes in the money stock on the nominal level of GNP takes place with a lag. An exhaustive study on this lagged relationship for the Turkish economy indicated that the lag lay in the region of twelve months [F25, pp. 103-106]. The simplest way of incorporating this lag is to define velocity as

$$V_t = \frac{Y_t}{M_{t-1}} \qquad (2.6)$$

where V_t is velocity in year "t", Y_t is GNP in year "t" and M_{t-1} is the money stock in year "t—1". Taking Equation 2.5 in which $a_1 = 1$, it is now possible to divide both sides by Y/P:

$$\left(\frac{M}{P}\right) \bigg/ \left(\frac{Y}{P}\right) = a_0 e^{a_2 i^*} \tag{2.7}$$

However,

$$\left(\frac{M}{P}\right) \bigg/ \left(\frac{Y}{P}\right) = \frac{M}{Y} = \frac{1}{V} \tag{2.8}$$

where V is velocity. Taking logarithms

$$- \log V = \log a_0 + a_2 i^* \tag{2.9}$$

or

$$\log V = m_0 + m_1 i^* \tag{2.10}$$

where $m_0 = - \log a_0$ and $m_1 = - a_2$. Thus, given values for the two constants m_0 and m_1 and the expected rate of inflation i^*, velocity can be calculated from Equation 2.10.

In a recent study, the expected rate of inflation, i^* or $\left(\dfrac{\Delta P}{P}\right)^e_t$, was calculated using the Almon lag technique in the relationship

$$\left(\frac{\Delta P}{P}\right)^e_t = \sum_{i=0}^{n-1} w_i \left(\frac{\Delta P}{P}\right)_{t-i} \qquad w_n = 0 \tag{2.11}$$

The average lag between a given rate of inflation and its effect on the nominal interest rate using Canadian data was found to be $1\frac{1}{2}$ to 2 years for the short term rate of interest and $2\frac{1}{2}$ to 3 years for the long term rate [C5, p. 593].

For the relationship between inflation and the medium term interest rate [C5, Table 1, p. 591], the expected rate of inflation, adjusted here for annual rather than quarterly observations, is

$$\left(\frac{\Delta P}{P}\right)^e_t = 0.249 \left(\frac{\Delta P}{P}\right)_t + 0.317 \left(\frac{\Delta P}{P}\right)_{t-1} + 0.278 \left(\frac{\Delta P}{P}\right)_{t-2}$$

$$+ 0.137 \left(\frac{\Delta P}{P}\right)_{t-3} \tag{2.12}$$

THE ECONOMY 35

Table 2.13

Actual and Expected Rates of Inflation 1311-1352

(Percentages)

Date	Actual Annual Inflation	Expected Inflation (100 i*)
1311	7.69	
1312	−20.41	
1313	20.51	
1314	6.38	3.47
1315	−1.00	4.68
1316	6.06	5.78
1317	5.71	3.94
1318	4.50	4.48
1319	11.21	6.64
1320	10.85	8.29
1321	29.37	14.49
1322	28.65	21.00
1323	28.99	25.95
1324	29.32	28.48
1325	30.48	28.87
1326	8.69	23.95
1327	4.09	16.26
1328	22.01	13.37
1329	7.83	11.25
1330	0.00	9.16
1331	2.71	5.87
1332	−1.13	1.65
1333	13.71	3.81
1334	7.70	6.32
1335	22.90	11.80
1336	3.54	12.16
1337	2.52	9.17
1338	−14.69	1.26
1339	−12.29	−6.53
1340	6.16	−6.10
1341	21.70	1.93
1342	−3.12	6.13
1343	24.26	11.93
1344	20.75	14.96
1345	4.86	14.10
1346	0.16	10.67
1347	0.32	4.32
1348	4.77	2.00
1349	16.59	5.75
1350	2.99	7.37
1351	−1.92	5.74
1352	0.00	2.50
Average	8.65	9.15
Standard Deviation	12.21	8.21

Note: Expected inflation rates derived as described in the text. Actual inflation for
1352 has been assumed nil.
Source: Figures in Table 2.7 have been used to calculate actual annual rates of
inflation.

Using this relationship to calculate expected rates of inflation in Afghanistan, the figures in Table 2.13 have been produced.

Because there has been a large subsistence component in GNP throughout the period, which has not been affected by inflation, the wartime
decline in foreign trade, etc., an attempt has been made to derive estimates
for this component separately from the monetary estimates. Ideally
precipitation would have been used as a variable, as it has been the main
determinant of short run changes in this sector, but data are only available
for the past 15 years. It has, therefore, simply been assumed that in 1314
(1935), 60 per cent of GNP originated in the subsistence sector and that
this sector has grown at the same rate as population.

For the money economy component, a value of $m_0 = 1.6094$ in
Equation 2.10 has been assumed. This gives a velocity of 5 in the absence
of any expected change in the price level. Assigning a value for m_1 is
somewhat more difficult since considerable variation has been found in
empirical tests. Nevertheless, a value of $m_1 = 0.5$ could be accepted
taking comparative studies (e.g. [H3]) and the relatively modest expected
rate of inflation in Afghanistan over this period. Having calculated V in
this manner, the following transformation was made to Equation 2.6:

$$Y_t^* = V_t M_{t-1} \tag{2.13}$$

where Y_t^* is the non-subsistence component of GNP. The estimates are
shown in Tables 2.14 and 2.15 and Figure 2.1 below.

There are three simple methods of assessing the validity of the monetary GNP estimates. All are approximate in the extreme but nevertheless
can allow a modicum of confidence to be placed in the monetary estimates
where they indicate a reasonable degree of positive correlation. The first
method compares the estimates with other economic indicators. The
second method uses the impressionistic assessments of the rate of economic growth by foreign experts visiting Afghanistan on regular missions.
The third is based on recent work on fluctuations in currency/money
ratios over the business cycle.

The GNP estimates are consistent with the indicators presented in
Tables 2.9 and 2.10 above in that the 1330s (1950s) show the most rapid
growth, the 1320s (1940s) indicate recession and the 1340s (1960s)

Table 2.14

An Estimate of Gross National Product 1314-1352

(Millions of Afghanis)

Date	Expected Percentage Inflation $(100\,i^*)$	Velocity	Money Stock $(M2)$	Money Economy	Subsistence Economy at 1314 Prices	Subsistence Economy at Current Prices	Gross National Product
1313			196				
1314	3.47	5.09	209	997	1,496	1,496	2,493
1315	4.68	5.12	224	1,070	1,503	1,488	2,558
1316	5.78	5.15	240	1,153	1,511	1,587	2,740
1317	3.94	5.10	257	1,224	1,518	1,685	2,909
1318	4.48	5.11	275	1,314	1,526	1,770	3,084
1319	6.64	5.17	292	1,421	1,533	1,978	3,399
1320	8.29	5.21	338	1,522	1,541	2,204	3,726
1321	14.49	5.38	420	1,817	1,549	2,866	4,683
1322	21.00	5.55	502	2,332	1,557	3,706	6,038
1323	25.95	5.69	582	2,858	1,564	4,801	7,659
1324	28.48	5.77	684	3,355	1,572	6,241	9,596
1325	28.87	5.78	797	3,951	1,580	8,184	12,135
1326	23.95	5.64	850	4,492	1,588	8,940	13,432
1327	16.26	5.42	855	4,610	1,596	9,353	13,963
1328	13.37	5.35	907	4,571	1,604	11,469	16,040
1329	11.25	5.29	1,040	4,797	1,612	12,509	17,306
1330	9.16	5.23	1,168	5,444	1,620	12,571	18,015
1331	5.87	5.15	1,274	6,014	1,636	13,039	19,053
1332	1.65	5.04	1,339	6,423	1,653	13,026	19,449
1333	3.81	5.10	1,593	6,824	1,669	14,954	21,778
1334	6.32	5.16	2,097	8,221	1,686	16,270	24,491
1335	11.80	5.30	2,473	11,122	1,703	20,198	31,320
1336	12.16	5.31	2,481	13,140	1,720	21,122	34,262
1337	9.17	5.23	2,417	12,987	1,737	21,869	34,856
1338	1.26	5.03	2,587	12,161	1,754	18,838	30,999
1339	-6.53	4.84	2,728	12,519	1,772	16,692	29,211
1340	-6.10	4.85	2,981	13,230	1,789	17,890	31,120
1341	1.93	5.05	3,565	15,050	1,816	22,101	37,151
1342	6.13	5.16	4,405	18,380	1,844	21,741	40,121
1343	11.93	5.31	5,393	23,379	1,871	27,410	50,789
1344	14.96	5.39	6,160	29,059	1,899	33,593	62,652
1345	14.10	5.37	6,355	33,050	1,928	35,764	68,814
1346	10.67	5.27	6,289	33,516	1,957	36,361	69,877
1347	4.32	5.11	6,538	32,132	1,986	37,019	69,151
1348	2.00	5.05	7,341	33,019	2,016	39,372	72,391
1349	5.75	5.15	8,181	37,776	2,046	46,587	84,363
1350	7.37	5.19	8,759	42,440	2,077	48,706	91,146
1351	5.74	5.15	9,954	45,070	2,108	48,484	93,554
1352	2.50	5.06		50,396	2,140	49,220	99,616

Note: The money stock data are the averages of beginning and end of year figures, thus providing a mid-year estimate. Velocity is assumed to equal $Y_t^*/M2_{t-1}$. Therefore, velocity is multiplied by the money stock figure of the preceding year to obtain estimates for Y_t^*, the non-subsistence component of Gross National Product.

Source: Expected inflation data are taken from Table 2.13. Money stock data are taken from Table 2.9. Velocity is calculated in the manner described in the text.

Table 2.15

An Estimate of Gross National Product at Constant Prices, 1314-1352
(Millions of Afghanis, 1340 Prices)

Date	Gross National Product	Annual Percentage Growth Rate
1314	24,930	
1315	25,838	3.6
1316	26,095	1.0
1317	26,207	0.4
1318	26,586	1.4
1319	26,349	−0.9
1320	26,056	−1.1
1321	25,314	−2.8
1322	25,370	0.2
1323	24,948	−1.7
1324	24,171	−3.1
1325	23,427	−3.1
1326	23,858	1.8
1327	23,828	−0.1
1328	22,434	−5.9
1329	22,302	−0.6
1330	23,215	4.1
1331	23,906	3.0
1332	24,681	3.2
1333	24,306	−1.5
1334	25,379	4.4
1335	26,408	4.1
1336	27,901	5.7
1337	27,685	−0.8
1338	28,863	4.3
1339	31,010	7.4
1340	31,120	0.4
1341	30,527	−1.9
1342	34,030	11.5
1343	34,668	1.9
1344	35,417	2.2
1345	37,096	4.7
1346	37,609	1.4
1347	37,098	−1.4
1348	37,067	−0.1
1349	37,050	0.0
1350	38,868	4.9
1351	40,676	4.7
1352	43,311	6.5
Average Annual Percentage Increase	1.46	

Source: Figures in Table 2.14 have been deflated by the modified purchasing power parity price index in Table 2.7. The average annual growth rate is the annually compounded rate of growth in GNP in real terms.

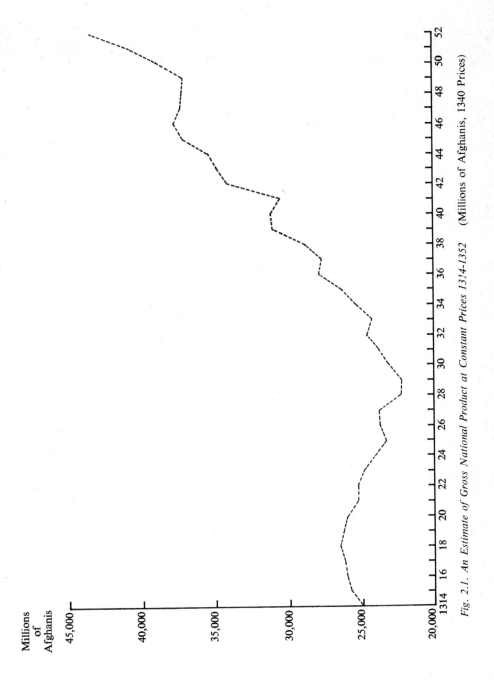

Fig. 2.1. An Estimate of Gross National Product at Constant Prices 1314-1352 (Millions of Afghanis, 1340 Prices)

moderate growth. A more detailed comparison is given in Table 2.16. Over the entire period, Government domestic revenue has increased at a slightly faster rate than GNP which is consistent with expectations based on a detailed evaluation of fiscal developments in Chapter VI. Exports have increased considerably more rapidly than GNP, also a reasonable expectation given the substantial improvement in transport facilities over the past four decades.

Table 2.16

Average Annual Percentage Rates of Change in Gross National Product, Government Domestic Revenue and the Money Stock at Constant Prices 1314-1351
(Percentages)

Date	Average Annual Percentage Change in GNP	Average Annual Percentage Change in Government Revenue	Average Annual Percentage Change in the Money Stock	Average Annual Percentage Change in Per Capita GNP
1314-1351	1.3	1.4	2.0	0.4
1314-1329	−0.7	−6.2	−2.9	−1.2
1329-1351	2.8	7.0	5.5	1.5
1329-1335	2.9	8.0	7.6	1.9
1335-1340	3.3	16.8	7.4	2.3
1340-1345	3.6	1.8	2.8	2.0
1345-1350	0.9	1.5	1.7	−0.6

Source: Figures in Tables 2.1, 2.10 and 2.15 have been used to compute average annually compounded annual rates of change.

The effects of the Second World War, most pronounced on Government revenue, caused a fall in GNP over these years. A report written in 1319 (1940) indicates that they were, in part, anticipated:

> It is probable that the present war will cause a serious curtailment of the program for the development of Afghan resources. Europe will no longer be interested in buying karakul skins, which have been the most valuable article of export. When we left Kabul the Government was carefully considering which items of the program were least essential and might be first abandoned. Public works and industrial projects are almost sure to suffer as funds are diverted to a military use. In times like these the demands of national defense come first. [H11, p. 122]

The results of the decline in GNP from a level barely above subsistence are vividly described in Akhramovich's history of the post-war period [A13, pp. 8-28].

On a cyclical basis, the movements in Government domestic revenue and GNP are also consistent with one another. Thus, the recessions of

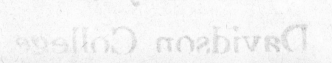

1318-1321 (1939-1942), 1339-1341 (1960-1962), and 1346-1349 (1967-1970) are matched by declines in Government revenue as is the rapid decline from 1321 (1942) to 1328 (1949). The booms of 1329-1332 (1950-1953), 1337-1339 (1958-1960) and 1341-1342 (1962-1963) also correspond to significant increases in Government domestic revenue at constant prices.

Regular visits of foreign experts to Afghanistan have taken place since 1335 (1956); the first pronouncements on economic growth were apparently made in 1341 (1962). In that year, the conclusion was reached that there had not been much growth over the past six years. Given the absence of statistics, six years is a long time span over which to draw comparisons. One would in fact expect such an assessment to be biased towards greater emphasis on the nearer events and less emphasis on developments occurring in the earlier part of the period. On this assumption, the monetary estimates are confirmed. Real growth was significantly negative in 1341 (1962) and stagnant in 1340 (1961).

The stagnation reported at this time was attributed to excessive levels of deficit finance. Using data from International Financial Statistics [I2, pp. 40-41; I3, pp. 228-29], it would appear that this phenomenon occurred in the last three years of this period and was considerable only by 1341 (1962). This again supports the monetary estimates if deficit finance did in fact retard growth.

At the time, the fiscal and foreign exchange reforms at the beginning of 1342 (1963) were thought to have stimulated agricultural production and raised the rate of growth. The monetary estimates indicate rapid growth during this year. The less satisfactory performance reported in the following year, attributed to the increase in inflationary pressures, is again indicated. Improvement reported in the following few years is also consistent with the monetary estimates. Finally, a recession from the latter part of 1345 (1966) to 1347 (1968) was reported by a mission in 1348 (1969).

In conclusion, fluctuations in the rate of growth during the 1340s (1960s) reported by teams of foreign experts have all been forecast by the monetary estimates, thus providing considerable support to their validity.

The third method is based on recent evidence on the cyclical behaviour of the currency/money ratio provided by Hess:

> In the early part of a business expansion income rises, increasing the demand for demand deposits. However, since currency is related to consumption expenditures which in turn are dependent on permanent income, and permanent income has a muted response to changes in measured income, the demand for currency rises little if at all. Hence, the currency

ratio initially falls. As the expansion proceeds, the demand for currency starts to rise faster than the demand for demand deposits in response to the earlier increases in income. This is because the cumulative response of currency to consumption is larger than that of demand deposits to income. Coupled with this is the delayed response of demand deposits to interest rates, which further depresses the demand for demand deposits relative to currency. Hence, midway through the expansion the lagged responses take effect and currency rises relative to demand deposits. This is reinforced as economic activity moves past its peak. After the peak, the demand for currency falls less than for demand deposits, causing the currency ratio to continue to rise. However, as during the expansion, the delayed responses of currency to consumption and consumption to income and demand deposits to interest rates results in an eventual fall in the relative demand for currency. The currency ratio starts to fall midway through the contraction which continues past the trough when the cyclical process repeats itself. In summary, the cyclical pattern of the currency ratio is effectively explained in terms of the cyclical pattern of the ratio of consumption to income in conjunction with interest-induced changes in the velocity of demand deposits. [H8, p. 673]

From the currency/money ratios for the period 1331-1351 (1952-1972) given in Table 2.12, business cycle upswings should have occurred in 1335 (1956) and 1345 (1966) and downswings in 1341 (1962) and 1349 (1970). From Table 2.15 and Figure 2.1, it can be seen that the expected movements in GNP at constant prices have taken place in these years according to the monetary estimates.

iv. *Conclusion*

The consistency of the monetary estimates of GNP with other economic indicators reinforces the assumption made at the outset that there has been no significant decline in velocity over the past four decades. Average velocity for 1314-1316 (1935-1937) was 11.6 and for 1349-1351 (1970-1972), 10.0. The significance of this lies in the fact that velocity can be used to measure financial development. As shown in Chapter I, the latter was found to be the most important economic determinant of growth [A2; M7].

The inverse of velocity measures the proportion of income held on average in the form of money. Thus, any decrease in velocity is an increase in this proportion, i.e. is an increase in the demand for money per unit of income. In a country like Afghanistan, where money is the only important financial claim, an increase in the demand for money per unit of income increases financial savings and results in a relative expansion of the financial sector which provides such financial claims.

The causal links between financial development and economic growth are twofold: first, an increase in savings is a concomitant of financial development; second, a higher proportion of savings is held in financial form. In turn, these have two effects on investment: first, investment increases; second, its productivity rises. The increase in savings occurring with financial development frees additional resources for investment. The increase in the proportion of savings held in financial form means that a greater portion of those savings can be allocated to the most productive investment opportunities by the financial system, thus reducing fragmentation in the capital market. Since the real interest rate is the critical variable in financial development, a positive relationship exists between it and both the quantity and quality of investment. As shown in Chapter V, institutional interest rates have generally fluctuated around zero in real terms. The financial constraint is discussed at length in this chapter. Interest rate policy within the context of financial development is the subject matter of a large part of Chapter VIII.

CHAPTER THREE

A FRAGMENTED ECONOMY

i. *Introduction*

Dubious though data used elsewhere in this book to support the analysis are, at least some information is available. In this chapter, however, the propositions put forward have almost no statistical support. Nevertheless, because of its importance in the minds of a number of economists in Afghanistan to an understanding of the economy, the idea of a fragmented economy is considered here. The central hypothesis is that the economy has consisted of distinct segments which have been only very loosely linked to one another. This fragmentation has occurred in three ways. The first is the separateness of the public sector from both the modern private sector and the bazaar economy. The second is the lack of cohesion between economic sectors, particularly agriculture, construction, industry and foreign trade, and the isolation of the subsistence economy. The third is the separation by distance of Afghanistan from the rest of the world and of regions within the country itself.

Had it not been for the recent appearance of a book containing arguments in a theoretical context along the same lines as those pursued here [M7], the importance of this phenomenon to economic development would have been underestimated. However, in many ways it is intimately related to all the critical constraints to economic development discussed in Chapter I in circular relationships.

ii. *Government, Modern Sector and the Bazaar Economy*

A comparison of developments in Goverment, modern and the bazaar sectors of the economy reveals strong countervailing forces at work throughout the past forty years. As soon as Bank Millie, the only private commercial bank, rose to prominence in the 1310s (1930s) as the leader of the modern private sector, it turned to restrict the bazaar economy with the weapons of exchange control and monopoly concession. In the 1330s (1950s), a strong Government restricted both the Bank Millie Group and the bazaar in its single-minded attempt to pursue an étatist economic policy. During the 1340s (1960s), increased liberalism witnessed a boom in the bazaar economy, a near collapse of the public sector, and a consolidation and retraction of Bank Millie.

Details of the relationship between Bank Millie and the Government are presented in Chapter V. Here it suffices to point out that the Bank was established with equity participation of the Government. The Bank and the Government cooperated in various ways until after the Second World War. In the early 1330s (1950s) the Bank was torn apart by Abdul Malik, the Minister of Finance, in his étatist purge. Bank Millie has not flourished since then, despite the absence of open antagonism between it and the Government during the past decade.

Other post-war industrial development in the private sector has also suffered at the Government's hands. In general, since the early 1330s (1950s) the Government has not supported and in many instances has actually deterred private industry:

> The Afghan policy known as "guided economy" may in fact be instrument-
> al in precluding so large an amount of achievement rewards for the econo-
> mically active segment of the population as to have a serious dampening
> effect on economic development. Pragmatically, "guidance" can be and
> more often is a tool for obstructing than facilitating economic activity.
> [N3, pp. 5-6]

The "mixed guided economy" philosophy has meant in practice participation and involvement in private sector activities as well as a programme

Table 3.1

Sources of Industrial Finance in 1337

(Millions of Afghanis)

Name	Government Equity Participation	Private Equity Participation	Loans	Total Funds
Government Depot	211	0	600	811
Afghan Textile Company	12	624	68	704
Electricity Company	365	139	102	606
Cotton Company	107	81	74	262
Transport Company	82	0	8	90
Government Monopolies	41	0	40	81
Slaughter House	30	0	5	35
Government Printing Press	30	0	0	30
Medicine Depot	29	0	0	29
Government Cooperatives	16	5	51	72
Hotel Company	0	14	0	14
Ariana Airline Company	5	5	0	10
Fruit Company	4	1	1	6
Kolmo Company	2	1	0	3
De Boto Company	2	0	3	5

Source: Ministry of Planning, *A Survey of Progress 1958* (Kabul: Ministry of Planning, 1958), Volume II, Table Industry (6).

of public enterprise, as illustrated in Table 3.1. The latter has been unsuccessful and was not greatly expanded after 1342 (1963). Although resulting in the establishment of unprofitable enterprises, this did no great harm to other sectors of the economy. Interference in the private sector, on the other hand, has had an extremely damaging effect not only by making legitimate profit hard to earn but also by increasing uncertainty in what was already an uncertain environment:

> Another problem the private sector has always encountered relates to the lack of satisfactory communication with the Government concerning varied industrial policies. In turn, this lack has inhibited the development of such a policy .... The Government is prone to intervene in industrial and business decisions without having an adequate basis for determining the effects of such intervention. [N3, pp. 144 and 156]

Under such circumstances, it is hardly surprising that the private sector has not exhibited much enterprise. Further, the absorption of domestic credit by the public sector to the point where institutional credit extended to the private sector actually declined in real terms greatly inhibited what initiatives there were. A distinct picture of the economy as a battlefield emerges.

During the 1330s (1950s), the embryonic entrepreneurial class within the modern private sector began to express grave doubts as to the viability of the Government's development strategy and, in particular, the country's increasing dependence on the U.S.S.R.:

> In its opposition to the new foreign policy alignment, the business group has predicted disastrous economic consequences of the commitment of so many Afghan resources to the repayment of Soviet loans .... [F18, p. 13]

As shown in Chapters IV and VI these fears were far from groundless.

The distance between the Government and other sections of the community is not confined to Bank Millie and the modern private sector. In fact, one of the critical constraints to development in Afghanistan in that it has caused low potential for development is the lack of identification of the public with the Government's development programme:

> .... those who have most to gain from policies designed to achieve economic development which would raise the standard of living of the Afghan people (an officially accepted objective) are not heard and have relatively little influence on the course of events. Their lot tends to remain largely unaffected by the development efforts of the RGA [Royal Government of Afghanistan]. Such efforts are rarely directed to the objective of optimum growth and a wider degree of sharing in the increased income flowing from such development efforts .... After 16 years of

5-year plans, this sense of participation by a significant number of people
in the various regions of the country is notably lacking. This is particularly
distressing when the Government should be asking for increased contributions from the people to support a continuing program. [N3, pp. 4 and 56]

Perhaps because it is further removed from the Government, the bazaar
economy, i.e. traditional, small scale entrepreneurial activities, has not
been so adversely affected by the Government as the modern private
sector. Where it has been involved in areas of Government interest, e.g.
foreign exchange and trade, intervention has occurred. Apart from the
1310s (1930s) when Bank Millie persuaded the Government to curb the
Kabul foreign exchange market and to institute foreign exchange controls,
intervention also took place during the 1330s (1950s) as the exchange
system became increasingly complex and non-market oriented and again
in 1352 (1973). Further details of the history of the foreign exchange
markets is given in Chapter VII.

Little information on other sections of the bazaar economy is available.
It was therefore one of the first tasks of this study to conduct a small
survey in 1351 (1972). What is now reported is largely drawn from that
survey. It must be emphasised at the outset that the sample was not
randomly selected. The author and his assistant simply walked round
sections of all the major towns in Afghanistan and picked what was
hoped to be a reasonably representative sample. Some attempt was made
to evaluate the accuracy of information obtained through cross-check
questions and intuitive assessment on the part of the interviewers. It was
found, for example, that respondents who had been on the *haj*, i.e.
pilgrimage to Mecca, were far less willing to discuss prevailing rates of
interest than others. There is also no doubt that sales figures collected
were grossly underestimated and questions on the respondents' own
credit arrangements biased heavily in favour of interest free loans both
given and received. Nevertheless, most of these same respondents seemed
well aware of the prevailing rates of interest. There was almost unanimous
agreement on a number of issues, particularly on the upward movement
of interest rates over the past decade, and some interesting regional
differences emerged. A strong degree of optimism regarding business
conditions and standards of living was encountered throughout the field
trip which conflicted strongly with accepted views on Afghanistan's
economic stagnation.

The impression obtained from interviews and observations during this
survey was that economic conditions in the Afghan bazaar have improved
considerably over the past ten years. Making a regional comparison, the

northern part of the country seemed to have experienced the most rapid development as a result of the new asphalt roads and increased trade with the U.S.S.R. The only town visited on this survey which both appeared less prosperous than reported in the past and whose inhabitants indicated that business conditions had deteriorated was Faizabad. The droughts in 1349 (1970) and 1350 (1971), distance from the asphalt road, and declining handicraft industries, the consequence of competition from the importation of cheap manufactured goods and used clothes, all appear to have contributed to this situation. In the south, Lashkar Gah seemed to have experienced, not surprisingly, the greatest boom, while business in Herat, Jalalabad and Kandahar has seen reasonable expansion.

Kabul has attracted the major part of Afghanistan's embryonic industrial sector, the availability of cheap electricity, a local market, labour force and credit facilities, as well as Kabul's position as the capital city, all acting as magnets. There is hardly any need to record that most respondents in Kabul thought that business conditions and the general standard of living had improved considerably over the past ten years.

Despite the impression of increased prosperity, not all have benefited from the economic boom. The asphalt roads have had enormous impact on the towns through which they pass. However, by providing a comparative advantage for many forms of economic activity in these locations, enterprise has been attracted away from other areas such as Chakcharan, Faizabad and Maimana. A predictable concomitant of modernisation is the decline of traditional forms of economic activity. The fact that people engaged in handicrafts, such as shoes, kitchen utensils, etc., and traditional forms of trade reported that their economic position had deteriorated over the past decade lends support to the veracity of statements by the majority of respondent on the improvement in business conditions. Carpet making has not been affected in the same way as other handicrafts since carpets are still an important export. Interestingly, in a study of the bazaar economy in Iran, Thaiss found that it was here that "some of the more dynamic (traumatic) changes are occurring" [T2, pp. 210-11]. One of the less favourable findings of the survey was that respondents frequently felt that income distribution was becoming less equal; standards of living at the bottom end of the scale had declined. The rich had become richer, the poor poorer.

The survey findings documented here as well as in the Appendix to this chapter and in Chapters V and VII are consistent both with one another and with basic economic principles. They present a picture of an economic boom, a new awareness of economic opportunities and the growth of an entrepreneurial cadre in the bazaar. The concomitants of these have been increasing inequality in the distribution of income, a decline in traditional forms of economic activity and higher costs of borrowed funds.

The prosperity of the bazaar economy stands in sharp contrast to developments in both the modern and the Government sectors. Between 1339 (1960) and 1351 (1972) Government domestic revenue did not grow at all on a per capita basis at constant prices, while capital and reserves of Bank Millie actually declined. Increased liberalisation of foreign trade and reduction of Government control have in part been responsible for the economic boom in the bazaar. The contrast is also another indication of the fragmented economy.

iii. *Economic Sectors*

The agricultural sector is thought to contribute about 50 per cent of the total value of Gross Domestic Product. In this respect and even more in that about 80 per cent of the labour force works in it, the predominant position of agriculture in the Afghan economy cannot be neglected. Despite the concentration of development expenditure in the agricultural sector, neither output nor productivity has risen substantially. Indeed, domestic wheat production has generally been barely sufficient to feed the population. Prior to the Second World War, bad harvests resulted in famine. In 1326 (1947), 1331 (1952) and 1332 (1953), wheat was imported commercially [F18, p. 17]. Since 1335 (1956) wheat importation through commodity aid programmes has greatly alleviated the effects of bad harvests. This sector has for a number of reasons remained largely a subsistence economy with strong barriers between it and the money economy.

Price controls on bread have not encouraged wheat production, again illustrating the unfavourable effects of Government intervention. Comparing the average price of wheat for 1312 (1933), 1330-1332 (1951-1953) and 1347-1349 (1968-1970) with the average modified purchasing power parity price index for the same years, the following results emerge. Average wheat prices were Afs 1.00, Afs 19.15 and Afs 45.00 per seer and the price index 7.8, 78.7 and 203.1. Thus, between 1312 (1933) and 1330-1332 (1951-1953) wheat prices increased slightly faster than the rise in the modified purchasing power parity price index. Thereafter, they did not increase as rapidly as the index. In other words, price controls may have been effective. To the extent they were, wheat production was deterred. At the same time, Commodity Assistance itself by increasing supply also contributed to keeping prices down and so to deterring domestic production.

The experience of 1352 (1973) provides another example of Government actions which were not likely to provide incentive for future cash crop production. An increase in fertiliser use combined with a more important factor, above average and well distributed precipitation, led to a bumper wheat crop and the cancellation of Commodity Assistance in the form of wheat. A price support programme was announced early in the year. This was soon abandoned and at harvest time farmers in many areas were receiving prices so low that neither could they afford to buy fertiliser for the next year's crop nor was there incentive to do so. The Government's granaries, the only commercial storage facilities since the Anti-Hoarding Law prohibits private storage, remained unfilled.

In general, farmers have not been given great incentive to move from subsistence to cash crop farming. Farmers in the North have at various times been obliged to grow cotton by the Government because the price differential between it and wheat has generally failed to provide economic incentive for cotton production. This has had unfortunate results. As early as 1325 (1946) a failure of the wheat harvest forced the Government to allow farmers to grow wheat instead of cotton and sugar beet. Consequently, "the textile factory was starved and the sugar factory had to close down" [S15, p. 12]. During the first half of the 1340s (1960s), the failure of the Government to raise cotton prices greatly deterred production as the cotton/wheat price ratio was halved over a five year period [U3, pp. 29-30]. Government intervention in 1335 (1956) resulted in a ban, later lifted, on privately owned cotton gins and the establishment of conditions of virtual monopsony. Although this ban was purportedly for the benefit of farmers, cotton prices have never been raised by the Government to sufficient levels to encourage more farmers to transfer resources into cotton production, except in 1352 (1973). The increase in this year, combined with low wheat prices, began to increase production again, though still not to the levels of the early 1340s (1960s). This has been unfortunate in that cotton exports have been an important foreign exchange earner and domestic textile manufacturers have consistently been unable to operate at full capacity due to shortages of raw cotton.

Apart from unfavourable Government action which has also included the surrender requirements at below free market rates on foreign exchange earned from cotton, karakul and wool exports, high transport costs from farm to market have also deterred cash crop production. This is considered in some more detail later. The incentive to remain isolated has recently been expressed as follows:

In effect, as long as the farmer has no debts and is producing crops for self-consumption his own living conditions are preserved at a relatively high level compared with conditions in other Asian countries. As far as the economy as a whole is concerned, the real problem is to encourage the farmers to produce a marketable surplus to feed that part of the population which lives in towns or does not own land. In this, the country's agricultural policy has failed. Indeed, the more interference from the government in the agricultural sector, the more the Afghan farmer seems to retreat into the shell of self-consumption or barter. [B26, p. V/22]

Involvement with the money economy by way of trade with the nomads has also resulted in unsatisfactory experiences for the farmer:

The result of this trade is clear; the Hazaras are sinking deeper and deeper into debt, and even if they wish to try to get straight economically they are seldom able to do so, being as it were compelled by their earlier financial engagements to continue trading with the nomads, a vicious circle. As settlement of an unredeemed debt the nomads take over sheep, cows and, in the last resort, land. [F3, p. 132]

Indeed, contact with both the Government and the bazaar economy has not provided much incentive for farmers to improve agricultural productivity so as to produce a marketable surplus. In 1348 (1969), one observer opined that in any Government initiative to improve agricultural productivity

.... the obstacles appear almost insurmountable: if the Government cannot even collect the land taxes on the books, how can it hope to make the necessary concerted efforts to engage the farmers in a nationwide campaign to attain self-sufficiency in foodstuffs in so short a period [i.e. by the end of 1351 (1972)]? [D9, p. 277]

Productivity has not risen significantly and, in the words of a report written in 1311 (1932), "it will be long before the Afghan peasant pays much heed to the advice of experts" [T3, p. 11].

The failure of agricultural productivity to rise, as shown in Table 3.2, is another result of economic fragmentation in both capital and product markets. The underlying cause is again an inadequate information system. In some areas where efforts have been concentrated on demonstrating new inputs and techniques and on providing the necessary credit facilities for the farmers to follow suit, the results have been striking. Only because the catchment areas for demonstration projects are so small and credit so limited have these not been reflected in a general upward trend in overall agricultural productivity. A greatly increased effort is needed under such conditions to affect significantly the total

Table 3.2

Wheat Yield in Tons per Hectare 1335-1351

Date	Output (Thousands of Tons)	Hectares Sown (Thousands)	Yield per Hectare
1335	2,200	2,200	1.00
1336	1,983	2,204	0.90
1337	2,234	2,212	1.01
1338	2,240	2,218	1.01
1339	2,279	2,230	1.02
1340	2,279	2,230	1.02
1341	2,279	2,341	0.97
1342	1,947	2,341	0.83
1343	2,250	2,343	0.96
1344	2,282	2,346	0.97
1345	2,033	2,346	0.87
1346	2,280	2,030	1.12
1347	2,354	2,036	1.16
1348	2,454	2,070	1.19
1349	2,081	2,176	0.96
1350	1,915	2,350	0.81
1351	2,401	2,897	0.83

Source: Ministry of Planning, *Survey of Progress 1962-64* (Kabul: Ministry of Planning, 1964) Tables A-26 and A-27, pp. 132-33; Ministry of Planning, *Survey of Progress 1968-1969* (Kabul: Ministry of Planning, 1969), Table S-20; Ministry of Planning, *Survey of Progress 1971-1972* (Kabul: Ministry of Planning, 1972), Table S-27; and Ministry of Planning.

picture. This is doubly important not only because self-sufficiency in grain production is a sensible goal from an economic viewpoint but also because rising agricultural productivity is one of the Adelman-Morris indicators of development potential. Its failure to rise in Afghanistan thus acts as a critical constraint to economic development.

Industry has already been mentioned in the discussion of the modern private sector's conflicts with the Government. However, as an economic sector it comprises both public and private sector enterprises. The Government started industrialisation in Afghanistan with the munitions (*Machine Khanah*), match and military supplies factories established before 1310 (1931) [A11, p. 120]. It played a paternalistic role during the 1310s (1930s) by approving projects and providing financial assistance. It was not until the late 1330s (1950s) that industrialisation by the public sector was decided upon:

> Experience has shown that private enterprise does not possess adequate resources and experience for undertaking large-scale investment of the type required for achieving a rapid rate of growth. [M15, p. 37]

With this, the public sector industrial programme was expanded and credit extended at such a rate to this end that the private sector was even more severely restricted in obtaining adequate resources to finance enterprise. Life was not made easy for private enterprise [U20, pp. 6-7].

The results have not been successful. Protected from competition, isolated from market forces, staffed and run by civil servants, most public sector enterprises failed to contribute to development:

> This is not surprising since, typically, public industrial enterprises operate at 30 to 40 percent of capacity. [N3, p. 54]

Interestingly, import substitution activities in Afghanistan had been strongly attacked by Strickland as far back as 1311 (1932) [S19, pp. 719-20]. Eltezam showed in some detail why specific import substitution industries, e.g. matches and sugar, failed and suggested that export promotion was the only viable strategy for foreign trade policy [E2, pp. 100-102]. Import substitution industries have also been criticised more recently [I1; P11; S11]. Again, the fragmentation phenomenon is highlighted by the fact that great waste in these industries has been possible in an economy with so few resources.

The mid-1340s (1960s) saw a reversal of the étatist policies of the previous decade. The 50 public enterprises had failed to contribute to economic development as had most other investment under the first two development plans. Thus, a decision was taken to promote private industry and in 1345 (1967) the Foreign and Domestic Private Investment Law was enacted to this end. This law and the underlying rationale embodied the import substitution philosophy. Firms established under the law were given tax and tariff exemptions for their first five years and plans were made for the establishment of an Industrial Development Bank to provide low cost credit. The Bank was eventually established after a number of setbacks in 1351 (1973). By mid-1352 (1973) 84 firms had been established and were producing under the provisions of the law [C15, Table 1, p. 50]. They had, however, predictably created only 6,000 jobs since incentives were for capital rather than labour intensive methods of production:

> In common with other countries in the early stages of economic develop-ment, Afghanistan has protected import-saving industries using imported machinery and in some cases (rayon weaving, for example) imported raw materials. The few benefits that have come from these projects have remained largely in the hands of the owners of the enterprises and in some cases have found their way out of the country. [P11, p. 10]

There has throughout the post-war period been a neglect of small scale enterprise which could have contributed highest returns [F18, p. 26].

Lack of widespread benefits from industrialisation is no new complaint. The First Five Year Plan's commenting on industrial finance says:

> In some cases the participation of banks have no other result except leading to its own profit. [M14, p. 273]

At the same time, indiscriminate participation is also criticised [M14, p. 275]. Rather than condemning self-interest (e.g. [K2, p. 2]), the observed phenomenon might be explained simply as an aspect of fragmentation. In other words, the multiplier effects of expenditure are low because economic linkages are weak.

The lack of any multiplier process emanating from foreign aid expenditure is due particular consideration in this regard. Foreign aid whether it is actually used for investment expenditure or syphoned off into private consumption expenditure has no multiplier effect simply because in both cases imports increase by the amount of foreign aid with no parallel increase in exports. In the case of expenditure on capital goods the investment has no direct income generating effect within the country. There is, however, an indirect effect to the extent that domestic labour, previously unemployed, is employed to install or operate the equipment. On the other hand, not even indirect effects occur when foreign aid is used to import luxury consumer goods. In any case, strong doubt as to the general applicability of the multiplier model to underdeveloped economies was expressed over two decades ago by Rao [R4].

The disappointing performance of both private and public industry can also be attributed to another fragmented market, namely, the capital market. As this is considered in relation to investment as a whole in Chapter VI, it is not discussed in detail here. However, there has been a general belief, stated here by Strauss, that:

> Perhaps there is no greater stimulus to industrial development than credit availability .... [S18, p. 3]

One might go further than this to say that there is probably no greater stimulus to *efficient* industrial and other types of economic development than an efficient, unified capital market. It is clearly market imperfection which on the one hand results in miniscule institutional credit being provided for small scale, high yielding on-farm investment in the agricultural sector and the acquisition of foreign funds to establish an Industrial Development Bank when, on the other hand, capital flight is thought to be substantial because real returns on financial assets in Afghanistan have been negative [G3, p. 4]. In Afghanistan, as in India:

> The assumption that in an underdeveloped economy all savings may be thought of as a 'pool', which is related to the entire national product in some more or less defined manner and may be readily drawn upon either by the public or the private sector, is scarcely borne out by the facts. [S12, p. 184]

The same point is made in a more formal theoretical exposition by Khatkhate [K9].

The modern private industrial sector then is another fragmented part of the Afghan economy. With the recent introduction of minimum wage legislation, there is additional incentive for industrialists to withdraw into the urban enclave and build walls between them and the rest of the community.

In conclusion, neither public nor private sector approach to industrialisation has affected the population at large either by offering a large number of jobs or by providing cheaper products. In fact, as discussed in more detail in Chapter VI development strategy appears to have been one of deliberately bringing change and therefore disruption to as small a number of people as possible.

The construction sector, in which over-investment has occurred in so many underdeveloped countries, has grown apace in Afghanistan. As expected, investment in this traditional outlet for urban savings yields low returns. In a recent survey of finance in this sector, the point was made that the poor were much better off renting than borrowing money to build a house because market interest rates were so high and rents so low that the latter were less than one-eighth of the cost of borrowing the necessary funds to build [K1, pp. 13-14]. This is a dramatic illustration of a fragmented capital market, given the evidence that large amounts of money are funnelled into the construction sector in which even allowing for capital appreciation expected returns are far below the market interest rate. On the other hand, the same study produced evidence to suggest that funds borrowed at market rates to finance motor car purchases for use as taxis could be used so productively as to enable repayment within a few months [K1, p. 9].

iv. *Geographic Fragmentation*

In 1308 (1929), there were 200 motor cars and 150 lorries in Afghanistan [G22, p. 180]. King Amanullah had himself driven a Rolls Royce from

Tehran to Kabul at the end of his European tour the previous year [F9, p. 214]. Six months later it enabled him to escape to Kandahar from Bacha Saqao. Despite appalling road and weather conditions, he reached safety just ahead of the bandit's horsemen [F9, p. 218]. By 1333 (1954), there were 1,350 cars and 4,000 buses and lorries [W3, p. 250]. Internal air services were started in the second half of the 1330s (1950s) [M21, p. 126]. But in 1335 (1956), transport facilities were still bad:

> Transportation is a bottleneck. When northern karakul breeders complain about low returns for their lamb skins or when Qandahar consumers resent high prices for wheat and barley shipped from the southwest, they can blame the high cost of freight, due to terrible roads .... Half the total annual freight was hauled by animals. [W3, pp. 247-48]

> Transportation facilities were primitive. There were no paved roads, bridges were mainly temporary, air transport was practically non-existent and river transport was very limited. The gravel and dirt roads were rendered impassable by any heavy snow or rainfall even between major centres of population. [M22, p. i]

The effects of poor transportation facilities on economic organisation are predictable:

> Most of the industrial activities are on a modest scale and are not geared to supply a national market. Both the localization and the small scale are due to a lack of integration between various economic regions. More often than not one region may have surplus production (or at least unused capacity) for which it has no outlet, while another may suffer from dire shortages and be forced to import supplementary supplies from abroad. The economic organization of Afghanistan resembles a wide sea dotted with islands of economic activity, each one more or less limited to its own local market, primarily because of inadequate transportation. [W3, p. 162]

Road building in the southern regions of Afghanistan during the late 1330s (1950s) met with considerable opposition and was one factor contributing to the Kandahar riot of 1339 (1960) [W6, p. 288]. The reasons appear to have been twofold:

> The extension of the central government's power into the hitherto autonomous tribal areas resulted in serious internal revolts. A revolt of Mangol tribesmen in the Khost area was sparked by the government's road-building efforts in the South. Such road construction threatened the autonomy of the tribe and removed its local livelihood derived from caravan traffic. [R6, p. 160]

By 1352 (1973), caravan trade only flourished in the less accessible areas of Afghanistan such as the mountainous Hazarajat region of central Afghanistan [F3]. The improvements in transport and communication have in fact been motivated primarily by strategic necessities. As mentioned above, these improvements have not been particularly beneficial to the rural community.

The 2,500 kilometres of paved road constructed between 1355 (1956) and 1351 (1972) have had a striking impact. There have been sharp reductions in transport costs which have had important repercussions on both foreign and domestic trade. Paved roads now connect Afghanistan with Iran, Pakistan and the U.S.S.R., although ferries still have to be used to cross the Amu Darya (River Oxus). Eltezam calculated that Afghanistan's terms of trade had declined during the second half of the 1330s (1950s) [E2, pp. 99-100]. However, between 1338 (1959) and 1347 (1968) import prices fell by 40 per cent, while export prices rose by 15 per cent. The resulting 80 per cent improvement in the commodity terms of trade was due in considerable part to the fall in transport costs though these are still high [U3, pp. 24 and 37]. Hansen has estimated that the improvement in income terms of trade during the 1340s (1960s) added about one per cent annually to real National Income [U3, p. 38].

A study of the three land locked countries in the region covered by the United Nations Economic Commission for Asia and the Far East, Afghanistan, Laos and Nepal, pinpointed the inadequacies in transport, banking, and agricultural productivity as the critical constraints to economic development. In all three countries "rugged topography" is the main factor impeding the development of transportation and the cause of high cost transport [U8, p. 183]. It is of interest to note that this study appeared long before the cross-country analysis of Adelman and Morris [A1; A2].

The opening up of Afghanistan to the outside world has not only been a result of road improvements. As shown in Chapter VI, foreign aid has been solicited on a large scale over the past two decades which in part has been used to send Afghans abroad for training. Many have not returned. It has also resulted in a large number of technical advisors and administrators residing in Afghanistan. There has been a liberalising of the foreign trade regime, discussed in Chapter VII, which has had an additional impact on exports as seen by the figures in Tables 2.9 and 2.10.

The effects of improved transport on domestic trade has similarly been striking. The north, south and east are all connected by paved roads to Kabul, thus linking all major urban centres by a day's drive. The impact has been so pervasive that one observer concluded in the mid-1340s (1960s):

> If any single sector of the economy is to be named the main lever of intensified economic activity today, it is undoubtedly transport. Development of roads in recent years has lowered cost of haulage, widened the market, made mining of coal and movement of labour easy and profitable, and has created an increasing demand for petroleum .... [G21, p. 439]

Seven years later, however, doubt was being voiced as to the unmitigated benefits brought by improved transport because

> .... construction of feeder roads connecting production centers to the main trunklines to capitalize on the heavy financial outlays have so far been neglected. [N3, p. 46]

The result has been to provide a competitive advantage to the movement of agricultural surplus to the major towns and an even greater disadvantage to its movement into the hinterland where areas of wheat deficit have existed [B14, p. 7; E2, p. 102]. Indeed, it has been suggested that Operation Help, launched in 1351 (1972) to bring wheat into the areas suffering acute distress after two years of drought, was necessary not because there was insufficient wheat in the country as a whole but rather because there had been less and less economic incentive for the private sector to transport wheat in these directions [B14, p. 7].

Differentials in wheat prices both on a geographical and temporal basis indicate fragmentation between regions and over time. Part of the latter has undoubtedly been aggravated by the anti-hoarding legislation. Table 3.3 presents some wheat price data collected in eight provinces on a monthly basis over the past nine years. The interesting aspect of these data is that there has been no region of consistently high or low prices. The ranking of the provinces on this basis changes from year to year. The coefficients of variation have also fluctuated randomly. The latter is a clear indication of a fragmented economy. However, in no year during the 1343-1351 (1964-1972) period was the coefficient of variation nearly as high as it was in 1303 (1924), also given in Table 3.3, or even in 1340 (1961):

> The mountainous nature of the country has been a serious obstacle to national economic integration, as indicated by the substantial differences in prices as between various parts of the country. For instance, in 1961, wheat prices in the most expensive towns were 150 per cent higher than in the cheapest towns. Thanks to the improvement in transport facilities, the price differentials fell to about 30 per cent by 1966. [U3, p. 24]

Thus, although improved roads have resulted in some reduction in price differentials and have had an important effect in linking up the major urban markets, there is much to be done before the fragmentary

Table 3.3

Harvest Period Wheat Prices in Eight Provinces 1303, 1343-1351

(Average Afghanis per Seer over Five Months Saratan to Aqrab)

Province	1303	1343	1344	1345	1346	1347	1348	1349	1350	1351	1343-51
Herat	.70	25.2	31.8	39.2	47.4	34.8	32.4	55.2	84.6	52.0	44.73
Faryab	.80	21.1	33.4	46.0	42.2	27.4	33.6	58.4	86.4	51.6	44.46
Balkh	.60	25.6	30.6	46.4	46.6	32.0	40.2	64.4	75.8	47.4	45.44
Kunduz	.90	24.6	33.4	41.8	55.4	34.4	32.4	59.6	75.0	43.6	44.47
Badakhshan	1.00	27.4	29.6	39.2	40.6	32.2	39.6	58.6	61.4	48.6	41.91
Kabul	1.60	33.0	36.6	42.4	59.2	42.4	40.1	58.8	57.6	48.8	46.54
Kandahar	1.20	32.8	37.8	41.0	67.6	46.8	45.6	57.2	81.0	43.4	50.36
Nangarhar	1.20	32.4	41.8	40.2	62.0	46.0	40.4	54.8	72.0	43.8	48.16
Average	1.00	27.76	34.38	42.03	52.63	37.00	38.04	58.38	74.23	47.40	45.76
Standard Deviation	0.33	4.47	4.10	2.82	9.86	7.15	4.74	2.98	10.36	3.50	2.59
Coefficient of Variation	32.5	16.1	11.9	6.7	18.7	19.3	12.5	5.1	14.0	7.4	5.7

Source: 1303—A. Guha, "The Economy of Afghanistan during Amanullah's Reign, 1919-1929," Journal of International Studies, 9 (2), October 1967, p. 167; 1343-1351—N. Koenig and H. V. Hunter, A Wheat Stabilization Program for Afghanistan (Kabul: United States Agency for International Development, mimeo, September 1973), Table 12, pp. 53-54.

features still observed are eliminated. In particular, the construction and improvement of minor roads to join small villages to the major roads is vital. Even this will only achieve partial success unless it also acts as a catalyst to produce greater cohesion within the society.

It has been pointed out that although notionally a centralised Government, there is much local autonomy within each province. This has been a contributory factor in producing fragmentation. The army, however, ensured that secession of the tribal areas has not been a serious threat during most of the Musahiban period [G12, p. 2; R6, pp. 160-86]. Some movement in the direction of political integration, compared to the heterogeneous tribal society of 1311 (1932) [T3, p. 11], has taken place. Nevertheless, change in the opposite direction has also been detected:

> Increased educational opportunities and literacy, plus an improved infrastructure (radio, telephone, telegraph, roads, internal airfields, airports) have not, as many people predicted, furthered the creation of an Afghan nation-state, but have initially intensified regional and tribal schisms. [D9, p. 277]

Communication within the Government has been so poor as to have produced a fragmented Government:

> As a result of missing information flow, each province applies its own techniques and procedures for tax collection .... Even within the precincts of one department or an authority the communication is unsatisfactory .... The consequence is administrative confusion. [I1, pp. 15-16]

Poor information channels have also been observed in the commercial field:

> Market information on prices and supplies reaches producers and consumers too late or in garbled form, if disseminated at all. But even if the interchange of commercial information were more efficient, the costly and slow means of transport would make it difficult for supply to adjust to commercial intelligence. [W3, p. 275]

In conclusion, all means of communications, whether it be in the form of transport, price reports or Government directives, are still so limited that the effect is to maintain the archipelago-like structure of the economy. It was Adam Smith who stressed the twin notions of division of labour and economies of scale. Market size, however, is the essential determinant of the benefits which can be reaped from their application. There is considerable room for expanding market size in Afghanistan. The transport factor is still therefore one of the critical constraints to economic growth in that it contributes to the low development potential for Afghanistan shown in the Adelman-Morris study [A2].

v. *Generalisation and Explanation of Fragmentation*

Fragmentation is not unique to the Afghan economy. Recently, a generalised description of this phenomenon has been put forward by McKinnon [M7]. The distance between economic units, which has been illustrated above in the case of Afghanistan, is viewed by McKinnon in terms of price differentials:

> The economy is "fragmented" in the sense that firms and households are so isolated that they face different effective prices for land, labor, capital, and produced commodities and do not have access to the same technologies. [M7, p. 5]

The effect of a wide scatter in prices of the same product is that any one of these has low probability of being a real indicator of economic scarcity. Because some governments have perceived this, they have often intervened to manipulate market prices in various ways in attempts to persuade the private sector to take up what is assumed to be socially profitable investment opportunities. The result has been greater fragmentation:

> Consequently, the market mechanism has become no better, and perhaps even worse, as an indicator of social advantage.
> Modern fragmentation, therefore, has been largely the result of government policy and goes beyond the old distinction between the export enclave and the traditional subsistence sector. One manifestation is the often-noted existence of small household enterprises and large corporate firms—all producing similar products with different factor proportions and very different levels of technological efficiency. Continuing mechanization on farms and in factories in the presence of heavy rural and urban unemployment is another. Excess plant and equipment with underutilized capacity are commonly found in economies that are reputed to be short of capital and that do suffer from specific bottlenecks .... While tangible land and capital are badly used, fragmentation in the growth and use of human capital can be more serious and no less visible. [M7, pp. 6-7]

In McKinnon's theory, the critical aspect of fragmentation from the viewpoint of economic development lies in the fragmented capital market:

> It is hypothesized here that fragmentation in the capital market—endemic in the underdeveloped environment without carefully considered public policy—causes the misuse of labor and land, suppresses entrepreneurial development, and condemns important sectors of the economy to inferior technologies .... The resulting dispersion in real rates of return reflects the misallocation of existing capital and represses new accumulation. [M7, pp. 8 and 11]

Examples of these effects in Afghanistan are given in Chapter VI. McKinnon further suggests that the unification of the capital market is a prerequisite for the elimination of other forms of fragmentation [M7, p. 9].

The fragmented capital market which is again reflected in price disparity, in this case taking the form of wide dispersion in the availability and
cost of capital, facing different sections of the population misallocates
investible funds. Therefore, economic development is impeded not only
by fragmented product markets but more seriously by fragmented
capital markets. The correct prescription in all cases is the improvement
rather than the circumvention of the market mechanism. Prices must be
made to reflect economic scarcity and not dismissed or ignored because
they do not reflect true scarcity when markets are fragmented.

Having examined the fragmented Afghan economy from three stand-
points and put forward McKinnon's description and analysis of the
phenomenon, a fundamental cause can now be suggested. It springs from
the lack or inadequate use of modern information systems in Afghanistan
and other underdeveloped countries. It would seem that information
channels in a traditional society are ill-suited and rarely used to convey
economic information necessary for business decision making.

The rural population in Afghanistan shuns contact with the outside
world because, in the past, most encounters have been unsatisfactory.
This tends to perpetuate

> . . . . the "*inward-looking*" *society*, into which men and women are born
> into a *set of answers*. In the pluralistic, ultra-specialized developed world,
> a man is born into a *set of questions*, but he finds that the answer to any
> given question opens a Pandora's Box of other questions as the half-
> truths of tomorrow replace the half-truths of today.
> Therefore, developing and developed societies have polar scales of values,
> attitudes and time, and these must be altered as well as technology, in
> order to bring about permanent changes in a society. For example, if a
> woman dies because of a *jinn* (or the will of Allah) instead of childbed
> fever, the introduction of public health measures *alone* will help but little.
> If a tractor or a truck runs because of the will of Allah instead of preventive
> and corrective maintenance, breakdown renders the tractor doubly useless.
> In an inward-looking society functioning at a subsistence level, dissidence
> cannot be tolerated. For any questions asked, the answers are known and
> parroted from generation to generation. [D11, pp. 17-18]

This would also seem to be the case in the political field:

> There is relatively limited articulation of policy views by professional,
> occupational, sectoral, or aligned economic interest groups since the
> mechanisms and channels for articulation frequently follow tribal lines,
> or other lines where the more obvious economic group interests are sub-

sumed by other interests. The poor articulation stems from a lack of adequate comprehension and cohesion of class interest within the more numerous classes, as well as from a lack of discussion processes from which leaders and spokesmen can emerge. There has been little or no tendency to encourage such articulation through the encouragement of social intercourse. [N3, pp. 3-4]

Given that change itself in, for example, the lack of social, political and economic mobility [D11], is alien to traditional societies, information is not sought on matters relating to alternative uses of scarce resources. Nor are the information channels suitable for conveying such data:

Afghanistan's stratification has been based almost solely on the ascriptive model .... This creates a lack of willingness to act on independent judgment. The right questions are not asked and the right answers are not obtained. [N3, p. 5]

This would explain the random nature of wheat price differentials even between markets with good transportation links. The latter are not used because information has not been received or acted upon which would indicate profitable haulage activities.

The wheat price data which exist have been collected by branch employees of Da Afghanistan Bank. One might hazard a guess that the procedure was instituted because either a foreign advisor or an Afghan returning from abroad recommended it. In any case, little use has been made of them and there is no demand for such information from private businessmen. Given that over 90 per cent of the population cannot read or write, printed market information can of necessity reach only a few. Furthermore, the existence of three major language groups divided into some ten sub-families and further into dialects in different regions of the country is an obvious constraint to information flow.

In the critical capital market, the same information problem exists. McKinnon makes the general statement that:

Reliable information on any one contemplated loan or investment may be costly, relative to its size, for outsiders to obtain. Repayment records are not well established, and many units operate with little liquidity. The fear of bankruptcy or default—which hardly enters at all into conventional uncertainty theory—pervades the underdeveloped economy. [M7, p. 18]

But this does not go far enough. Banking practices in many underdeveloped countries are typified by the absence of any attempts at obtaining information to make rational loan decisions. These are more often made on the basis of non-economic criteria such as the social status of the potential borrower and his personal relationship to the banker. Information

necessary for loan appraisals on economic criteria does not exist in
Afghanistan because not only is it expensive to provide but also there has
been little demand for it.

Accepting the Adelman-Morris finding that financial development is
one of five critical determinants of development potential and McKinnon's
explanation of why this is so leads to the recommendation that considerable development effort should be directed towards improving the capital
market as well as the road network. An improved capital market is a
necessary condition for widespread improvement in agricultural productivity. Financial development, in turn, has to start by changing the
traditional information system and teaching borrowers and lenders how
to use newly provided information for business decision making. It is not
sufficient in a country like Afghanistan simply to remove the constraints
which may in part have been imposed by the Government. This is
necessary but not sufficient. In addition, non-traditional information
systems must be created and their use encouraged through education.
Where the former is provided but not the latter, the wheat price example
above has shown that it will not necessarily be used. The important
aspects of a programme of financial development for Afghanistan and
direct benefits which can be expected therefrom are outlined in Chapter
VIII below. Here, it has simply been the aim to describe and explain the
underlying cause of this particular critical constraint to development
by placing it in the context of the wider phenomenon of a fragmented
economy.

APPENDIX

Bazaar Finance

With the exception of respondents in Lashkar Gah, almost all respondents in the survey described in the body of this chapter indicated that
credit was more difficult to obtain and was more expensive in 1351 (1972)
than it had been ten years previously. The reasons given for this phenomenon varied but increased demand for funds, reduced supply of idle
money, decline in trustworthiness and abandonment of religion were the
more popular explanations. Lashkar Gah is in the centre of the Helmand
Valley and many private pockets have been well lined with funds allocated
to the Helmand project. Thus, it is not surprising to find credit conditions
there easier than elsewhere.

Rising interest rates are a normal concomitant to conditions of economic boom [L5, p. 505]. This finding is therefore consistent with the conclusion that business conditions in the bazaar have generally improved

over the past decade. The reported rates of interest, however, varied widely not so much as a function of region but of credit worthiness of the borrower. Well-to-do businessmen all over the country mentioned rates of between one and two per cent per month, whereas small artisans, tenant farmers and shopkeepers were reported to pay up to 30 per cent per month, the most commonly quoted figure however being five per cent. Almost all the respondents had no expectations of increasing prices in the future. Hence, the rise in reported interest rates does appear to represent an increase in real as opposed simply to nominal rates.

At the top of the scale a slight regional disparity may exist, with businessmen in Kabul able to obtain funds somewhat cheaper than their counterparts in the provinces. Credit seemed most expensive in Faizabad, the town furthest from both the asphalt road and (by time and cost) Kabul. Such regional disparity is predictable given a banking system which channels all its funds into the head offices [L7].

Information on credit conditions ten years ago cannot be expected to be as reliable as information on the present situation. Nevertheless, it appears that the prime rate was probably only a few percentage points lower in 1341 (1962) than it was in 1351 (1972): bank rates have remained constant. However, when respondents stated that the rate of interest now was 100 per cent per annum they usually reported a rate of 50 per cent for ten years ago. Rates above 100 per cent per annum were considerably less than half their present level then. This differential effect is also a predictable concomitant to a period of tight money. A differentially greater increase in the cost of "low-safety-factor" loans occurs because the expected profitability of the project being financed is reduced, the stability of the expected rate of profit is lower and leverage tends to be higher on these projects during such cyclical phases [G23, p. 836].

The credit squeeze which existed in Afghanistan in 1351 (1972) suggests that a new business outlook has been developing throughout the country. Respondents frequently explained the increase in interest rates by the fact that people no longer held idle cash balances to the extent they did ten years ago. Instead, it was reported, money is now re-invested in stocks or new business ventures or otherwise employed. Since the differential between bank and non-bank interest rates has widened, it can be assumed that the allocation of resources amongst different uses has become less rather than more efficient.

In response to questions on the number of professional moneylenders in the respondent's town and province, answers indicated that most towns contained 50 to 100, with about ten times that number in each province. Quite predictably, the larger the town, the larger the number of moneylenders estimated by respondents. Many, however, admitted that they did not know how many such individuals lived in their town and/or province. Some of the more religious respondents denied the existence of this occupation in Afghanistan.

In the absence of a customary bank chequing system, the only way of transferring money between one town and another through the banks has been by telegraphic transfer which is expensive, complicated and not totally reliable. It is not surprising, therefore, to discover that a traditional financial instrument, the *hawala*, is commonly used in lieu of a cheque drawn on a bank account, to transfer funds between towns as an alternative to carrying cash. The *hawala* is a simple draft requesting a trading associate in another locality to pay the bearer a specified sum of money. A facsimile of a typical *hawala* is shown in Figure 3.1 with a translation underneath. *Hawalas* are used by many medium and large scale traders and shopkeepers to settle debts in other towns between regular trading partners. Small scale traders and others can buy *hawalas* when they do not want to carry large amounts of money when travelling to purchase stock, etc.

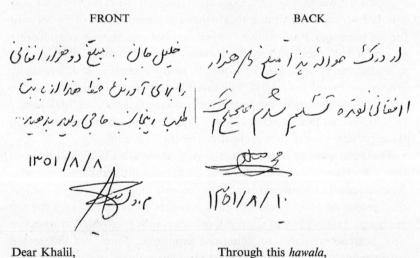

FRONT   BACK

Dear Khalil,   Through this *hawala*,
Give the sum of Afs 2,000 to the   I have received Afs 2,000 in cash.
bearer of this letter from my account. It is correct.
Haji Walid
                                                (Signature)
8.8.1351 (Signature)   10.8.1351

Fig. 3.1. *A Typical Hawala (Endorsed)*

Hawalas and their counterpart in India and Pakistan, *hundis*, are commonly used in foreign trade, particularly with India, Iran and Pakistan. There is a slight difference in the form of *hundis* used in Afghan-Indian trade, since the transfer of funds in this way is illegal in India. To avoid detection such *hundis* make use of code names in the form of fruits and vegetables to denote currencies and quantities. In all other respects they resemble the *hawala* illustrated in Figure 3.1.

Hawalas and *hundis* have the same disadvantage as that of bilateral trade in that balance must ultimately be achieved between each pair of traders drawing drafts on one another. A bank cheque system has the advantage of multilateral trade in that only an overall balance is required.

CHAPTER FOUR

RESOURCE MOBILISATION UNDER THE
DEVELOPMENT PLANS

i. *Financial, Fiscal and Foreign Sectors in Resource Mobilisation*

Development expenditure can be financed from domestic resource mobilisation through the financial sector and/or the fiscal system as well as from a deficit on current account in international trade. The extent to which domestic resource mobilisation is used in preference to foreign aid is important for two reasons. First, growth in the real volume of domestic credit is an indicator of financial development, one of the critical factors determining development potential. Thus, a rapidly expanding real volume of domestic credit will, *ceteris paribus*, not only provide resources for development expenditure but will also indicate high prospect development potential. Second, domestic resource mobilisation through the fiscal system too will be an indicator of development potential as well as provide funds for investment expenditure. This acts as an indicator because it suggests not only that there is a real commitment by a country's leadership to economic development but also, under a great variety of political systems, an acceptance of higher taxes by the population at large as a necessary sacrifice for development.

Thus, the effectiveness of a country's development programme will be determined not only by the magnitude of investment in relation to Gross National Product (GNP) but also by the method in which it is financed. *A priori*, one can conclude that a development programme, no matter how large, which is predominantly financed by foreign aid will not result in a high rate of growth. This is because low levels of domestic resource mobilisation, irrespective of per capita income, indicate low development potential.

Heavy reliance on foreign aid when this indicates lack of commitment to and acceptance of development has several disadvantages from the recipient's point of view [G16; L1; M7, Chapter 11]. First, the low development potential which heavy reliance indicates results in small if not negligible return from development expenditure leading eventually to a debt problem to the extent that aid received has been provided in loan form. The debt problem occurs despite concessionary terms whenever returns to foreign aid financed projects fail to exceed the interest rate on the loan to some significant degree. But it is precisely when foreign aid is used to a predominant extent indicating low development potential that returns will be low.

The second disadvantage to the recipient in using foreign aid as a substitute for domestic resource mobilisation lies in the fact that foreign aid inflows which sustain higher imports than exports actually penalise the tradable goods sector of the economy consisting both of export and import substitution enterprise [M7, p. 160]. Under such circumstances, the provision of extra foreign exchange ensures that the domestic currency is over-valued in comparison to its equilibrium market rate in the absence of foreign exchange supplying foreign aid. This, in turn, reduces earnings in domestic currency from exports and makes imports cheaper, thereby lowering prices of import substitutes. The importance of export promotion for development is discussed in Chapter VII. Cohen has shown empirically that extra exports are a more important determinant of economic growth than foreign aid [C17]. To the extent that the latter depresses the level of the former growth is, therefore, retarded. As suggested in Chapter III, the trade imbalance created by foreign aid inflows produces a leak in the circular flow of income of the same magnitude as the injection. There is, therefore, no multiplier effect from foreign aid financed investment.

Finally, excessive reliance on foreign aid may shorten the period over which assistance will be forthcoming. Not only will donors be disillusioned by the low rate of growth their perhaps sizable contributions have produced, but they may also become reluctant to allow the recipient country's leverage to exceed a given multiple of net worth. This can best be viewed from the traditional balance sheet analysis used by a bank contemplating a loan to a business firm. When net worth remains constant, i.e. domestic or internal savings are zero, and borrowing continues, leverage increases as do risks to creditors. They then become reluctant to offer new loans which will increase their own risk even further. It can, of course, be argued that aid should not be looked at in banking terms.

Afghanistan has received one of the highest levels of technical assistance on a per capita basis of any country in the world [B31, p. 158]. Indeed, the competition in the provision of aid between the U.S.A. and the U.S.S.R. during the late 1330s (1950s) has led Dupree to use the phrase "an economic Korea" to describe the situation in Afghanistan at that time [D10, Chapter 23]. The difference in the effects of foreign aid in these two countries could not, of course, have been greater. Afghanistan has relied heavily on foreign aid for financing the post-war development programme. The result of this has been all the disadvantages enumerated above. The remainder of this chapter examines the Afghan development programme since the First Plan of 1335 (1956).

ii. *The Five Year Development Plans*

Afghanistan has a relatively long history of development planning dating back to Abdul Majid Zabuli's plan for economic recovery which he prepared in three months in 1308 (1930) [B7].

> The seven-year Over-all Economic Development Plan (1932/33-1938/39) reformed the currency, introduced corporate business organization, encouraged private investment in textiles, sugar and leather-goods manufacture, but did little for transport or power. [U5, p. 58]

The first plan which fits, though imperfectly, the present day conception of an economic development plan was that prepared in 1328 (1949). It was not however formally adopted by the Government [U5, p. 58]. It is with the four five year plans starting with the First Plan of 1335 (1956) that this

Table 4.1

Planned Financing of Development Expenditure 1335-1355
(Millions of Afghanis)

	First Plan 1335-1339 (1334 Prices)	Second Plan 1341-1345 (1340 Prices)	Third Plan 1346-1350 (1345 Prices)	Fourth Plan 1351-1355 (1350 Prices)
Development Expenditure	10,499	39,369	33,000	30,930
Public Sector	10,499	39,100	31,000	27,730
Private Sector	0	269	2,000	3,200
Finance of Public Sector	10,499	39,100	31,000	27,730
Budget Current Account Surplus	2,750	3,000	6,600	6,570
Borrowing from Da Afghanistan Bank	241	3,583	1,200	1,720
Commodity Assistance	} 7,508	5,818	4,200	6,100
Foreign Project Aid		26,699	19,000	13,340

Note: All foreign exchange expenditure and receipts have been converted throughout at Afs 45 = $ 1.

Source: Ministry of Planning, *First Five Year Plan 1956/57-1961/62* (Kabul: Ministry of Planning, mimeo, 1956), pp. 312-20; Ministry of Planning, *Second Five-Year Plan 1341-45* (Kabul: Ministry of Planning, 1342), pp. 11 and 13; Ministry of Planning, *The Third Five Year Economic and Social Plan of Afghanistan 1967-1971* (Kabul: Ministry of Planning, 1967), pp. 21 and 48; Ministry of Planning, *Draft Fourth Five Year National Development Plan for Afghanistan 1351-1355* (Kabul: United Nations Development Programme, mimeo, July 1973), p. 45.

Table 4.2

Planned Financing of Development Expenditure at Constant Prices 1335-1355
(Millions of Afghanis, 1340 Prices)

	First Plan 1335-1339	Second Plan 1341-1345	Third Plan 1346-1350	Fourth Plan 1351-1355	Total First Three Plans	Total All Four Plans
Development Expenditure	11,182	39,369	25,539	18,562	76,090	94,652
Public Sector	11,182	39,100	24,461	17,197	74,743	91,940
Private Sector	0	269	1,078	1,365	1,347	2,712
Finance of Public Sector	11,182	39,100	24,461	17,197	74,743	91,940
Budget Current Account Surplus	2,850	3,000	3,558	2,802	9,408	12,210
Borrowing from Da Afghanistan Bank	250	3,583	647	733	4,480	5,213
Commodity Assistance	⎰ 8,082	⎰ 26,699	2,264	2,601	⎰ 60,855	⎰ 74,517
Foreign Project Aid	⎱	⎱	17,992	11,061	⎱	⎱

Note: Foreign project aid has been deflated by the U.S. wholesale price index in Table 2.6. All other figures have been deflated by the modified purchasing power parity price index in Table 2.7.

Source: Figures in Table 4.1 were adjusted in the manner described in the Note above.

Table 4.3

Actual Financing of Development Expenditure at Constant Prices 1336-1350

(Millions of Afghanis, 1340 Prices)

	First Plan		Second Plan		Third Plan		Total	
	Millions of Afghanis	*Percentage of Plan*	*Millions of Afghanis*	*Percentage of Plan*	*Millions of Afghanis*	*Percentage of Plan*	*Millions of Afghanis*	*Percentage of Plan*
Development Expenditure	13,031	116.5	21,824	55.4	14,154	55.4	49,009	64.4
Public Sector	13,031	116.5	21,485	54.9	13,284	54.3	47,800	64.0
Private Sector	0	100.0	339	126.0	870	80.7	1,209	89.8
Finance of Public Sector	13,031	116.5	21,485	54.9	13,284	54.3	47,800	64.0
Budget Current Account Surplus	1,364	47.9	1,871	62.4	991	27.9	4,226	44.9
Borrowing from Da Afghanistan Bank	1,443	577.2	2,091	58.4	1,724	266.5	5,258	117.4
Commodity Assistance	827	} 126.5	1,789	30.7	1,740	76.9	4,356	} 63.0
Foreign Project Aid	9,397		15,734	58.9	8,829	49.1	33,960	

Note: The First Plan ran from mid-1335 to mid-1340. Actual financing data are taken from Government accounts for the five years 1336-1340. Foreign project aid has been deflated by the U.S. wholesale price index in Table 2.6. All other figures have been deflated by the modified purchasing power parity price index in Table 2.7.

Source: Private sector development expenditure from Ministry of Planning, *The Third Five Year Economic and Social Plan of Afghanistan 1967-1971* (Kabul: Ministry of Planning, 1967), p. 46; Ministry of Planning, *Draft Fourth Five Year National Development Plan for Afghanistan 1351-1355* (Kabul: United Nations Development Programme, mimeo, July 1973), p. 45.

All other figures from Tables 6.4 and 6.6 below.

chapter is concerned. The scope, however, is restricted to a survey of
resource mobilisation in macroeconomic terms under these plans.
For details on all other aspects of the plans, the interested reader is
referred to [J1; M14; M15; M16; M17; M18; N3; S4].

Planned development expenditure and its sources of finance are shown
in Tables 4.1 and 4.2. The outcome of the first three plans is given in
Table 4.3. Comparing figures in Table 4.2 and 4.3, a number of interesting
points emerge. The First Plan saw more than the planned level of investment as a result of a greater foreign aid inflow than had been anticipated.
However, fiscal savings contributed less than half the planned level of
investible funds and deficit finance was nearly six times that which had
been planned, highlighting the absence of any financial planning.

The Second Plan, far more ambitious than the First Plan, realised
only 55 per cent of planned investment with shortfalls in all sources of
finance, particularly in the expected level of Commodity Assistance.
Public sector savings only reached 62 per cent of the planned level.

The Third Plan experienced the same shortfall in realised over planned
investment as had the Second Plan, despite its more modest scope.
Foreign project aid obtained was less than half the planned level. Public
sector savings reached only half the level of the Second Plan and less than
one-third of the planned level. This was offset temporarily, as in the First
Plan, by deficit finance of over $2\frac{1}{2}$ times the level planned.

The three five year plans saw realisation of less than two-thirds of the
planned level of investment matched by the same shortfall in foreign aid.
Public sector savings failed to reach even half the planned amount thus
leading the Government to use deficit finance at a level greater than
planned and to an excessive extent from the macroeconomic and longer
term viewpoints.

The planning period can be analysed not only through an examination
of divergences of actual from planned savings and investment but also
through comparisons of the latter with Gross National Product (GNP)
magnitudes. This is shown in Table 4.4. The weak fiscal effort, discussed
at length in Chapter VI, is particularly apparent from these figures.
Public sector savings averaged less than one per cent of GNP during the
planning period and financed only 8.6 per cent of total investment. There
was a noticeable decline in even this small level of savings in the Third
Plan.

Private sector savings took the form almost entirely of forced
financial savings resulting from the increase in the stock of money.
The inflation tax which produced forced savings averaged 4.6 per cent

Table 4.4

Actual Financing of Development Expenditure at Constant Prices in Relation to Gross National Product 1336-1350

(Millions of Afghanis, 1340 Prices)

	First Plan 1336-1340		Second Plan 1341-1345		Third Plan 1346-1350		Total 1336-1350	
	Millions of Afghanis	Percentage of GNP	Millions of Afghanis	Percentage of GNP	Millions of Afghanis	Percentage of GNP	Millions of Afghanis	Percentage of GNP
Gross National Product	146,579	100.0	171,738	100.0	187,692	100.0	506,009	100.0
Investment	13,031	8.9	21,824	12.7	14,154	7.5	49,009	9.7
Public Sector Savings	1,364	0.9	1,871	1.1	991	0.5	4,226	0.8
Private Sector Savings	1,443	1.0	2,430	1.4	2,594	1.4	6,467	1.3
Foreign Savings	10,224	7.0	17,523	10.2	10,569	5.6	38,316	7.6

Source: Gross National Product—Table 2.15 above.
Investment and Savings—Table 4.3 above.

annually between 1336 (1957) and 1350 (1971). Over the three five year plans, this tax on money-holding averaged —3.4, 13.2 and 4.8 per cent annually, respectively. Because no financial development occurred partly attributable to an annual average rate of inflation over the decade 1340-1350 (1961-1971) of 8.9 per cent considerably above the time deposit rate of 6 per cent, thus giving all types of money holding negative returns, this source of funds has not been large, averaging only 1.3 per cent of GNP over the period of the three five year plans.

The interdependence between financial and fiscal savings has been stressed by Shaw:

> Strong emphasis is due to the interdependence of fiscal and monetary policy. A weak fiscal effort during 1341-1350 (1962-1971) forced Afghanistan to tax money. In the degree that fiscal savings are reduced by price-level inflation, the taxation of money can make the weak fiscal effort weaker still. By the end of this decade, Afghanistan teetered on the edge of a process that would close the flow from both fiscal and financial sources of savings to capital formation and economic development. [S11, p. 8]

It has been foreign savings in the form of commodity and project assistance that provided the largest source of funds for investment expenditure over this period. For various reasons, this source began to decline during the Second Plan and not much hope can be held out for any sizable increase in the future without a much higher proportion of investible funds coming from domestic resource mobilisation. As Shaw points out:

> Several factors may account for the decline in foreign savings. One factor must be that Afghanistan's own fiscal and financial efforts were lax. If, in the country's own estimation, its development did not deserve a substantial input of domestic savings, why should savers elsewhere take up the slack? Another factor must be the accelerating rise in Afghanistan's foreign debts for accruing interest and amortization. On the national balance sheet, debt to the outside world has been rising relative to the national equity, and that is always the warning signal that makes creditors back away from new commitments. [S11, p. 9]

Thus, interdependence exists not only between private sector financial savings and public sector total savings but also between both these channels of domestic resource mobilisation and foreign savings. That the decline in public sector savings has been accompanied by a decrease in forced private sector financial savings over the Third Plan was predictable. Neither can it be a surprise to find that foreign savings have fallen too. In sum:

Processes of drawing savings to investment in Afghanistan appeared to have reached a critical juncture by the end of 1350 (1972). Each of the three that have been discussed here seems to have been regressing, and weakness in any one is contagious for the others. Declining real fiscal savings give a signal for more inflation in the financial process, and both are deterrents to savings inflow from abroad. [S11, p. 10]

iii. *Investment and Growth during the Three Five Year Development Plans*

An attempt can be made to analyse the macroeconomic impact of the development plans through the simple Harrod-Domar growth model (e.g. [A19, pp. 197-206]). Assuming an elastic supply of labour, the production function or the multiplier-accelerator version can be used to express the rate of growth in GNP as a function of the incremental capital/output ratio (ICOR) and the proportion of investment in GNP:

$$\frac{1}{Y} \cdot \frac{dY}{dt} = \frac{i}{v} \tag{4.1}$$

where Y is GNP measured at constant prices, i the proportion of investment in GNP, and v the ICOR.

Despite deficiencies in the investment and savings data presented in Table 4.5, five year average annual ICORs have been calculated for the period 1331-1351 (1952-1972) and are given in Table 4.6. For the three plans, average annual growth rates were 3.3, 3.6 and 0.9 per cent, respectively. The percentages of investment in GNP for the same three periods were 11.3, 16.0 and 10.8 per cent. The resulting ICORs follow: 3.4, 4.5 and 11.5, respectively. If a lag of a year between investment outlay and initial productivity is assumed, the relevant ICORs are 2.6, 4.6 and 12.6. The growth rate rose only marginally during the Second Plan despite a considerable increase in the proportion of investment in GNP because the ICOR was much higher. The lowest growth rate which occurred during the Third Plan was caused by the lowest investment ratio and the highest ICOR. The latter has been considerably more volatile than the former.

The ICOR is measured as a residual and simply incorporates all influences on the growth rate other than the proportion of investment in GNP. It does not therefore exclusively measure investment efficiency. Nevertheless, when ICOR accelerates to the extent it has in Afghanistan over the period of the three five year plans, an assumption of economic mismanagement must be made. In Chapter VI, further evidence is introduced to support the conclusion that much investment during this period

Table 4.5

Investment and Savings at Constant Prices 1331-1351
(Millions of Afghanis, 1340 Prices)

Date	Private Sector Investment	Private Sector Savings	Private Sector Financial Savings	Public Sector Investment	Public Sector Savings	Public Sector Financial Savings	Total Investment	Total Domestic Savings	Foreign Sector Savings
1331	654	733	79	213	-58	-271	867	675	192
1332	661	665	4	218	138	-80	879	803	76
1333	668	675	7	229	155	-74	897	830	67
1334	674	534	-140	339	363	24	1,013	897	116
1335	681	718	37	321	201	-120	1,002	919	83
1336	688	394	-294	958	391	-567	1,646	785	861
1337	695	653	-42	1,728	251	-1,477	2,423	904	1,519
1338	702	876	174	2,308	209	-2,099	3,010	1,085	1,925
1339	709	1,314	605	3,529	384	-3,145	4,238	1,698	2,540
1340	716	1,637	921	4,508	208	-4,300	5,224	1,845	3,379
1341	1,158	2,030	872	4,323	224	-4,099	5,481	2,254	3,227
1342	1,174	1,983	809	4,385	221	-4,164	5,559	2,204	3,355
1343	1,191	1,674	483	4,269	343	-3,926	5,460	2,017	3,443
1344	1,207	1,157	-50	4,382	607	-3,775	5,589	1,764	3,825
1345	1,225	1,202	-23	4,126	476	-3,650	5,351	1,678	3,673
1346	1,348	1,667	319	3,555	322	-3,233	4,903	1,989	2,914
1347	1,366	1,683	317	3,060	113	-2,947	4,426	1,796	2,630
1348	1,384	1,941	557	2,749	181	-2,568	4,133	2,122	2,011
1349	1,402	1,648	246	1,823	239	-1,584	3,225	1,887	1,338
1350	1,420	1,705	285	2,097	136	-1,961	3,517	1,841	1,676
1351	1,445	1,605	160	2,904	210	-2,694	4,349	1,815	2,534

Note: Private investment consists of investment in both the subsistence economy and the modern private sector. The estimate of investment in the subsistence economy has been calculated by assuming an incremental capital/output ratio of 4 and then deriving the investment required to raise output in the subsistence economy at the same rate as assumed population growth. Investment in the modern private sector is taken to be that given in the five year plan estimates. Annual investment of Afs 68 million has been taken for the Second Plan period, Afs 174 million for the Third Plan and Afs 180 million for 1351.

Source: Private Sector Investment—Calculated in the manner described in the Note above. Modern sector private investment from Table 4.3 above.

Private Sector Savings—Total investment less public and foreign sector savings.
Public Sector Investment—Table 6.4 below.

Public Sector Savings—Table 6.4 below.
Foreign Sector Savings—Table 6.4 below.

78   RESOURCE MOBILISATION UNDER THE DEVELOPMENT PLANS

has yielded neither significant direct nor indirect returns. Below, an examination of the planning process leads to the conclusion that if investment was inefficient, part of the blame lies with the increasingly inadequate planning process.

Table 4.6

Five Year Average Annual Incremental Capital/Output Ratios 1331-1351

Date	Five Year Total GNP (Millions of Afghanis)	Five Year Total Investment (Millions of Afghanis)	Five Year Average Percentage Investment in GNP	Five Year Average Percentage Growth in GNP	$ICOR_t$	$ICOR_{t-1}$
1331-35	124,680	4,658	3.74	2.61	1.43	—
1332-36	128,675	5,437	4.23	3.14	1.35	1.19
1333-37	131,679	6,981	5.30	2.32	2.28	1.82
1334-38	136,236	9,094	6.68	3.50	1.91	1.51
1335-39	141,867	12,319	8.68	4.09	2.12	1.63
1336-40	146,579	16,541	11.28	3.34	3.38	2.60
1337-41	149,205	20,376	13.66	1.82	7.51	6.20
1338-42	155,550	23,512	15.12	4.21	3.59	3.24
1339-43	161,355	25,962	16.09	3.73	4.31	4.05
1340-44	165,762	27,313	16.48	2.69	6.13	5.98
1341-45	171,738	27,440	15.98	3.58	4.46	4.60
1342-46	178,820	26,862	15.02	4.26	3.53	3.75
1343-47	181,888	25,729	14.15	1.74	8.13	8.63
1344-48	184,287	24,402	13.24	1.35	9.81	10.48
1345-49	185,920	22,038	11.85	0.91	13.02	14.55
1346-50	187,692	20,204	10.76	0.94	11.45	12.61
1347-51	190,759	19,650	10.30	1.58	6.52	6.81

Note: $ICOR_t$ has been calculated by dividing the five year average percentage investment in GNP by the five year average annual percentage growth in GNP (annually compounded). $ICOR_{t-1}$ has been calculated by dividing the investment figure for one period by the growth rate figure for the following period. Thus, the 1331-35 investment figure of 3.74 has been divided by the growth rate figure for 1332-36 of 3.14 to give 1.19.

Source: Gross National Product—Table 2.15 above.
Investment—Table 4.5 above.

The general picture presented above is similar to that given in a recent United Nations' survey conducted by Hansen. During the 1340s (1960s) he estimates that the ICOR was over 6, compared to a ratio of over 3 for the 1330s (1950s) [U3, p. 26]. His explanation for the doubling of the ICOR is as follows:

The apparent reasons for this high capital-output ratio are the building of the infrastructure and the large-scale irrigation projects, in particular the Helmand River Valley Project, which yielded much less than originally envisaged. The development projects undertaken during the 1960s consisted to a large extent of modern paved highways connecting the country with the USSR and Pakistan. While the highways linked the major regions of the country, they were not planned entirely on economic grounds and, in any case, they cannot yield their full potential until further developments in the economy have taken place. Similarly, the commodity production projects and the electric power generation stations are producing far below full capacity utilization. [U3, p. 26]

On the assumption that a sustainable incremental ICOR of about 3 could be achieved through a relatively efficient investment programme, investment in relation to GNP would have to reach 15 per cent for a modest annual rate of growth of 5 per cent. Although this investment ratio was reached towards the end of the First and beginning of the Second Plan, it declined thereafter and ICOR rose rapidly. In the future, a return to the 15 per cent investment ratio is unlikely without a considerably greater contribution from domestic savings.

iv. *The Commitment to and Process of Planning*

The First Plan was prepared by a planning unit within the Ministry of Finance [N3, p. 9]. The plan was prepared without foreign assistance

.... after a series of studies and investigations which have taken into consideration the lack of statistical data and experience in planning. Without this data and experience but with the help of God Almighty this plan has been formulated. [M14, p. 2]

Although foreign assistance was used in the preparation of subsequent plans, deficiencies in statistical data were as serious a constraint to the Fourth Plan preparation as they had been to the First Plan.

Deficiencies in planning have arisen not only as a result of over-reliance on foreign aid and insufficient mobilisation of domestic resources, but also as a result of the planning process itself. The absence of cost-benefit analysis, project evaluation and continuous assessment, and project supervision have also been responsible for the poor performance. The results of these failures have been described recently as follows:

Some projects were poorly conceived or designed, such as the Kandahar Airport (U.S.) and the Mahipar power generation project (German), and may never be productive. Others were overly costly, such as the Balkh textile mill (French) or involve outdated technology, such as the Mazar fertilizer plant (U.S.S.R.), which is still not completed. Most of the factories built in the public sector are operating far below capacity or have ceased operations because of inadequate availability of raw materials (cotton ginning, textile, vegetable oil and sugar mills) and very poor administration and management. [N3, p. 47]

The five year plans have appeared to be more lists of projects for which foreign assistance was to be solicited than attempts to lay foundations for overall economic policies. But donors have become disillusioned with such an approach:

> Unlike the First and Second Plan periods, foreign assistance in the Third Plan was primarily in the form of loans. There seemed to be a hardening of lender attitudes and terms during the Third Plan, brought on in part by the lack of economic performance in earlier periods, disappointment in the Afghan revenue effort, lack of sound feasible projects and deep concern over the general absence of progress and of convincing evidence that improved administration and better performance would be forth-coming. [N3, pp. 100-101]

Despite strong statements to the contrary in the Fourth Plan [M18, pp. 12-17], probably written by foreign advisors in any case, performance does not indicate that Afghanistan has yet like

> .... one country after another come to perceive that the principal sources of rapid growth and development are to be found within its own structure of production, institutions, technology and ways of adaption and functioning. [S12, p. 181]

The Ministry of Planning was established in 1335 (1956) with the Prime Minister holding the portfolio [N3, p. 9]. However, partly as a result of personnel deficiencies, the Ministry never played more than a coordinating role. It has not conducted any project evaluations nor required other ministries and agencies to do so. The administrative constraint was stressed at various times by the Nathan Team which advised the Ministry of Planning throughout the 1340s (1960s):

> Afghanistan was and still is one of the most traditional of the less developed countries. Over the years it became increasingly apparent that, if the available domestic and foreign resources were to yield significant results, the highest priority and greatest concentration of efforts in Afghanistan had to be focused on the implementation of modern principles of ad-ministration and management and the building of development institutions. [N3, p. 11]

With this, the German Economic Advisory Group also attached to the Ministry of Planning strongly agrees.

Since the mid-1340s (1960s) the Ministry of Planning appears to have lost authority and respect, partly because the Prime Minister no longer acted as Minister of Planning and partly because the planning process did not improve:

During the period covering the first three plans, there appeared to be either steady deterioration or no perceptible improvement in the degree of attention given to plan preparation and plan execution, in the sorting out and establishment of priorities at high policy levels, in the preparation of more carefully conceived and detailed annual budgets, in the formulation and coordination of sectoral programs in the operating Ministries and agencies, in project preparation, and perhaps even more importantly, in the formulation and execution of policy and in the vigor and firmness with which the nation's development effort was pursued. [N3, p. 22]

Thus, the question is raised as to the real extent of the commitment to planned economic development. Three factors suggest that it has not been great. First, the low level of domestic resource mobilisation to finance development expenditure points to low priority to such efforts as does the low achievement ratios of planned investment, a result primarily of low fiscal effort. Second, there was heavy reliance not only on foreign aid to finance planned investment but on foreign advisors to draw up the plans:

Particularly in the first two plans, there was a tendency on the part of Afghans to relinquish much of the responsibility for development by permitting the donors considerable latitude in identifying and financing projects. This was the result of less than appropriate efforts by Afghans to do their own planning with the help of advisors .... With the exception of the First Plan, foreigners were depended upon to prepare the first drafts of each plan. [N3, pp. 29-30]

There is the serious danger that such dependence has produced a deepening expectation among Afghan politicians, officials and—to a lesser extent—ordinary citizens that the effort and expenditure for development is the business of the donors; that development does not require sacrifice or the willingness to modify the ways and attitudes of the Afghans themselves. [N4, p. 171]

Third has been the declining prestige of the Ministry of Planning, the failure to establish the required data collecting procedures and to train capable planners, and the disintegration of the planning process by the end of the Third Plan. The

.... tendency to take the plans less seriously as the years went by .... [N3, p. 27]

combined with the other factors mentioned above, suggests that there has been weak, if any, commitment to planned economic development. This, in turn, has been a critical constraint to development since it has contributed with the other four Adelman-Morris factors to an extremely limited potential for development in Afghanistan.

CHAPTER FIVE

THE FINANCIAL SECTOR

i. *Introduction*

In 1295 (1916) an American working in Afghanistan noted:

> No Afghan would trust his money in a bank, nor would he take paper
> money—except, of course, a merchant who uses and is familiar with the
> Indian paper money. Most of them have Russian notes (which could be
> got for a song in Kabul during the last years of the war). Barats are issued
> on the treasury for money, and the mirzas pay all salaries in rupees; no
> Afghan ever receives his pay without the mirza getting a percentage.
> [B19, p. 285]

Rupees were hauled up from India on donkeys for pay day and
hauled down again to buy commodities on the Indian market. The
route through the Khyber Pass was particularly hazardous for these
convoys.

The situation which existed only 50 years ago must be borne in mind
when examining the developments of the financial system since then. The
complete absence of foreign banks (and indeed of any foreigners working
in the domestic banks until very recently), the strong religious antagonism
towards the business of banking, the lack of social prerequisites such as a
code of business ethics, attitudes favouring cooperative endeavours,
mutual trust, etc., and a legal system ill-suited to the task of supporting
modern business transactions and enforcing contracts have combined to
produce an environment which could hardly have been less conducive to
financial development. Nevertheless, Afghanistan produced one man who
not only tried but succeeded in laying the foundations of the present
financial system.

The history of banking in Afghanistan is intimately related to the
activities of Abdul Majid Zabuli who founded the first joint-stock
company in Afghanistan in 1303 (1924) together with other associates
from Herat to engage in trade with Russia. Between 1304 (1925) and
1308 (1929) Zabuli lived in Moscow as the company's representative.
The political riots in 1307 (1928) against Amanullah's reforms and the
brief reign of the bandit, Bacha Saqao, 1307-1308 (1929), resulted in
severe economic disruption and almost complete cessation of foreign
trade [G15, pp. 263-75; G21, p. 424].

The political upheaval and military conflict that took place in 1929 led
to a flight of capital from the country mostly in the form of gold and silver
coins that constituted the only form of money at that time. [M21, p. 182]

Four weeks after Bacha Saqao was overthrown, Zabuli returned to Kabul
[B7]. On arrival, he was summoned before the new king, Nadir Shah, and
asked to prepare a plan for economic recovery. According to Zabuli, the
king told him:

> Today we see in our own country export, import, transportation, brokerage
> and everything else are all done by foreigners; only shopkeeping is left
> for our people. This situation is intolerable and we must have our own
> nationals engaged in all these activities throughout the country. We must
> find a way to cut off the hands of the foreigners. [B7]

Zabuli stayed in Kabul for three months to prepare an economic plan
which included a scheme to establish a bank. To this proposal, the
Minister of Justice, who had been directed to enforce Islamic law,
strongly objected [B7; G15, p. 295]. Nadir Shah, who was well aware of
the religious opposition to a similar plan of Amanullah, also opposed the
scheme, although he supported the rest of Zabuli's plan [B7]. The plan
was completed by the end of 1308 (1930) and Zabuli left Afghanistan to
run the Berlin office of his trading company. Meanwhile, the Shirkat-i-
Sahami-i-Afghan had been established as a trading company rather than
as the bank Zabuli had proposed. Permission to establish the joint-stock
company, Shirkat-i-Sahami-i-Afghan, to regulate foreign trade and
develop the domestic economy was granted by Nadir Shah in 1309 (1930)
to the group of merchants from Herat led by Abdul Majid Zabuli. As part
of the arrangement, they were given the monopoly for sugar, petrol and
motor vehicle imports and cotton, karakul and wool exports [B7; C9,
p. 411; M27, p. 1]. The Shirkat-i-Sahami-i-Afghan was founded with a
capital of Afs 2.5 million, of which Afs 1.7 million was subscribed by the
Government [M21, p. 182]. The company opened for business in the
following year [G15, p. 316].

In 1310 (1931) after Zabuli's economic plan had run into difficulties, he
was asked to return to Afghanistan. His prescription was once again the
foundation of a bank and investment in the northern part of the country.
As part of his conditions for remaining in Afghanistan, he required
Government support for his scheme to establish the bank. Zabuli returned
to Afghanistan towards the end of 1310 (1931) and directed his first efforts
to reviving his and Amanullah's scheme to found a bank which could issue
paper currency, provide credit and, above all, form the nucleus for the
development of entrepreneurial and managerial talent in the country. The

vehicle used was the Shirkat-i-Sahami-i-Afghan. Reorganisation took place in 1311 (1932) in which the name of the company was changed. "In Saur 1312 (April/May 1933), Bank Millie was established with capital invested by the Government as well as founders of the Bank" [B6, p. 6]. This reorganisation involved raising the capital to Afs 7.1 million. By 1316 (1937), this figure had been increased by stages through Afs 35 million to Afs 60 million [M21, p. 182]. Thereafter, the Bank's capital was progressively raised to Afs 500 million by 1329 (1950) [C10, p. 39]. There has been no increase in capital since then and total capital and reserves have risen slowly from Afs 519 million in 1330 (1952) to Afs 839 million in 1350 (1972), a considerable decline in real terms [B5; B8].

Bank Millie was something of a hybrid in that its founder had obtained both support and finance from the Government. As in other areas of Government interest or intervention since 1311 (1932), the relationship was informal. The Government appeared to show enthusiasm for economic development but no clear views on how this should be achieved. Assisting Bank Millie was just one of several *ad hoc* measures in this direction.

One of the main difficulties encountered at the beginning was the religious prohibition against interest. The opposition was led by the Minister of Justice. However, an ingenious solution was found whereby loans could be made interest free but the borrower obliged to buy a stamp, *pule tiket* (money ticket), to be attached to each repayment receipt thus providing the bank with profit rather than interest, the former not in violation of Islamic law. The term, though not the stamps, is still used.

For the first six years, the success of Bank Millie was dramatic, particularly when viewed against the backcloth of the Great Depression.

> When people were introduced to the idea of pooling their resources and interests, when representative money and large-scale commercial credit were introduced and the first results obtained, the effect was amazing. During the first six years the Afghan National Bank [English translation of Bank Millie Afghan] increased its capital one hundredfold. [C9, p. 411]

During the 1310s (1930s), Bank Millie's operations expanded rapidly with Government help. The latter consisted of the accedence to requests from the Bank for monopoly concessions and the control over foreign exchange dealings as well as financial support. In 1314 (1935) Afghanistan adopted a fixed exchange rate and foreign exchange transactions were supervised by Bank Millie [B6, p. 7]. Due to a deteriorating balance of payments situation thereafter, the Bank recommended tighter exchange control regulations. In 1317 (1938) earnings from karakul exports had to be surrendered to the Bank and importers were obliged to export an equal value of commodities before placing their import orders [O4, pp. 123-33]. Bank Millie was instrumental in an attempt to disband the Kabul money bazaar and did take over a large part of Afghanistan's foreign trade from bazaar dealers. In part, this followed a deliberate policy to break the domination of foreign trade by ethnic minorities (Hindus and Jews) [B7].

The fixed exchange rate system adopted in 1314 (1935) was designed in part to eliminate seasonal fluctuations in the rates. Bank Millie agreed to buy 100 Rupees for Afs 396 and to sell for Afs 400. As a result of a continuous debasement of the currency, this rate soon overvalued the Afghani and necessitated increasingly stringent exchange controls. Responsible by this time for the country's exchange rate system, the Bank supplied all Government requirements of foreign exchange at the fixed rate from 1314 (1935) onwards [M21, p. 182]. A preferential exchange rate for the Government was a feature of the exchange system until 1352 (1973).

Bank Millie assisted the Government with the issue of Treasury currency notes which started in 1315 (1936). The paper currency was convertible into silver Afghanis at the Bank; initially, soldiers and civil servants who received payment in currency notes immediately converted them into coins. However, after the first year silver coins began to be accumulated by the Bank. Within three years Afs 60 million of Afghan and Iranian coins had been collected. Gold was also used to back the paper currency [B7]. By 1352 (1973), Afghanistan's international liquidity consisted in most part of gold, thus presenting the Government with a sizable windfall profit on the abandonment of the two tier gold system in that year.

Despite problems of trade imbalance in the pre-war period, considerable growth in the volume of both imports and exports took place. The expansion of Afghanistan's foreign trade and level of economic activity during the Great Depression can to a large extent be attributed to the dynamic and unfettered development of Bank Millie [N5, pp. 60-62]. Activities were wide ranging, though largely dependent on the success of its banking business:

> Along with these fundamental measures, the Banke Milli diverted special attention towards organizing banking affairs. It afforded facilities in carrying out financial transactions and executing drafts in the shortest possible time. It offered prompt and satisfactory service to customers. The

Bank also offered facilities in granting loans to traders. It introduced cheques as well as exchange and transfer drafts. All this attracted customers in a wonderful way, enabling fixed deposits and current and deposit accounts to increase considerably within a short period. [B6, pp. 8-9]

The most important activity of Bank Millie in these years was its involvement and participation in industry. Joint-stock companies were established to engage in trade (cotton, karakul and wool exporting), cotton ginning, oil extracting, sugar refining and textile manufacturing [B6, pp. 9-30]. Between 1311 (1932) and 1313 (1934), 30 joint-stock companies were organised under the auspices of Bank Millie [G15, p. 315]. By 1317 (1939), the total capital of these subsidiary companies had reached Afs 292 million [O4, pp. 123-33]. By 1325 (1947), Bank Millie held interests in 50 trading and industrial companies:

> The same important merchants who held shares in the bank were the majority stockholders of these companies. In addition to a virtual monopoly in the major commodities of the Afghan export-import trade, the Bank-i-Milli and its president, Abdul Majid Zabuli, gained control of most of the industry of the kingdom, both the well-established state-owned enterprises and the budding new firms. [G15, p. 363]

Bank Millie also extended credit, granting loans of all kinds at 12 per cent interest. For example, after it had received the monopoly over motor vehicle imports it extended credit to purchasers:

> The first vehicle owners were people from the Jaji tribe. Vehicles were sold for Afs 12,000 on instalments over 18 months. The Jajis did a great job and took over the transportation business from the Indians. [B7]

There was, of course, no insurance on the vehicles, appalling road conditions and unskilled drivers. Bank Millie contended with the latter problem by establishing a special driving school.

The relationship between the Bank and the Government during these early years has been described as follows:

> It took a government franchise for the establishment of the first successful joint stock company (shirkat) with limited liability for the contributors. This company, Shirkat-i-Ashami, promoted the Bank Melli Afghan .... It not only assumed the position of the government's banker and handled its note issue, but also promoted the establishment and participated in the financing of at least 125 shirkats. In each case, the government would approve the new company and thereby protect the investment of the Bank Melli. [W3, p. 186]

In 1318 (1939), Da Afghanistan Bank, the central bank, was established with a capital of Afs 120 million, of which 93 per cent was subscribed by the Government. Bank Millie apparently cooperated with the Government in this. Exactly what lay behind the move cannot be ascertained. However, Bank Millie took the opportunity to repay the Government's equity interest in the Bank and in this way contributed to the financing of the new institution [B7]. As the only trained bankers in the country, Bank Millie employees were provided to staff the new central bank. The issue of possible conflict of interest was never raised. By the end of the 1320s (1940s), there was no distinction between the interests of Bank Millie, Da Afghanistan Bank and the Government:

> The operations of Bank Melli became so all-embracing that it was only natural that at the end of World War II the president of the Bank, Abdul Majid Zabuli, became the Minister of National Economy and also Governor of the State Bank. [W3, p. 187]

The interlocking ownership and control still existing within the financial sector is discussed below.

Reports suggest that relations between Bank Millie and the Government had, however, begun to deteriorate by 1317 (1938) [C9, pp. 412-13; G15, pp. 367-68]:

> During its first years of existence relations were good, but in 1938, when it became obvious that the new venture was developing well and its leaders were pocketing handsome profits which were not all shown in the books of their companies, the Government took away most monopolies from the Bank and ordered a first investigation into the group's activities. The official reason given was a shortage of foreign exchange. "Invisible" exports of foreign exchange, in which the Bank was involved, were discovered and a leading personality of the group was sentenced to six years of imprisonment for too skilful disposal of karakul skins . . . . The Government opened a bank of its own and put it in charge of foreign exchange control . . . . [C9, pp. 412-13]

The dispute of 1317 (1938), whether or not it led to the establishment of Da Afghanistan Bank as a retaliatory gesture, was soon resolved. Abdul Majid Zabuli was appointed Minister of National Economy in the following year [W3, p. 239] but left Afghanistan immediately to spend the War years in Switzerland [C9, p. 413]. The imprisoned member of the Bank Millie hierarchy was released and appointed president of one of the Bank's manufacturing companies [C9, p. 413].

The Second World War so disrupted the Afghan economy that it is not surprising to find Bank Millie and the Government working in harmony to salvage whatever possible of the pre-war industries and trading concerns. Further, because Afghanistan had accumulated foreign exchange during the War, this was no longer a critical issue. With Zabuli as Minister of National Economy and Governor of Da Afghanistan Bank, peaceful co-existence prevailed during the 1320s (1940s).

It was once again Bank Millie's success which drew the Government's ire. For all private enterprise, this has been a threat of varying severity throughout the post-war period. Too much private sector expansion appears to have been anathema to most Governments. Profit has been considered undesirable and excessive profit immoral. Government assistance during attempts at recovery was replaced in the 1330s (1950s) by strong opposition:

> A live-and-let-live policy prevailed under H. R. H. Shah Mahmoud, who succeeded his brother H. R. H. Hashim Khan as Prime Minister in 1946. As part of this policy, the government allocated practically all the foreign exchange needed by the industrial group and maintained a special exchange rate (the "industrial" rate) at a level between the official and the free rates. But the underlying economic rivalry between the Banke Millie group and the government (which had political overtones because of the absence of tribal and dynastic ties with Abdul Majid's industrial-mercantile group) broke out into the open when he left the Cabinet in 1950 over a controversial exchange allocation. The break was completed in September 1953, when Shah Mahmoud's resignation ended the line of the King's uncles serving as Prime Ministers. Under his successor, H. R. H. Mohammed Daoud Khan, cousin of the King and a former Minister of War and Ambassador to France, and the Deputy Prime Minister, H. R. H. Mohammed Naim Khan, also a cousin and a former Minister of Public Works and Ambassador to the U.S., a new economic policy of more stringent government control of business took hold. The cousins had not been so closely associated with the Banke Millie group as the uncles and were less impressed with the merits of a free enterprise system within the framework of an underdeveloped economy than they were.
>
> The new approach to economic planning is perhaps best represented by the policies of Abdul Malik, the new Minister of Finance (since the beginning of 1955 also Minister of National Economy) who, perhaps under the influence of his previous experience as Quartermaster General of the Army, has been inspired by Turkey's "étatism," with which he had become familiar. He found the policies of Banke Millie no longer suited to the country's best interests.
>
> Within the first years of his regime the following curbs on Banke Millie were put through:
>
> (a) The government forced Banke Millie to sell 63 percent of the stock in the Northern Cotton company to the Ministry of Finance, which in turn engaged private merchants to enforce a new cotton buying policy.
>
> (b) The government continued to control textile selling prices and the profit rate of the Banke Millie-owned Textile Co.
>
> (c) The government set domestic minimum prices to be paid the breeders

for karakul skins which left too narrow a margin for processing, handling, and selling in New York.

(d) The government forced Banke Millie to sell it 51 percent of the stock in the General Electric Co. (which is building the new Sarobie power plant) and assumed control over that construction.

(e) The government took over the Cement Co. (which long had made plans for the first plant) and negotiated the construction contract involving machinery and a $ 5-million credit from Czechoslovakia.

(f) The government charged Banke Millie with tax evasion in connection with capital gain derived from the sale of stock and land.

(g) The government extended exchange control to all proceeds from karakul, wool, and cotton, but raised the buying rate from 16.8 afghanis to between 21 and 26 afghanis to the dollar. This permitted the government to broaden its control over new plant investment, since proceeds from cotton and wool exports could no longer be used to make foreign purchases without government approval. At the same time, by making available what exchange it wanted at a lower than the free market rate, the government cheapened foreign investment goods.

The impact on business volume and public opinion was such that Banke Millie shares, once scarce at 1,000 afghanis, were now available at 500 afghanis. Moreover, the Bank could no longer obtain ready cash from its shareholders to defray the local cost of the Gulbahar textile plant, thus delaying the plant's completion. The bank's dividends were reduced to 5 percent in 1954, and prospects for 1955 seem dark. [F17, pp. 47-49]

Share prices had only climbed back to Afs 1,000, their par value, by 1352 (1973).

Measured in 1340 (1961) prices, Bank Millie's capital and reserves have declined from Afs 669 million in 1330 (1952) to Afs 358 million by the end of 1350 (1972). It is not surprising that Bank Millie has felt disinclined to invest additional resources to any significant extent in the Afghan economy since the 1330s (1950s). The "controlled economy" programme announced in 1333 (1954) seemed designed to curtail the Bank's activities as did the threatened appointment of Government supervisors to the board of each private company to restrict entrepreneurial initiative.

Part of the cause of these phases of hostility appears to have sprung from the Bank's concentration of its investment in the north [F19, p. 318]. The Pushtun majority in the Government from the south wanted investment in its area. This pressure eventually resulted in the Helmand Valley project, a scheme opposed by Zabuli on economic grounds from its conception [P14, p. 7].

Perhaps Da Afghanistan Bank was established to allay some of the fears of a Bank Millie take-over of the country. In any event, the name is Pushtu rather than Dari thus tending to support the racial interpretation

of Bank Millie/Government disputes. Da Afghanistan Bank was given
responsibilities of acting as the fiscal agent of the Ministry of Finance,
controlling the currency issue, regulating bank credit, controlling foreign
exchange dealings and promoting investment in the national interest
[D1]. In 1319 (1940), Da Afghanistan Bank started to issue banknotes
[A3, p. 98] and by mid-1327 (October 1948) had an outstanding issue of
Afs 800 million [F15, p. 436]. The foreign exchange business was transferred from Bank Millie in 1322 (1943) [B6, p. 7].

One of the early bones of contention between Bank Millie and the
Government had been over foreign exchange transactions. When one of
Bank Millie's ex-directors was Governor of Da Afghanistan Bank,
another enquiry into the use of Bank Millie's foreign exchange earnings
was initiated. Such was the storm which blew up between the Governor
and Zabuli that the former resigned. Within a few months he had returned
to Bank Millie. In 1334 (1955) the Government again accused Bank
Millie of illegal expropriation of foreign exchange earnings from cotton,
karakul and wool sales. To eliminate further possibilities of such misdeeds,
Da Afghanistan Bank opened branches in London and New York to
supervise the surrender of foreign exchange proceeds itself.

During the Daoud administration, 1332-1341 (1953-1963), a banking
boom took place in Afghanistan. Each Government ministry wanted a
bank. The Ministry of Public Works already had the Mortgage and
Construction Bank established in 1326 (1948). The Ministry of Commerce
set up Pashtany Tejaraty Bank in 1333 (1954) and the Ministry of Agriculture formed the Agriculture and Cottage Industries Bank in the same
year. The Ministry of Mines and Industries under its Minister, Dr.
Yousuf, apparently asked Bank Millie to become its industrial bank.
Although willing to participate in the establishment of such an institution,
Bank Millie was quite naturally uninterested in the original proposition.
Thus, the Industrial Development Fund set up in 1336 (1957) was the
last in the field.

In a decade, one commercial (Pashtany Tejaraty Bank) and three
specialised banks had opened their doors alongside Bank Millie and the
central bank, Da Afghanistan Bank. By 1336 (1957), however, the
fortunes of this infant financial sector were already on the decline. The
currency/money ratio, an indicator of the stage of financial development,
had reached its lowest point, i.e. highest level of financial development,
in 1334 (1955) at 0.64; thereafter it rose to 0.81 in 1341 (1962), only
falling to 0.75 by 1351 (1972) as can be seen from Table 2.12. A serious
bout of inflation hit the economy in 1333 (1954) continuing until 1337

(1958), which in part both explains and is explained by the trend in the currency/money ratio.

In an inflationary situation, never conducive to financial development, and with a rising currency/money ratio, it is not surprising to discover that the new financial institutions were not performing as well as had been hoped. Political interference, weak management and legal impediments to securing loans in addition to unconducive economic conditions resulted in a high rate of attrition. The Agriculture and Cottage Industries Bank ceased its lending activities in 1337 (1958), the Industrial Credit Fund had virtually exhausted its resources by the end of its first year of operation, the Mortgage and Construction Bank gradually contracted its business until it was only providing small, medium term loans to Government employees, and Pashtany Tejaraty Bank appears to have maintained only a tenuous existence for many years which any significant net deposit withdrawals would seriously jeopardise. Indeed, even a year after its establishment, the observation was made that "it is hard to see how it can earn enough to pay dividends" [W3, p. 185].

Foreign aid to the financial sector in the form of technical assistance started in 1349 (1970) after the establishment of the Agricultural Development Bank (AgBank) in 1348 (1970) under German management financed by a grant from the United Nations. The AgBank has also received a loan from the World Bank. The AgBank replaced the defunct Agriculture and Cottage Industries Bank. Similarly, the Industrial Development Bank was finally incorporated in 1351 (1973), years after plans had been drawn up to replace the Industrial Credit Fund by a new institution to provide finance to the industrial sector. This sector has seen some expansion since the enactment of the Foreign and Domestic Private Investment Law of 1345 (1967) but lack of credit has inhibited development at a faster pace. The new Industrial Development Bank is a World Bank project.

Although the banks dominate the limited financial sector in Afghanistan, an historical sketch would not be complete without reference to the insurance companies, the Pension Fund, the credit cooperatives in Baghlan and Kohdaman and, most important, the money bazaars of Kabul and Kandahar. Prior to the formation of the Afghan Insurance Company in 1342 (1963) there were three very small insurance agencies in Kabul, one representing the Sterling Insurance Company of New Delhi, one for the Northern Insurance Company, the third for Ingosstrakh, the overseas branch of the Soviet Insurance Trust. Most marine insurance, which constituted virtually the only type of insurance in Afghanistan, was placed on the foreign insurance markets [W7, p. 1; Z3, pp. 28-33]. These three agencies are still in operation, although the Northern Insurance Company was taken over by the Commercial Union in 1348 (1969) [T5, p. 40]. The insurance market in Afghanistan is still minute. Nevertheless, all the institutions have fared well, perhaps as a result of strong links with parent companies abroad which have provided ex-patriate management from the start.

The Pension Fund was established in 1323 (1944). Its total assets at the end of 1351 (1973) were Afs 169 million. As contributions are not sufficient to finance all Government pensions, an additional Afs 100 million was provided by the Government in both 1350 (1971) and 1351 (1972).

The Project on Agricultural Credit and Related Services through Cooperatives in Afghanistan (PACCA), a joint venture of the Food and Agriculture Organisation of the United Nations and the Swedish International Development Authority began in 1347 (1968). By 1351 (1972) the Kohdaman cooperative had 812 members and capital and reserves of Afs 253,797 and the Baghlan cooperative which began in 1350 (1971) had 354 members in 1351 (1972), although it has still not raised any equity or become a fully-fledged cooperative [B27, pp. 4-8].

Information on the money bazaars of Kabul and Kandahar with respect to the relative size of their assets is unavailable. Their operations are described in Chapter VII. A non-institutional credit network of considerable magnitude exists in Afghanistan. However, nothing resembling rotating credit associations or the like has been found. Various studies have presented information on the mechanics of these non-institutional networks [N2; N8]. Because bazaar interest rates are higher than those of the financial institutions, it is thought that over half the total loanable funds is supplied by money lenders in the bazaar [S13, p. 315], who offer "nearly the same services as the commercial banks" [Z3, p. 71]. In fact, the situation in Afghanistan is similar to that in Iran over a decade ago:

> Iranians have observed that the main distinction between the bazaar and modern Persian commercial banks is the impressive buildings housing the latter. To an important extent, this statement is true. [B21, p. 65]

In both countries, the situation resulted from the absence of modern banking practices.

This brief historical sketch of the financial sector has described two periods of apparent expansion during the decades of the 1310s and 1330s (1930s and 1950s) and two of contraction during the 1320s and 1340s

(1940s and 1960s). Bank Millie grew rapidly during its first years but met with increasing opposition later. The Government sponsored developments in the 1330s (1950s), which were shorter lived because collection rates remained well below the survival threshold. There are several reasons for these apparent fluctuations. The first is there was in reality only one period of growth—the dynamic early years of Bank Millie. The second is that all banks established after Bank Millie until 1348 (1970) were Government banks closely linked to parent ministries and staffed by ill-trained, badly paid civil servants. Given that the environment itself was unconducive to financial development, these additional internal handicaps made survival virtually impossible.

Afghanistan has embarked on the second round in the institution building process within the financial sector. Internal conditions of the Ag-Bank and the Industrial Development Bank are a vast improvement over those of the Agriculture and Cottage Industries Bank and Industrial Credit Fund, as a result of both ex-patriate management and a reasonable degree of autonomy from the Government ministries. Nevertheless, collection rates on AgBank loans, now a reflection only of the external environment, are still too low for complacency. The problems of lending, i.e. the

Table 5.1

Financial Institutions of Afghanistan

Institution	Date of Establishment
Banks	
Private	
Bank Millie	1311 (1932)
Industrial Development Bank	1351 (1973)
Government	
Da Afghanistan Bank	1318 (1939)
Mortgage and Construction Bank	1326 (1948)
Pashtany Tejaraty Bank	1333 (1954)
Agricultural Development Bank	1348 (1970)
Other Financial Institutions	
Private	
Afghan Insurance Company	1342 (1963)
Three Insurance Agencies	
Kohdaman Credit Cooperative	1348 (1969)
Baghlan Credit Cooperative	1350 (1971)
Kabul Money Bazaar	
Kandahar Money Bazaar	
Government	
Pension Fund	1323 (1944)

Table 5.2

Total Assets of the Financial Institutions in Afghanistan 1340-1351

(Millions of Afghanis, End of Year Figures)

	1340	1341	1342	1343	1344	1345	1346	1347	1348	1349	1350	1351
Da Afghanistan Bank	5,482 (77%)	7,741 (81%)	9,288 (82%)	8,689 (79%)	9,103 (76%)	9,467 (76%)	9,269 (75%)	10,704 (77%)	13,927 (80%)	15,107 (80%)	16,498 (78%)	17,082 (74%)
Other Commercial Banks	1,512 (21%)	1,631 (17%)	1,794 (16%)	2,079 (19%)	2,612 (22%)	2,689 (22%)	2,907 (23%)	3,004 (21%)	3,172 (18%)	3,328 (18%)	4,130 (19%)	4,578 (20%)
Specialised Banks	104 (1%)	100 (1%)	102 (1%)	113 (1%)	129 (1%)	122 (1%)	137 (1%)	127 (1%)	134 (1%)	131 (1%)	497 (2%)	1,087 (5%)
Pension Fund	75 (1%)	76 (1%)	78 (1%)	79 (1%)	87 (1%)	93 (1%)	107 (1%)	108 (1%)	121 (1%)	135 (1%)	152 (1%)	169 (1%)
Afghan Insurance Company				23 (—)	30 (—)	25 (—)	28 (—)	32 (—)	66 (—)	55 (—)	66 (—)	75 (—)
Total	7,173 (100%)	9,548 (100%)	11,262 (100%)	10,983 (100%)	11,961 (100%)	12,396 (100%)	12,448 (100%)	13,975 (100%)	17,420 (100%)	18,756 (100%)	21,343 (100%)	22,991 (100%)

Source: International Financial Statistics: 1972 Supplement, p. 229; Research Department, Da Afghanistan Bank; and balance sheets of the financial institutions.

Table 5.3

Total Assets of the Financial Institutions in Afghanistan at Constant Prices, 1340-1351

(Millions of Afghanis, 1340 Prices, End of Year Figures)

	1340	1341	1342	1343	1344	1345	1346	1347	1348	1349	1350	1351
Da Afghanistan Bank	5,482 (77%)	6,361 (81%)	7,878 (82%)	5,931 (79%)	5,146 (76%)	5,104 (76%)	4,989 (75%)	5,742 (77%)	7,131 (80%)	6,635 (80%)	7,035 (78%)	7,427 (74%)
Other Commercial Banks	1,512 (21%)	1,340 (17%)	1,522 (16%)	1,419 (19%)	1,477 (22%)	1,450 (22%)	1,565 (23%)	1,612 (21%)	1,624 (18%)	1,461 (18%)	1,761 (19%)	1,990 (20%)
Specialised Banks	104 (1%)	82 (1%)	87 (1%)	77 (1%)	73 (1%)	66 (1%)	74 (1%)	68 (1%)	69 (1%)	58 (1%)	212 (2%)	473 (5%)
Pension Fund	75 (1%)	62 (1%)	66 (1%)	54 (1%)	49 (1%)	50 (1%)	58 (1%)	58 (1%)	62 (1%)	59 (1%)	65 (1%)	73 (1%)
Afghan Insurance Company				16 (—)	17 (—)	13 (—)	15 (—)	17 (—)	34 (—)	24 (—)	28 (—)	33 (—)
Total	7,173 (100%)	7,846 (100%)	9,552 (100%)	7,497 (100%)	6,761 (100%)	6,682 (100%)	6,700 (100%)	7,497 (100%)	8,920 (100%)	8,237 (100%)	9,101 (100%)	9,996 (100%)

Source: Figures in Table 5.2 have been deflated by the modified purchasing power parity price index in Table 2.7.

external environment, are discussed below. A major improvement in this environment could be achieved by the enactment of banking laws which would include both a Negotiable Instruments and a Security Interest Act.

ii. *Overall View of the Financial System*

The existing financial system is dominated by the three commercial banks, Bank Millie, Da Afghanistan Bank and Pashtany Tejaraty Bank, and by the Kabul money bazaar. Table 5.1 gives a list of Afghanistan's financial institutions. Omitting the money bazaars for which data are unavailable, Tables 5.2 and 5.3 provide a rough quantitative comparison at current and constant prices, respectively, of the financial institutions, and Table 5.4 shows the numbers of people working in them.

It can be seen that the three commercial banks hold virtually all the assets of the financial system. Da Afghanistan Bank, which combines certain central banking functions such as the issue of banknotes with commercial banking activities, alone holds over three-quarters of the total assets of the financial system.

Table 5.4

Number of Persons Working in the Financial Institutions at the End of 1351
(Excluding Servants)

Institution	*Number*	*(of which Foreigners)*
Da Afghanistan Bank	1,803	6
Other Commercial Banks	615	—
Specialised Banks	237	10
Credit Cooperatives	92	5
Money Bazaars	110[a]	—
Pension Fund	58	—
Afghan Insurance Company	24	3
Insurance Agencies	10	2
Total	2,949	26

[a] Approximate.
Source: Information provided by the financial institutions themselves.

In 1900, the banking system in the U.S.A. accounted for 63 per cent of total assets of the financial institutions. By 1963 this had fallen to 38 per cent [G13, Table 1-3, pp. 24-25]. A comparative picture of the percentage of assets of central and commercial banks in a selection of countries is provided in Table 5.5. The high proportion of total assets held by the banks in Afghanistan reflects both the low stage of economic evolution and the even lower level of financial development. The expectation of a declining share of banks' assets in the total of the financial system as economic and financial development proceeds has been elaborately reasoned in the works of Gurley and Shaw [G25; G26].

Table 5.5

Percentage of Total Assets of the Financial Institutions Held by Central and Commercial Banks in 16 Countries in 1963

Country	Percentage
Afghanistan[a]	97
Israel	53
Jamaica	66
Japan	49
Mexico	35
Pakistan	78
Philippines	67
Puerto Rico	58
Rhodesia	40
Spain	65
Sweden	35
Thailand	88
Trinidad	77
Turkey[b]	71
U.S.A.	38
Venezuela	56

[a] 1350 (1972).
[b] 1968.
Source: Afghanistan—Table 5.2 above.
Turkey—M. J. Fry, *Finance and Development Planning in Turkey* (Leiden: Brill, 1972), Table 1, p. 38.
All other countries—R. W. Goldsmith, *Financial Structure and Development* (New Haven and London: Yale University Press, 1969), Appendix IV.

Over the period 1340-1351 (1962-1973) there has been an increase in the proportion of total domestic credit allocated to the public sector from 53 per cent at the end of 1340 (March 1962) to 68 per cent at the end of 1351 (March 1973) as can be seen from the figures in Table 5.6. Indeed, domestic credit in real terms extended to the private sector has fallen from Afs 2,162 million at the end of 1340 (March 1962) to Afs 1,710 million at the end of 1351 (March 1973) in 1340 (1961) prices, as shown in Table 5.7.

Table 5.8 provides a broad picture of the volume of domestic credit in Afghanistan over the past twenty years. In Table 5.9 these figures have been deflated by the modified purchasing power parity price index in Table 2.7 to produce estimates of domestic credit expressed in constant

Table 5.6

Monetary Survey, 1340-1351

(Millions of Afghanis, End of Year Figures)

	1340	1341	1342	1343	1344	1345	1346	1347	1348	1349	1350	1351
Foreign Assets	1,007	1,100	2,279	2,279	2,443	2,374	1,891	2,226	2,203	2,211	2,888	2,986
Domestic Credit	4,573	5,426	6,083	5,964	6,261	6,034	6,798	6,773	8,921	9,377	10,671	12,110
Net Claims on Government	2,411	3,312	4,376	4,009	4,063	3,745	4,449	4,013	6,058	6,605	7,142	8,177
Claims on Private Sector	2,162	2,114	1,707	1,955	2,198	2,289	2,349	2,760	2,863	2,772	3,529	3,933
Money	2,920	3,688	4,538	5,300	5,338	5,194	5,529	5,931	7,011	7,383	7,693	9,117
Quasi-Money	285	236	348	600	1,081	1,096	759	857	882	1,085	1,356	1,741
Foreign Liabilities	190	233	235	478	547	731	525	771	758	828	678	635
Other Items (Net)	2,185	2,065	3,205	1,868	1,788	1,388	1,871	1,387	2,416	2,293	3,834	3,516

Source: *International Financial Statistics*, 26 (10), October 1973, pp. 40-41; and *International Financial Statistics: 1972 Supplement*, pp. 228-29.

Table 5.7

Monetary Survey at Constant Prices, 1340-1351

(Millions of Afghanis, 1340 Prices, End of Year Figures)

	1340	1341	1342	1343	1344	1345	1346	1347	1348	1349	1350	1351
Foreign Assets	1,007	904	1,933	1,556	1,381	1,280	1,018	1,194	1,128	971	1,232	1,298
Domestic Credit	4,573	4,459	5,159	4,071	3,539	3,253	3,659	3,634	4,568	4,118	4,551	5,265
Net Claims on Government	2,411	2,721	3,712	2,737	2,297	2,019	2,395	2,153	3,102	2,901	3,046	3,555
Claims on Private Sector	2,162	1,737	1,448	1,334	1,243	1,234	1,264	1,481	1,466	1,217	1,505	1,710
Money	2,920	3,030	3,849	3,618	3,018	2,800	2,976	3,182	3,590	3,242	3,281	3,964
Quasi-Money	285	194	295	410	611	591	409	460	452	477	578	757
Foreign Liabilities	190	191	199	326	309	394	283	414	388	364	289	276
Other Items (Net)	2,185	1,697	2,718	1,275	1,011	748	1,007	744	1,237	1,007	1,635	1,529

Source: Figures in Table 5.6 have been deflated by the modified purchasing power parity price index in Table 2.7.

Table 5.8

Domestic Credit, 1330-1351

(Millions of Afghanis, End of Year Figures)

Date	Claims on Government (Net)	Claims on Private Sector	Total
1330			1,126
1331			1,209
1332			996
1333			1,510
1334			1,816
1335			2,084
1336			2,014
1337	832	1,527	2,359
1338	421	2,037	2,458
1339	1,063	2,244	3,307
1340	2,411	2,162	4,573
1341	3,312	2,114	5,426
1342	4,376	1,707	6,083
1343	4,009	1,955	5,964
1344	4,063	2,198	6,261
1345	3,745	2,289	6,034
1346	4,449	2,349	6,798
1347	4,013	2,760	6,773
1348	6,058	2,863	8,921
1349	6,605	2,772	9,377
1350	7,142	3,529	10,671
1351	8,177	3,933	12,110

Source: 1330-1336 from J. R. Brooks, *Recommendations for a Bank for Industrial Development of Afghanistan* (Washington, D.C.: International Cooperation Administration, Office of Private Enterprise, mimeo, 1960), p. 8.

1337-1351 from *International Financial Statistics*, 26 (10), October 1973, pp. 40-41 and *International Financial Statistics: 1972 Supplement*, pp. 228-29.

prices. To the extent that the deflator is accurate, an indication of movements in the real volume of credit is given; it appears to have increased from 1330 to 1342 (1952 to 1964), downward fluctuations then occurred, but a rapid increase in 1351 (1972) however leaves a final figure for the end of 1351 (1973) virtually the same as that for 1342 (1964).

The proportion of domestic credit absorbed by public and private sectors has changed substantially over the years 1337-1351 (1959-1973), the period for which sectoral data are available. In 1337 (1959) the public sector received 35 per cent of total domestic credit. By 1351 (1973), the proportion had risen to 68 per cent, one of the highest figures to be found in any non-socialist country.

Table 5.9

Domestic Credit at Constant Prices, 1330-1351

(Millions of Afghanis, 1340 Prices, End of Year Figures)

Date	Claims on Government (Net)	Claims on Private Sector	Total
1330			1,451
1331			1,517
1332			1,264
1333			1,685
1334			1,882
1335			1,757
1336			1,640
1337	661	1,213	1,874
1338	392	1,897	2,289
1339	1,128	2,382	3,511
1340	2,411	2,162	4,573
1341	2,721	1,737	4,459
1342	3,712	1,448	5,159
1343	2,737	1,334	4,071
1344	2,297	1,243	3,539
1345	2,019	1,234	3,253
1346	2,395	1,264	3,659
1347	2,153	1,481	3,634
1348	3,102	1,466	4,568
1349	2,901	1,217	4,118
1350	3,046	1,505	4,551
1351	3,555	1,710	5,265

Source: Figures in Table 5.8 have been deflated by the modified purchasing power parity price index in Table 2.7.

The result of the shift in the proportion of domestic credit allocated to public and private sectors between 1340 (1962) and 1350 (1972), a 50 per cent increase in the real volume of credit for the public sector and a 30 per cent decrease for the private sector, was noted in a recent Survey of Progress:

> The full brunt of credit restriction is placed on the private sector, the result of which is that private enterprises which need short-term credit must either do without or borrow from other sources at unnecessary high rates. [M30, p. 18]

The effects of the contraction in the real volume of institutional credit to the private sector on economic growth have also received attention:

> Some of the near-failures could have been avoided if the companies concerned had been able to obtain additional working capital to finance inventories and to carry initial operating losses. The underlying projects

were basically sound and could have been salvaged if normal commercial banking facilities had been available. [R3, p. 3]

The scarcity of domestic financial resources was a major factor behind the slow rate of growth during the Third Plan. [M18, p. 14]

Some of the reasons for the decline in private sector credit are considered in more detail in Section vii below.

Rates of interest offered on deposits in and levied on loans from the financial institutions have remained virtually unchanged over the past two decades. Interest is not offered on demand deposits, but a tax free return of 6 per cent is paid on savings deposits in all the banks. Time deposits opened by business firms with Bank Millie carry a taxable return of between 3 and 6 per cent. On the loan side, the Government and Government industries pay 2 to 6 per cent on loans from Da Afghanistan Bank and the private sector nominally pays 8 to 10 per cent, although additional charges raise the rates by about one per cent in most cases.

In the bazaar economy, on the other hand, rates have apparently been rising sharply over the past decade. The great dispersion in interest rates, as seen in Chapter III, indicates a fragmented capital market. Perhaps nowhere has this phenomenon had a more deleterious effect than in the agricultural sector. High rural interest rates have been a strong deterrent to any move from subsistence to cash crop farming. This problem has been recognised for many years and one of the objectives of the bank expansion in the 1330s (1950s) was the reduction in interest rates [W3, p. 190]. Unfortunately, the attempt failed because institutional rates were set too low to attract the necessary funds with which to expand lending activities. The result was further fragmentation.

Despite relatively low and unchanged institutional interest rates, non-price credit rationing does not appear to have been prevalent. There is little, if any, excess effective demand for loans from the financial institutions, primarily because there are few borrowers who can meet minimum requirements of credit worthiness. This in turn springs from legal inadequacies connected with the securing of loans and expropriation of collateral on default. The unfavourable external environment is exacerbated by the institutions' own inadequacies in terms of untrained personnel, poor pay and absence of incentives to improve the situation.

Despite the unfavourable environment within which banks have to operate, changes have occurred which make the stagnant financial sector, partly reflected in unchanged interest rates, an increasingly serious bottleneck to economic development in Afghanistan. The two most important are the absorption of larger and larger proportions of the limited supply of domestic credit by the public sector and the developments within the embryonic industrial sector since the Foreign and Domestic Private Investment Law of 1345 (1967) and the boom in the bazaar economy. Since the differential between bank and non-institutional interest rates has widened, it can be assumed that the allocation of resources amongst different uses has become less rather than more efficient.

Table 5.10

Yield on Government Bonds in 22 Countries

Country	1950	1960	1970
U.S.A.	2.32	4.02	6.58
U.K.	3.00	5.77	9.22
Belgium	4.42	5.48	7.81
Denmark	4.53	5.76	10.57
France	6.52	5.15	8.06
Germany	—	6.40	8.30
Italy	5.73	5.01	9.01
Netherlands	3.28	4.20	7.76
Norway	2.58	4.58	6.29
Sweden	3.11	5.19	7.39
Switzerland	2.67	3.09	5.82
Canada	2.78	5.26	9.82
Ireland	—	5.45	9.56
Portugal	3.92	3.46	5.27
Australia	3.14	4.99	6.75
New Zealand	3.07	4.83	5.51
South Africa	3.63	5.29	7.15
Uruguay	5.64	8.50	—
Jamaica	1.50	3.80	4.03
Ceylon	3.04	2.90	7.57
India	3.11	4.07	5.00
Pakistan	2.99	3.50	5.50
Unweighted Average	3.55	4.85	7.28

Source: *International Financial Statistics: 1972 Supplement.*

Over the past two decades, interest rates throughout the world have risen. An indication of this is provided in Tables 5.10 and 5.11 in which government bond yields in 22 countries and discount rates in an additional 19 countries are presented. On average both the yields on government bonds and discount rates have doubled. Interest rates in the Afghan bazaar have followed a similar course. Institutional interest rates in Afghanistan, however, have remained unchanged.

The rise in nominal interest rates throughout the world is in large

Table 5.11

Discount Rate in 19 Countries

Country	1950	1960	1970
Turkey	4.00	9.00	9.00
Brazil	6.00	8.00	20.00
Chile	4.50	16.55	20.00
Colombia	4.00	5.00	14.00
Costa Rica	4.00	5.00	5.00
Ecuador	8.00	5.00	8.00
El Salvador	3.00	5.50	6.10
Honduras	—	2.00	4.00
Nicaragua	4.00	6.00	6.00
Peru	6.00	9.50	9.50
Venezuela	2.00	4.50	5.00
Egypt	3.00	3.00	5.00
Iran	4.00	6.00	8.00
Syria	—	3.50	5.00
S. Korea	5.84	10.22	19.00
Philippines	2.00	5.00	10.00
Thailand	7.00	5.00	5.00
Ghana	—	4.00	5.50
Tunisia	—	3.00	5.00
Unweighted Average	4.49	6.09	8.90

Source: *International Financial Statistics: 1972 Supplement.*

part a reflection of the rise in the expected rate of inflation [F8, Chapter 19; G9]. Using the very simple model

$$i_t = b_0 + b_1 \left[\left(\frac{\Delta M}{M}\right)_t - \left(\frac{\Delta M}{M}\right)^e_{t-1}\right] + b_2 \left(\frac{\Delta P}{P}\right)^e_t \qquad (5.1)$$

where i_t is the nominal rate of interest, M is the money stock, P the price level, e denotes an expected value, and b_0, b_1 and b_2 are constants [C5, p. 588], Carr and Smith find that a change in the expected rate of inflation, $\left(\frac{\Delta P}{P}\right)^e_t$, has a significant positive effect on i_t, the nominal rate of interest [C5, p. 590].

With an average expected rate of inflation over 9 per cent in Afghanistan, together with its high standard deviation shown in Table 2.13 which increases the risk of real loss from holding money, a nominal rate of 6 per cent on savings accounts implies a negative real rate of interest from the standard Fisher equation

$$r_t = i_t - \left(\frac{\Delta P}{P}\right)^e_t \qquad (5.2)$$

where r is the real rate of interest and i the nominal rate. Furthermore, it has been a highly risky negative return with the standard deviation over 8.

In a recent survey of studies on the determinants of savings in underdeveloped countries, the conclusions were reached that:

A. Measured savings are responsive to changes in the real rate of interest [M10, p. 19].
B. The rate of interest is more important in determining the channels into which savings will flow, however, than in altering the propensity to save itself [M10, p. 17].

Hence, the real rate of interest is the key factor in financial development. Naturally, the negative real rate has not promoted financial development in Afghanistan.

Institutional interest rates in Afghanistan are low for two main reasons. First, the effective demand for loans is small because of the legal inadequacies which make loans difficult to secure. Thus, lending is not such an attractive proposition as it could be. Legal reform to secure loans and enforce collection might produce a strong incentive to expand banking operations.

The second basic reason why interest rates are low lies in the nature of the market structure of Afghanistan's financial sector. The interlocking ownership and control throughout the financial system is worth documenting. As of the beginning of 1352 (1973), the Supreme Council of Da Afghanistan Bank consisted of the Minister of Finance (Chairman), the Minister of Mines and Industries, the Minister of Planning, the Acting Minister of Commerce, the President of the Industrial Development Bank, a representative of the Prime Minister's Office, the Governor, Deputy Governor and the two Vice Presidents of Da Afghanistan Bank. The Board of Directors of Pashtany Tejaraty Bank included the Minister of Finance, the Acting Minister of Commerce, the President of the Pension Fund, the Governor of Da Afghanistan Bank, the President of the Agricultural Development Bank, the President of Bank Millie, a member of Bank Millie's Board and four other traders. The members of the Board of Directors of Bank Millie naturally did not include any representative of the Government but three members of its Board also sat on the Boards of other banks. The members of the Supreme Council of the Agricultural Development Bank were the Minister of Finance, the Minister of Planning, the Acting Minister of Commerce, the Minister of Agriculture and Irrigation, the Governor of Da Afghanistan Bank, the

Vice Chairman of the Board of Directors of Bank Millie, the President and General Manager of the Agricultural Development Bank and three other elected members. The Board of Directors of the Industrial Development Bank consisted of the President of Pashtany Tejaraty Bank (Chairman), the President of Bank Millie, the President and General Manager of the Industrial Development Bank, representatives of Chase, National Westminster and the World Bank and two industrialists. The Supreme Council of the Mortgage and Construction Bank consisted of the Minister of Finance, the Minister of Public Works, the Governor of Da Afghanistan Bank and four elected members. The Board of Directors of the Afghan Insurance Company included the President of Pashtany Tejaraty Bank (Chairman), the Vice Chairman of the Board of Directors of Bank Millie and a representative of the Guardian Assurance Company. The Pension Fund has invested funds in the form of equity participation in the Afghan Insurance Company, the Mortgage and Construction Bank and Pashtany Tejaraty Bank, and has a loan from Da Afghanistan Bank. Shares of the Mortgage and Construction Bank are held by Da Afghanistan Bank.

This rather lengthy documentation of inter-locking directorships and equity participation simply indicates that not one financial institution in Afghanistan is independent from the others. There have, furthermore, been informal links between the institutions including, apparently, representation of Bank Millie's views on the Supreme Council of Da Afghanistan Bank. One can, therefore, assume that there has been no competition between the financial institutions. Hence, interest rates have remained low and stable, advertising is negligible and there is no search whatsoever for business. Bankers wait for customers, who on the loan side have had to meet increasingly stringent collateral requirements, and do not contemplate any innovations or other action which might disturb the market share balance. So far, the equilibrium has been preserved from any external disruptions, the most serious of which would be competition inside Afghanistan from a foreign bank. The banking fraternity has to date ensured that no serious threat of this kind has materialised.

The result has been financial stagnation over the past two decades. The early years of Bank Millie have long been forgotten as bankers have settled down to a stable, low level, non-competitive equilibrium. This has been facilitated not only by inter-locking ownership and control within the financial institutions but also by complacency on the part of the Ministry of Finance and the conspicuous lack of indigenous credit arrangements such as rotating credit associations, pawnbrokerage, and simple

Table 5.12

Banks, Branches, Assets and Deposits in Afghanistan, Iran, Pakistan and Turkey

(Millions of Dollars)

Country	Bank Assets	Bank Deposits	Number of Banks	Number of Branches	Assets per Bank	Assets per Branch	Deposits per Bank	Deposits per Branch
Afghanistan A (1350 = 1972)	49.940	23.785	2	33	24.970	1.513	11.892	0.721
Afghanistan B (1350 = 1972)	158.960	73.386	3	93	52.987	1.709	24.462	0.789
Iran (1346 = 1968)	2,817.333	1,734.667	25	3,407	112.693	0.827	69.387	0.509
Pakistan (1967)	1,926.150	962.960	36	2,285	53.504	0.843	26.749	0.421
Turkey (1967)	2,774.056	1,167.500	46	2,210	60.306	1.255	25.380	0.528

Note: Bank assets are total consolidated balance sheet figures. Afghanistan A provides figures for Bank Millie and Pashtany Tejaraty Bank. Afghanistan B includes assets of Da Afghanistan Bank excluding those covering currency and bankers' deposits. Iran and Turkey include all banks other than the central bank. Pakistan refers only to the scheduled banks.
Bank deposits include both public and private sector demand and time deposits. Inter-bank deposits are excluded.
Domestic currency figures were converted into U.S. Dollars using the following exchange rates:

Afghanistan $ 1 = Afs 82.70
Iran $ 1 = Rls 75.00
Pakistan $ 1 = Rs 10.00
Turkey $ 1 = TL 18.00

Source: Afghanistan—International Financial Statistics: 1972 Supplement, p. 229; and balance sheets of the banks for number of branches. Iran, Pakistan, Turkey—Regional Cooperation for Development, Manual on Banking (Tehran: Regional Cooperation for Development Secretariat, 1969).

financial instruments such as promissory notes, etc. This is not to imply that non-institutional credit is unimportant but that there are no sophistications to basic lending operations such as an indigenous negotiable instrument, elementary cooperative groups, etc. In fact, the only traditional financial instruments are essentially non-negotiable. They include the *hawala*, a simple draft, the *barat*, a bill of exchange, the *hujat*, a promissory note and the *sanad*, a receipt. These are only known to a small proportion of urban traders. The majority of the population has never even heard the words.

The lack of even simple indigenous financial instruments and institutions highlights one of the major obstacles faced by the embryonic modern financial system should an attempt at expansion be made, namely, the total lack of understanding by the vast majority of the population of basic concepts of credit. As the Agricultural Development Bank has discovered, when the distinction between a loan and a grant is unclear even an aggressive, German-managed financial institution is still in a precarious position when it attempts to expand rapidly its lending activities.

Two matters of significance in analysing Afghanistan's financial system have received much attention in the literature of recent years. The first concerns economies of scale in banking, the second competition. Table 5.12 provides a comparative picture of Afghanistan's banking system with those of the neighbouring countries of Iran, Pakistan and Turkey. Total assets and total deposits of the banking system are extremely small on any criterion. At the end of 1967, for example, Kaufman lists 171 banks in the world with total assets over $1 billion. Of the 151 banks for which further data were available, assets per bank averaged $3,239 million and assets per branch $8.626 million [K6, Table 2, pp. 104-109].

Population per bank branch was 4,618 in Iran in 1350 (1972), 53,039 in Pakistan in 1967 and 14,957 in Turkey in 1967. Using the official population estimate of 17.5 million for Afghanistan gives 188,172 people per branch. The population estimate of 10 million gives 107,527—still considerably greater than even Pakistan.

Benston recently estimated a cost elasticity for banking of 0.93 indicating that a 10 per cent increase in deposits resulted on average in a 9.3 per cent increase in costs [B22]. He explained the economies of scale by the fact that large banks were able to use a larger proportion of lower skilled labour, needed fewer processing and administrative officers and could shift to technology only economical for large scale operations [B22, p. 339]. In another recent publication, Baltensperger showed that the existence of uncertainty also produced economies of scale:

.... if it is true that uncertainty is a major source of economies of scale in banking, then, since the degree of uncertainty involved in different types of banking activities varies widely, the extent of these economies should be considerably different for different types of banking services. This again, it seems, should show up in the relative degrees of concentration of different types of services. We should expect that in the long run those services with relatively large scale economies become much more concentrated in the hands of a few large banks than those having only insignificant economies. [B4, p. 475]

In an empirical analysis of the Swiss banking system, Baltensperger found support for his hypothesis. He concluded:

.... the fact that the high-risk services are more concentrated in the hands of the largest firms than the low-risk services implies that, on average, a relatively large part of a large bank's business takes place in the high-risk department, and a relatively large part of a small bank's business in the low-risk department. [B4, pp. 484-85]

From the work of Baltensperger and Benston, it could be expected that even if Afghanistan's financial system were competitive and efficient, banking would be relatively high cost and prone to greater risk aversion than other financial systems simply because of its small size.

The fact that Afghanistan's financial system is not competitive suggests, a priori, that it is unlikely to be efficient and furthermore has remained much smaller than a competitive system would have done. This alone suggests advantages from competition might accrue. Recent work on American and British banking suggests that the absence of competition has produced high social costs [G17; G18; G19; R8]. In both countries, regulations and restraints on competition are in the process of being removed since the recognition of the facts that the dangers of competition are much less serious than the banking communities try to make out and that the benefits of competition are considerably greater. Afghanistan could well take note of this move towards competitive banking in any attempt at financial development.

iii. The Central Bank

Da Afghanistan Bank, founded in 1318 (1939), is the central bank of Afghanistan in that it "has the monopoly and privilege of issuing bank-notes throughout Afghanistan" [D1, Article 1, p. 1] and acts as banker to "the Government, Municipalities and all other Governmental Departments in Afghanistan as well as abroad" [D1, Article 11 (b), p. 3]. However, the Bank has no powers to control in any way other financial institutions. In the absence of standard central and commercial bank

Table 5.13

Assets and Liabilities of Da Afghanistan Bank, 1340–1351

(Millions of Afghanis, End of Year Figures)

	1340	1341	1342	1343	1344	1345	1346	1347	1348	1349	1350	1351
ASSETS												
Foreign Assets	989	1,063	2,205	2,177	2,370	2,263	1,789	2,059	1,815	1,833	2,633	2,604
Claims on Government	3,058	4,380	5,759	5,162	5,239	5,472	5,870	6,661	9,068	9,870	10,947	11,390
Claims on Private Sector	1,017	968	552	538	560	581	584	842	979	927	1,052	936
Claims on Commercial Banks	122	70	70	71	72	175	91	73	432	724	239	430
Unclassified Assets	296	1,260	702	741	862	976	935	1,069	1,633	1,753	1,627	1,722
ASSETS = LIABILITIES	5,482	7,741	9,288	8,689	9,103	9,467	9,269	10,704	13,927	15,107	16,498	17,082
LIABILITIES												
Reserve Money	2,957	3,707	4,632	5,325	5,445	5,270	5,592	5,832	7,123	7,657	7,803	8,976
Quasi-Money Deposits	204	147	198	203	361	436	161	156	192	172	156	358
Foreign Liabilities	190	233	235	478	547	731	525	771	758	828	678	573
Government Deposits	478	863	1,171	1,016	1,070	1,607	1,267	2,439	2,827	3,085	3,625	2,995
Counterpart Funds	104	81	242	102	43	6	94	74	29	0	4	4
Capital Accounts	733	826	668	741	804	666	673	703	1,087	986	1,404	1,522
Unclassified Liabilities	816	1,923	2,336	891	920	753	957	674	1,854	2,380	2,711	2,654

Source: International Financial Statistics: 1972 Supplement, p. 229; and Research Department, Da Afghanistan Bank.

legislation, there is in fact no special control over other financial institutions. This is unnecessary at present for monetary policy purposes for
two reasons. First, there is essentially no money multiplier process, i.e.
multiplied relationship between high powered money and the money
supply, since three-quarters of the money supply, broadly defined to
include time deposits, is currency. Furthermore, 31 per cent of the
deposit component of the money supply is held at Da Afghanistan Bank;
Table 5.13 presents balance sheet data for 1340-1351 (1962-1973). Second,
in the absence of borrowing possibilities for the public sector outside the
financial system, monetary policy is determined almost exclusively by
fiscal policy.

Da Afghanistan Bank opened its first branch office in 1321 (1942) in
Kandahar and established five more during the 1320s (1940s). During the
1330s (1950s), 14 branches were started and 35 in the 1340s (1960s). At
present in 1352 (1973), there are eight branches in Kabul, 51 provincial
branches together with the Trading Company of Afghanistan, Incorporated, established in 1333 (1954) in New York and the Trading Company
of Afghanistan, Limited, established in 1334 (1955) in London.

Despite the steady increase in branches, the facilities normally offered
by a branch network are absent. No branch makes any loans, only a dozen
accept savings accounts and there is no cheque clearing system. By and
large, the branches of Da Afghanistan Bank serve almost exclusively as
the Ministry of Finance's cashier. During the first six months of 1351
(1972), there were 930 transactions totalling Afs 1,763 million between
the head office and the branches and 747 transactions totalling Afs 1,359
million between the branches and the head office. There was an average of
43 chequing accounts, eight fiduciary, i.e. temporary non-chequing, non-
interest bearing accounts, and 27 savings accounts per branch at the end
of 1351 (March 1973). While 17,222 savings accounts were held at the
head office, only 1,600 were held in the branches. In certain other respects,
including the salary scales of its employees, Da Afghanistan Bank is
treated as an organ of the Ministry. The problems created by less than
subsistence salaries which the Bank is obliged to pay are no different
from those in all Government offices.

One of the internal constraints to expansion and greater autonomy lies
in the quality of the Bank's personnel. Generally, the staff have had
inadequate education before joining the Bank and little methodical
on-the-job training after recruitment. Hence, there is general recognition
that to improve the efficiency of operations on-the-job training must be
given to almost the entire staff. Staff at the very top have generally

received considerable training abroad but are thwarted in any efforts to apply their high level training by the eternal stream of mundane tasks which they are obliged to perform, including for example writing simple business letters and deciding which damaged banknotes are exchangeable. It is therefore doubly important to initiate training at lower and middle levels not only to increase the Bank's operational efficiency but also to free senior staff to devote more of their time to policy issues, etc.

Da Afghanistan Bank plays a relatively important role in foreign trade with offices in London and New York established primarily to facilitate and supervise the karakul trade. As shown in Table 7.12, Da Afghanistan Bank accounts for 28 per cent of the total annual turnover of foreign exchange, excluding clearing currencies. In addition to the $71 million foreign currency exchanged in 1351 (1972) there was business in clearing currencies amounting to over $50 million. Da Afghanistan Bank not only has a monopoly in clearing currency accounts but also in $36 million of foreign exchange bought and sold at the official rate.

In its foreign exchange operations and in its private sector credit policy, Da Afghanistan Bank is surprisingly unfettered. Although obliged to provide all funds required by the Government subject only to the physical constraint of banknote availability, foreign exchange reserve policy and private sector credit are matters entirely within the Bank's responsibility. Efforts seem to have been made to counteract the more violent swings in Government funding through compensating changes in reserves and private sector credit supply. This is taken up again in the subsequent section.

iv. *Money Supply*

The Afghani was introduced as the monetary unit of Afghanistan in a law passed on 23 Hoot 1304 (14 March 1925) [B29, p. 427]. It was a silver coin weighing 10 grams and replaced the Kabuli Rupee at an exchange rate of 11 Kabuli Rupees to 10 Afghanis. Under the same law, two gold coins, the Amani and half Amani weighing 6 and 3 grams respectively were prescribed and valued at Afs 20 and Afs 10 [B29, p. 427]. With the decline in the price of silver shortly afterwards these coins went out of circulation.

The first batch of Afghani coins contained silver of the same fineness (0.99) as the old Kabuli Rupees, thus equating intrinsic values with the official rate of exchange [G22, p. 173]. In subsequent mintings, less silver was used:

.... on the face of it, no material profit could have been derived from recoining eleven old coins into ten new ones. The percentage of the alloy in the old coin is, however, exceedingly small, especially in the older "raw" rupees, whereas in the *afghani* the alloy, though probably not exceeding the limit considered as legal, is an unknown quantity and is certainly comparatively high. [B29, p. 433]

That further debasements took place was suggested in Chapter II on the evidence of implicit exchange rate calculations. At this time, Indian and Iranian gold and silver coins also circulated in Afghanistan.

The Law on Banknotes in Circulation in Afghanistan, enacted 4 Aqrab 1314 (26 October 1935), authorised the issue of currency notes. The Law enabled the Ministry of Finance to issue paper notes itself or through Bank Millie. The arrangement actually reached between Bank Millie and the Ministry resulted in an issue of Treasury notes in 1315 (1936) which according to Article 6 of the Law could be converted "..... into Afghan coins in all government treasuries and in Bank Millie with no difficulty." A previous attempt in the 1300s (1920s) to introduce paper currency had been unsuccessful. A contemporary account provides an interesting description:

There being no bank in Afghanistan, no bank-notes or treasury-notes are issued and the currency is limited to the silver and copper coins above described. That state of things is very trying when larger sums are involved in some transaction. The usual method of avoiding that drawback is by having recourse to some foreign currency (English gold and treasury-notes, Indian currency notes, and the like) or to cheques on some bank in India, the amount being calculated in accordance with the rate of exchange of the day.

A timid attempt at introducing *sub rosa* some kind of currency-note into circulation was, however, made some time ago. A kind of promissory note was issued by the Treasury of Daru-l-Aman (the new capital of Afghanistan, still under construction, some ten miles to the South of Kabul). These notes were to serve for the payment of the workmen employed on its construction, but not being accepted as money in the bazar of Kabul (or anywhere else), these notes very soon died a quiet, natural death. [B29, pp. 425-26]

Notes issued by the end of 1315 (1937) equalled Afs 20 million. By the end of 1318 (1940) Treasury notes totalled Afs 180 million. In this year Da Afghanistan Bank was founded with the right to issue banknotes. Article 19 of its Statutes states:

The Bank, in order to cover its short-term liabilities, shall be in possession of at least 30% of their face-value in the form of gold, silver, free foreign currencies, commercial bills payable within 15 days and bank-notes delivered by the "Committee of Bank-note Reserves" in accordance with clause 63 of these Statutes. [D1, p. 6]

Section H of the Statutes also contains provisions on note issue and cover:

H. THE COMMITTEE OF BANK-NOTE RESERVES

62. In order to control the reserve of Bank-notes a special Committee composed of seven members is to be formed at the Bank as under:

> Two members of Parliament
> A member of the Cabinet
> The President of the Supreme Court
> The Governor of the Da Afghanistan Bank
> The Chief Treasurer
> The Government Auditor at the Bank

Term of Service

The term of office of the Government delegates and representatives is two years. Their appointment shall take place every year in the month of Hamal (March/April) at the occasion of the first session of Parliament and of the Cabinet. If Parliament does not sit at the aforesaid time, their nomination shall be postponed till the first session of the House is held.

63. This Committee has the following duties and powers:
(a) Inspecting and receiving the Bank-notes newly printed.
(b) Safe-keeping the Bank-notes and effecting their delivery to the Bank after examining the Legal Reserves and ascertaining that it is in proper ratio to the notes printed. The delivery of the Bank-notes to the Bank denotes, with regard to their cover, that such notes are considered to be in circulation.
(c) Receiving the Bank-notes withdrawn from circulation as well as the worn and defaced Bank-notes; keeping the respective accounts for the same and proceeding to their incineration with all necessary precautions. At the time of incinerating Bank-notes a protocol with full particulars of the procedure must be made in a special book. A copy of the protocol shall be forwarded to the Finance Minister.
(d) Controlling the account regarding the cover for the Bank-notes in accordance with the Rules and Regulations concerned. This Control Committee shall prepare a report at least once a month on the total value of notes in circulation and the coins, gold and silver bullions kept as cover for the same. This report shall be submitted to the Government which in its turn publishes it for the information of the public.
[D1, pp. 15-16]

Incineration of worn banknotes has taken place at regular intervals with some ceremony in the gardens of Da Afghanistan Bank. On one such occasion, a wind sprang up during the proceedings and notes swept up from the garden rained down outside on lucky by-standers in Pushtunistan Square, the Piccadilly Circus of Kabul.

When Da Afghanistan Bank started issuing notes, it had them printed in Kabul on machinery imported from Germany and operated with the help of technical assistance from German experts. The product was of high quality and considerable beauty. When the Germans were forced to leave Afghanistan during the Second World War, the machinery fell into disrepair. Notes are now printed by De La Rue in Newcastle. The antique machinery for minting coins has also broken down and the Mint, although still employing quite a number of people, is now unproductive.

By the end of 1319 (1941) Afs 60 million of Da Afghanistan Bank notes were circulating alongside the Treasury notes. The latter had become the liability of Da Afghanistan Bank. They were virtually all withdrawn from circulation by the end of 1327 (1949) by which time there were nearly Afs 700 million of Da Afghanistan Bank notes in circulation.

In 1317 (1938), the Afghan currency note lost its convertibility:

.... the National Assembly authorized the Ministry of Finance to hold gold, silver, and foreign exchange as a reserve equivalent to half the value of the notes in circulation. [F15, p. 436]

Nevertheless, there was clearly a strong desire for currency backing to prevent irresponsible recourse to the printing presses. The 1343 (1964) Constitution of Afghanistan follows up this concern with monetary stability. Article 64 provides that "the authorization to issue money . . . . . are within the competence of the Shura (Parliament)." By then, however, the note cover had been reduced to 20 per cent [M22, p. 77].

Valued at either official or free market exchange rates, there has always been ample excess cover. In fact, the official exchange rate is used and maintenance of the prescribed cover was the predominant factor behind the devaluation of this rate in 1342 (1963). Gold and silver reserves had previously been revalued at the official rate introduced in 1328 (1949) during 1332 (1954) for the same purpose [W3, p. 194]. Between 1341 (1963) and 1349 (1971), the gold and foreign exchange backing of currency in circulation averaged 45 per cent [M25, Table 6, p. 81; M32, Table 94, p. 156].

Although the depreciating Afghani/Dollar exchange rate suggests that domestic inflation has been generally greater than inflation in the U.S.A., the average annual rate of inflation has, in fact, only been 5.6 per cent between 1329 (1950) and 1351 (1972). This can be compared with 3.1 per cent in Iran, 1951-1970, 2.9 per cent in Pakistan, 1950-1970, and 7.2 per cent in Turkey, 1950-1970 [F26, Table 19.3, p. 377]. Many underdeveloped countries have suffered considerably higher rates of inflation over this period.

Unfortunately, the relatively modest average rate of inflation during the past two decades has been accompanied by high variance. The standard deviation of the annual rates of inflation between 1329 (1950) and 1351 (1972) is 10.6. High variance produces uncertainty as to future directions of change and so makes money an extremely risky asset. As already pointed out, if inflation *per se* has not been a major deterrent to money holding, the variance in it certainly has. As the critical objective in any programme of financial development is to increase the demand for money in real terms, efforts must in the future be directed at reducing not only the level of inflation but, more important in the Afghan context, also the variance.

For this task it is essential to understand the factors which have contributed to this high variance. The major exogenous factor against which it is difficult, though certainly not impossible, to take counteracting measures is fluctuations in agricultural output. Indeed, this is particularly well illustrated at the present (1973) when, for example, the price of wheat flour is 28.5 per cent lower than it was a year ago and the price of mutton 46.4 per cent higher [C8]. Although the stabilisation of meat prices is a long and complicated process, grain prices which are much more important in the cost-of-living index can be stabilised to a considerable extent through repeal of the Anti-Hoarding Law of 1346 (1967) and the implementation of a Government reserve stock programme.

Agricultural fluctuations and seasonalities are probably the major cause of short run (up to 18 months) price fluctuations. However, it is significant that a calculated series of expected inflation rates which uses a weighted average of inflation over four year periods yields a standard deviation of 6.0 [F31, pp. 13-15]. Thus, even if agricultural fluctuations contribute a maximum of 4.6 to the standard deviation of annual inflation rates the major cause is still to be discovered. This is, in fact, undoubtedly changes in the money supply. Between 1331 (1952) and 1350 (1971), the average three year increase in the money stock was 38.7 per cent; the standard deviation of the 18 observations is 26.9.

Regression of the simple relationship

$$\dot{P}_t = a + b\,\dot{M}_{t-1} \tag{5.3}$$

where P_t is the three year percentage rate of inflation over period t and M_{t-1} is the three year percentage change in the money stock over period t—1, yields the following results for the period 1331-1351 (1952-1972):

$$\dot{P}_t = -8.88 + 0.77\,\dot{M}_{t-1} \tag{5.4}$$

which, with $R^2 = 0.76$ and $t = 6.9$, is a highly significant relationship, well over the 99.9 per cent confidence level. Thus, over three-quarters of the change in the price level during a three year period is accounted for by changes in the money stock. The data used in this analysis are presented in Table 5.14. There are high standard deviations for both changes in the money stock and changes in the price level. Table 5.15 presents a somewhat longer series for currency and money stock on an annual basis. For an average annual increase in currency in circulation since 1318 (1949) of 12.7 per cent, the standard deviation is 9.6, while for an average annual increase in the money supply over the same period of 11.9 per cent the standard deviation is 10.3. Both standard deviations are extremely high. Table 5.17 provides a comparison with Iran, Pakistan and Turkey.

Differences between the size of changes in the money supply and changes in demand for money in real terms will influence not only the

Table 5.14

Three Year Moving Average Percentage Changes in the Money Stock and Modified Purchasing Power Parity Price Index, 1331-1351

(Percentages)

Date	Money Stock	Purchasing Power Parity Price Index
1331-34	64.6	
1332-35	84.7	50.51
1333-36	55.7	37.05
1334-37	13.9	30.47
1335-38	4.6	−9.44
1336-39	10.0	−23.29
1337-40	24.8	−20.57
1338-41	37.8	13.31
1339-42	61.5	25.16
1340-43	80.9	46.50
1341-44	72.8	45.36
1342-45	44.3	57.34
1343-46	16.6	26.83
1344-47	6.1	5.37
1345-48	15.5	5.28
1346-49	30.1	22.55
1347-50	34.0	25.80
1348-51		17.77
Average	38.70	20.94
Standard Deviation	26.87	23.76

Source: Money Stock—Table 5.15.
Purchasing Power Parity Price Index—Table 2.7.

118 THE FINANCIAL SECTOR

Table 5.15

Currency and Money Stock 1310-1351

(Millions of Afghanis, End of Year Figures)

Date	Currency in Circulation	Money Stock (M2)	Percentage Change in Currency	Percentage Change in Money Stock
1310		165		
1311		177		7.3
1312		189		6.8
1313		202		6.9
1314		216		6.9
1315		231		6.9
1316		248		7.4
1317		265		6.9
1318	180	284		7.2
1319	240	300	33.3	5.6
1320	300	375	25.0	25.0
1321	372	465	24.0	24.0
1322	430	538	15.6	15.7
1323	500	625	16.3	16.2
1324	594	743	18.8	18.9
1325	680	850	14.5	14.4
1326	680	850	0.0	0.0
1327	687	859	1.0	1.1
1328	764	955	11.2	11.2
1329	900	1,125	17.8	17.8
1330	940	1,210	4.4	0.8
1331	978	1,338	4.0	10.6
1332	989	1,339	1.1	0.1
1333	1,193	1,848	20.6	38.0
1334	1,474	2,345	23.6	26.9
1335	1,760	2,601	19.4	10.9
1336	1,889	2,360	7.3	−9.3
1337	1,849	2,473	−2.1	4.8
1338	1,881	2,700	1.7	9.2
1339	2,155	2,756	14.6	2.1
1340	2,607	3,205	21.0	16.3
1341	3,158	3,924	21.1	22.4
1342	3,884	4,886	23.0	24.5
1343	4,722	5,900	21.6	20.8
1344	4,644	6,419	−1.7	8.8
1345	4,624	6,290	−0.4	−2.0
1346	4,804	6,288	3.9	0.0
1347	5,238	6,788	9.0	8.0
1348	6,144	7,893	17.3	16.3
1349	6,532	8,468	6.3	7.3
1350	6,785	9,049	3.9	6.9
1351	8,180	10,858	20.6	20.0
Average			12.7	11.0
Standard Deviation			9.6	9.4

Note: See Note to Table 2.9. Currency figures for 1318-1329 include vault cash. It can be assumed that this was very small during these years.

Source: Same as Table 2.9.

Table 5.16

Currency and Money Stock at Constant Prices 1310-1351

(Millions of Afghanis, 1340 Prices, End of Year Figures)

Date	Currency in Circulation	Money Stock (M2)	Percentage Change in Currency	Percentage Change in Money Stock
1310		1,813		
1311		1,806		-0.4
1312		2,423		34.2
1313		2,149		-11.3
1314		2,160		0.5
1315		2,333		8.0
1316		2,362		1.2
1317		2,387		1.1
1318	1,552	2,448		2.6
1319	1,860	2,326	19.8	-5.0
1320	2,098	2,622	12.8	12.7
1321	2,011	2,514	-4.1	-4.1
1322	1,807	2,261	-10.1	-10.1
1323	1,629	2,036	-9.9	-10.0
1324	1,496	1,872	-8.2	-8.1
1325	1,313	1,641	-12.2	-12.3
1326	1,208	1,510	-8.0	-8.0
1327	1,172	1,466	-3.0	-2.9
1328	1,069	1,336	-8.8	-8.9
1329	1,160	1,450	8.5	8.5
1330	1,211	1,559	4.4	7.5
1331	1,227	1,679	1.3	7.7
1332	1,255	1,699	2.3	1.2
1333	1,331	2,063	6.1	21.4
1334	1,527	2,430	14.7	17.8
1335	1,484	2,193	-2.8	-9.8
1336	1,538	1,922	3.6	-12.4
1337	1,469	1,964	-4.5	2.2
1338	1,751	2,514	19.2	28.0
1339	2,288	2,926	30.7	16.4
1340	2,607	3,205	13.9	9.5
1341	2,595	3,224	-0.5	0.6
1342	3,294	4,144	26.9	28.5
1343	3,223	4,027	-2.2	-2.8
1344	2,625	3,629	-18.6	-9.9
1345	2,493	3,391	-5.0	-6.6
1346	2,586	3,384	3.7	-0.2
1347	2,810	3,642	8.7	7.6
1348	3,146	4,041	12.0	11.0
1349	2,869	3,719	-8.8	-8.0
1350	2,893	3,859	0.8	3.8
1351	3,557	4,721	23.0	22.3
Average			3.2	3.0
Standard Deviation				12.0	12.1

Source: Figures in Table 5.15 have been deflated by the modified purchasing power parity price index in Table 2.7.

general level of prices but also the demand for money itself. Hence, the double importance of regulating the money supply. Reasonable price stability is a necessary condition for increasing demand for money in real terms. Depositors desire security not only in the form of the certainty that they will always be able to get their money back but also in the form of the certainty that the money which is eventually withdrawn will be worth at least the same in real terms as it was when deposited. The latter condition is also required by currency holders. Thus, the paramount importance of

> .... the crucial contribution that central banks can make to economic development by achieving—and maintaining—reasonable stability in domestic prices and equilibrium in the balance of payments. A central bank that uses its powers to discharge effectively these traditional central banking responsibilities makes a fundamental contribution to development because these are contributions that encourage and sustain economic growth. [B32, p. 781]

In all central banking activities designed to promote financial development, i.e. increase the real demand for money, the same two prerequisites appear, namely, the need to ensure security and the need to provide

Table 5.17

Average Annual Percentage Changes and Standard Deviations in Money and Prices in Afghanistan, Iran, Pakistan and Turkey

(Percentages)

		Money Stock (M2)		Price Level	
		Average Annual Percentage Change	Standard Deviation	Average Annual Percentage Change	Standard Deviation
Afghanistan	1331-1340	11.0	13.6	3.1	11.1
	1341-1351	12.1	9.2	8.3	10.4
Iran	1950-1960	14.0	7.3	4.5	9.7
	1961-1971	16.3	5.3	1.9	2.1
Pakistan	1950-1960	8.6	5.1	2.7	15.1
	1961-1971	11.2	5.5	3.9	4.8
Turkey	1950-1960	18.4	5.1	8.5	8.8
	1961-1971	16.3	4.9	6.2	4.1

Source: Afghanistan—Tables 2.7 and 5.15.
Iran, Pakistan and Turkey—*International Financial Statistics: 1972 Supplement; Pakistan Monthly Statistical Bulletin*, 12 (1), January 1964 (Pakistan Central Statistical Office); Pakistan Institute of Development Economics, *A Measure of Inflation in Pakistan, 1951-60* (Karachi: Pakistan Institute of Development Economics, Monograph No. 4, 1961).

attractive earnings in real terms to money holders. Regulating the money supply must be designed, therefore, to ensure that supply does not deviate from real demand, i.e. that the money supply is increased so that any increase in demand is satisfied or decreased to compensate for any decrease in demand. It must not be increased faster than any increase in demand or decreased slower than any decrease in demand, both of which would cause inflation which in turn would produce uncertainty and negative returns to money holding.

Given the importance of regulating the money supply, the next step is to examine the way in which a central bank can do this. Work on money supply functions has followed two distinct paths in recent years. The first approach, followed among others by Meltzer [M8] and Cagan [C2], separates three direct determinants of the money supply, namely, high powered money, the currency/money ratio and the reserve/deposit ratio, and analyses their movements. High powered money or the cash base is defined here as currency in circulation and vault cash of the commercial banks. "This total is called 'high-powered money' because one dollar of such money held as bank reserves may give rise to the creation of several dollars of deposits" [F24, p. 50]. The second method, followed by Bell and Berman [B18], concentrates on an accounting framework through which the Government's financial deficit can be linked to changes in the money supply. These two approaches are by no means mutually exclusive. The Government's financial deficit may well be, and in Afghanistan certainly has been, the major contributor to increases in high powered money.

The three determinants approach, as the first method of analysis referred to above will hereafter be called, starts with an equation giving the money supply expressed in terms of the three determinants:

$$M = \frac{H}{\dfrac{C}{M} + \dfrac{R}{D} - \dfrac{CR}{MD}} \qquad (5.5)$$

where M is the money supply, H high powered money, C currency in circulation, R holdings of reserves by the banking system, and D deposits included in the definition of money. Contributions of each factor to changes in the money supply can be computed after a minor transformation of the above equation has been made. It may then be possible to study the determinants of the determinants, i.e. of the two ratios and high powered money. The relationship between the Government's deficit and increases in high powered money has already been mentioned.

In the process of economic development, the currency/money ratio can be expected to follow a secular downward path. However, certain factors may accelerate or retard this trend, which may or may not move smoothly. Confidence both in the economic and political stability of the country will be an important factor. Other factors may include the geographical spread of bank branches, the interest paid on deposits, lottery prize inducements, bank advertising, and general measures associated with financial development.

The reserve/deposit ratio may also depend on the same variables as the currency/money ratio, but will also be influenced by any changes in legal minimum reserve requirements. Where legal minimum reserve requirements exist, reserves can be separated into those which are required and those in excess of this requirement, i.e. usable reserves. A secular downward trend in the latter might be expected during times of economic and political stability. Evidence from the U.S.A. suggests that changes in these two ratios have tended to be small and, when they did occur, to move in the opposite direction [C2, pp. 19-20].

In Afghanistan, changes in high powered money or the cash base are caused by the borrowing of the Government from Da Afghanistan Bank, the Bank's lending to the private sector and changes in its foreign exchange holdings. When Da Afghanistan Bank assumes the role of banker to the commercial banks and discontinues its own commercial banking operations, lending to the private sector will only occur through its extension of credit to the commercial banks. By controlling the provision of credit to the public sector and the commercial banks and either accurately forecasting or controlling its foreign exchange position, Da Afghanistan Bank could determine overall changes in high powered money.

In the industrial countries of the west, there has been a generally accepted view until recently that changes in high powered money affect the money supply in a multiplier fashion through fractional reserve banking practices. Elementary textbooks on money and banking invariably provide examples of this process (e.g. [N6, Chapter 2]). In a country such as Afghanistan, where the liquidity position of the commercial banks is known to be both high and variable, no such mechanistic relationship can be assumed. Nevertheless, it is frequently found in empirical investigations that, because of the greater importance of high powered money in money supply as a whole, the relationship between changes in the latter to changes in the former is actually closer in underdeveloped countries than is the case in countries possessing highly sophisticated financial systems.

Eventually, when bank deposits do become the dominant element of the money supply in Afghanistan, fluctuations in the currency/money and reserve/deposit ratios will be potentially much more important determinants of changes in the money supply than they are now; at present, deposits represent only a small fraction of the money supply. Then, it will be important for Da Afghanistan Bank to pursue a rediscount policy which both creates a strong dependence of the commercial banks on it and produces such confidence that reserves are held around the legal minimum requirement. In this situation, changes in credit extended to the commercial banks by Da Afghanistan Bank will have a predictable, multiplier effect on the level of their deposits. As Dorrance points out:

> .... this instrument of monetary control is likely to be most powerful in the developing countries. It is likely to be effective in that the deposit-money banks will probably respond to any easing of central bank policy, while the central bank retains the initiative to restrict its operations if such a policy is appropriate at any time. It is an instrument that is consistent with the institutional situation in most developing countries. It need not lead to countervailing speculative reactions by the community. Finally, it is, by itself, independent of the fiscal and other requirements of a developing country. [D7, p. 278]

In the brief discussion of a money supply function presented earlier, the public sector deficit approach was incorporated into the more general three determinants approach as one of the factors influencing the quantity of high powered money. It may well be that high powered money is the most important determinant of the money supply and that the public sector deficit is the most significant factor producing changes in high powered money. Nevertheless, it is useful to keep the more general approach in mind as it does indicate all possible sources of fluctuations in the money supply, some of which, although not important in the past, might become so in the future. Furthermore, the three elements are controlled by three different economic sectors, the currency/money ratio by the private, non-bank sector, the reserve/deposit ratio by the banking sector and high powered money by the central bank and/or public sector. The reactions of these three groups may differ from one another and yet be predictable. The importance of each determinant and the precise effects of each of their own determinants becomes crucial in an assessment of the extent to which the money supply is a policy variable of the central bank.

To estimate the contribution of the three elements, high powered money, the currency/money and reserve/deposit ratios, Equation 5.5

requires some modification before it can be applied. A number of
alternatives are possible, the one chosen here being to convert it to a log
differential form:

$$\frac{d \log M}{dt} = \frac{d \log H}{dt} + \frac{M}{H}\left(1 - \frac{R}{D}\right)\frac{d\,(-\,C/M)}{dt}$$

$$+ \frac{M}{H}\left(1 - \frac{C}{M}\right)\frac{d\,(-\,R/D)}{dt} \tag{5.6}$$

and to approximate this continuous function by annual averages. Thus,
$\dfrac{d \log M}{dt}$ is approximated by $(\log M_t - \log M_{t-1})$ and similar adjustments
are made for all the differential terms. The ratios $\dfrac{M}{H}\left(1 - \dfrac{R}{D}\right)$ and
$\dfrac{M}{H}\left(1 - \dfrac{C}{M}\right)$ are calculated by averaging their beginning and end of year
values. For the entire period, the averages of all the annual rates of
change have been used.

Table 5.18

Sources of the Rates of Change in Afghanistan's Money Stock 1338-1351
(Percentages)

Date	Total Percentage Change in the Money Stock	Percentage Rates of Change Contributed by		
		High Powered Money	Currency/ Money Ratio	Reserve/ Deposit Ratio
1338	8.78	1.66	5.42	1.72
1339	2.05	12.47	-8.94	-1.53
1340	15.09	21.64	-2.65	-3.92
1341	20.24	20.21	0.61	-0.57
1342	21.93	21.92	0.66	-0.66
1343	18.86	14.13	-0.43	5.16
1344	8.43	-0.65	7.84	1.27
1345	-2.01	-1.31	-1.27	0.56
1346	-0.05	6.83	-2.87	-4.03
1347	7.65	4.12	-0.76	4.29
1348	15.08	20.51	-0.65	-4.78
1349	7.03	8.22	0.55	-1.74
1350	6.64	0.88	1.84	3.93
1351	18.22	14.38	-0.38	4.22

Note: All figures given in this table are the annual percentage rates of change. Not
all lines add up to the total because of rounding and approximation errors.

Source: International Financial Statistics, 26 (10), October 1973, pp. 40-41; and
International Financial Statistics: 1972 Supplement, pp. 228-29.

Over the period 1338-1351 (1959-1972), the money supply increased at an annual average rate of 10.57 per cent. Annual average contributions from changes in high powered money, the currency/money and reserve/ deposit ratios were 10.36 per cent, —0.07 per cent and 0.28 per cent, respectively. In other words, over the entire period changes in the money supply were the result of changes in high powered money. There were virtually no effects from changes in the currency/money or reserve/ deposit ratios.

Table 5.19

Sources of the Rates of Change in the Money Stock
in Iran, Pakistan and Turkey, 1961-1970

IRAN

Date	Total Percentage Change in the Money Stock	Percentage Rates of Change Contributed by		
		High Powered Money	Currency/ Money Ratio	Reserve/Deposit Ratio
1962	12.8	13.1	2.2	−2.5
1963	17.0	10.0	1.0	6.0
1964	16.6	9.4	3.1	4.1
1965	13.1	15.1	2.6	−4.6
1966	13.1	5.0	3.8	4.3
1967	15.5	12.4	2.4	0.7
1968	18.2	13.7	2.9	1.5
1969	17.3	17.6	3.2	−3.5
1970	15.5	15.2	1.6	−1.3
1962-70	15.5	12.4	2.5	0.5

PAKISTAN

Date	Total Percentage Change in the Money Stock	Percentage Rates of Change Contributed by		
		High Powered Money	Currency/ Money Ratio	Reserve/Deposit Ratio
1961	4.7	2.7	2.0	0.1
1962	6.3	1.3	5.2	−0.3
1963	13.6	8.1	6.1	−0.6
1964	16.6	12.9	4.5	−0.7
1965	12.4	7.9	4.8	−0.3
1966	14.2	13.0	0.7	0.6
1967	9.0	4.2	6.4	−1.7
1968	9.0	3.3	4.4	1.3
1969	10.5	11.3	−1.0	0.2
1970	9.6	7.5	2.1	−0.1
1961-70	10.6	7.2	3.5	−0.1

Table 5.19 (Continued)

TURKEY

Date	Total Percentage Change in the Money Stock	Percentage Rates of Change Contributed by		
		High Powered Money	*Currency/ Money Ratio*	*Reserve/Deposit Ratio*
1961	7.7	9.3	−1.4	−0.2
1962	11.6	10.2	2.0	−0.5
1963	8.8	8.5	1.2	−0.8
1964	11.8	14.0	−1.5	−0.7
1965	17.9	16.0	3.4	−1.4
1966	18.1	14.7	4.7	−1.3
1967	15.8	15.1	2.5	−1.7
1968	14.4	12.6	3.8	−2.0
1969	15.8	13.2	4.0	−1.3
1970	13.5	13.1	0.0	0.4
1961-70	13.6	12.7	1.9	−1.0

Note: All figures given in this table are the annual percentage rates of change. Not all lines add up to the total because of rounding and approximation errors.

Source: *Bank Markazi Iran Bulletins*, 3-10, 1962-1971; *Pakistan Monthly Statistical Bulletins*, 1962-1971; *Türkiye Cumhuriyeti Merkez Bankası Aylık Bülteni*, 1962-1971.

The same picture, however, does not emerge when the changes in the individual years are analysed. The figures presented in Table 5.18 above indicate that the short run influence of high powered money on the money supply is much less predictable than the long run influence. Both currency/money and reserve/deposit ratios are much more volatile in the short run and from inspection do not appear easily explicable. Detailed work by the author on Turkish monetary statistics suggested that a lag between an increase in high powered money and the corresponding increase in the money supply of about five months existed [F25, p. 89]. Unfortunately, the lack of data makes a similar test on the Afghan monetary system impossible. Table 5.19 provides comparative figures for Iran, Pakistan and Turkey. Declining currency/money ratios in all three countries have provided positive contributions to changes in the money supply. There is no noticeable trend in the Afghan currency/money ratio, an indication of the absence of financial development in Afghanistan. This is brought out more clearly from the figures given in Tables 2.11 and 2.12 above.

The question which must now be answered is:

Does control over the monetary base and other instruments provide the central bank with sufficient powers to fit the behavior of the money stock into a given program? [F2, p. 221]

Regressing the annual changes in the money supply against changes in high powered money produces a coefficient of determination of 0.56, indicating that 56 per cent of the variance in the money supply is accounted for by changes in high powered money. Lagging the relationship by one year, i.e. hypothesising that changes in high powered money affect the money supply a year later, gives a coefficient of determination of 0.39, somewhat worse than that resulting from the unlagged analysis. In a similar exercise on Turkish monetary statistics, the author found that without taking account of any lagged adjustment changes in high powered money explained 70 per cent of the fluctuations in the rate of change in the money supply. With a five month lag, 88 per cent of the variance was accounted for by changes in high powered money [F25, pp. 89-90]. In France, another study found that less than 50 per cent of the variance was explained in this way [M8, p. 283]. It should be mentioned, however, that these results were for quarterly rather than annual differences.

Taking the analysis to have provided an affirmative answer to the question posed above, i.e. concluding that the largest part of the fluctuations in changes in the money supply are determined by changes in high powered money in Afghanistan, two further questions require examination: Can Da Afghanistan Bank control the stock of money on a month-to-month or a quarter-to-quarter basis? Does Da Afghanistan Bank, or at least the central Government authorities as a whole, hold control over the volume of high powered money?

A glance at Afghanistan's monthly and quarterly monetary data suggests that short run control over the money supply is considerably more difficult than long run control. Evidence from the U.S.A. has also shown that seasonal forces severely reduce the authorities' ability to control the quantity of money in the short run [A25; F2, p. 225]. In Afghanistan, the importance of agriculture accentuates this short run disability in that seasonal fluctuations cannot be accurately predicted; counteracting measures to maintain a target figure for the money supply cannot therefore be taken in advance. Any agricultural price support programme will compound this difficulty. Thus, a negative answer to the first question posed above is reached.

The second question produces a considerable statistical problem to which only a partial and far from perfect solution exists. It arises from the fact that the annual public sector deficits produced using monetary data are by no means consistent with those derived from the Government accounts. The reasons for the difference spring from the fact that there is a serious time lag in the compilation of Government accounts, these accounts are not strictly on a cash basis and further do not include Government enterprises. The discrepancy appears to find its way into "other items" in the monetary surveys. Therefore, if changes in the Government position *vis-à-vis* the financial system are required, a more realistic figure may be obtained by including "other items" with "Claims on Government (net)." This procedure is followed here. Table 5.20 presents absolute as well as percentage changes in both high powered money and the public sector debt calculated by the method described above. It is clear that little relationship exists. Changes in public sector debt have been much more volatile than changes in high powered money, fluctuations in the latter being to some extent ironed out by compensating changes in credit extended by Da Afghanistan Bank to the private sector. Over the entire period, public debt increased by Afs 9,169 million, whereas high powered money only increased by Afs 6,452 million. Reductions in foreign exchange holdings enabled this to occur. Furthermore, private sector credit increased only very modestly and in real terms actually declined.

Table 5.20
Annual Changes in High Powered Money and Public Sector Debt 1338-1351

Date	High Powered Money		Public Sector Debt	
	Change in Millions of Afghanis	*Percentage Change*	*Change in Millions of Afghanis*	*Percentage Change*
1338	33	1.7	−11	−1.3
1339	267	13.3	642	78.2
1340	550	24.2	567	38.8
1341	633	22.4	1,351	36.3
1342	848	24.5	2,144	42.3
1343	654	15.2	−1,011	−14.0
1344	−32	−0.6	−355	−5.7
1345	−64	−1.3	−717	−12.3
1346	344	7.1	1,185	23.1
1347	219	4.2	−919	−14.5
1348	1,236	22.8	3,074	56.9
1349	571	8.6	424	5.0
1350	64	0.9	2,078	23.4
1351	1,129	15.5	717	6.5
Average		11.3		18.8
Standard Deviation		9.6		28.8

Source: *International Financial Statistics*, 26 (10), October 1973, pp. 40-41; and *International Financial Statistics: 1972 Supplement*, pp. 228-29.

Changes in high powered money have not moved in mechanistic response to changes in the public sector debt. Hence, even if Da Afghanistan Bank could control the latter this would not automatically ensure control over high powered money and through this the money supply. The absence of any mechanistic relationship between public sector deficits and changes in high powered money does not, fortunately, imply a negative answer to the second question. It simply means that the other determinants of changes in high powered money, namely, changes in Da Afghanistan Bank's lending to the private sector and changes in its foreign exchange holdings, must either be controlled or predicted so that compensating changes in public sector credit can be arranged. In fact, the public sector deficit at present takes precedence and compensations in terms of changes in credit extended to the private sector and official foreign exchange holdings are made. Ideally, the foreign exchange situation should be predictable or planned and a policy to make necessary changes in public and private sector credit extended by Da Afghanistan Bank so that high powered money changed in the appropriate way worked out in advance. This is where forecast monetary surveys can play such a useful role in monetary policy.

Where Government borrowing requirements are neither planned nor predictable, as is shown to have been the case in the following chapter, monetary policy of the type discussed above is doomed so long as the Government borrows solely from the central bank and the central bank is powerless to refuse. When such a situation is foreseeable, the only alternative which can allow monetary policy to be planned and implemented efficiently to promote financial development both by maintaining stable prices and avoiding violent and unexpected contractions of credit to the private sector is for the Government to raise loans through a free auction of treasury bills. Agreement can be reached in advance on the annual acquisition of bills by the central bank and on some expected interest rate on these bills. In this way, the independence of monetary policy is ensured and any variation in interest rate on the bills from that expected will occur only when the Government sells more than the central bank has agreed to buy. Such variation will not only deter the Government from increasing its borrowing beyond the amount which the central bank has agreed to finance, but ensure that such extra borrowing is non-inflationary and furthermore force the Government to bid competitively for the economy's scarce resources.

The ultimate aim of money supply regulation is the maintenance of stable prices, full employment and an economic climate conducive to development. It is therefore essential for effective implementation of monetary policy that the relationship between the money supply and the level of Gross National Product at current prices be examined. From projections of the real growth rate, an optimal money supply policy can then be calculated. The framework for such analysis has been presented in Chapter II. Here, it is simply assumed that in general control of the money supply over the long run is the most important weapon for the maintenance of relative price stability.

The question which now arises is: Who was responsible for the erratic behaviour in the money stock? It has been shown that the greater part of the fluctuations in the money supply are determined by changes in high powered money. Furthermore, changes in public sector debt were found to have been even more volatile than changes in high powered money, as can be seen in Table 5.20. Over the period 1338-1351 (1959-1972) the average annual increase in high powered money was 11.3 per cent with a standard deviation of 9.6. Over the same period the average annual increase in public sector domestic debt was 18.8 per cent with a standard deviation of 28.8. The greater variability of changes in public sector domestic debt than in high powered money is due to the fact that Da Afghanistan Bank made compensating changes in the credit it extended to the private sector and in its foreign exchange reserves. Net reductions in foreign exchange reserves enabled public sector domestic debt to increase at a considerably faster rate than high powered money.

Given that the Government's financial requirements have always taken precedence over all other considerations, it would appear that the extraordinarily high annual variations in public sector domestic borrowing has been ultimately responsible for the variability in the money supply, with Da Afghanistan Bank attempting to and partially succeeding in dampening these fluctuations through private sector credit and reserve policies. The causes of the volatile public sector domestic borrowing requirements are analysed in the following chapter.

High variance in the rate of inflation, caused by the extreme volatility of public sector domestic borrowing, has been one factor contributing to financial stagnation. In addition, the rate of inflation itself, which can also be attributed to excessive public sector domestic borrowing, has suppressed financial development. Such borrowing can be regarded as a tax on money holdings since the inflation it has created reduced the real value of money held. The consequences of this tax on one of the most important products of the financial sector have been succinctly analysed by Shaw in the following extract:

Real money balances can be regarded not merely as wealth from the stand-point of the money-holder but as social wealth, deserving a place on the social balance sheet with wealth in machines, inventories, structures, natural resource endowments and human skills. A fully monetized eco-nomic system can extract the highest yield from its productive capacities. Incomplete monetization constrains productivity. Afghanistan is among the least monetized of economies, yet it was public policy to tax money more severely than other forms of wealth. Put another way, it seems that policies were pursued to ensure that Afghanistan would remain a barter society. [S11, p. 8]

v. *Bank Millie and Pashtany Tejaraty Bank*

Of the three non-specialised banks, Bank Millie is generally regarded as the most efficient, Pashtany the least. Bank Millie is the only private bank, yet in several ways it resembles a Government agency. For example, its personnel policy bears similarities with the Government's in that great emphasis is placed on security and little on payment according to merit. Salary scales themselves are not much above the Government's and again senior staff bemoan the lack of trained staff at the lower and middle levels. Not surprisingly, Bank Millie's lending policy is now the most conservative of the three banks.

Pashtany Tejaraty Bank suffers from Government civil service person-nel policies and Government intervention since it is a Government bank, yet lacks note issuing powers and/or rediscount facilities with Da Afghan-istan Bank to ensure the maintenance of liquidity. This is likely to create a major problem at some future date.

Tables 5.21 and 5.22 provide some balance sheet data and banking ratios for these two institutions. The former generally indicates the small size of the two banks. Of interest in the latter has been the steady increase in the deposit/asset ratio, the wildly fluctuating reserve/deposit ratio and the apparent decline in the credit/asset ratio until 1349 (1971). The latter is not too informative in that a large proportion of Bank Millie's loans go to firms in which it has major equity interests.

There are many similarities between Bank Millie, Pashtany Tejaraty Bank and Da Afghanistan Bank. Lending is concentrated in the foreign trade sector, branches are no more than deposit and collection agencies, efficiency is low and, in certain Government banks, corruption has been reported. In general, the commercial banks present a sorry picture of stagnation.

The provinces have suffered from Afghanistan's highly centralised banking system. No loans have been granted by the branches without the

Table 5.21

Assets and Liabilities of Bank Millie and Pashtany Tejaraty Bank, 1340-1351

(Millions of Afghanis, End of Year Figures)

	1340	1341	1342	1343	1344	1345	1346	1347	1348	1349	1350	1351
ASSETS												
Reserves	220	302	424	240	286	242	406	191	521	704	515	249
Foreign Assets	18	37	74	102	73	111	102	167	169	200	186	292
Claims on Private Sector	1,145	1,146	1,155	1,417	1,638	1,708	1,765	1,918	1,884	1,845	2,477	2,997
Unclassified Assets	129	146	141	320	615	628	634	728	598	579	952	1,040
ASSETS = LIABILITIES	1,512	1,631	1,794	2,079	2,612	2,689	2,907	3,004	3,172	3,328	4,130	4,578
LIABILITIES												
Demand Deposits	191	339	408	319	392	292	431	443	515	491	587	477
Quasi-Money Deposits	81	89	150	397	720	660	598	701	690	913	1,200	1,383
Government Deposits	169	205	212	137	106	120	154	209	183	180	180	280
Capital Accounts	984	1,006	1,019	1,035	1,061	1,117	1,203	1,264	1,283	1,195	1,217	1,201
Unclassified Liabilities	92	-5	7	194	332	498	516	389	501	550	946	1,236

Source: International Financial Statistics: 1972 Supplement, p. 229; and Research Department, Da Afghanistan Bank.

Table 5.22

Banking Ratios of Bank Millie and Pashtany Tejaraty Bank, 1340-1351

(Percentages)

	1340	1341	1342	1343	1344	1345	1346	1347	1348	1349	1350	1351
Ratio A	29	39	43	41	47	40	41	45	44	48	48	47
Ratio B	50	48	55	28	23	23	34	14	38	44	26	12
Ratio C	76	70	64	68	63	64	61	64	59	55	60	65

$$\text{Ratio A} = \frac{\text{Total Deposits}}{\text{Total Assets}} \times 100$$

$$\text{Ratio B} = \frac{\text{Reserves}}{\text{Total Deposits}} \times 100$$

$$\text{Ratio C} = \frac{\text{Outstanding Credit}}{\text{Total Assets}} \times 100$$

Source: *International Financial Statistics*, 26 (10), October 1973, pp. 40-41; *International Financial Statistics: 1972 Supplement*, p. 229; and Research Department, Da Afghanistan Bank.

decision being first taken in Kabul. Most branches of Da Afghanistan Bank have not even accepted loan applications. A further deprivation in the provinces with respect to banking facilities springs from the lack of a bank clearing system. Thus, cheques cannot, in general, either be cashed or even paid into an account in any branch other than that on which the cheques are drawn. An exception appears to be Bank Millie's head office branch which has accepted cheques from other branches and other banks for payment into an account after they have been cleared.

This strong deterrent to the use of banking facilities in the provinces has resulted in the possession of bank accounts by only a very limited number of people, e.g. wealthy foreign traders, and joint stock companies. Virtually no one else uses the banks. Indeed, when asked whether they would like to borrow from a bank, several respondents in the survey mentioned in Chapter III replied that they already had enough trouble with the Government and indebtedness to it would be disastrous. The association of Da Afghanistan Bank with the Government is not surprising given the fact that the smaller branches undertake almost no business apart from the collection and disbursement of public funds. Information collected thus suggests that the banking system has done little to facilitate the transfer of funds throughout the country and has failed to administer the payments mechanism. Improved transport between the major towns has made it easier to transfer cash. This has apparently actually retarded the growth of bank deposits.

Mixed feelings were expressed by respondents on the desirability of the establishment of foreign bank branches in Afghanistan. At one extreme, nationalistic sentiments were exhibited and the view that all profitable ventures should be in Afghan hands was propounded. At the other extreme, however, there was a frequently expressed hope that foreign banks would be more willing than domestic banks to lend money and so would be a considerable asset. This sentiment often took the form of a feeling that Moslem banks were generally unhelpful. There were, of course, a number of respondents who viewed the establishment of foreign banks in Afghanistan quite neutrally, stating that as long as there were more banks willing to lend, it did not matter whether they were domestic or foreign.

vi. *Specialised Banks*

The history of specialised banking in Afghanistan has been less than satisfactory. A new period, however, started in 1348 (1970) with the reconstitution of the former Agriculture and Cottage Industries Bank into the new Agricultural Development Bank (AgBank) with help from the United Nations and the World Bank. There are several striking differences between the activities of the AgBank and the commercial banks. Despite the fact that it is a Government institution, the AgBank has been operating under new personnel policies, which take some major departures from the civil service procedures previously followed, since the beginning of 1352 (March 1973). Pay scales have been considerably raised, the civil service promotion system and titles abolished and an incentive scheme introduced.

The AgBank also differs from the commercial banks in that it is expanding rapidly as can be seen from the data in Table 5.23. These figures can be compared to those of the Mortgage and Construction Bank given in Table 5.24. Recently, the AgBank solicited the problematic job of distributing credit for fertiliser purchases and has devised new ways and means of increasing the probability of prompt collection. Due to the lack of market intelligence, the former did not meet expectations in 1352 (1973) because effective demand for such credit was considerably lower than forecast, again illustrating the endemic communications problem discussed in Chapter III.

The accounting procedures used by the AgBank differ from those of the commercial banks and the Mortgage and Construction Bank not only in the fact that they are much more accurate and are audited by external auditors of international repute, but also in the important fact that bad debts are written off. No debt in any of the other banks has ever been written off. This alone results in such distortions as to make the balance sheets and profit and loss statements extremely misleading.

The Mortgage and Construction Bank has so reduced the scope of its activities that it is virtually defunct. A few small loans to Government employees are all that are now made.

The Industrial Development Bank of Afghanistan (IDBA) established after many years of planning and negotiations in 1351 (1973) has just started operations and hopes to make its first loans in 1352 (1973). Like the AgBank, the IDBA is managed by a foreign management team funded by the UNDP with the World Bank as executing agency. Unlike the AgBank, the IDBA is a private corporation with 40 per cent foreign participation. Bank Millie, Pashtany Tejaraty Bank and the Chamber of Commerce hold another 40 per cent of the equity. In relation to the equity capital of Afs 240 million, the IDBA is to receive an enormous subsidy from the Government in the form of an Afs 560 million loan at 2 per cent interest with repayment over 25 years, which includes a 10 year grace period, from Da Afghanistan Bank. The World Bank, through IDA, has

Table 5.23

Assets and Liabilities of the Agricultural Development Bank, 1350-1351
(Millions of Afghanis, End of Year Figures)

	1350	1351
ASSETS		
Cash and Deposits	118	229
Claims Abroad	24	49
Domestic Loans	91	384
Participations	16	16
Inventories and Goods in Transit	65	56
Other Assets	8	13
ASSETS = LIABILITIES	322	747
LIABILITIES		
Deposits	15	156
Loans from Government and Da Afghanistan Bank	6	142
Foreign Liabilities	53	18
Other Liabilities	32	13
Paid-up Capital	215	395
Reserves and Undistributed Profits	1	23

Source: Accounts Department, Agricultural Development Bank.

Table 5.24

Assets and Liabilities of the Mortgage and Construction Bank, 1334-1350

(Millions of Afghanis, End of Year Figures)

	1334	1335	1336	1337	1338	1339	1340	1341	1342	1343	1344	1345	1346	1347	1348	1349	1350
ASSETS																	
Deposits	5	4	4	4	9	8	9	5	6	19	18	9	22	6	14	19	25
Loans	66	62	64	66	62	63	67	66	71	68	79	85	87	92	90	86	85
Investments	2	2	2	2	2	2	4	4	4	4	5	5	6	6	6	6	6
Other Assets	29	31	34	35	31	29	24	25	21	22	27	23	22	23	24	20	20
ASSETS = LIABILITIES	102	99	104	107	104	102	104	100	102	113	129	122	137	127	134	131	136
LIABILITIES																	
Capital	61	61	61	61	61	61	61	61	61	61	61	61	61	61	61	65	65
Loan from Pension Fund	13	9	9	9	6	5	0	0	0	0	0	0	0	0	0	0	0
Loan from Da Afghanistan Bank	0	0	0	0	0	0	0	4	4	4	4	3	3	0	0	0	0
Deposits	0	0	0	0	0	0	0	0	0	0	5	5	5	5	5	5	5
Other Liabilities	28	29	34	37	37	36	43	35	37	48	59	53	68	61	68	61	66

Source: Mortgage and Construction Bank, *Reports of the Executive Committee to the Annual General Assembly on the Activities for the Years 1334-1350* (in Dari) (Kabul: Mortgage and Construction Bank, 1335-1351).

provided a $2 million loan to the Government with a 50 year term, 10 year grace period, at a service charge only of three-quarters of a per cent on the amount outstanding. The Government, in turn, is to extend foreign exchange to the IDBA at rates of $5\frac{1}{4}$ and $7\frac{1}{4}$ per cent, the former for relending at 8 per cent to small scale firms, i.e. firms with less than $100,000 worth of equipment, the latter at 10 per cent to other borrowers. The foreign exchange conversion risk is in both cases borne by the borrower. Lending policy is likely to be conservative. The expected return on IDBA capital in the short run is 12-18 per cent. The anomalous effect of the spread of interest rates and returns in terms of income distribution has been noted by Shaw:

> .... if the IDBA achieves a portfolio equal only to funds initially committed and earns upon them, after allowing for expenses, a return of 7 per cent, the yield to stockholders will exceed 18 per cent. That is hardly comparable with the yield to taxpayers of 2 per cent on the Government's loan, through Da Afghanistan Bank, to the IDBA. [S11, p. 20]

vii. *Problems of Bank Lending*

Not only has the volume of credit measured at constant prices which has been received by the private sector declined considerably over the past decade, but the variety of loans has also contracted. Because of difficulties experienced by the banks in collecting loans on maturity, the types of collateral which are now acceptable against secured loans have been reduced. The difficulties in collecting debts have been mentioned in several publications:

> .... the banks are reluctant to widen their range of borrowers or to extend credit facilities to industry and agriculture, owing to inadequate protection under existing laws. [U12, p. 106]

> Since the rights, duties and obligations of both borrower and lender are not clearly defined by law, neither commercial bankers as lenders nor the private sector as borrowers can be expected to fully mobilize the credit resources of the country to accelerate economic development. [M30, p. 19]

> The lack of suitable laws as for example a civil code, credit security laws, a general banking law and the inexperienced administrative staff of the banks as well as that of the different commercial courts makes it difficult for the banks to promote the lending business .... [G3, p. 8]

> .... the banking institutions have not been successful in distributing and collecting loans .... The failure of the banking system in the distribution and collection of loans is mostly due to poor management, untrustworthiness of borrowers and the use of bank credit for consumption and non-productive purposes. [M31, p. 19]

The three recurring problems which emerge from reports and interviews with the managers of credit departments in all the banks are:

A. Legal
B. Management
C. Political

The legal problems appear to arise from the influence owners continue to hold over the disposal of their collateral, slow and inefficient court procedures, the political and social influence of the borrower, incompetent court officials and corruption. Management problems arise from inadequate training in audit and inspection procedures for bank employees, nepotism in promotion and incompetence in both branch and head offices. Similar defects in the borrowing institutions themselves and in the customs houses compound these difficulties. Political influence has been exerted on state owned financial institutions to extend specific loans.

The histories of the specialised Government owned banks well illustrate the problems of institutional lending in Afghanistan. One of the major problems has been postponement of interest and instalment payments. The Industrial Credit Fund was established at the beginning of 1336 (1957) with a capital of Afs 205 million. By the end of its first year it had lent out almost all its funds and thereafter "ceased to operate to all intents and purposes" [B34, p. 15]. The Fund was later wound up when it became evident that loans would never be repaid. The same fate has befallen all the other specialised banks. The Agriculture and Cottage Industries Bank established in 1333 (1954) had exhausted its funds by 1337 (1958):

> The Agricultural Bank continued giving loans till the end of 1337, but as many of these loans were not utilized in productive enterprises and as the bank could not recover the major part of its loans and interest of six percent, at last it decided to close the chapter of giving loans. [M23, p. 12]

The peculiar problem faced by the Agricultural Bank in taking land titles as security is illustrated in the following passage on lending by nomads:

> In most cases the ordinary nomad today owns no land, but on the other hand often takes it on the so-called *gerawi* terms. This means that, against a once-for-all payment in the shape of a loan, the nomad takes a definite area of land as security. All rights to the land belong to the lender, and as he neither can nor will cultivate it, this is left to an Hazara on ordinary tenant conditions. If Islamic law is followed, the borrower (former owner of the ground) must not be employed as tenant. [F3, p. 133]

Thus, land can only be given as mortgage if it is then farmed by someone other than the owner.

The AgBank and the Mortgage and Construction Bank have turned to the Government to support collection. Until recently, the AgBank's lending activities were confined to tractor and water pump loans to large farmers. It is, however, attempting to extend activities. It tried with only limited success to distribute credit to groups of farmers for fertiliser purchases in 1352 (1973) and is planning to lend to small farmers under a system of supervised credit in the near future. In this, it is seeking assistance for supervision from Government extension services, PACCA, the Helmand-Arghandab Valley Authority (HAVA) and the cotton companies.

The main problems faced by the AgBank in its lending activities are best gleaned from two reports of the AgBank itself:

II *Existing Problems Faced by the AgBank*

A *Problems Related to the Distribution of Credit*

The AgBank in following general principles of banking and its own regulations does not extend loans to borrowers who cannot meet certain requirements. As security, the AgBank has accepted the following items: immovable property (land, shops, houses, etc.); movable property such as agricultural products, including animal products, merchandise and bonds; and guarantees from financial institutions and agro-business firms. To safeguard its loans, the AgBank has generally required immovable property as security for medium and long-term loans.

The provision of such security is still based on Government regulations concerning guarantees which were prepared by the Ministry of Finance and ratified by the Cabinet. To mortgage land, the owner swears in the presence of two witnesses in a court of law (mahkama-e-wasayeq) that he is placing a particular piece of his land under mortgage against the loan which is being provided by the Bank. On default, the Bank has the right to sell the mortgaged property without recourse to further judicial procedure.

In practice, a number of defects in this system does not encourage banks to accept such security (wasiqa) for the following reasons:

1 Since the cadastral survey has not been completed, the actual size and nature of the security is uncertain.
2 Incorrect land registration results in uncertainty as to whether the possessor of the title is in fact the owner of the land.
3 The variety of customary rights in different parts of the country over water use (haqaba) which is a major factor in determining the value of the property adds to the uncertainty of the security.
4 Various standards of measurement (tukhum raiz, paikal, quiba, etc.) further add to the problem.

5 Finally, legal promissory notes do not conform to the Bank's requirements. Unclear handwriting of court officials can easily prevent the document from being officially accepted.

B *Difficulties in Settling Loan Contracts*

1 Loans are extended in accordance with the conditions laid out in the contract which after the provision of adequate security is signed by both parties. The contract sets out the rights and duties of both sides. The Commercial Law establishes that disputes arising from such contracts should be taken to the commercial courts. However, as a result of various problems such as the non-attendance of borrowers or the bank's attorney, contracts have not been registered in the courts. This, of course, creates additional problems.
2 The absence of commercial courts in many parts of the country in any case makes registration of contracts impossible.
3 Registration departments (wasayeq) create obstacles preventing speedy registration.

C *Collection Problems*

Although the borrower vests the right to sell his security with the bank and his neighbours promise to buy the land in the case of default, the bank is often unable to sell the security because:

1 The inhabitants of the district refuse to buy the land through fear or compassion.
2 The immediate neighbours are not in a position financially to buy the land or they also want to help the borrower.
3 The judicial authorities will not transfer the security to the bank without the consent of the borrower. Even if it is transferred to the bank, the bank will not be able to manage the property: the establishment of a management team is too costly.
4 Loan collection is another area in which the bank does not possess any authority and at present this is undertaken by Government agencies. This has created many additional problems.

D *Borrowers' Difficulties*

In the absence of cooperatives, land titles and other securities, a large number of farmers are deprived of receiving agricultural loans. Even farmers with land titles who want to borrow are faced with severe difficulties arising from the costs of legal promissory notes and psychological factors.

IV *Problems Regarding Security for Medium-Term Loans*

Medium-term loans are generally given to farmers to help them buy immediate needs such as improved seeds, fertiliser, chemicals to combat insects, small tools, animals and to help them improve their marketing. In these cases, immovable property is held as security.

In this instance, the AgBank faces the following difficulties:

1 Preparation and distribution of credit for individual farmers possibly exceeding a million in number is a major problem.

2 Granting loans to farmers against their agricultural and animal products is not problem-free, both because the cooperative system is not common and also because the marketing system has not been developed, except for a few items such as sugar beet and cotton. Otherwise the sale of agricultural products is not controlled and the collection of loans is difficult.

3 Preparation of promissory notes for mortgages for short-term loans and also registration of the contracts related to these loans in the commercial courts create some problems in that they make the distribution of loans, which are increasing day by day, impossible. In particular, fertiliser will be needed by over half a million farmers in the next season. Although the Afghan Fertiliser Company has been established to satisfy the needs of farmers, there are not enough storehouses throughout the country and therefore fertiliser cannot be distributed to all the farmers.

[A10, pp. 3-12]

3.2 *Securities*

At present, the only utilized form of security is mortgage on land. Land security is established through a legal act undertaken in the courts. A mortgage on land can be given only by a landowner. The Bank also accepts land mortgage of a person other than the borrower. The procedure involved in getting a land mortgage confirmed by the court is time-consuming and troublesome. From the security document finally issued by the court on the basis of the "Qabala", which does not show the actual status of ownership, AgBank cannot be certain that the land mortgage obtained will be a valid guarantee, from which prosecution can be started without any difficulty.

It is the desire of AgBank that steps should be taken to simplify the legal documents and procedures involved in order to give further encouragement to the farmers and to enable AgBank to expand its loan activities. If the farmer does not pay the loan when it falls due the Bank's only remedy is the possibility of selling the mortgaged land. Under the present security system the sale of land not only involves legal problems but also problems in the practical aspects of the sale. Since the security is based on the signatures of neighbouring landowners, who have to state that they would be willing to purchase the land in the case of prosecution, this normally results in the neighbours' refusing to comply, claiming they have no cash available, that they maintain a good relationship with the present landowner and therefore do not want to take away his land, and that in cases where a neighbour signed the mortgage and has since died, his heirs are not willing to fulfill the obligations agreed to by the deceased. If it actually comes to a sale it is also very difficult for an outsider to buy the land as he will face difficulties in the future with the neighbours. The AgBank's taking over the land under the present system would add more problems to the already existing ones.

For these reasons many Bank loans have been long overdue. There are many cases available in the Bank as proof.

Generally, besides land, farmers do not have anything else—such as shares in companies, governmental bonds, warehouse receipts for goods placed in government warehouses, guarantees obtained from other banks, or other movable property—of great enough value to serve as security for AgBank. In addition to the difficulties arising from the legal procedures in obtaining land securities, the actual number of landowners in a position to obtain these securities on land is very limited, the reason being that only a minority of landowners has the land actually registered in their names and therefore can produce land titles. In many cases, the land belongs to several members of a family who have inherited the land from their father, grandfather, etc. In such cases, it would take the consent of all the family to put the land under mortgage. As experience has shown, this is also very difficult.

3.3 *Collection*

3.31 Short-term Loans

The collection rate of short-term credits disbursed to cotton companies, the PACCA Cooperative, and to agro-business enterprises with rates between 90 and 100 per cent is satisfactory. The collection rates for credits extended for fertiliser, however, are not at all satisfactory. For the disbursements of 1350, which were due on Mizan 1, 1351, up to Hoot 29, 1351, the average rate of collection was 63 per cent in the whole country, with variations from 28 per cent in Kabul Province to 100 per cent in Bamyan. The reason for this poor result is the fact that not enough efforts to collect have been made and more pressure should come from the RGA [Royal Government of Afghanistan].

3.32 Medium- and Long-term Loans

The collection rates of AgBank of individual loans are also not satisfactory. In the first nine months of 1351, for instance, the recovery rate of medium-term loans fallen due in that period was only 76 per cent. The loans not collected when they fell due are transferred to the category of "loans overdue" where the collection rate is even lower. The difficulties AgBank is having with the system of securities as described above result in farmers knowing exactly that prosecution on land mortgages is more or less fruitless for AgBank. Additionally, it is widely known that the Government does not take a strong position in the collection of fertiliser credit. This naturally has side-effects on AgBank's collections.
[A9, pp. 6-8]

The Mortgage and Construction Bank, established as the Construction Bank in 1326 (1947) and renamed the Mortgage and Construction Bank in 1333 (1954), enjoyed the longest period of activity amongst the specialised banks. However, operations have been severely contracted from a wide range of medium and long term lending operations for private housing, hotels, cinemas, etc., and participation in the construction business to a small volume of loans to Government employees only for a period of five years at a rate of interest of five per cent. It is probable that bad debts will be recognised in the near future and the Bank reorganised on the same lines as the AgBank was in 1348 (1970).

Various attempts at debt collection have been made by the Mortgage and Construction Bank but so far without success. The Bank received little help from the Ministry of the Interior which merely issued summonses on defaulters but did not facilitate the sale of the property. The result was that borrowers did not bother to repay their debts. In 1348 (1969), the Supreme Council of the Bank determined to take action by writing to all the defaulters demanding repayment within a month. Non-compliance would result in seizure and sale of their property by the Law Department of Kabul Province. Furthermore, the Council decided to hire a lawyer for a specific period. Defaulting borrowers were informed of these decisions but no other action was taken and the problem remained unchanged [M36].

In the Annual Report of 1349 (1971), the problem of defaulting borrowers was again brought to the attention of the shareholders. The compounded interest on many loans had reached a level at which the debt exceeded the value of the mortgaged property. When sales had been attempted third parties claimed an interest in the property and so prevented the sales. A further problem was created in 1349 (1970) when the Cabinet approved a motion prohibiting the Bank from holding the titles (qabala) of mortgaged property. Furthermore, the Bank had not insisted on insurance being taken out on mortgaged property. When uninsured mortgaged property had been destroyed, borrowers tended to assume that their obligations to repay were thereby dissolved [M37].

Again in the Annual Report of 1350 (1972) considerable attention is paid to collection problems. The Parliamentary Committee on Public Works and Communications had considered the Bank's problems and had directed it to force the sale of mortgaged property immediately. Two representatives from the Bank were assigned to work with the Collection Department of the Ministry of the Interior. The latter had been instructed to collect the Bank's outstanding loans by Cabinet Decree 962 which received the Royal Assent in Jauza 1345 (May/June 1966). It had made no steps to carry out these instructions and some ambiguity as to the intention of the Decree with regard to the responsibility for sale appeared to exist. The Parliamentary Committee again directed the Bank to make the appropriate sales itself. The Bank appealed to the Minister of Finance and there the matter rested with no one wishing to assume responsibility for debt collection [M38].

The commercial banks have also suffered from excessive loan defaults. In particular, Pashtany Tejaraty Bank has virtually exhausted its resources, faces a serious liquidity problem and is recognised to be in a difficult position as a result of the large number of loan defaults. The one private bank, Bank Millie, pursues very cautious lending policies and has not expanded its activities by any significant amount over the past twenty years. Apart from some foreign trade finance, most of its funds are used to finance its own companies. The choice of lending policies, as seen by the banking fraternity, appears to lie between ultra-conservatism and bankruptcy.

In the course of collecting a number of case histories of problematic loans, a pattern emerged of which the main elements are outlined below.

A. A loan is granted against collateral consisting of shares in a few specified joint stock companies, jewellery or real estate mortgage. Unsecured loans are also extended in a few cases. Most loans made by Da Afghanistan Bank are extended as a result of Cabinet decrees. This bank also discounts bills of exchange for exporters. In these cases, export licences can be withdrawn if bills are not honoured.

B. The loan is not repaid on the due date. After negotiation, an extension is usually agreed.

C. The bank finally decides to act upon the security. In the case of import finance, this should cause no difficulties in that documents needed for customs clearance of all bank financed imports should go directly to the bank concerned. Unfortunately, customs clearance without the necessary documents has been possible on occasions through the judicious distribution of relatively small sums of baksheesh. Where goods are held up at customs houses, there is the problem that no fixed period is specified in any law or regulation after which they become the property of the bank. No specific regulations exist concerning loans for exports.

In the case of other secured loans, the borrower still appears to retain control over the disposal of his collateral. Thus, he may insist that a minimum price be realised from and even on the timing of a sale. Partly for this reason, Bank Millie has discontinued its former practice of lending against gold and jewellery. Where shares form the collateral, written authorisation indicating the name of the new owner must be obtained from the shareholder before a bank can divest itself of them in the event of default. Land titles are often non-existent but where they do exist, and can form the basis for a mortgage loan, land valuation by the courts for the *tazmeen*, which is the legal document required for land mortgage, is arbitrary and can be influenced by the landowner to the disadvantage of the bank. In any event expropriation of land and resale is almost impossible in practice. Potential buyers of expropriated land, if they exist, can quite easily be dissuaded.

In the case of unsecured loans, no precise regulations exist for loan repayment in instances of bankruptcy of the borrower. There are apparently no clear provisions for seizure of property or expropriation of collateral on the default of a borrower.

D. In the few instances where a case reached the courts, decisions have again been influenced through the use of baksheesh, social pressure or political influence. The banks have generally not received satisfaction from the courts.

It cannot, however, be concluded that all the problems of banking arise from bad laws and legal practices. The banks themselves suffer from inadequately trained staff and faulty loan agreements. Thus, for example, in the case of mortgage loans the borrower is not required to insure his property; lack of expertise often results in finance being provided unknowingly for higher risk foreign trade, etc. Political interference in the lending activities of the Agriculture and Cottage Industries Bank, the Industrial Credit Fund and Pashtany Tejaraty Bank has also thwarted any pursuit of sound banking practices.

Bankers in Afghanistan are unanimous in the need for legal protection in their lending operations. The following specific legal requirements have been mentioned:

A. Law for securing bank loans
B. Registration Office for legal registration of all bank loans
C. Special court for enforcing repayment of bank loans
D. Legal provisions for chattel mortgage
E. Legal provisions for lien on crops
F. Legal provisions for loans against letters of credit
G. Cadastral survey
H. Legal provisions for all financial instruments
I. Detailed regulations concerning the absolute rights over and automatic transfer of ownership of collateral

J. Detailed regulations concerning expropriation of property on default

K. Legal provisions for real estate mortgage

L. Specification of responsibilities of customs officials to release imports under bank security only against all necessary documents and a time period after which goods become the property of the bank

M. Specification of how loans for barter imports should be secured

N. Detailed regulations concerning repayment of loans for exports

O. Detailed regulations concerning loan repayment in cases of bankruptcy

P. Detailed regulations obliging courts to seize property in cases of default

The present Commercial Law enacted in 1334 (1955) contains provisions on negotiable instruments, security interests, etc. The Law itself is defective in a number of important respects. For example, the use of cheques has not developed because there are no penalties specified for writing a cheque against insufficient funds. However, the basic provisions for negotiability exist, yet no negotiable instruments circulate in Afghanistan. The reason for this is simply that virtually no one knows the Commercial Law—certainly no one working in and with the commercial courts. There, cases are decided on elementary principles of fairness, Shariat law and the whims of the judge. No one in the Government, the judiciary or the legal profession understands, for example, that the key to negotiability lies in the provision that a transferee of an instrument can receive better rights than his transferor. In illustration of this, the Ministry of Finance recently decided to take a foreign exchange dealer to court in a case of disputed payment. The dealer was involved solely because he cashed an endorsed cheque by which the payment was made. This also illustrates the point that more than just a change in the law is required.

viii. *Non-Bank Financial Institutions*

Little space need be devoted to Afghanistan's non-bank financial institutions since the size of their operations is insignificant. It is surprising, however, to find both insurance and cooperative activities so alien in a trading and agriculturally based economy. Gross insurance premiums totalling under Afs 150 million in 1351 (1972), as can be seen in Table 5.25, are small in comparison to a money stock of Afs 9,954 million and an estimated Gross National Product (GNP) of Afs 93,554

million for the same year. The ratio of insurance premiums to GNP of
under 0.2 per cent can be compared with ratios for 14 developed countries
shown in Table 5.26 below. Insurance business, like bank business,
is not solicited in Afghanistan.

In terms of investible funds, insurance supplies almost nothing. None
of the agencies makes any investments in Afghanistan and the Afghan
Insurance Company holds most of its funds abroad. It has, however, an
equity interest of about Afs 1 million in the CAM (Coca Cola) Company
of Afghanistan and a nominal holding in the Inter-Continental Hotel.
The main problem of investing in Afghanistan is again the lack of security.
For example, the Afghan Insurance Company had a major task in
persuading the CAM Company to take out fire insurance on its plant.

Table 5.25

Gross Insurance Premiums 1343-1351

(Millions of Afghanis)

Institution	1343	1344	1345	1346	1347	1348	1349	1350	1351
Afghan Insurance Company	13	24	19	25	34	50	69	107	86
Commercial Union	—	—	—	5	5	8	9	10	10
Sterling General	—	—	6	7	8	7	8	10	12
Ingosstrakh	n.a.	n.a.	n.a.	n.a.	n.a.	n.a.	n.a.	n.a.	n.a.

Source: Information provided by each insurance institution.

Table 5.26

Insurance Premiums as a Percentage of Gross
National Product in 14 Developed Countries, 1971

(Percentages)

United States	7.1
Australia	5.5
New Zealand	5.4
Britain	5.0
Holland	5.0
Switzerland	4.9
Canada	4.8
S. Africa	4.6
Germany	4.5
Japan	4.2
Ireland	4.2
Denmark	3.6
Sweden	3.4
France	3.3

Source: The Economist, "Cinderella of the City: Insurance 1973—A Survey,"
The Economist, 9 June 1973, p. 28.

The lack of interest in and understanding of insurance is almost pathological in Afghanistan. Property, whether owner occupied or rented out, is virtually all uninsured and few vehicle owners take out any cover. It is surprising to find entrepreneurs, sophisticated in many other aspects of business, totally uninformed when it comes to insurance. Marine insurance, which accounts for by far the largest proportion, is taken out grudgingly at the banks' insistence before export or import loans can be received. One reason for the lack of awareness concerning insurance stems again from lack of competition. As Trosper concludes:

> If there is adequate competition among the insurors in a particular com-
> munity or country, the insurance companies will hire and train salesmen
> who themselves will do the job of educating the potential insurance buyer.
> [T5, p. 65]

There are no insurance salesmen in Afghanistan.

The Pension Fund receives about 43 per cent of its annual income from payments made by civil servants in the form of 3 per cent of their salaries, the first month's salary increment after promotion and any deductions from salaries for absence, etc. The remaining 57 per cent comes in the form of an annual allocation by the Government. Given that investment policy is non-profit seeking, e.g. it has equity holdings in the Afghan Insurance Company, the Mortgage and Construction Bank, Pashtany Tejaraty Bank and other Government enterprises, it can hardly be considered an attractive savings outlet to civil servants, even with the 57 per cent direct Government contribution. The return of perhaps 6 per cent in the inflationary environment of the past two decades implies that the return to civil servants is low in real terms despite the Government's contribution.

The Baghlan and Kohdaman cooperatives are small pilot projects (covering just over 1,000 farmers at present) designed to be models, if successful, for Government agricultural cooperative projects at a later date. What success the experiment has had so far has been due to the fact that it takes the form of an "integrated operation supplying credit, technical assistance and marketing advice" [N8, p. iv]. Credit for a sizable part of the necessary investment has been supplied by the AgBank at an interest rate of 10 per cent.

Despite favourable results, the possible extension of an agricultural cooperative movement is probably rather a long way off. PACCA has encountered serious impediments in working both with the farmers and the Government. The introduction of cooperatives throughout Afghanistan will require not only a far greater commitment than previous Governments have shown in this field but also a build-up of well trained and highly motivated extension agents before any programme of this kind could be launched. Hopefully, this will be an area of particular concern to the new Republican Government, since intensive efforts throughout the country to reach the farmer with demonstration projects, technical assistance, marketing advice and credit, whether by means of cooperative development or not, are essential if agricultural productivity is to be increased. The importance of the latter, because it determines in part development potential, was stressed in Chapter III.

ix. *Conclusion*

The picture of Afghanistan's financial institutions presented above is not one which can be viewed with complacency. Three forces have combined to prevent the development of a sound, efficient financial sector, namely, the external environment, the Government and the bankers themselves. The external environment has been unfavourable to financial development because of the absence of commercial laws, business ethics, wealth, etc., and the existence of a strong religious antagonism to interest. The Government has created an unfavourable environment by its inflationary and highly variable demands on the financial sector in the form of public sector domestic borrowing requirements. The bankers have done little to develop an efficient banking system through training programmes, etc., but have sustained instead uncompetitive market conditions by means of an interlocking network of ownership and control.

Towards the end of 1351 (1973), a Financial Development Committee was established in the Ministry of Finance. It was given a wide brief to prepare and implement a programme of financial development and reform. The most urgent measures were pinpointed; they included banking legislation and revision of the commercial law, training middle and lower level bank employees, and laying the foundations for a strong, independent central bank. It was recognised that the latter required a substantial training programme as well as central banking legislation. None of these measures has been implemented; their importance remains.

Recently, the rate of interest received some attention by Da Afghanistan Bank and a proposal to raise deposit rates in order to attract more funds was brought before its Supreme Council. Hopes were raised that at long last some competition might be generated to awaken the dormant financial institutions. Two reports supporting the Bank's initiative appeared urging it to take additional measures in conjunction with the deposit rate increase [F31; S9]. Hopefully this initiative will be revived under the aegis of the new Republican Government along with other vital components of the Financial Development Programme. These are outlined in Chapter VIII.

It has been shown that the extent to which financial development has been occurring is the most important economic variable determining a country's development potential [A2]. Afghanistan's low development potential can, therefore, be attributed in part to its stagnant financial system. Hence, the absence of financial development has acted as a critical constraint to economic development. This chapter has explored some of the causes and effects of the lagging financial sector.

The more developed the financial system, the more efficiently can it perform the function of channelling savings into the most productive investment opportunities. Given that past Governments and foreign aid donors have been singularly unsuccessful in this latter task, as shown in the following chapter, it is all the more imperative that it now be undertaken by Afghanistan's financial system. The importance of financial development in the Afghan context cannot be exaggerated. The metamorphosis of the financial system from a lagging to a leading sector is a necessary condition for economic development. Without this, Afghanistan's development potential will remain low.

CHAPTER SIX

PUBLIC FINANCE

i. *Introduction*

On the accession of Nadir Shah in 1308 (1929), a contemporary report states:

> It was probably the first case of a national exchequer being absolutely bankrupt, unlined with even a silver coin .... It was literally the case of a monarch ruling at Kabul without possessing so much as even the price of a meal for himself. [A15, p. 167]

Forty-four years later, on the proclamation of the Republic and deposal of Zahir, Nadir's son and successor, bankruptcy, albeit figurative, was again declared [D2, p. 1; D3, p. 2]. It is with the developments in public finance between these two years that this chapter is concerned.

Although data are almost non-existent for the earlier years, perhaps because of an unclear distinction between accounts of king and country, a series of revenue and expenditure figures for the entire period have been estimated and are presented in Table 6.1. For analytical purposes, the figures shown in Table 6.2 are of greater interest. These are domestic revenue and expenditure at constant prices.

In the first few years of the period, a small surplus was realised which was "utilized to build up a currency reserve" [A11, p. 75; M33, p. 866]. Although a smooth increase has been assumed together with a balanced budget from 1315 (1936) to 1318 (1939), the Statesman's Yearbook for 1934 says:

> The revenue of Afghanistan is subject to considerable fluctuations. The Government share of the produce recoverable is said to vary from one-fifth to one-tenth, according to the advantages of irrigation. The total revenue is estimated at about one hundred and fifty million (Afghani) rupees, a considerable portion of which is found from customs. [S17, p. 654]

In 1318 (1939), Bank Millie returned most of the Government's original share capital in the Bank and at the same time provided an additional Afs 16 million loan for the establishment of the central bank, Da Afghanistan Bank. There is doubt as to whether this loan was ever intended to be repaid since it is included in the sum mentioned by the President of Bank Millie when he stated that "the Government therefore obtained 21.1

PUBLIC FINANCE

Table 6.1

Government Domestic Revenue and Expenditure 1311-1352
(Millions of Afghanis)

Date	Domestic Revenue	Expenditure	Overall Balance
1311	140	138	+2
1312	145	143	+2
1313	150	148	+2
1314	160	158	+2
1315	175	175	0
1316	190	190	0
1317	210	210	0
1318	247	247	0
1319	250	331	-81
1320	260	278	-18
1321	270	324	-54
1322	280	297	-17
1323	290	253	+37
1324	300	290	+10
1325	310	314	-4
1326	315	433	-118
1327	319	400	-81
1328	387	461	-74
1329	473	669	-196
1330	548	712	-164
1331	614	830	-216
1332	775	838	-63
1333	964	1,030	-66
1334	1,283	1,260	+23
1335	1,149	1,291	-142
1336 (first half)	836	740	+96
1336/37	1,348	1,381	-33
1337/38	1,533	1,672	-139
1338/39	1,601	2,099	-498
1339/40	2,099	3,108	-1,009
1340 (second half)	721	1,398	-677
1341	2,123	3,296	-1,173
1342	2,677	4,246	-1,569
1343	3,061	4,180	-1,119
1344	3,976	4,622	-646
1345	4,285	5,131	-846
1346	4,211	5,320	-1,109
1347	4,465	6,074	-1,609
1348	5,085	6,652	-1,567
1349	5,702	6,889	-1,187
1350	5,823	7,420	-1,597
1351	6,172	7,789	-1,617
1352 (B)	7,037	9,082	-2,045

Note: Public finance data prior to 1328 (1949) are almost non-existent. The States-man's Yearbook gives a rough estimate of revenue for 1313 (1934) and the United

Nations Educational, Scientific and Cultural Organisation provides another benchmark revenue figure for 1318 (1939). The only other data source for the pre-1327 (1948)
period is Da Afghanistan Bank Economic Bulletin which provides gross borrowing by
the Government for 1319-1326 (1940-1947). It appears that the Budget showed a
surplus in the early 1310s (1930s) so a small positive balance is recorded. Revenues have
been extrapolated between benchmark years and the overall balance for 1319-1326
(1940-1947) was assumed to equal gross Government borrowing from Da Afghanistan
Bank. Domestic revenue excludes Commodity Assistance. Expenditure excludes
foreign aid expenditure. Throughout this chapter, the 1350 and 1351 (1971 and 1972)
figures shown are from provisional accounts. The data for 1352 (1973) are the Budget
figures (B) approved by Parliament. Before 1336 (1957) and after 1340 (1961) fiscal
years have been the same as the Afghan *Shamsi* (solar) calendar years. In 1336 (1957)
the fiscal year was altered to Mizan-Sunbula (September-September), exactly mid-
year to coincide with the planning period. Thus, two half-year periods occurred in
1336 (1957) and 1340 (1961).

Source: 1313 *Statesman's Yearbook 1934*, p. 654.

1318 United Nations Educational, Scientific and Cultural Organisation, *Educational
Missions-IV, Report of the Mission to Afghanistan* (Paris: United Nations Educational,
Scientific and Cultural Organisation, 1952), p. 65.

1319-1326 Overall balance from *Da Afghanistan Bank Economic Bulletin*, (in Dari),
5 (1), August 1961, Table 8-A.

1327-1330 D. N. Wilber (Ed.), *Afghanistan* (New Haven: Human Relations Area
Files, 1956), Table 6, p. 177.

1331-1352 Same as Tables 6.5 and 6.13 below.

million afghanis net profit from the bank" [C9, pp. 412-13; 19]. For
purposes of constructing Table 6.1, it has been treated as revenue. Thus,
until 1319 (1940) a balanced or surplus Budget has been recorded.

The Budgetary position throughout the 1310s (1930s) accompanied by
the increase in the world price of silver after 1311 (1932) ensured that the
domestic price level did not rise appreciably. Debasement of the currency,
on the other hand, offset any tendency for prices to decline [B29, p. 433;
G22, p. 173].

Fiscal problems really began with the decision in 1317 (1938) to
suspend convertibility of currency notes into silver coins [F15, p. 436],
previously guaranteed by the 1314 (1935) Law on Banknotes in Afghanistan, and to borrow heavily from the newly established central bank which
started activities in 1319 (1940). Between its establishment and 1326
(1948), loans totalling Afs 218 million were authorised by the National
Assembly, predecessor of Parliament [F15, p. 437]. The inflationary
impact of this can be gauged roughly through comparison with the size
of the money stock. An estimate for 1318 (1939) of Afs 275 million is
given in Table 2.9. By 1326 (1947) it had more than tripled to reach
Afs 850 million.

The rapid inflation caused by deficit finance, a balance of payments
surplus and wartime scarcities, played havoc with the fiscal system.

Table 6.2

Government Domestic Revenue and Expenditure at Constant Prices 1311-1352
(Millions of Afghanis, 1340 Prices)

Date	Domestic Revenue	Expenditure	Overall Balance
1311	1,428	1,408	+20
1312	1,859	1,833	+26
1313	1,596	1,575	+21
1314	1,600	1,580	+20
1315	1,768	1,768	0
1316	1,810	1,810	0
1317	1,892	1,892	0
1318	2,129	2,129	0
1319	1,938	2,566	-628
1320	1,818	1,944	-126
1321	1,459	1,751	-292
1322	1,176	1,248	-72
1323	945	824	+121
1324	756	731	+25
1325	598	606	-8
1326	560	769	-209
1327	544	682	-138
1328	541	645	-104
1329	610	862	-252
1330	706	917	-211
1331	770	1,041	-271
1332	983	1,063	-80
1333	1,076	1,150	-74
1334	1,330	1,306	+24
1335	969	1,089	-120
1336 (first half)	681	603	+78
1336/37	1,098	1,125	-27
1337/38	1,218	1,328	-110
1338/39	1,491	1,954	-463
1339/40	2,228	3,299	-1,071
1340 (second half)	721	1,398	-677
1341	1,744	2,708	-964
1342	2,270	3,601	-1,331
1343	2,089	2,853	-764
1344	2,248	2,613	-365
1345	2,310	2,766	-456
1346	2,266	2,863	-597
1347	2,395	3,258	-863
1348	2,604	3,406	-802
1349	2,504	3,025	-521
1350	2,483	3,164	-681
1351	2,683	3,386	-703
1352 (B)	3,060	3,949	-889

Source: Figures in Table 6.1 have been deflated by the modified purchasing power parity price index in Table 2.7.

Revenue increased modestly between 1318 (1939) and 1327 (1948) from Afs 247 million to Afs 319 million as can be seen in Table 6.1. In real terms, however, Table 6.2 shows that revenue was reduced to just over one-quarter of its pre-war level, which was not in fact exceeded until 1339 (1960). Domestic revenue in 1351 (1972) was only 26 per cent higher in real terms than in 1318 (1939).

The wartime experience highlights the major deficiency of the revenue system, namely, specific rather than *ad valorem* tax rates on land, live-stock and *de facto* on most imports, together with excessive reliance on foreign trade taxation. In 1305 (1926) soon after Amanullah had sub-stituted cash payment for taxes in kind, land and livestock taxes contri-buted 62½ per cent or Afs 30 million to the total revenue of Afs 48 million [G22, p. 173]. In 1327 (1948) taxes on land and livestock totalling Afs 83 million represented 26 per cent [U17, p. 65]. By 1351 (1972) the contribu-tion had declined to 1 per cent of total domestic revenue. Despite the fact that land tax rates had been doubled in 1344 (1965), revenue from land and livestock taxes actually fell to Afs 78 million in 1351 (1972), partly as a result of the abolition of the livestock tax in 1345 (1966).

A law following the 1310 (1931) Constitution made it illegal for new taxes to be imposed or radical changes made without the consent of the *Loya Jirgah* (Great Council), which had to be convened at least once every three years [G15, p. 305]. Prior to 1343 (1964), the Budget was presented to the *Shura* (National Assembly). The 1343 (1964) Constitution also gave this power to the *Shura* (both houses of Parliament) [C18, Article 75]. Since the Great Council, National Assembly and Parliament were composed predominantly of landlords who were not permitted to form any political parties, it is not so surprising that by 1352 (1973) the agricultural sector was paying virtually no direct taxes.

The reason for the powerful position of the landowners lies in the fact that it was tribal support which brought Nadir Shah to power. To maintain this support for the critical years during which the army was rapidly being strengthened, various concessions were made. Six serious tribal revolts since 1309 (1930) attest to the potential threat posed by the tribes to a central authority in Kabul [W3, p. 103]. The fiscal concession was zealously guarded by Parliament until its disbandment by the Republican Government in 1352 (1973).

Modernising the army was a continuous objective of those in power during the Musahiban period [H11, p. 121; R6, pp. 160-86; S15, p. 11]. In pursuing it, a number of changes of a developmental nature, e.g. in the areas of communications, education and transport, occurred. With

Soviet help, military capability was strengthened under the Daoud administration [F18, p. 6; G12, p. 2] to a point where by 1344 (1965):

> With its long sought goal to modernize the military accomplished, the royal family faced the continuing imperative that it preserve and strengthen the loyalty and allegiance to the regime of an officers' corps which had been educated to operate a modern military organization and which, in the process, had also acquired modernizing perspectives and roles. In effect, those Afghan leaders who in the future would be able to secure the allegiance and control of the military establishment would be the individuals upon whom would devolve the power and authority to define the policies and goals of Afghanistan's modernization and to guide its destiny as a nation. [R6, p. 197]

The establishment of the Republic in 1352 (1973) lends credence to this analysis.

Budget expenditures were not divided between ordinary and development outlays until 1331 (1952). Since then, a somewhat arbitrary, though consistent, distinction has been made. However, the information on education, health and road construction presented in Chapter II indicates that development expenditure during the 1310s (1930s) was not insignificant. Since the First Plan, inaugurated in 1335 (1956), development expenditure has increased rapidly. Whether the vastly increased outlays of the 1340s (1960s) achieved much greater results than those of the 1310s (1930s) is debatable. What certainly differed were the methods of finance.

Balanced budgets were the norm in the 1310s (1930s) and few foreign loans were sought in the pre-war period. Afghanistan's first foreign debts were incurred during Amanullah's reign. He ordered a substantial quantity of military and other commodities on credit during his European tour in 1306 and 1307 (1927 and 1928). In 1311 (1932), the debt to Germany which had still been outstanding in 1308 (1929) was being repaid in eight annual instalments [A11, p. 116]. A few relatively small loans were obtained in the pre-war period from Britain, Czechoslovakia and Germany. By 1328 (1949), however, there only remained a small fraction of the British loan outstanding [F14, pp. 312-13]. In 1328 (1949), Afghanistan's position and prospects for future foreign aid looked good:

> In all these credit arrangements, as in the commodity barter agreements with other countries, including the Soviet Union, the Afghan Government displayed a strictly businesslike attitude and today offers a field for investment free from international mortgages and commitments. [F14, p. 313]

By 1350 (1971) Afghanistan felt it necessary to request some rescheduling of its foreign debt, despite the fact that a considerable part of the credit still available had not been used [U14, p. 94]. Another request was submitted in 1351 (1973). Without further agreements in this respect, the cost of debt servicing could reach SDR 45.3 million by 1355 (1976) or, at the 1351 (1972) rate of exchange, Afs 3,597 million, a figure approaching 50 per cent of total exports in 1351 (1972) and well over 50 per cent of total domestic revenue in that year.

ii. *The Fiscal System*

Tables 6.3 and 6.4 present the basic structure of the Government's budgetary position since 1331 (1952), four years prior to the First Plan. Domestic revenue and ordinary expenditure have increased steadily over the period, the latter at a slightly faster rate than the former. In real terms, there has also been an upward trend except during and immediately after the two periods of relatively high rates of inflation, 1333-1335 (1954-1956) and 1343-1344 (1964-1965). The much more dramatic effect of wartime inflation on real revenue and expenditure was discussed in the previous section.

The current account balance, which for 1332-1334 (1953-1955) represented 20 per cent of domestic revenue, has fluctuated considerably on an annual basis over this period. By 1349-1351 (1970-1972) it had actually declined in real terms and represented only $7\frac{1}{2}$ per cent of domestic revenue. One aspect of the fiscal system, apart from the need to obtain legislative approval for the Budget, which has bedevilled the Government, is the greater price elasticity of ordinary expenditure than of domestic revenue. This feature of the system has produced self-perpetuating inflationary pressure requiring constant vigilance to stop it getting out of hand. Section v below considers this problem in more detail in relation to deficit finance.

A substantial increase in development expenditure, in both real and nominal terms, took place between 1331 (1952) and 1344 (1965), a result of rapidly expanding domestic expenditure and foreign aid inflows. Given the failure of the current account balance to increase in real terms, domestic development expenditure had to be financed to an increasing extent from Commodity Assistance and even more so from domestic borrowing. Since most project assistance has been received only after the local currency component has been allocated, it is not surprising to find project assistance increasing in parallel with domestic development expenditure until 1344 (1965). In real terms, the latter reached a peak in 1342 (1963). Two years later, project assistance peaked and by 1349 (1970) was only one-third its 1344 (1965) level. In real terms, domestic development expenditure was by 1349 (1970) less than half its 1342 (1963) level. During the 1350s (1970s) some recovery has been achieved.

Between 1336/37 (1957) and 1351 (1972) project assistance contributed over 70 per cent of total development expenditure at constant prices and one-third of domestic development expenditure was financed through Commodity Assistance. Despite the substantial foreign aid input which in total contributed over 80 per cent of the development budget, raising funds for the remainder of the local currency component of the development budget has been a continual problem. The fiscal system has not been modified by anything like the extent necessary to allow sufficient current account surpluses to be achieved. In the short run, the problem was solved by recourse to excessive domestic borrowing from Da Afghanistan Bank. Efforts to curb the ensuing inflationary impact resulted in cut backs in planned development expenditure. This pattern is well exemplified by events during the 1340s (1960s).

Table 6.3

Budgetary Position 1331-1352

(Millions of Afghanis)

Item	1331	1332	1333	1334	1335	1336 (first half)	1336/ 37	1337/ 38	1338/ 39	1339 4•
Domestic Revenue	614	775	964	1,283	1,149	836	1,348	1,533	1,601	2,09
Ordinary Expenditure	660	666	825	933	910	526	1,007	1,251	1,394	1,55
Current Expenditure	660	666	825	933	910	526	867	1,077	1,215	1,37
Foreign Debt Service	0	0	0	0	0	0	140	174	179	18
Current Account Balance	−46	109	139	350	239	310	341	282	207	54
Development Expenditure	170	172	205	327	381	214	1,620	1,977	2,783	4,24
In Local Currency	170	172	205	327	381	214	374	421	705	1,55
Project Assistance	0	0	0	0	0	0	1,246	1,556	2,078	2,69•
Overall Balance	−216	−63	−66	23	−142	96	−1,279	−1,695	−2,576	−3,70
Commodity Assistance							128	149	113	20
	153	60	60	112	98	219				
Project Assistance							1,246	1,556	2,078	2,69
Loans							925	1,071	1,034	1,10
Grants							321	485	1,044	1,58
Net Domestic Borrowing (Residual)	63	3	6	−135	44	−315	−95	−10	385	8C

Note: Project assistance excludes most technical assistance. In 1351 (1972), there were about 2,300 foreign experts working on 300 projects in Afghanistan. The residual item, Net Domestic Borrowing, as explained in Chapter V, differs substantially

Declining foreign aid since 1344 (1965) can in small part be attributed to the inability of the Government to meet local currency financing requirements of projects for which the foreign exchange component had already been provided. The reduction in foreign aid since 1344 (1965) can also be attributed to donors' disillusionment with Afghanistan's overall development achievements, the inability of the Government to mobilise domestic resources through either the Budget or the financial sector, the increasing debt/equity ratio of the Government, the end of the Cold War aid race, and the completion of some major infrastructure projects. By far the most important factor, however, has been the failure on the Government's part to prepare projects.

The summary budgetary position shown in Tables 6.3 and 6.4 indicates a rapid increase in the negative overall balance. A more useful way of analysing this is to reduce it by the grant component of foreign aid. Until the late 1340s (1960s), most Commodity Assistance was obtained in

Table 6.3

Budgetary Position 1331-1352
(Millions of Afghanis)

1340 (second half)	1341	1342	1343	1344	1345	1346	1347	1348	1349	1350	1351	1352 (B)
721	2,123	2,677	3,061	3,976	4,285	4,211	4,465	5,085	5,702	5,823	6,172	7,037
878	1,850	2,416	2,558	2,902	3,403	3,613	4,254	4,732	5,158	5,504	5,689	6,538
745	1,592	1,873	2,179	2,646	2,929	2,948	3,653	3,865	4,144	4,364	4,634	5,067
133	258	543	379	256	474	665	601	867	1,014	1,140	1,055	1,471
−157	273	261	503	1,074	882	598	211	353	544	319	483	499
2,343	4,590	4,663	4,790	5,205	5,101	4,496	4,079	3,910	2,972	3,460	4,609	4,780
520	1,446	1,830	1,622	1,720	1,728	1,707	1,820	1,920	1,731	1,916	2,100	2,544
1,823	3,144	2,833	3,168	3,485	3,373	2,789	2,259	1,990	1,241	1,544	2,509	2,236
2,500	−4,317	−4,402	−4,287	−4,131	−4,219	−3,898	−3,868	−3,557	−2,428	−3,141	−4,126	−4,281
104	112	615	411	734	889	517	1,018	479	627	929	1,250	1,245
1,823	3,144	2,833	3,168	3,485	3,373	2,789	2,259	1,990	1,241	1,544	2,509	2,236
593	1,556	1,150	1,859	2,539	2,918	2,477	1,854	1,552	924	1,339	1,842	n.a.
1,230	1,588	1,683	1,309	946	455	312	405	438	317	205	667	n.a.
573	1,061	954	708	−88	−43	592	591	1,088	560	668	367	800

from figures provided in the monetary surveys. Also, see Notes to Tables 6.5 and 6.13.

Source: Same as Tables 6.5 and 6.13.

Table 6.4

Budgetary Position at Constant Prices 1331-1352

(Millions of Afghanis, 1340 Prices)

Item	1331	1332	1333	1334	1335	1336 (first half)	1336/ 37	1337/ 38	1338/ 39	1339 4
Domestic Revenue	770	983	1,076	1,330	969	681	1,098	1,218	1,491	2,22
Ordinary Expenditure	828	845	921	967	768	429	820	994	1,298	1,65
Current Expenditure	828	845	921	967	768	429	706	856	1,131	1,46
Foreign Debt Service	0	0	0	0	0	0	114	138	167	19
Current Account Balance	−58	138	155	363	201	252	278	224	193	57
Development Expenditure	213	218	229	339	321	174	1,567	1,888	2,728	4,33
In Local Currency	213	218	229	339	321	174	305	334	656	1,64
Project Assistance	0	0	0	0	0	0	1,262	1,554	2,072	2,68
Overall Balance	−271	−80	−74	24	−120	78	−1,289	−1,664	−2,535	−3,75
Commodity Assistance							104	118	105	21
	192	76	67	116	83	178				
Project Assistance							1,262	1,554	2,072	2,68
Loans							937	1,070	1,031	1,10
Grants							325	484	1,041	1,58
Net Domestic Borrowing (Residual)	79	4	7	−140	37	−256	−77	−8	358	85

Note: Project assistance figures have been deflated by the United States wholesale price index in Table 2.6. All other figures have been deflated by the modified purchasing power parity price index in Table 2.7.

grant form. Thus, adjusting the overall balance to show only that part for which debts were incurred shows a rapidly accelerating negative balance towards the end of the period. This, in turn, is a reflection of the considerable reduction in the grant component of project assistance since 1342 (1963). Given that Commodity Assistance has also been offered on a loan rather than a grant basis in recent years, the acceleration in the accumulation of debt has been somewhat understated. The request by Afghanistan for debt rescheduling negotiations in 1350 (1971) could not, therefore, have come as much of a surprise.

The Government's external debt is taken up again in Section vi, where a brief review of project assistance is presented. Here, it is simply the intention to indicate the magnitude and source of what has now come to be regarded as a problem. The existence of a problem essentially lies in the fact that returns from projects for which debt has been incurred have been unsatisfactory. In anticipation of this, finance for a number of

Table 6.4

Budgetary Position at Constant Prices 1331-1352

(Millions of Afghanis, 1340 Prices)

1340 (second half)	1341	1342	1343	1344	1345	1346	1347	1348	1349	1350	1351	1352 (B)
721	1,744	2,270	2,089	2,248	2,310	2,266	2,395	2,604	2,504	2,483	2,683	3,060
878	1,520	2,049	1,746	1,641	1,834	1,944	2,282	2,423	2,265	2,347	2,473	2,843
745	1,308	1,589	1,487	1,496	1,579	1,586	1,960	1,979	1,820	1,861	2,015	2,203
133	212	460	259	145	255	358	322	444	445	486	458	640
−157	224	221	343	607	476	322	113	181	239	136	210	217
2,343	4,323	4,385	4,269	4,382	4,126	3,555	3,060	2,749	1,823	2,097	2,904	2,881
520	1,188	1,552	1,107	972	932	919	976	983	760	817	913	1,106
1,823	3,135	2,833	3,162	3,410	3,194	2,636	2,084	1,766	1,063	1,280	1,991	1,775
2,500	−4,099	−4,164	−3,926	−3,775	−3,650	−3,233	−2,947	−2,568	−1,584	−1,961	−2,694	−2,664
104	92	522	281	415	479	278	546	245	275	396	543	541
1,823	3,135	2,833	3,162	3,410	3,194	2,636	2,084	1,766	1,063	1,280	1,991	1,775
593	1,552	1,150	1,855	2,484	2,763	2,341	1,710	1,377	791	1,110	1,462	n.a.
1,230	1,583	1,683	1,307	926	431	295	374	389	272	170	529	n.a.
573	872	809	483	−50	−23	319	317	557	246	285	160	348

Source: Figures in Table 6.3 have been deflated by the price indices referred to in the Note above.

projects should have only been accepted on a grant basis. Social rates of return appear to have been low on many aid financed projects and yield in the form of increased Government revenue nil. The latter state of affairs has been a result of the firm refusal of the landowning members of Parliament to pay direct taxes and the failure of the Government to collect revenues from the users of one of the largest and most profitable projects from the users' standpoint, namely, road building and improvement. In the 1330s (1950s) and early 1340s (1960s), a deliberate policy was pursued to make transport as cheap as possible so that economic and social integration would proceed rapidly. In the second half of the 1340s (1960s), when attempts were made to raise revenue from road users, the vehicle licence proposal was rejected by Parliament. Furthermore, the road toll system has not yielded even the modest revenue anticipated because a simple baksheesh system has been substituted for the revenue raising toll ticket by road users and toll collectors to their mutual benefit.

Finally, there has been a reluctance to raise petrol prices to tax road users, partly because until 1351 (1973) the Government believed that this needed Parliamentary approval and did not want to annoy Parliament by submitting such a proposal, and partly because all price increases have been anathema.

The bureaucracy and the Government appear to have had a strong preference for price stability, the former because it has always been penalised during periods of inflation in that salaries have not been adjusted commensurately, the latter because its revenue has been inelastic with respect to the price level. Parliament, in fact, has used inflation to reduce real tax burdens, although it has generally been opposed to inflationary deficit finance.

This overview of the budgetary position ends with a brief comment on the residual item, net domestic borrowing. Apart from the one bond issue in 1331 (1952) which raised Afs 6 million [F16, pp. 41-42], all domestic borrowing has been directly from Da Afghanistan Bank. Excessive recourse to central bank credit has been discussed in some detail in the previous chapter. There, consideration was particularly given to the effects of the extreme volatility of public sector domestic borrowing requirements and the credit squeeze imposed on the private sector. The factors which caused these fluctuations are discussed in Section v below. Here, the macroeconomic impact of fiscal policy is considered.

Although the estimates of Gross National Product (GNP) are unreliable and may be misleading for long run comparisons, some attempt at analysing the effects of the fiscal situation on the general level of economic activity is warranted if only because of the variability in public sector net domestic borrowing which can be assumed to have had a destabilising influence. It must, however, be emphasised at the start that Government activities in relation to GNP are small. Domestic revenue and total local currency expenditure represented 3.2 and 3.6 per cent of GNP in 1331 (1952) and 6.6 and 8.3 per cent in 1351 (1972), respectively. Public sector savings represented only —0.2 and 0.5 per cent of GNP in 1331 (1952) and 1351 (1972), respectively, and the residual, net domestic borrowing, for the same years equalled 0.3 and 0.4 per cent. Nevertheless, because public sector net domestic borrowing requirements in many years have been of significant magnitudes in comparison to the money stock, this in itself has had important impact on the latter's rate of change and hence on prices and the general level of economic activity.

Comparing changes in the Government's net domestic borrowing position with broad movements in GNP shown in Tables 2.14 and 2.15, it can be seen that the period of negative net domestic borrowing in the mid-1330s (1950s) is associated with a stable level of GNP at current prices. In real terms, however, growth was fairly rapid. The large increase in domestic borrowing at the beginning of the 1340s (1960s), although accompanied by a rapid increase in GNP at current prices, has been widely blamed for the poor growth in real terms between 1339 (1960) and 1344 (1965), despite the fact that these were the years of largest foreign aid input. Fiscal stringency in the mid-1340s (1960s), however, has also been held responsible for the recession between 1346 (1967) and 1349 (1970). Most analyses of these years have regarded the stabilisation programme or at least its outcome as an over-reaction to earlier fiscal irresponsibility. Indeed, by the time the first drafts of the Fourth Plan were being prepared in 1351 (1972), a target of no deficit finance was being planned for the second year onwards as if any positive level were undesirable. Foreign advisors urged that positive levels should be planned for each year but should be held within a non-inflationary limit. However, by 1352 (1973) the net domestic borrowing requirements had again reached high levels, although GNP in real terms was expanding so fast that prices actually fell.

Excess deficit finance in the early 1340s (1960s) and excessive fiscal stringency in the mid-1340s (1960s) have both been held responsible for periods of recession. Evidence from international comparisons does support the view that both too little and too much inflation retards economic growth. Periods of rapidly accelerating deficit finance followed by sharp over-reactions which have forced sizable reductions in planned development expenditure appear to have been damaging not only for this reason but also because erratic Government behaviour has increased uncertainty in the economic environment and added considerable variability to the development effort.

Because public sector net domestic borrowing requirements have been met only by central bank lending largely in the form of an increase in the money stock and because velocity is high in Afghanistan, relatively small fluctuations in these requirements in comparison to GNP have had important impact on the rate of inflation and hence the general level of economic activity.

There is also another macroeconomic effect of changes in the budgetary position which might be anticipated. This is the effect of rapidly increasing development expenditure on the rate of economic growth. This expectation is, however, not fulfilled. Over the four five year periods since 1331 (1952), the average annual real rates of growth were 2.6, 3.3, 3.6 and 0.9

per cent, respectively, despite investment as percentages of GNP over
the same periods of 3.7, 11.3, 16.0 and 10.8 per cent, as shown in Table
4.6. The summary conclusion which seems to emerge is that the investment has not been as productive as might have been hoped. This is taken
up again in some detail in Sections vi and vii below.

This section ends with a brief discussion of the administrative shortcomings of the fiscal system. Its economic defects from the macroeconomic viewpoint have been covered above and in Chapter IV. From a
microeconomic standpoint, they will be dealt with in subsequent sections
of this chapter. Since administrative shortcomings can be held responsible
for the erratic fiscal impact of the past and must in large part determine
the feasible set of alternative recommendations for fiscal reform, it is
doubly appropriate to touch upon some of the problems in this area at
this point.

Despite considerable technical assistance from the Public Administration Service since 1336 (1957) and the Robert Nathan Team between 1340
(1961) and 1351 (1972), both financed by the United States Agency for
International Development, fiscal administration and policy in Afghanistan is still weak. There have been some improvements, e.g. more accurate
and speedier accounting, and improved budgeting procedures. Tax
collection procedures are now being standardised and a training programme for provincial revenue collectors has been initiated. However,
by 1352 (1973) the results had been limited. Standardisation, a prerequisite
for an equitable system, had not been achieved:

> With the exception of taxes paid by aliens and foreign firms operating in
> Afghanistan, the entire non-customs revenue area is decentralized to the
> provincial level. Each of the 28 provinces has its own out-dated system
> for the enforcement and collection of revenues. The system is based on past
> practices and custom without regard to present day needs and existing
> legislation. Knowledge of the provisions of law is practically non-existent.
> This applies equally to land, income or business taxes. [U18, pp. 6-7]

> A lack of proper knowledge about the tax laws and decrees on the part
> of officials often causes decisions, taken at random, involving tax-liability.
> This arbitrary manner of fixing tax-liability results in special harassment
> of less well-off tax-payers . . . . A part of the landlords living in Kabul
> successfully refused to pay taxes. This problem must be solved in a manner
> that all tax-payers are forced to pay their tax-liabilities irrespective of
> their social position. [I1, pp. 16-17]

> Revenue-maximization and the principle of equity, the two common charac-
> teristics of any modern income tax are not realizable in the Afghan situation
> because of a lack of necessary technical preconditions involving both the

tax assessees and tax-bureaucracy. In addition, there persists a low level of tax morality on the part of tax-payers, who are unwilling to disclose details of their revenue. [I1, p. 2]

Revenue from non-tariff taxes has failed to rise substantially, the number of assessments is low and delinquency rates are high; in 1352 (1973) it was estimated that Afs $1\frac{1}{2}$ billion tax liabilities were outstanding [I1, p. 17].

An example of the low level of administrative capability is the experience under the new income tax law enacted in 1344 (1965). Despite much assistance over the preceding five years from the two advisory teams in drafting this law, revenue collected under it dismally failed to reach anticipated levels. By 1347 (1968) income tax collected was exactly half the amount collected prior to enactment of the new law. Apparently, administrative capacity was well below that required to enforce the new and more complex law. Recently, this constraint has been given more explicit recognition and the simplest tax systems recommended. It has also received more attention in the general literature on public finance in underdeveloped countries. Thus, for example, Hart has urged that

.... the most important criterion of good tax policy in the next few years is whether a proposed tax measure helps towards the goals of mutual respect [—where the taxpayer and the tax official will deal with each other on a footing of respect for each other and of respect for facts—] and of objective tax information. [H5, p. 872]

So severe is the constraint imposed upon fiscal policy by administrative capability in most underdeveloped countries that objectives have to be modest:

The traditional tactical goals of fiscal policy—continuity of employment, tax equity, internal price stability, and a workable foreign-exchange situation—are on a modest scale good things in themselves; yet except as they are instrumental toward development, they might well be viewed as luxuries. [H5, p. 871]

With respect to the objective of equity, standardisation and uniform enforcement of assessment and appeal procedures would contribute far more than any changes in the tax structure in Afghanistan.

Mention has already been made of the substitution of baksheesh for taxes in connection with road toll revenues. The same has applied to all other taxes; customs is an important case in point. When the author had occasion to visit the Kabul Customs House in 1351 (1972), baksheesh was required as standard payment for various essential documents and signatures for customs clearance. The system operated quite openly on a fixed price basis. Corruption apparently increased significantly during the

1340s (1960s). This can in part be explained by declining salaries in real terms received by civil servants. In 1352 (1973), only a small minority of Government employees were paid salaries above the subsistence level calculated in a recent cost-of-living study by the Agricultural Development Bank as a basis for its own salary structure. In this year, a report concludes:

> Wide fluctuations in incomes from different sources of revenue can be superficially seen wholly as an outflow of economic trends but are, in fact, partly related to a widespread corruption. It is doubtful whether all endeavours aimed at improvement of fiscal administration can really succeed if corruption is not curbed. [I1, p. 18]

Explicit recognition of this problem has been given by the Public Administration Service which has advised against higher tax rates. These would only create greater incentives for evasion and might actually lower revenue yields.

Corruption is not a problem unique to Afghanistan. It has apparently been increasing throughout South Asia in recent years and Myrdal suggests that " . . . . . corrupt practices are highly detrimental from the point of view of the value premises applied in the present study, namely, the modernization ideals" [M39, pp. 951-52]. In particular, corruption has had the effect of slowing down administrative procedures, thus contributing to inertia and inefficiency within these societies [M39, pp. 951-55]. Given the generally held view that corruption in Afghanistan increased substantially over the past decade, it is interesting to recall Myrdal's introductory comments on this subject:

> The significance of corruption in Asia is highlighted by the fact that wherever a political regime has crumbled—in Pakistan and Burma, for instance, and, outside South Asia, in China—a major and often decisive cause has been the prevalence of official misconduct among politicians and administrators, and the concomitant spread of unlawful practices among businessmen and the general public. The problem is therefore of vital concern to the governments in the region. Generally speaking, the habitual practice of bribery and dishonesty tends to pave the way for an authoritarian regime, whose disclosures of corrupt practices in the preceding government and whose punitive action against offenders provide a basis for its initial acceptance by the articulate strata of the population. The Communists maintain that corruption is bred by capitalism, and with considerable justification pride themselves on its eradication under a Communist regime. The elimination of corrupt practices has also been advanced as the main justification for military takeovers. Should the new regime be unsuccessful in its attempts to eradicate corruption, its failure will prepare the ground for a new putsch of some sort. [M39, pp. 937-38]

Much of this analysis is directly applicable to the coup in Afghanistan on 26 Saratan, 1352 (17 July, 1973), and the subsequent strategy of the Republican Government. In his first address to the nation, the President stated:

> .... the regime and system became so corrupt that no hope or expectation for its reform existed. Consequently all patriots, specially the patriotic armed forces of Afghanistan, decided to put an end to this rotten system and deliver the nation from their plight. [D2, p. 1]

Daily reports of uncovered corruption have since appeared.

Apart from the prevalence of corruption, incompetence and lack of motivation have also played their parts in reducing administrative capability and capacity. As with bank employees discussed in the previous chapter, so lower and middle level civil servants have received inadequate training to carry out even simple, routine work. This has been recognised and the Public Administration Service has channelled a considerable part of its efforts into establishing what it is hoped will become a self-sustaining training programme. Also of critical importance among senior level civil servants is the lack of trained auditors:

> .... the auditing of enterprises' accounts is carried out by officials who possess very little knowledge of accountancy. This phenomenon, which has bad effects on tax morality, arises mainly because of lack of training for the officials. [I1, p. 13]

A serious problem in this respect has been the capricious transfer of professionals between one type of job and another. Thus, under its present programme the Public Administration Service is to send five times the number of trainees required to the U.S.A. in the hope that one-fifth will be recovered to work in the field for which they will have specifically been trained. The remaining four-fifths may never be called upon to use their expertise acquired during expensive two year courses.

Lack of motivation has been caused in part by inadequate salaries and a promotion system unrelated to merit. The importance of this was stressed in 1331 (1952) by a United Nations expert in public finance who drafted a civil service law to provide for promotion on merit; he also recommended the establishment of training programmes [F16, p. 39]. The problem has not yet been tackled although the Public Administration Service has given attention to it and suggested various possible remedies [P18].

In 1335 (1956), 1344 (1965) and 1351-1352 (1972-1973) concerted efforts were made to improve collection and reduce the proportion of tax delinquency. A Finance Committee established within the Economic Planning Commission in 1334 (1955) proposed a major overhaul of the

tax system. In particular, suggestions were put forward for a more
progressive income tax, higher corporate taxes, a progressive retail tax
based on the rental value of the retail outlet, a progressive livestock tax to
replace the straight Afs 2 per animal, a progressive land tax and an
increase in tariff rates [W3, pp. 171-77]. The National Assembly was not
favourably disposed and combined with administrative constraints
ensured that no significant increase in revenue occurred. As can be seen
from Table 6.3, a considerable increase in domestic revenue was achieved
in 1344 (1965) and measures taken towards the end of 1351 (1973) held
high probability of achieving a substantial rise in revenue in 1352 (1973).
Thus, determination on the Government's part has at times been effective
in raising both taxes and collection rates. Whether a longer term effort
would have been effective in producing a distinct upward trend in non-
tariff tax revenue is questionable. The evidently low administrative
capability, as witnessed in the income tax debacle, and the increased
incentive to evasion which significantly higher effective tax rates would
have produced might have seriously limited the results of sustained efforts
in the directions so far tried.

Within the new milieu created by the establishment of the Republic and
the disbandment of Parliament, possibilities for the long run are broad-
ened. In particular, there may be a higher probability that agriculture
and transport sectors will be made to contribute directly to domestic
revenue. The major constraint to revised land taxes in the past has been
the absence of a cadastral survey. This again highlights administrative
shortcomings in that the survey was started in 1337 (1958) on the recommendation and with the help of the newly arrived Public Administration Service. By 1352 (1973), the survey had been completed for between
one-quarter and one-third of total agricultural land in the country but
no firm plans had been prepared for using the data obtained. The serious-
ness of the administrative constraint has been stressed yet again in a
recent report of the German Economic Advisory Group:

> The experience with the first three development plans clearly shows that
> the public administration was unable, and still is so, to induce the social,
> economic, and technical progress of the country. Especially during the last
> years an increasing decline in discipline can be noticed everywhere. The
> hope that the public administration would be able to accelerate the
> development of the country further declined. In our opinion, the low
> efficiency of the public administration is the most momentous obstacle
> of the country's development. If the efficiency of the public administration
> is not increased there will be no chance for a fundamental improvement
> in the country's performance. [G4, p. 1]

Kaldor's general assertion in this regard is totally applicable to the situation in Afghanistan:

> It cannot be emphasized too strongly that the efficacy of the tax system is not just a matter of appropriate tax laws but of the efficiency and integrity of tax administration .... Any additional outlay incurred in improving the status and pay of the officials of the revenue department is likely to yield a very high return in terms of increased revenue. [K3, p. 189]

iii. *Domestic Revenue*

A Sources

Government revenue is composed of domestic revenue, Commodity Assistance and project aid, the last two being provided on a variety of terms and conditions by foreign governments and international agencies. Their relative magnitudes have been compared in the previous section. Although project aid cannot be regarded as exogenously determined, it would be generally true to assume that its magnitude has been only indirectly subject to Government control. It has been essentially by improving domestic resource mobilisation and the overall effectiveness of the development effort, of which project preparation has been the most critical element, that any desire to increase project assistance could be realised. It is for this reason that discussion of project aid is limited to an analysis of its effectiveness in Sections vi and vii. However, because of its importance in the Government's budgetary position, Commodity Assistance as a source of revenue is discussed here.

A selective breakdown of Government revenue for the period 1331-1352 (1952-1973) is presented in Tables 6.5 and 6.6. As can be seen from these tables, by far the most important and rapidly expanding source of revenue has been foreign trade taxes. Table 6.7 shows that considerably more reliance has been placed on indirect taxes, particularly taxes on foreign trade, in Afghanistan than in other countries at a similar stage of development.

Taxes on Afghanistan's foreign trade sector have taken the form of export and import duties, the requirement on exporters of cotton, karakul and wool to surrender their foreign exchange earnings at fixed rates below the fluctuating free market rate, fixed taxes on exports and imports, and special monopoly taxes on imports of items such as cigarettes which were imported prior to 1348 (1969) by the Government Monopoly. Since then, a 10 per cent monopoly tax has been substituted for the monopoly privilege except for petrol products and sugar which are still imported solely by the Government. More analysis of the tariff structure and other aspects of foreign trade regulation is presented in the next

Table 6.5

Government Revenue 1331-1352

(Millions of Afghanis)

Item	1331	1332	1333	1334	1335	1336 (first half)	1336/ 37	1337/ 38	1338/ 39	1339/ 40
Direct Taxes	192	208	216	215	225	158	287	267	242	301
Income Tax	⎰ 81	99	98	98	153	109	192	161	⎱ 84	106
Corporate Tax	⎱								⎰ 51	82
Land Tax	77	77	77	77	31	2	35	43	40	40
Livestock Tax	34	32	41	40	41	48	60	63	67	73
Other	0	0	0	0	0	0	0	0	0	0
Indirect Taxes	288	339	513	469	608	314	789	874	766	1,121
Foreign Trade Taxes	244	302	461	417	534	296	777	851	732	991
Other	44	37	52	52	74	18	12	23	34	130
Income from State Sales	n.a.	n.a.	22	26	26	18	37	101	79	93
Natural Gas	0	0	0	0	0	0	0	0	0	0
Other	n.a.	n.a.	22	26	26	18	37	101	79	93
Other Income	74	149	117	362	262	341	173	290	198	337
Road User Taxes and Tolls	0	0	0	0	0	0	0	0	0	1
Other	74	149	117	362	262	341	173	290	198	336
Income from Government Enterprises	60	79	96	211	28	5	62	1	316	247
Less: Commodity Assistance included above	—	—	—	—	—	—	—	—	—	—
Total—Domestic Revenue	614	775	964	1,283	1,149	836	1,348	1,533	1,601	2,099

Note: Foreign Trade Taxes include Duties (210), Export Duties (220), Tax on Commercial Transactions (240), Fixed Taxes on Imports (260), Fixed Taxes on Exports (270) and Monopoly Taxes (250). The tax on commercial transactions is mainly profit on Da Afghanistan Bank's foreign exchange operations, i.e. from the difference between free and official exchange rates. Revenue from Government enterprises (610) is almost exclusively profit from the Government's petrol and sugar monopolies. As these are essentially revenue raising activities, this revenue should really be treated as indirect tax. The monopoly taxes consist predominantly of a special tax on cigarette and tea imports.

Source: 1331-1332 Tudor Engineering Company, *Report on Development of Helmand Valley* (Washington, D.C.: Tudor Engineering Company, 1956), Table 9, p. 153; and Ministry of Finance.

chapter. In broad terms, some of the economic disadvantages of heavy reliance on indirect taxation have been stressed by Hinrichs:

> Concentration on indirect taxation has led to a system of built-in incentives that tend to depress production, trade, exports and, thus, the general growth of the economy .... This practice retards the growth of production of those commodities which are more heavily taxed and rewards the holding of land for speculative increases in value. Hence, the incentive

Table 6.5

Government Revenue 1331-1352

(Millions of Afghanis)

1340 (second half)	1341	1342	1343	1344	1345	1346	1347	1348	1349	1350	1351	1352 (B)
81	313	376	448	575	603	556	372	411	464	428	574	648
38	114	157	238	324	390	318	162	208	234	216	230	300
6	77	79	81	81	123	145	120	118	138	138	165	200
34	39	50	44	82	89	93	90	83	88	70	78	88
3	83	90	85	88	1	0	0	0	0	0	0	0
0	0	0	0	0	0	0	0	2	4	4	101	60
317	1,131	1,712	1,917	2,176	2,645	2,495	2,083	2,549	2,806	2,974	2,942	3,262
282	1,059	1,622	1,719	2,084	2,565	2,432	2,032	2,424	2,689	2,860	2,821	3,042
35	72	90	198	92	80	63	51	125	117	114	121	220
45	114	151	198	245	279	214	651	721	989	886	1,051	1,192
0	0	0	0	0	0	60	429	453	714	589	726	847
45	114	151	198	245	279	154	222	268	275	297	325	345
115	236	300	320	382	380	333	351	408	493	562	675	625
1	2	2	0	0	0	31	33	36	54	59	63	80
114	234	298	320	382	380	302	318	372	439	503	612	545
163	390	570	347	768	378	613	1,008	996	950	973	930	1,310
—	61	432	169	170	—	—	—	—	—	—	—	—
721	2,123	2,677	3,061	3,976	4,285	4,211	4,465	5,085	5,702	5,823	6,172	7,037

1333-1336 (first half) Ministry of Planning, *Survey of Progress 1959* (Kabul: Ministry of Planning, 1959), Volume IV, Table 54, pp. 226-31; and Ministry of Finance.

1336/37-1340 (second half) Ministry of Planning, *Survey of Progress 1962-64* (Kabul: Ministry of Planning, 1964), Table A-1, p. 89.

1341-1343 Ministry of Planning, *Survey of Progress 1967-1968* (Kabul: Ministry of Planning, 1968), Tables S-1 and S-2; and Ministry of Finance.

1344-1347 Ministry of Planning, *Survey of Progress 1970-1971* (Kabul: Ministry of Planning, 1971), Tables S-1 and S-2; and Ministry of Finance.

1348-1349 Ministry of Planning, *Survey of Progress 1971-1972* (Kabul: Ministry of Planning, 1972), Tables S-1 and S-2; and Ministry of Finance.

1350-1352 Ministries of Finance and Planning.

structure is contrary to good economic development strategy. The results have followed logical expectations: widespread export smuggling (especially karakul and wool) and little or no growth in production of these commodities, while the value of land in favored locations has increased as much as tenfold in the past two decades. [H9, pp. 12-13]

Hansen has actually estimated the loss in output resulting from the discriminatory export taxes [U3, Table 19, p. 47].

Table 6.6

Government Revenue at Constant Prices 1331-1352

(Millions of Afghanis, 1340 Prices)

Item	1331	1332	1333	1334	1335	1336 (first half)	1336/ 37	1337/ 38	1338/ 39	1339/ 40
Direct Taxes	241	264	241	223	190	129	234	212	225	319
Income Tax	102	125	109	102	129	88	156	128	78	113
Corporate Tax									48	87
Land Tax	97	98	86	80	26	2	29	34	37	42
Livestock Tax	42	41	46	41	35	39	49	50	62	77
Other	0	0	0	0	0	0	0	0	0	0
Indirect Taxes	361	430	572	486	512	256	643	694	713	1,190
Foreign Trade Taxes	306	383	514	432	450	241	633	676	681	1,052
Other	55	47	58	54	62	15	10	18	32	138
Income from State Sales	n.a.	n.a.	25	27	22	15	30	80	74	99
Natural Gas	0	0	0	0	0	0	0	0	0	0
Other	n.a.	n.a.	25	27	22	15	30	80	74	99
Other Income	93	189	131	375	221	277	141	231	185	358
Road User Taxes and Tolls	0	0	0	0	0	0	0	0	0	1
Other	93	189	131	375	221	277	141	231	185	357
Income from Government Enterprises	75	100	107	219	24	4	50	1	294	262
Less: Commodity Assistance included above	—	—	—	—	—	—	—	—	—	—
Total—Domestic Revenue	770	983	1,076	1,330	969	681	1,098	1,218	1,491	2,225

Source: Figures in Table 6.5 have been deflated by the modified purchasing power parity price index in Table 2.7.

The more than proportionate increase in non-tax domestic revenue between 1333 (1954) and 1351 (1972) is partly illusory and partly a result of gas sales. The illusory feature is the classification of revenue from monopoly sales of petrol and sugar as non-tax revenue. There has been virtually no revenue forthcoming from the other Government enterprises despite substantial investment over the period. The investments have not yielded any significant return. The proceeds from natural gas sales which have increased sharply since 1346 (1967) are used exclusively for debt repayment to the U.S.S.R., the purchaser of the gas.

Finally, Commodity Assistance has become an increasingly important support to the Budget. Given that its magnitude depends on agricultural conditions in the recipient country, it has been an unstable and unpredictable revenue source. This in turn has been partly responsible for the high

Table 6.6

Government Revenue at Constant Prices 1331-1352

(Millions of Afghanis, 1340 Prices)

1340 (second half)	1341	1342	1343	1344	1345	1346	1347	1348	1349	1350	1351	1352 (B)
81	257	319	306	325	325	299	200	211	204	183	250	282
38	94	133	163	183	210	171	87	107	103	92	100	131
6	63	67	55	46	66	78	65	60	60	59	72	87
34	32	43	30	46	48	50	48	43	39	30	34	38
3	68	76	58	50	1	0	0	0	0	0	0	0
0	0	0	0	0	0	0	0	1	2	2	44	26
317	929	1,452	1,308	1,230	1,426	1,343	1,117	1,305	1,232	1,268	1,279	1,418
282	870	1,376	1,173	1,178	1,383	1,309	1,090	1,241	1,181	1,220	1,226	1,322
35	59	76	135	52	43	34	27	64	51	48	53	96
45	94	128	135	139	150	115	349	369	434	378	457	518
0	0	0	0	0	0	32	230	232	313	251	316	368
45	94	128	135	139	150	83	119	137	121	127	141	150
115	194	254	218	216	205	179	188	209	217	239	293	272
1	2	2	0	0	0	17	18	18	24	25	27	35
114	192	252	218	216	205	162	170	191	193	214	266	237
163	320	483	237	434	204	330	541	510	417	415	404	570
—	50	366	115	96	—	—	—	—	—	—	—	—
721	1,744	2,270	2,089	2,248	2,310	2,266	2,395	2,604	2,504	2,483	2,683	3,060

degree of volatility in net domestic borrowing requirements. Good harvests in Afghanistan have reduced Commodity Assistance and so thrown the Government into unexpected and usually excessive reliance on domestic borrowing. Bad harvests have generally been a boon to the Budget. This particular problem could be solved by raising tax revenue from the agricultural sector. Then, a good harvest year, while resulting in a reduction in Commodity Assistance revenue, would show an offsetting increase in agricultural taxes provided that demand was kept elastic through stock management activities. The latter could be carried out by the private sector were the 1346 (1967) Anti-Hoarding Law, unjustifiable anyway on economic grounds, repealed or through a Government wheat reserve programme. This, however, would absorb the additional revenue it was designed to raise.

Table 6.7

Tax Revenue Sources in 51 Underdeveloped Countries

Per Capita GNP (Dollars)	Number of Countries	Indirect Taxes as Percentage of Total Tax Revenue	Foreign Trade Taxes as Percentage of Total Tax Revenue
100 or less	20	68	41
101-200	11	64	39
201-500	19	64	35
Afghanistan (1351)	1	86	67

Source: R. I. McKinnon, *Money and Capital in Economic Development* (Washington, D.C.: The Brookings Institution, 1973), Table 10-3, p. 140; and Table 6.5 above.

Neither taxing the agricultural sector nor contriving demand elasticity for agricultural products are new ideas. The Nathan Team stressed the importance of land tax [L4, p. 16] and in its final report stated:

> Whatever the incidence and equities and complexities of a land tax, it must be a significant source of revenues in Afghanistan where agriculture is so overwhelmingly important a part of the total economy. The land tax seems the best means of tapping this sector for needed revenues. [N3, p. 109]

Hansen also makes the same recommendation [U3, pp. 49-50].

The issue of price stabilisation policies for agricultural products received renewed interest in 1352 (1973). The Government announced a support price of Afs 45 per seer for wheat at the beginning of the year and various reports on immediate and future problems and requirements of price support policies were prepared (e.g. [F30; K11]). The abandonment not only of the price but more important of any substantial Government purchases later in the year seriously exacerbated the problem of raising agricultural productivity, as mentioned above in Chapters II and III.

B   Elasticities

The concessions to the tribes which had rallied behind Nadir Shah in 1308 (1929) consisted in part of abrogation of power to increase taxes without their approval. Virtually no initiative since then has succeeded in persuading the legislature to raise land and livestock taxes. Neither the problem of declining tax revenue in real terms from the agricultural sector nor the power of the legislature to impede fiscal reform are unique to Afghanistan. On the former, Kaldor comments:

> An annual tax on land, expressed as a percentage of the value of the produce per acre, is the most ancient form of taxation both in Europe and

in Asia. Up to the beginning of this century the land tax still provided the principal source of revenue in the countries of the Middle East, in India and many other areas .... Since that time, however, political pressures, combined with monetary changes, have succeeded almost everywhere in 'eroding' the weight of this tax almost completely, and its rehabilitation now faces heavy political and administrative obstacles .... the low 'coefficient of utilization' of that [taxation] potential—due to bad tax laws, bad tax administration, or both—which in turn is only partly to be explained by lack of knowledge, understanding or of administrative competence—it is also the result of resistance by powerful pressure groups who block the way to effective tax reform. [K3, pp. 171 and 178]

He also points out that

.... it is the taxation of the agricultural sector that has a vital role to play in accelerating economic development; the disproportionate taxation of the 'monetized' or market sector tends to retard economic progress by reducing both the sources and the incentives to accumulation .... The importance for economic development of an efficient system of taxation of the agricultural or subsistence sector of the community cannot be over-estimated. [K3, pp. 176 and 180]

Nor has its important potential been ignored in Afghanistan.

On the second problem, namely that of powerful legislatures, Hart suggests the following solution:

.... the first step toward reform in cases where legislatures have real autonomy should be to develop an adequate professional staff (largely, but not exclusively, of economists) for the legislature .... [Without such a precondition] attempted substantive reforms will fail. [H5, pp. 874-75]

Indeed, one might suggest that the Nathan Team was preaching to the converted when

Throughout the contract period the team endeavored to create within the RGA [Royal Government of Afghanistan] an awareness of the need for and the capability of developing a domestic revenue base sufficient to support sustained and increasing economic development. [N3, p. 89]

Redirected efforts to convince the legislature of this were what was needed.

The demise of direct agricultural taxation together with administrative constraints, the rising ordinary expenditure, and yet a desire on the Government's part, particularly during the Daoud era of 1332-1341 (1953-1963), to sustain a development programme have combined to force the Government to resort to foreign trade taxes and deficit finance as interim measures. Excessive recourse to both these sources of revenue which have been necessitated by these circumstances have had unfortunate consequences in the longer run.

Taxes on the foreign trade sector have distorted resource allocation through discrimination against the major traditional exports, with the exception of carpets and fruit, in which comparative advantages have been greatest. As mentioned earlier, Hansen has calculated the actual effects of the discriminatory export taxes on the level of output [U3, Table 19, p. 47]. The specific price system employed in Afghanistan has made foreign trade taxes price inelastic. Thus, in order to raise revenue the tax rates have had to be revised. This has not only acted as a deterrent to exports, no matter whether taxes have been levied directly on exports or imports [L2; M6; M7], but with inefficient administration has increased smuggling. The allocative inefficiencies of the latter have recently received attention [B24; J3]. The additional distortions created by tax exemptions have also been reviewed:

> The existing provision regarding the 5-year exemption from customs has resulted in serious distortion of competitive conditions without achieving a rapid industrial growth .... Therefore, we recommend that the remission of customs under the private investment law should be put off. [I1, pp. 8-9]

The problems Afghanistan will face in the future from continued heavy reliance on foreign trade taxes as a source of revenue are the same as those to be faced by Ethiopia:

> Obviously as Ethiopia matures and capital becomes available for industrialization, these revenue tariffs of long standing become protective and can attract domestic resources into the manufacture of these same consumer "luxuries." (This was not a problem in the earlier, more pristine state.) The government then loses revenue as the volume of imports of final consumer goods is reduced when domestic manufacture begins. The tax system has become inelastic to the rising income that is associated with industrialization. [M7, p. 141]

In other words, although tariffs have been price inelastic in the past, occasional revaluations and rate changes together with an increasing volume of trade have enabled a substantial increase in revenue to take place. In the future, income elasticity may become negative and the tax base decline. Attempts simply to maintain revenue from this source might then create a vicious circle in which rate increases reduce the tax base and revenue declines.

Income and price inelasticities are of particular concern in a country where changes in rates have had to be approved by the non-party, car driving members of Parliament, most of whom derived their income from land ownership. Dupree proffers the following analysis:

The elections [of 1344 (1965)] produced one paradox which plagues the centre. Many regionally strong, conservative religious leaders, gradually losing power in Kabul since 1953, became parliamentary deputies. Now they have a *national* platform on which they can stand and attempt to stymie reform programmes which threaten their economic, political and social power. [D9, p. 275]

The unwillingness of the legislature to permit higher taxation might not, however, have been due solely to selfish motives. Had Government expenditure provided more tangible benefits to a larger fraction of the population, more cooperation might have been found in this quarter. But expenditure has not produced widespread benefits. The statement that "the peasantry ..... gained nothing by the enhanced revenues" made in 1312 (1933) [A15, pp. 10-11] still applied in 1352 (1973). Perhaps Gilbert's report reflects more accurately the legislature's position in the following extract:

What was needed 15 or 20 years ago, at the inception of the program, was a wide diffusion of the benefits of development, to lay the basis for widespread support of the development program and the willingness to make sacrifices, to pay taxes for it. What was required for the unification of the country was a sense of universal benefit from which no area and no ethnic group was excluded. Instead, the program and its benefits were highly concentrated. Even the road program, which was truly national in scope, had less than national visibility in the absence of feeder roads. On the other hand, the costs of the program, the pains of development were widely diffused. The inflation of food prices may be cited as an example. And the rapid decline of aid in recent years with the decrease in construction and in employment flowing from it must have had a negative effect.

On the internal side it must be remembered that the democratic process is a recent phenomenon. It was only in 1342 that the King promulgated the Constitution which limited his powers and set the stage for a substantial enlargement of democratic development. The members of the Jirga represent what are still tribal and local influences. There are as yet no political parties with national outlook and responsible programs. The result, unfortunately, has been a near paralysis in the government. The members of the Jirga, seeing for the most part little benefit from development for the people they represent, and charging and seeing corruption and waste in government operations, have resisted and obstructed measures of self help. The government has not had the means to provide the kind of program with widely spread benefits that could have appealed to the Jirga. [G10, p. 10]

The Nathan Team's final report says roughly the same thing:

.... most Afghans can rightfully say that they are paying for the exclusive benefit of a privileged minority in privileged areas of the country. [N3, p. 56]

Whether or not such altruistic motives can be attributed to Parliament, inelasticity of revenue sources to rising income and prices has been the most acute budgetary problem over the past two decades. Effort has been required just to prevent slippage, let alone move forward. Price inelasticity has been the result not only of the specific value system but also of lags in tax collection [H5, pp. 867-69]. Because rates have been raised too little and too late, excessive deficit finance has been used which has simply exacerbated the problem in subsequent years. Necessary effort to avoid the vicious circle has been forthcoming. No energy has been left, however, to make the effort needed to move out of the low level trap. Compared to many underdeveloped countries, inflation in Afghanistan has not been high during the post-war period. Yet, because the fiscal system has been so adversely affected by any rise in prices it has been a constant threat to the development effort.

The failure of domestic revenue to rise appreciably in real terms has been attributed by a number of observers to economic stagnation. It has already been argued in Chapters II and III that this conclusion, reached by circular reasoning from analysis of the Government's budgetary position, is erroneous. Here, it has been suggested that the Government's domestic revenue sources have been income and price inelastic and for this reason have failed to increase substantially. Furthermore, over the past decade, the tax collection effort seems to have deteriorated. This has been particularly noticeable with respect to direct tax receipts.

C   Incidence

The two most obvious gaps in the tax structure appear, at first sight, to lie in the exemption of the agricultural and transport sectors from direct taxation. It has been taxes on these two sectors which have been most strongly resisted by the legislature. Indeed, this is well exemplified by the Parliamentary debate on the 1352 (1973) Budget. Finally approved on 25 Saratan 1352 (16 July 1973), it was returned to the Government with the following amendments: Afs 112 million off the proposed land tax, Afs 100 million off the livestock tax, and Afs 10 million off the vehicle registration tax. These cuts reduced the agricultural taxes to their 1351 (1972) levels, namely, Afs 88 million and nil, and halved the proposed vehicle licence tax. Given that agriculture and transport have received well over 50 per cent of the local currency development expenditure and a considerably higher proportion of foreign aid disbursements, the question of equity is clearly raised.

The two sectors must be treated separately in this regard because tax incidence and benefits differ. In the case of the agricultural sector, although true that no direct tax burden is borne, to the extent that exports are primarily agricultural products, foreign trade taxes are passed back to the agricultural sector to some extent. This has been particularly apparent in the case of cotton, karakul and wool, the production of which has been directly deterred by the export taxes. However, in that foreign trade taxes have counteracted the depreciation of the exchange rate to some extent, fruit and nut producers have also been affected. One of the anomalies springing from an incidence-benefit analysis is that the recipients of Government expenditure, primarily in the Helmand-Arghandab Valley Region, have not in the main been producing exportable commodities. The concentration of effort by the Helmand-Arghandab Valley Authority has been on wheat production. However, on the benefit side results have been meagre even in this area as will be shown in Sections vi and vii.

Transport presents a different picture in that benefits arising from the sharp decline in transport costs have been high and tax incidence, even indirectly, negligible. The changes produced by the extensive road building programme of the past four decades were discussed at some length in Chapter III. Sections vi and vii deal with the high direct user benefits. Here it suffices to point out that these benefits have been provided virtually free.

Despite unique factors determining the revenue structure in Afghanistan, it is far from atypical:

> By one device or another, including marketing boards, substantial revenues are collected from traditional exports. Excises on some items of luxury consumption and duties on imports of goods that compete with products of capital-intensive industry are other ranking revenue sources. Real property is taxed lightly, if at all; various tax concessions are arranged for the industrial enclave; and public enterprise supplies cheaply, or at a loss, various utilities that, like savings and foreign exchange, are rationed in some degree of compliance with a plan of industrialization. Total revenues tend to be inelastic to both inflation and growth in real national output. [S8, p. 13]

In Afghanistan, the industrial sector has been nurtured under the 1345 (1967) Foreign and Domestic Private Investment Law which has provided a five year tax holiday and tariff exemptions.

D Regressivity

Data do not exist for any firm statements on the regressivity or otherwise of the tax structure. Certain taxes are undoubtedly regressive—the

tax on shopkeepers which takes the form of a poll tax and the tax based
on the number of vehicles owned for transport companies are two obvious
examples. The applicability of the following comment made in 1333
(1954) still stands:

> When the nature of the tax system is considered, officials of the present
> government have agreed that the tax revenue system has not served to work
> towards an equilibrium in the distribution of income among the different
> classes of the people. Moreover, because of many haphazard policies
> enacted in the past, the tax system as of 1954 has led to an unbalanced
> growth of the economy in that it encouraged capital investments in one area
> and discouraged them in others. In particular, there has been too much
> dependence on indirect taxes instead of on direct ones. The changeover
> to more reliance on the income tax, so encouragingly initiated in 1943,
> failed to make much progress after 1952, despite a growth in national
> income. Finally, the tax administration was poor, so that even such
> relatively simple levies as customs tariffs failed to rise in proportion to
> the rise in prices and in the volume of production and trade. [W3, p. 171]

The narrowness of the tax base and the political constraints have
forced the Government to pursue only the one fundamental objective of
preventing erosion. Equity considerations have had to take a low priority
in the Government's objective function.

Afghanistan's fiscal system exhibits many characteristics common
amongst the underdeveloped countries. Inelasticity of revenue with
respect to both income and inflation is just one:

> Tax bases have ways of eroding relative to income and wealth: without
> increases in rates of tax, revenues can fall absolutely or relatively ....
> First, the values of products subject to indirect taxation decline relative
> to total output because sources of supply are depleted, because demand
> is income-inelastic or because substitutes appear. In one sense or another,
> components of the base are inferior goods. Second, monetary values
> assessed for the tax base are not adjusted to inflation so that the real value
> of the base diminishes when the price level rises .... Inflation yields real
> revenues from a part of the financial base—the money supply, for example
> —but it reduces real revenues from parts of the fiscal base. When the
> fiscal base is both income-inelastic and inflation-inelastic, the peak-
> employment fiscal surplus becomes smaller as rates of growth in real
> income and the price level are higher, especially if revenues from the
> inflation tax are counted in the surplus. Such a fiscal base automatically
> constrains capital accumulation and is automatically destabilizing in the
> short run. [S8, pp. 171-72]

In reforming fiscal systems in underdeveloped countries, the traditional
preference for direct over indirect taxation has been dropped. Part of
the reason lies in the questionable usefulness of the distinction [P16],

part in the high administrative costs of collecting and difficulties of enforcing direct taxation. Strong arguments have recently been presented in favour of the value added tax [H5, p. 884; M7, Chapter 10; S8, pp. 179-80]. Despite its relative simplicity, administrative capabilities will have to be vastly improved before Afghanistan could administer such a tax successfully.

iv. *Fiscal Effort*

A rapidly growing body of literature has been produced recently presenting the view that there is something called a country's fiscal or tax effort and that this can be measured. That more fiscal effort is better than less springs from the premise stated forcefully by Kaldor that:

> .... the importance of public revenue from the point of view of accelerated economic development could hardly be exaggerated .... taxation provides the most appropriate instrument for increasing savings for capital formation. [K3, pp. 170-71]

On this assumption, two bases for measuring fiscal effort suggest themselves. The first and more usual approach is to examine the ratio of a country's tax revenue to GNP. The other is to analyse public sector savings, again as a ratio to GNP. An important qualification to Kaldor's statement is essential in the Afghan context. *Per se*, strong fiscal effort is irrelevant. It is important only to the extent that this would signify a real interest in development on the part of the Government and a far better performance on the expenditure side of the coin.

A few years ago, the International Monetary Fund initiated studies on the tax effort of underdeveloped countries; several articles reporting various results have now appeared. The two concerned with measuring tax effort make comparisons between 49 countries [B1; B2]. The method used in the first article is to measure taxable capacity and then to compare this with achievements. In the empirical work taxable capacity is determined by the stage of development, the composition of National Income and the size of the foreign trade sector. The indicators used are Ay, the percentage of agricultural income in GNP, and Ny, the percentage share of the mining sector in GNP. Elaborate justification for using these two variables is provided. The results of the regression analysis are as follows. For the 49 countries, taxable capacity is measured by the equation

$$\hat{T}y = 14.95 - 0.0742(Ay) + 0.2951(Ny) \qquad (6.1)$$

$$(9.682) \quad (2.074) \qquad (3.678)$$

where $\hat{T}y$ is taxable capacity as a percentage of GNP. Figures in brackets are "t" values. The adjusted coefficient of determination, $\overline{R}^2$, is 0.411 [B1, p. 592], giving a higher explained variance than previous studies of this kind.

Tax effort, E, is measured by the ratio of actual to capacity tax revenues as percentages of GNP:

$$E = \frac{Ty}{\hat{T}y} \qquad (6.2)$$

From Equations 6.1 and 6.2, the results shown in Table 6.8 were obtained. Afghanistan was not amongst the 49 countries included in this study. However, using Equation 6.1 and GNP data estimated by a team of economists from the World Bank, tax capacity and achievement can be measured. With an estimated GNP for 1346 (1967) of Afs 62, 268 million, gross agricultural and mining sector income of Afs 30,214 million and Afs 284 million, respectively, and tax revenue of Afs 3,082 million, the taxable capacity, $\hat{T}y$, is 11.31 per cent of GNP and tax actually collected 4.95 per cent. This gives a tax effort, E, of 0.44 which would place Afghanistan last in the ranking given in Table 6.8 were it not for an even lower effort of 0.32 recorded for Nepal.

The result implies that, given Afghanistan's low stage of economic development, unconducive composition of income from a taxability viewpoint and relatively small foreign trade sector, less than half the taxes which could be collected through an exertion of only average effort were in fact collected in 1346 (1967). Some of the reasons for such a low score have been discussed in the previous section.

Table 6.8

Taxable Capacity and Tax Effort in 50 Underdeveloped Countries

Country	Taxable Capacity as a Percentage of GNP	Tax Effort E
Ivory Coast	12.09	1.63
Brazil	13.50	1.53
Chad	9.86	1.39
Zaire	16.97	1.38
Senegal	13.24	1.37
Egypt	13.41	1.34
Mali	11.36	1.32
Ceylon	12.03	1.30
Tunisia	16.69	1.24
Tanzania	11.83	1.22

Table 6.8 (Continued)

Country	Taxable Capacity as a Percentage of GNP	Tax Effort E
Sudan	11.01	1.18
Upper Volta	11.01	1.18
Zambia	24.47	1.17
Malaysia	14.46	1.16
Morocco	14.48	1.14
Guyana	18.24	1.13
Kenya	12.47	1.11
Turkey	12.79	1.10
Chile	17.84	1.09
Taiwan	13.81	1.08
Ghana	12.32	1.08
Vietnam	12.85	1.07
Argentina	14.34	1.03
India	11.44	1.01
Jamaica	16.93	1.00
Venezuela	22.06	0.99
Thailand	13.15	0.98
Iran	19.95	0.97
Ecuador	13.00	0.97
Burundi	9.94	0.96
South Korea	12.73	0.93
Peru	15.60	0.88
Singapore	14.71	0.85
Honduras	12.63	0.83
Ethiopia	10.32	0.83
Costa Rica	13.23	0.83
Colombia	13.30	0.78
Paraguay	12.50	0.76
Philippines	13.01	0.76
Rwanda	10.93	0.75
Togo	13.52	0.75
Lebanon	14.17	0.75
Pakistan	11.55	0.72
Trinidad and Tobago	21.52	0.70
Mexico	14.20	0.69
Indonesia	12.08	0.62
Guatemala	12.91	0.61
Bolivia	17.74	0.51
[Afghanistan	11.31	0.44]
Nepal	10.12	0.32

Note: Afghanistan was not included in the 49 country comparative study in which taxable capacity was calculated. Measurement of Afghanistan's taxable capacity and tax effort is described in the text.

Source: R. W. Bahl, "A Regression Approach to Tax Effort and Tax Ratio Analysis," *International Monetary Fund Staff Papers*, 18 (3), November 1971, Table 2, p. 596.

Other measures of tax effort have been used by various investigators. Some of the equations which have been estimated are listed below:

$$\hat{T}y = 10.48 + 0.0026(Yp) + 0.0614(Xy + My) \tag{6.3}$$

$$\hat{T}y = 10.05 + 0.0031(Yp - Xp) + 0.3973(Ny) + 0.0881(Xy - Nxy) \tag{6.4}$$

$$\hat{T}y = 15.98 - 0.1077(Ay) + 0.0350(Xy + My) \tag{6.5}$$

where Yp is per capita income, Xy exports as a percentage of income, My imports as a percentage of income, Xp per capita exports, Ny the share of Gross Domestic Product (GDP) generated in the mining sector, Nxy mining exports as a percentage of income, Ay the share of GDP generated

Table 6.9

Data for Calculating Afghanistan's Tax Effort, 1346

Item	Estimate
Population	9.15 million
Per Capita Income	$ 88
Gross National Product at Market Prices	Afs 62,268 million
Gross Domestic Product at Factor Cost	Afs 59,355 million
National Income	Afs 58,076 million
Gross Agricultural Income at Factor Cost	Afs 30,214 million
Gross Nonagricultural Income at Factor Cost	Afs 29,141 million
Gross Mining Income at Factor Cost	Afs 284 million
Gross Manufacturing Income at Factor Cost	Afs 1,071 million
Commercial Imports	Afs 5,778 million
Exports	Afs 5,018 million
Per Capita Exports	$ 7.26
Mining Exports	Afs 241 million
Exports of Agricultural Products	Afs 4,344 million
Net Foreign Aid (excluding Commodity Assistance)	Afs 2,124 million
Commodity Assistance	Afs 517 million
Total Tax Revenue	Afs 3,082 million
Taxes Related to Nonagricultural Income	Afs 412 million
Taxes Related to Total Income	Afs 93 million
Taxes Related to Basic Sector Income	Afs 1,174 million
Taxes Related to Imports	Afs 1,403 million
Gross Public Sector Savings	Afs 598 million
Net Public Sector Savings	Afs 453 million

Source: Population—Table 2.1 above.

Per Capita Income—United Nations, *World Economic Survey, 1969-1970: The Developing Countries in the 1960s—The Problem of Appraising Progress* (New York: United Nations, 1971), Table A.1, p. 177.

National Income Data—World Bank estimates provided by the Ministry of Planning.

Foreign Trade Data—Ministry of Commerce, *A Summary of Afghanistan's Foreign Trade, 1343-1348* (Kabul: Ministry of Commerce, mimeo, December 1971).

Tax Data—Table 6.5 above.

Table 6.10

Ratios for Calculating Afghanistan's Tax Effort, 1346

Item	Percentage
Gross Agricultural Income / Gross Domestic Product	50.904
Gross Nonagricultural Income / Gross Domestic Product	49.096
Gross Mining Income / Gross Domestic Product	0.478
Gross Manufacturing Income / Gross Domestic Product	1.804
Commercial Imports / Gross National Product	9.279
Exports / Gross National Product	8.059
Exports of Agricultural Products / Gross National Product	6.976
Exports of Nonagricultural Products / Gross National Product	1.082
Exports of Mined Products / Gross National Product	0.355
Net Foreign Aid / Gross National Product	3.411
Commodity Assistance / Gross National Product	0.830
Total Tax Revenue / Gross National Product	4.950
Taxes of Nonagricultural Income / Nonagricultural Income	1.230
Taxes of Basic Sector / Basic Sector Income	20.600
Taxes of Imports / Imports	24.282
Taxes of Total Income / Gross National Product	0.149

Note: Nonagricultural income is income generated outside the agricultural sector plus the value of agricultural exports on which personal income tax, sales taxes, excises and other internal indirect taxes are levied. Taxes related to total income comprise property, poll and personal, and unclassified tax collections as a percentage of GNP. The basic sector consists of mining and manufacturing sectors and agricultural exports on which corporate income tax and export taxes are levied.

Source: Table 6.9 above.

in the agricultural sector, and $\hat{T}y$ taxable capacity as a percentage of income [B2, p. 109]. Taking the data provided in Tables 6.9 and 6.10, the following results are obtained for Afghanistan:

$$\text{Equation 6.3} \quad \hat{T}y = 11.773 \quad E = 0.420$$
$$\text{Equation 6.4} \quad \hat{T}y = 11.168 \quad E = 0.443$$
$$\text{Equation 6.5} \quad \hat{T}y = 11.104 \quad E = 0.446$$

These results support the conclusion that less than half the tax receipts which could have been collected by an average effort were actually collected in 1346 (1967). This year is not atypical. It is not surprising to find that this poor tax effort has been accompanied by low levels of public sector saving.

An alternative way of measuring tax effort on the tax revenue criterion involves the use of the representative tax system approach. This method uses the average tax rate structure for all countries in the sample and

computes the tax revenue which would be collected by each country had
it applied these average or representative rates. A recent study employing
this technique [B2] produced the following representative tax structure:

$$\hat{T} = 0.0869(Y - A + Ax) + 0.1430(N + I + Ax) + 0.1725(M)$$
$$+ 0.0132(Y) \tag{6.6}$$

where $\hat{T}$ is the yield from the representative tax system, Y is GNP, A total
income generated in the agricultural sector, Ax total value of agricultural
exports, N total income generated in the mining sector, I total income
generated in the manufacturing sector, and M the total value of imports
[B2, p. 104]. Data required to compare Afghanistan's tax effort on this
basis are given in Tables 6.9 and 6.10. The results are presented in Table
6.11 below. In this case, the tax effort, E, is 0.556, indicating that just
over half the taxes which could be collected through applying the representative tax structure were collected.

The representative tax approach enables a more detailed analysis of
the tax effort. In Afghanistan's case, as indicated in Table 6.11, of the
44.40 per cent shortfall in expected revenues, 45.06 per cent can be
attributed to below average personal income and internal indirect taxes
and 13.15 per cent to below average property taxes. On the other hand,
import taxes are higher than would have been the case had Afghanistan
adopted the representative tax system. This offsets the 58.21 per cent
shortfall contributed by the other tax groups by 7.33 per cent. The higher
value of taxes collected on corporate and export taxes (mainly the latter)
also offsets the shortfall created by low internal tax collection by 6.48
per cent. These findings are consistent with the analysis presented in
Section iii.

Unfortunately, data on public sector savings are not as easily available
as data on tax revenues. However, a comparison of a small selection of
countries for which figures could be obtained is given in Table 6.12
below. From a glance at this table, the conclusion is again drawn that
Afghanistan's tax effort based on the savings criterion has been extremely
low. In 1346 (1967), public sector net savings represented 0.8 per cent of
National Income.

An analysis of domestic savings rates has been attempted in a recent
cross-country study [P1]. Based on 85 observations, the following result
from regression analysis was obtained:

$$S = 11.4 - 1.00(A) + 0.20(P) + 1.50(E) \tag{6.7}$$
$$(12.1) \quad (-7.1) \quad (5.4) \quad (7.0)$$

Table 6.11

A Representative Tax System Applied to Afghanistan, 1346

	Income (Millions of Afghanis)	Tax Receipts (Millions of Afghanis)	Effective Tax Rates (Percentage)	Representative Tax Rates (Percentage)	Representative Tax Receipts (Millions of Afghanis)	Contribution to Shortfall (Percentage)
Non-Subsistence Sector Income	33,485	412	1.230	8.69	2,910	45.06
Basic Sector Income	5,699	1,174	20.600	14.30	815	-6.48
Imports	5,778	1,403	24.282	17.25	997	-7.33
Gross National Product	62,268	93	0.149	1.32	822	13.15
Total	—	3,082	—	—	5,544	44.40

Tax Effort, E = 0.556

Note: The non-subsistence sector includes all non-agricultural income and agricultural exports. The basic sector consists of mining and manufacturing sectors and agricultural exports.

Source: Data from Table 6.9 above used in Equation 6.6.

Table 6.12

*Public Sector Net Savings as a Percentage of National Income in 15
Underdeveloped Countries, 1968*

(Percentage)

Country	Public Sector Net Savings	Tax Effort
Argentina	2.7	(1.03)
Brazil	3.2	(1.53)
Chile	9.6	(1.09)
Taiwan	3.6	(1.08)
Colombia	5.8	(0.78)
India	1.9	(1.01)
South Korea	9.5	(0.93)
Philippines	1.2	(0.76)
Thailand	3.2	(0.98)
Tunisia	5.8	(1.24)
Venezuela	7.8	(0.99)
Iran	4.1	(0.97)
Pakistan	4.1	(0.72)
Turkey	9.5	(1.10)
Afghanistan	0.8	(0.44)

Note: For Iran, Pakistan and Turkey, gross public sector saving as a percentage of Gross National Product is used. For Afghanistan, public enterprises are assumed to yield no net savings. Therefore, the Government current acount balance of Afs 598 million for 1346 (1967) is taken as gross savings and Afs 145 deducted for depreciation. Gross public sector savings as a percentage of Gross National Product is 0.96 per cent for Afghanistan. Tax effort, E, from Table 6.8 is shown in brackets.

Source: Afghanistan—Table 6.3 above.

Iran, Pakistan and Turkey—M. J. Fry, *Money, Exchange Control and Bank Regulation in Iran, Pakistan and Turkey* (London: City University, mimeo, March 1972), Statistical Appendix.

All other countries—Development Centre, *National Accounts of Less Developed Countries 1959-1968* (Paris: Organisation for Economic Co-operation and Development, 1970).

where A is foreign aid, P exports of primary products, and E other exports, all expressed as percentages of GNP. Figures in brackets are "t" values. The adjusted coefficient of determination, $\bar{R}^2$, equalled 0.62 [P1, Table 5, p. 127]. Inserting values for Afghanistan given in Table 6.9 into Equation 6.7 gives S = 9.67 which is a relatively low figure compared to domestic savings achieved in many of the underdeveloped countries. However, from figures in Tables 2.15 and 4.5, it can be calculated that domestic savings reached 5.29 per cent of GNP in 1346 (1967) but had declined to 4.46 per cent, less than half the level predicted by Equation 6.7, by 1351 (1972). Equation 6.7 and additional results published by

Papanek [P1] lend support to the contention in Chapter IV that foreign aid is not so effective as exports in stimulating growth. Equation 6.7 illustrates one reason, namely that foreign aid acts as a substitute for domestic savings whereas exports generate it. Papanek's results also show that foreign aid represses exports [P1, Table 6, p. 129]. It is interesting to note that on the basis of the tax effort calculations (E = 0.44), had the tax effort in 1346 (1967) been of average strength, i.e. E = 1, and had all extra revenue been saved for development expenditure, public sector savings alone might have been raised to Afs 4,521 million or 7.3 per cent of GNP.

If Afghanistan is classified as an underachiever in relation to some expected rate of economic growth, it might be grouped with a number of other countries "..... whose governments put a very low priority on economic performance ....." [P1, p. 124]. This was the conclusion reached in Chapter IV. That the Government has failed to raise revenue for development expenditure supports this contention. It is strengthened by analysis presented below in which investment is examined in more detail.

v. *Deficit Finance*

Noticeable for their omission in both this and the preceding chapter have been references to monetary or fiscal policy; in the Afghan context they would represent two sides of the same coin. The omission springs from the fact that no deliberate policies have been pursued. Domestic borrowing has been a balancing item and not a part of either monetary or fiscal policy. The uncertain outcome of the budgetary position would in any case have made the preparation of fiscal policy a sterile exercise. As for monetary policy:

> Unfortunately, in Afghanistan it is difficult to formulate and make effective monetary policy, since the Government has to rely solely on the Da Afghanistan Bank to finance its deficit since there is no private sector market from which the Government can borrow.   [M30, p. 18]

It was suggested in Chapter V that Da Afghanistan Bank had done what it could to mitigate the effects of violent fluctuations in public sector net domestic borrowing requirements. Periods of excessive recourse to deficit finance can easily be pinpointed from the money supply series presented in Table 2.9. 1333-1335 (1954-1956), 1340-1344 (1961-1965) and 1351-1352 (1972-1973) are picked out in this way. Using monetary data, the public sector deficit for the three years 1333-1335 (1954-1956) appears to have been Afs 726 million or 26 per cent of total revenue. This differs greatly from the residuals given in Table 6.3 since most of it consisted of loans to the new Government enterprises established at this time. From Table 5.8, it can be seen that during the five years 1340-1344 (1961-1965) net claims on the Government by the financial sector increased by Afs 3 billion or 21 per cent of total revenue. In 1351 (1972), net claims on the Government by the financial sector increased by Afs 1,035 million or 34 per cent of total revenue and the estimated outcome for 1352 (1973) is likely to be of a similar order of magnitude and proportion. In relation to the initial money stock, the average annual deficits for the periods 1333-1335 (1954-1956) and 1340-1344 (1961-1965) represented 18 and 19 per cent, respectively. The 1351 (1972) deficit of Afs 1,035 million represented 11 per cent.

The balance between revenue and expenditure has been large enough in relation to the money stock to have had a strong effect in terms of increasing the latter. In the previous chapter, the relationship between changes in the money stock and changes in the price level was analysed. That a strong relationship appears to have existed and that domestic revenue has been price inelastic suggest that any level of deficit finance which increases the money stock annually by more than 4 per cent leads to further imbalance in the future. Roughly, this implies that the deficit should be held within 4 per cent of the money stock.

Using Equation 5.4 from the previous chapter, the maximum non-inflationary increase in the money stock over a three year period is 11.5 per cent. The average three year increase between 1331 (1952) and 1350 (1971) shown in Table 5.14 has, in fact, been 38.7 per cent; it has already been argued that increases in net claims on the Government by the financial sector have been the primary determinant of changes in the money stock.

Not all expenditures are price elastic. In particular, throughout the period civil servant salaries have been adjusted only very irregularly. Thus, for example, in 1328 (1949) a mission from the United Nations Educational, Scientific and Cultural Organisation stated:

> It seems clear from our study that in 1938 a family of four could live reasonably well on 300 afghanis per month. At present the same family would need about 1,600 afghanis per month. [U17, p. 67]

Yet, the mission found that teachers were receiving between Afs 150 and Afs 712 per month, the latter being the salary of a university professor [U17, p. 68], and concluded:

> The Mission is of the opinion that the tragic financial situation of the teaching profession is one of the principal reasons for the poor results achieved by Afghanistan in the sphere of education. [U17, p. 68]

A similar situation occurred in the 1340s (1960s), there having been no general increase in salary scales for civil servants between 1344 (1965) and 1352 (1973). Most civil servants receive salaries generally regarded as below the subsistence level.

For illustrative purposes, one might perhaps reasonably assume that in the short run revenue price elasticity has been about 0.5 and expenditure price elasticity about 0.7. For the years 1339-1342 (1960-1963), the part of the Government's deficit financed by the financial sector was Afs 3,313 million. Total revenue for those years was Afs 7,061 million and total expenditure Afs 10,493 million. The money stock increased by Afs 2,130 million, the difference being financed in equal part by a reduction in domestic credit to the private sector and a depletion of international reserves [I3, p. 229]. Despite countermovements which offset the effect of the increase in Government borrowing on the money supply, the latter increased by 61.5 per cent. From Equation 5.4, this increase would have caused an increase in the price level of 38.5 per cent. The actual increase shown in Table 5.14 is 46.5 per cent.

A 38.5 per cent increase in the price level would, on the basis of the assumed price elasticities, increase revenue by Afs 1,359 million and expenditure by Afs 2,828 million and thus increase the deficit for the subsequent three year period by Afs 1,469 million. At the end of 1342 (1964), the money stock totalled Afs 4,886 million. Hence, even the increase in the gap between expenditures and revenues created by price increases alone over the 1339-1342 (1960-1963) period would have necessitated a 30 per cent increase in the money stock over the subsequent three year period 1342-1345 (1963-1966), adding a further 23 per cent to the rise in the price level, had new revenue measures not been forthcoming to prevent the perpetuation of this vicious circle.

This example serves to illustrate the potentially self-generating nature of the inflationary process in Afghanistan. A strong pressure group which can hold its taxes to very modest increases, if any, in nominal terms, a revenue structure which is less price elastic than expenditures, despite civil service pay freezes, and a desire at certain times stronger than at others to promote economic development have combined to produce a circle of inflationary pressures which eventually have had to be cut by unpopular action on the revenue side of the equation and growth retarding cuts on the expenditure side. That such actions have been too late and too weak is evinced from the inflationary picture presented in Table 2.7.

Afghanistan's case is not unique:

> Because government expenditures *are* elastic to income growth even if revenues are not, the problem of relieving financial repression is made much more difficult. Growth brings with it a tendency toward budgetary deficits. Public saving does not keep pace, and governments either allow more non-neutral small taxes to proliferate or turn to central banks for financing, given the absence of capital markets for absorbing long-term public debt. Excessive issue of nominal money can then cause inflation and a reduction in the real stock of money .... [M7, p. 142]

Various other aspects of deficit finance, including its drawbacks, have been discussed elsewhere by others, e.g. in [E6; R5; U4; V1].

An important aspect of the deficit finance issue in Afghanistan has been the extreme variability in the level of public sector domestic borrowing from one year to the other. The effects of this in terms of the variance of changes in the money stock and hence of the price level were covered in the last chapter. Here, an examination of the causes of the high variance in the Government's domestic borrowing requirements is due. Turning back to Table 6.3 it can be seen that current account balances have not fluctuated to anything like the extent of the residual domestic borrowing requirements. Omitting the two half years, the coefficient of variation of the current account balance in constant prices is 61 per cent over the period 1331-1351 (1952-1972), while over the same period the coefficient of variation of net domestic borrowing is 123 per cent. The causes of the high variability of net domestic borrowing would at first sight appear to lie in the capital account and in other financing items. Project assistance cancels out, thus leaving development expenditure in local currency and Commodity Assistance. The former appears to have followed a fairly steady path (coefficient of variation 56 per cent for 1331-1351 (1952-1972) omitting the two half years) which leaves Commodity Assistance. In fact, this item has not been particularly volatile (coefficient of variation 54 per cent for 1336/37-1351 (1957-1972) omitting the one half year). But it has been unpredictable since it depends primarily on agricultural conditions for any particular year. Thus, it has been impossible to budget accurately for this item and so take measures in advance to counteract its fluctuations. Apart from unpredictable Commodity Assistance, the fact that net domestic borrowing requirements is a residual further contributes to its own variability. Small movements in opposite directions of the major revenue and expenditure items have a relatively large percentage effect on the small residual. That such movements have not been anticipated has been a result of the primitive budgeting procedures, lack of implementation checks, and other aspects of the weak administrative system which impinges on the Government revenue and expenditure outcome.

A need for some system of controls on levels of deficit finance in Afghanistan has been recognised. A report by the German Economic Advisory Group suggests:

> .... there should at least exist regulations for all credit relations between Government and Central Bank. Such regulations should fix limits, purpose, procedure, term structure, repayment, interest rates for government debt to the Central Bank.
> Da Afghanistan Bank too feels that such regulations are unavoidable, if uncontrolled monetary expansion by government deficit spending should be prevented (see Da Afghanistan Bank's reply to the Ministry of Planning's enquiry of 29.2.1350). During the last four years the Government has neither paid loan instalments nor interest on loans. [G3, p. 3]

Regulations of this type would be unnecessary were fiscal and monetary policies rationally formulated and then accurately implemented. Such a situation has not existed in Afghanistan, where instead immediate financing requirements have driven the Government to the only available source. An appreciation of the idea that even this source should not be used when the longer run consequences are likely to be detrimental was clearly recognised by the Government and Da Afghanistan Bank in 1352 (1973). A Cabinet policy statement on banking legislation stated:

> Loans by the central bank to the Government will be limited by law to a maximum percentage of the Budget. Each year, consultation will take place between the central bank and the Government on the optimum level of deficit finance within this limit for that particular year. [C1, p. 3]

This was incorporated into the laws which were then drafted by the Financial Development Committee with assistance from the International Monetary Fund and the United States Agency for International Development. The draft legislation awaits further consideration by the new Republican Government.

vi. *Expenditure*

As can be seen from the figures in Tables 6.13 and 6.14, ordinary expenditure has increased steadily over the past two decades in both nominal and real terms. In 1349 (1970) personnel, debt servicing and defence accounted for 78 per cent of ordinary expenditure. The only new and accelerating component has been debt service. This has clearly had a strong negative effect on the Government's current account balance. However, it was its predicted effect on the balance of international payments that was in fact used as primary justification in the request to

Table 6.13

Government Expenditure 1331-1352

(Millions of Afghanis)

Item	1331	1332	1333	1334	1335	1336 (first half)	1336/ 37	1337/ 38	1338/ 39	1339/ 40
Ordinary Expenditure	660	666	825	933	910	526	1,007	1,251	1,394	1,558
National Defence and Security	249	281	211	294	259	181	420	510	522	640
Debt Service	0	0	0	0	0	0	140	174	179	183
Other	411	385	614	639	651	345	447	567	693	735
Development Expenditure	170	172	205	327	381	214	374	421	705	1,550
Education	26	28	19	22	28	20	44	35	47	154
Health	n.a.	n.a.	7	7	9	6	10	3	18	66
Transport and Communications	n.a.	n.a.	49	71	133	82	167	233	434	949
Agriculture	n.a.	n.a.	10	8	15	8	99	85	91	114
Industry and Mines	n.a.	n.a.	0	15	11	5	43	47	113	183
Other	144	144	120	204	185	93	11	18	2	84
Development Expenditure in Foreign Currency (Project Assistance)	—	—	—	—	—	—	1,246	1,556	2,078	2,697
Total	830	838	1,030	1,260	1,291	740	2,627	3,228	4,177	5,805

Note: Classifications follow Ministry of Finance procedures and are in some cases arbitrary. Thus, for example, higher figures might well be assigned to education and health development expenditures. In 1336/37, only 33.5 per cent of total education expenditure and 23.2 per cent of health expenditure were classified as development. For transportation and communications, agriculture, and mines and industries, the proportions of total expenditure classified as development expenditure were 53.0, 88.0 and 79.7 per cent, respectively. As no distinction between ordinary and development expenditures was made prior to 1336/37, these proportions were assumed for the period 1333-1336 (first half) and expenditures of the appropriate ministries and agencies partitioned accordingly. The resulting estimates agree reasonably well with figures in Tudor Engineering Company, *Report on Development of Helmand Valley* (Washington, D.C.: Tudor Engineering Company, 1956), Table 9, p. 153.

Throughout, project assistance has been converted into Afghanis at Afs 45 to the United States Dollar.

Education includes Ministry of Education, Kabul University and the Faculty of Medicine.

Health includes Public Health and Health Institutions.

Transport and Communications includes Communications, Public Works, Civil Aviation and Transport.

donors for debt rescheduling made in 1350 (1971). The U.S.S.R., the largest creditor, agreed. The U.S.A. felt that the request was unjustifiable because the appreciation of the Afghani since 1349 (1970) and Afghanistan's ample foreign exchange reserves did not suggest an imminent

Table 6.13

Government Expenditure 1331-1352

(Millions of Afghanis)

1340 (second half)	1341	1342	1343	1344	1345	1346	1347	1348	1349	1350	1351	1352 (B)
878	1,850	2,416	2,558	2,902	3,403	3,613	4,254	4,732	5,158	5,504	5,689	6,538
297	693	759	925	1,044	1,285	1,370	1,501	1,577	1,651	1,637	1,657	1,785
133	258	543	379	256	474	665	601	867	1,014	1,140	1,055	1,471
448	899	1,114	1,254	1,602	1,644	1,578	2,152	2,288	2,493	2,727	2,977	3,282
520	1,446	1,830	1,622	1,720	1,728	1,707	1,820	1,920	1,731	1,916	2,100	2,544
34	81	117	51	82	125	127	130	128	96	57	82	108
21	18	21	14	15	21	11	33	34	57	49	82	112
308	844	938	878	403	362	314	338	386	410	390	316	345
50	117	173	136	437	467	681	681	842	711	927	953	1,113
98	367	442	445	645	586	428	368	328	328	334	340	367
9	19	139	98	138	167	146	270	202	129	159	327	499
,823	3,144	2,833	3,168	3,485	3,373	2,789	2,259	1,990	1,241	1,544	2,509	2,236
3,221	6,440	7,079	7,348	8,107	8,504	8,109	8,333	8,642	8,130	8,964	10,298	11,318

Agriculture includes Agriculture, Helmand Valley Authority, Rural Development, Water and Soil, Nangarhar, Paktia, and Land Reclamation and Settlement.

Industry and Mines includes only the Ministry.

Source: 1331-1332 Tudor Engineering Company, *Report on Development of Helmand Valley* (Washington, D.C.: Tudor Engineering Company, 1956), Table 9, p. 153; and Ministry of Finance.

1333-1336 (first half) Ministry of Planning, *Survey of Progress 1959* (Kabul: Ministry of Planning, 1959), Volume IV, Table 56, pp. 242-44; and Ministry of Finance.

1336/37-1340 (second half) Ministry of Planning, *Survey of Progress 1962-64* (Kabul: Ministry of Planning, 1964), Table A-2, p. 91 and Table A-4, pp. 94-95.

1341-1343 Ministry of Planning, *Survey of Progress 1967-1968* (Kabul: Ministry of Planning, 1968), Tables S-2, S-3 and S-4.

1344-1347 Ministry of Planning, *Survey of Progress 1970-1971* (Kabul: Ministry of Planning, 1971), Tables S-2, S-3 and S-4.

1348-1349 Ministry of Planning, *Survey of Progress 1971-1972* (Kabul: Ministry of Planning, 1972), Tables S-2, S-3 and S-4.

1350-1352 Ministries of Finance and Planning.

balance of payments crisis. The United States balance of payments situation, on the other hand, was not one under which the request could be viewed sympathetically.

Part of the reason behind the request lay in the composition of the

Table 6.14

Government Expenditure at Constant Prices 1331-1352

(Millions of Afghanis, 1340 Prices)

Item	1331	1332	1333	1334	1335	1336 (first half)	1336/ 37	1337/ 38	1338/ 39	1339 4(
Ordinary Expenditure	828	845	921	967	768	429	820	994	1,298	1,654
National Defence and Security	312	356	236	305	219	148	342	405	486	68(
Debt Service	0	0	0	0	0	0	114	138	167	194
Other	516	489	685	662	549	281	364	451	645	78(
Development Expenditure	213	218	229	339	321	174	305	334	656	1,64!
Education	33	35	21	23	24	16	36	28	44	16
Health	n.a.	n.a.	8	7	7	5	8	2	17	7(
Transport and Communications	n.a.	n.a.	55	74	112	67	136	185	404	1,00'
Agriculture	n.a.	n.a.	11	8	13	6	81	68	84	12]
Industry and Mines	n.a.	n.a.	0	16	9	4	35	37	105	19
Other	180	183	134	211	156	76	9	14	2	8(
Development Expenditure in Foreign Currency (Project Assistance)	—	—	—	—	—	—	1,262	1,554	2,072	2,68(
Total	1,041	1,063	1,150	1,306	1,089	603	2,387	2,882	4,026	5,98

Note: Development expenditures in foreign currency, i.e. project assistance, have been deflated by the United States wholesale price index in Table 2.6. All other figures have been deflated by the modified purchasing power parity price index in Table 2.7.

foreign exchange reserves, over 70 per cent of which was in the form of gold. The Government was naturally loath to use gold, which it would have had to have sold at well under half the world price following the rules of the two tier system, to support the Afghani. The abandonment of the two tier gold system in 1352 (1973) justified this reluctance.

Agarwal has recently measured the optimal monetary reserves for seven Asian countries [A4]. The model used is inapplicable to Afghanistan because the countries in Agarwal's study operated on fixed exchange rate systems in contrast to Afghanistan's floating rate. However, there is little doubt that Afghanistan's international reserves exceed the optimum level. Hopefully, the abandonment of the two tier gold system will provide the necessary incentive for Afghanistan to convert some of these unproductive reserves into productive investment goods.

For the future, the so-called debt problem looms large. The existence of a problem or a potential problem lies essentially in the fact that returns to the Government and in most cases to the country as a whole from

Table 6.14

Government Expenditure at Constant Prices 1331-1352

(Millions of Afghanis, 1340 Prices)

1340 (second half)	1341	1342	1343	1344	1345	1346	1347	1348	1349	1350	1351	1352 (B)
878	1,520	2,049	1,746	1,641	1,834	1,944	2,282	2,423	2,265	2,347	2,473	2,843
297	569	644	631	590	693	737	805	807	725	698	720	776
133	212	460	259	145	255	358	322	444	445	486	458	640
448	739	945	856	906	886	849	1,155	1,172	1,095	1,163	1,295	1,427
520	1,188	1,552	1,107	972	932	919	976	983	760	817	913	1,106
34	66	99	35	46	68	68	70	66	42	24	36	47
21	15	18	9	8	11	6	18	17	25	21	36	49
308	693	795	599	228	195	169	181	198	180	166	137	150
50	96	147	93	247	252	367	365	431	312	395	414	484
98	302	375	304	365	316	230	197	168	144	143	148	159
9	16	118	67	78	90	79	145	103	57	68	142	217
1,823	3,135	2,833	3,162	3,410	3,194	2,636	2,084	1,766	1,063	1,280	1,991	1,775
3,221	5,843	6,434	6,015	6,023	5,960	5,499	5,342	5,172	4,088	4,444	5,377	5,724

Source: Figures in Table 6.13 have been deflated by the price indices referred to in the Note above.

foreign aid financed projects have failed to produce yields sufficient even to cover the concessional interest rates charged on the loans, let alone reached levels anywhere near approximating those actually anticipated by the donors themselves. Given the admitted lack of expertise within the Afghan bureaucracy and the Government's reliance on the donors for project suggestions and appraisals, a somewhat more forceful argument for debt rescheduling or even some debt moratorium might have been based on attaching some responsibility for the unsatisfactory outcome of donor projects on the donors themselves. Their feasibility studies for potential loan financed projects have consistently produced wildly over-optimistic estimates of expected returns. A striking example of an over-optimistic estimate of returns made recently is the following:

From the research and practical on-farm work done, results show it is possible for wheat farmers in Afghanistan to receive up to 1,000 Afs for each 100 Afs spent for fertilizer if they use improved seed and recommended production practices. [K11, p. 13]

Defence and national security expenditures under the new Republic and, in the absence of successful debt rescheduling negotiations, debt service as well, are likely to increase sharply. Direct assistance for the former may be obtained from the U.S.S.R. Even so prospects for ordinary expenditure appear expansionary.

The distinction between ordinary and development expenditure has already been given some attention. The arbitrariness of some classifications throws doubt on the meaningfulness of comparisons within the development expenditure category. For example, the development proportion of expenditure on education and health is much lower than that on agriculture and transport. Nevertheless, the emphasis on infrastructure and particularly road building during the First Plan and the early years of the Second Plan stands out. Another major problem of analysing the sectoral breakdown of development expenditure arises from the fact that project assistance expenditure is not broken down in the Government accounts. Partly because accountability for project assistance expenditure does not rest with the Government and partly because such expenditure is for specific donor projects there seems to have been something approaching abrogation of responsibility for donor projects on the Government's part. As far back as 1328 (1949), the Afghan Delegation to the United Nations which had submitted a request for aid in 17 projects "left to the UN the task of selecting the most desirable projects" [F16, p. 15]. The same still appeared to be the case in 1352 (1973), as shown in Chapter IV.

Neither the Government nor the donors have been too concerned with *ex-post* rates of return analyses, despite the fact that benefits from both continuous project appraisal and *post mortems* would have been high. On the part of the Government this neglect seems to have been deliberate. Because most projects were of a long term nature, returns have not been expected in the short run. Thus, there appeared to be no urgency for relating expenditures to performance and no experience and expertise have been acquired for such analysis. Furthermore, there has been little incentive to complete projects which, while still uncompleted, have provided channels for siphoning off foreign aid funds into private pockets [B13, pp. 33-35].

In Chapter IV, macroeconomic analysis suggested that development expenditure as a whole had yielded low and declining returns, i.e. that the incremental capital/output ratio had been high and rising over the period since 1335 (1956) when the First Plan was started. Although an analysis of development expenditure at the microeconomic level is essential to an understanding of what has gone wrong, the mammoth task which a comprehensive study of this type would require has been beyond the resources allocated to the present enquiry. However, one example can be examined to illustrate some of the problems to which development projects in Afghanistan have been subject. Given the importance and longevity of the Helmand Valley project, it makes a natural case study. Since its inception in 1325 (1946), many reports have been prepared on this project. Of particular significance is that while most of them admit to the failure of the project to yield a satisfactory return to date, optimism has been shown for the future.

A brief historical sketch of the Helmand-Arghandab Valley projects can serve to produce specific examples of the most pervasive development problems in Afghanistan. A more detailed history can be found in Dupree's book [D10, Chapters 22-24]. Forty per cent of the country's total water resources flows through the Valley, which is situated in the southwest of Afghanistan and has many attributes conducive to highly productive agriculture [B10, p. 2]. However,

> .... what was once supposedly the "bread basket" of Central Asia was by the 20th century vast barren or scantily vegetated lands affected to varying degrees by salts, alkaline, ground water and erosion. [B10, p. 7]

Development efforts started in 1289 (1910) when part of the vast network of old irrigation canals was reconstructed. Foreign technical assistance was first introduced in the 1310s (1930s) when new canals were built with German and Japanese help [D10, pp. 478-81].

The Second World War brought not only the Helmand project to a standstill but all other development activities in the country because of a British-Soviet ultimatum on the Afghan Government to expel all German, Italian and Japanese personnel. The War also hit private industry by preventing the importation of essential supplies. Standards of living in the urban areas declined substantially [F14, p. 295; U17, p. 67-68; W3, p. 207].

In 1325 (1946), an American firm, Morrison-Knudsen, arrived in Afghanistan under contract with the Government to build two diversion dams, enlarge an irrigation canal and construct roads in the Valley. A loan was obtained from the Export-Import Bank in 1328 (1949) after rapid depletion of Afghanistan's foreign exchange reserves built up during the War on the first Morrison-Knudsen contract [D10, pp. 482-84]. Under a second contract, Morrison-Knudsen built the Arghandab and Kajakai Dams on the Arghandab and Helmand Rivers, respectively. The dams were completed by 1331 (1952).

The United Nations Preparatory Mission to Afghanistan recommended
in its 1329 (1950) report that the United Nations should provide assistance
to the Helmand Valley project [F16, p. 36]. However,

> .... UN headquarters entertained doubts about the economic soundness
> of the projects proposed and the Government's administrative capacity
> to complete them. Moreover, the economist of the first operational mission
> reported opposition from officials of the Afghan Department of Agri-
> culture, whose advice was not sought by those blueprinting the develop-
> ment of the Valley. It also seemed to him that the officials assuming
> responsibility for the undertaking attached too much weight to engineering
> feasibility and too little to economic and social usefulness. [F16, p. 36]

The United Nations economist suggested that on cost-benefit criteria
irrigation projects in the north of the country along the Amu Darya
(River Oxus) were far more promising. However, later studies were
considerably less enthusiastic about this alternative. Interestingly, he also
noted as long ago as 1329 (1950) that investment was seriously unbalanced,
there being too high a proportion allocated to the irrigation works and
too little to ancillary investment. This criticism can be applied to many
other foreign aid projects in Afghanistan, perhaps most tellingly to the
road building programme. Part of the reason for this has been the donors'
belief that the necessary ancillary investment should and/or would be
undertaken by the Government.

An important criticism in this early appraisal was that the Helmand
project as it stood "would be too expensive to pay for itself in terms of
foreign exchange" [F16, p. 37]. The same criticism has been made against
other large projects. Another United Nations expert expressed the view
in 1331 (1952) that the foreign exchange spent on the Helmand project
should instead have been spent on small scale agricultural schemes. He
further noted that Afghan officials failed to supervise and monitor the
contractors, Morrison-Knudsen, and that technical assistance should be
provided to the Government to increase its supervisory capacity:

> Only in this way, he implied, could the contractor be prevented from
> dotting the Afghan countryside with dams on every site that looked prom-
> ising to its engineers. [F16, p. 37]

The United Nations was not the only critic of the Helmand project even
in the early stages. Indeed, Abdul Majid Zabuli, Minister of National
Economy until his dismissal in 1329 (1950), stated that he opposed the
scheme on economic grounds from its inception [P14, p. 7]. This admission
is somewhat ironical in that his dismissal was based in part on the extra-

vagant use of foreign exchange used to pay Morrison-Knudsen for its work on the Helmand project under its first contract [F16, p. 17; F18, p. 39].

One feature of decisions relating to the Helmand project which has been apparent in other projects has been the importance attached to expenditure already made rather than an acceptance of the only economically justifiable approach to past expenditure of "bygones are bygones." To save face or simply on an erroneous understanding of economic principles, projects such as the Helmand have been continued despite admission of the low returns expected on future outlays. In the case of the Helmand project, such a pattern has been followed right from the first loan granted by the Export-Import Bank in 1328 (1949) which was designed to salvage something from efforts already expended. After a second loan from the Export-Import Bank in 1332 (1953) for more capital intensive irrigation work, the U.S.A. assumed tacit responsibility for a satisfactory outcome of the Helmand project.

> It became obvious to the U.S. government in mid-1953 that the project, without help from experienced extension workers and other experts, was headed for the worst. Since that time, U.S. technical assistance has been essential to the project's success. [F17, pp. 44-45]

Unfortunately, the two agricultural extension advisors provided under the Point IV Assistance Program were too late and too few.

The Morrison-Knudsen period ended in 1338 (1959) with recriminations on both sides:

> The Afghans blamed M-K [Morrison-Knudsen] publicly for the failures; privately, M-K blamed the Afghans ....
> Afghanistan's shortcomings in handling the projects can be attributed to the weakness characterizing underdeveloped government—lack of proper planning and administrative machinery. The latter depended on the agricultural planning which had run into snags. In addition to problems of settlement, insufficient attention had been given to that of reimbursing the government for land, water, and services. Production and settler income were low and squatters settled on nonirrigable land while thousands of applicants waited. All these inadequacies made the government turn to M-K for help above and beyond actual engineering.
> M-K's initial objective had been to build specified engineering works in the quickest and most effective way. Thanks to many improvised solutions to novel situations, the company lived up to its reputation as a fast, dependable construction firm. But gradually M-K had to assume additional responsibilities because of the government's unexpected lack of preparation, the uncertainty surrounding the physical and engineering features of the structures, and the considerable doubts developing over the economic

> merits of the reclamation and settlement program. These factors did not seem to be sufficiently allowed for in the company's agro-economic estimates—particularly projections and computations of cost-benefit ratios—with resultant deficiencies of resource allocation. To protect itself in the face of the Afghan government's desire for only perfunctory surveys, M-K had a clause in the contract which spared it legal consequences; but this clause could not protect it from public blame .... M-K could hardly escape the assumption of some responsibility. [F18, pp, 37-38]

The same allocation of responsibility is also made by Dupree [D10, pp. 500-501].

At this point, a team from the United States Bureau of Reclamation was brought in to help on the second stage—preparation of lands to be irrigated. New villagers were settled and given a 20 year loan for equipment and seed by the Government. By the early 1340s (1960s) even marginal land, reportedly only suitable for pasture [T6, Chapter 3], had been reclaimed. None of the Government loans to settlers has yet been repaid, an illustration of another major problem in Afghanistan, namely the failure on the part of the Government to collect payments from the fortunate minority which has benefited from developmental expenditure. This has been the case with electricity, in which even enough to cover operating costs has not been collected, roads, telephone facilities and almost all public enterprises whose pricing policies combined with low capacity utilisation of plant and inefficient management has resulted in a negligible return on capital estimated roughly at Afs 15 billion [F13, pp. 8-9; G6, p. 2].

One example of the acceptance of low returns even at the feasibility stage in Afghanistan, where capital is so scarce that as a general rule of thumb a 20 per cent return should be regarded as minimal, is the feasibility study of the Girishk and Kandahar electricity plants [B17]. The desired returns based on alternative capital structures vary between 5.25 and 6.25 per cent. Projected returns from both plants were expected to rise to 4.18 and 4.95 per cent, respectively, in 1349 (1970) and to 6.73 and 7.24 per cent in 1354 (1975) [B17, Volume I, Table II M1.2].

Between 1341 (1962) and 1349 (1970), total public sector investment in agriculture has been estimated at Afs 22 billion. The increase in value added in this sector by 1349 (1970) was supposedly Afs 4-4½ billion higher than in 1341 (1962). The incremental capital/output ratio of between 5 and 5½, high on any criterion, allows a maximum gross return of 20 per cent on capital had no additional labour been used in obtaining the increased output.

Complacency over low yielding investment might not have been so serious had a reasonable proportion of total development expenditure been spent on small, high yielding projects. But the Helmand again exemplifies in one project the overall picture—overemphasis on large scale, slow maturing, capital intensive infrastructure. The Nathan Team criticised agricultural development expenditure in general during the 1340s (1960s) along the same lines:

> [Analysis] .... does not support the claim that the pursuit of improved agricultural productivity has been a dominant goal of the government. The most effective means available are not being employed. Instead in 1350 (1971-1972) and in the Third Plan nearly seventy percent of the expenditures in the agriculture and related sectors went to large-scale irrigation projects, the construction of the Mazar urea plant, and rural roads and bridges. [N2, Chapter 2, p. 2]

> Although the central thrust of the Agricultural Plan was said to be the direct support of the farmer and increase of productivity, only one-tenth of the agricultural development budget was earmarked for that purpose. The RGA [Royal Government of Afghanistan] allocated Afs 221 million for agricultural development and Afs 2.1 billion for construction of dams and canals. [N3, p. 15]

The fertiliser plant in Mazar-i-Sharif, mentioned in the quotation above, was generally recognised to be obsolete even before its completion until the dramatic rise in the world price of fertiliser in 1352 (1973) gave it a positive value.

Part of the explanation for this contradictory emphasis between intention and budget allocation lies in the high proportion of uncompleted projects in total development expenditure. By the Fourth Plan, carry-over projects accounted for 68 per cent of total planned development expenditure [M18, Table 14, pp. 266-67]. For this, the Government cannot be held solely responsible. The first two requests for loans from the Export-Import Bank in the early 1330s (1950s) were partially rejected. In particular, finance for the ancillary investments was refused [B10, p. 22; F18, pp. 39-41]. In any case, the underestimates of the costs of canal construction due to the absence of engineering surveys beforehand "left insufficient funds for the irrigation and drainage systems which were to serve it" [F18, p. 43]. Another part of the explanation lies in social fragmentation: it is easier to work on projects not directly involving or affecting people. Thus, local opposition is unlikely to be encountered to a dam building project. There can naturally be considerable reluctance to disturbing a traditional *status quo* through land levelling, minor irrigation projects and on-farm assistance programmes:

Expectations for action and innovation among civil servants are low, and
condemned if the actions infringe on or are likely to disrupt local and
indigenous semi-autonomous systems of power and influence .... Major
changes in the directions of land reform or water control under government
authority are a clear threat to the *Khans* [feudal superiors] and the established system of order. These, along with other similar issues, are problem
areas government officials would prefer to leave alone. [B10, p. 103]

Where development projects occasionally encroach,

Officials can claim ignorance of the plan which is stated to be the work of
the foreigner. [B10, p. 104]

The lack of communication, already discussed in Chapter III as the
underlying cause of fragmentation, also plagues development projects:

.... counterparts have frequently and consistently resisted any sort of
major public information scheme, stating that they understand their own
people better than foreigners can and that they must use traditional
methods to inform and gain local support for their actions. Their method
was defined, by U.S. technical personnel, as being low-key gradual but
thorough, acceptable within our frame of reference. [B10, p. 99]

But,

Few literate Afghans, particularly government officials, really understand
their peasant villagers or tribal nomads. [D10, p. 501]

A result of this lack of understanding has been lack of communication.
In 1351 (1972), a survey of farmers living in the Helmand was conducted
by a sociologist with much experience in the area. He told the author:

To the man, I found no one who wanted the project as it involves land
leveling. There are numerous reasons for this position, the most basic being
the lack of understanding of the usefulness of the leveling for them as
farmers. There has been no systematic attempt to explain to farmers the
technical advantages of the proposed system, nor have individual farmers
been told how the scheme would affect their holdings.

Nevertheless, after 25 years there are indications that change has begun
in some parts of the Helmand area. The availability of modern agricultural
inputs, credit and technical advice has resulted in rapid increases in
productivity. A significant number of farmers in the region have started
double cropping and cash crop production. A popular cash crop has been
opium poppy. Some have engaged in land levelling. But as yet, these
men are few in number and the acreage affected small. However, the past
three years have witnessed a beginning of a process which could well
accelerate. If this were to happen, the effect on the general level of
agricultural productivity would be substantial.

The communications problem has not been confined to that between Afghan bureaucrat and Afghan farmer. It has been a serious problem in most technical assistance programmes. In the Helmand, Americans have not in the main bothered to learn the language even if they have expected to remain in the country for a considerable period of time. However, technical advisors from all donor agencies have not generally remained long in Afghanistan. Distance has been further increased by the great gulf in living standards between advisors and their counterparts:

> The standard of living of American technicians living in Afghanistan had to be at a relatively high level in order to attract them . . . . The depressing result has been the creation of a myth, which U.S. exhibits of fancy consumer gadgets have not helped to correct. It has created a barrier to close contacts, a truly artificial one, but nevertheless effective in the minds of the Afghans who otherwise might be seriously interested in establishing or maintaining contact with American institutions and ways of life. [F18, p. 48]

After comparing differences in living standards between American and Russian advisors in 1339 (1960), the same author continues:

> The average Afghan does not note the fact that the upkeep of the Americans of ICA projects is paid out of ICA grant funds while all Soviet aid is paid for out of credit, repayable by the Afghan government (as is the cost of M-K's employees). The most sensitive observers are higher government officials and intellectuals who see in this great difference between cost and ways of living a cultural gap, if not an unbridgeable barrier which they expect to last as long as Afghanistan does not have the resources to afford the American way. [F18, p. 63]

Thus, once again inadequate communication and information systems lie at the root of development problems in Afghanistan.

That high yielding alternative investment opportunities do exist in Afghanistan are suggested by direct and indirect evidence. Detailed plans for road improvement and maintenance prepared by an advisory firm, Kampsax, estimated the following returns from improving roads to the next grade: overall return to all proposed work, 33 per cent; improvement from B2 to B1 roads 41 per cent, from C to B2 roads 31 per cent and from D to C roads 33 per cent. On a geographic breakdown, highest returns were expected in the eastern region [K4, p. 6/02]. One proposed improvement was expected to yield an internal rate of return of 73 per cent [K4, Table 602]. For the initial selection of roads, a discount rate for future direct user benefits of 20 per cent was used. This rate was chosen because Ministry of Public Works' projects generally yielded a return of this magnitude and funds allocated were known to be insufficient to cover all improvements yielding more than 20 per cent.

Some of the public enterprises themselves need not be written off as inherent failures. Indeed, in the early 1340s (1960s) the Afghan Cement Company declared dividends of 25 per cent [R3, p. 10]. However, a major constraint has been inefficient management whose shortcomings are compounded by the fact that performance is not a criterion on which loans from Da Afghanistan Bank are made. These have generally been determined as a matter of Government policy with little regard to commercial factors. In fact, on a number of investments made by Da Afghanistan Bank, the Bank has not even obtained basic information such as the total capital of the enterprise.

Not all development expenditure in agriculture has produced poor results. The Project on Agricultural Credit and Related Services through Cooperatives in Afghanistan (PACCA) has already been mentioned in the previous chapter. A return of 33 per cent on its investment in improving yields on vines has been achieved. The Paktia project which has also concentrated on direct on-farm efforts also appears to have yielded satisfactory returns [B12, p. 2]. Potential social returns from cotton are evidently high and rising.

Private small scale agricultural investments of extraordinarily high yields have been recorded. In one set of case studies, returns from 75 to 200 per cent were found [N7; N8; N9; N10; N11]. Although returns in private industry are difficult to ascertain because accounts are misleading, rates in the order of 30 per cent have been estimated. Transport also appears to offer high returns if judged on the basis of the results of one case study [N7] and a recent survey of transport finance which suggests that profits are high enough to enable loan repayments for vehicle purchase within six to twelve months [K1, p. 9].

Seasonal price fluctuations suggest high time preference reflected in high market interest rates. Thus, for example, it is found in the next chapter that the average annual returns from foreign currency speculation between seasonal lows and highs resulting from the seasonal nature of the export trade have been 22, 27 and 24 per cent on holding Dollars, Indian and Pakistani Rupees, respectively, over the period 1332-1351 (1953-1972). Commodity holding, in general, has yielded roughly similar returns.

Thus, this section concludes in agreement with a paragraph from the Nathan Team Final Report:

> If a fraction of the money and effort spent over the years on large, expensive, poorly implemented, and slow-yielding irrigation and land development

projects and on Government farms in the poorest and most sparsely populated agricultural areas of the country had been devoted to assuring farmers in the best irrigated agricultural areas a larger and growing supply of fertilizer, improved seeds, pesticides, tractors, pumps, small self-help surface irrigation improvements, and technical assistance in crops and livestock practices, Afghanistan would today be self-sufficient in food grain production. [N3, p. 131]

To this list should also be added cooperative development, for even with the PACCA demonstration projects resistance to enacting cooperative legislation and promoting cooperative activity has been strong. This project, in fact, illustrates one of the main problems of the United Nations programme in Afghanistan:

> In general, UN teams were successful in using pilot operations to demonstrate the economic potential of new technology or of improvements grafted upon old ones .... It remained for Afghan private or public enterprise to exploit and enlarge the experiments. UN experts seldom stayed long enough to aid and complete that process. [F18, p. 52]

In many instances, it still remains for Afghan initiative to exploit successfully demonstrated opportunities. Again, this can be interpreted as yet another problem in communications and information as well as of economic fragmentation, as shown in Chapter III. It also illustrates the reluctance on the part of Governments in the past to change existing institutions and systems. Had Governments been keener on instigating social and economic changes for development and less interested in obtaining foreign aid for large scale projects which were not a threat to the traditional social order, Afghanistan could not only have become self-sufficient in food grain production, but also acquired fewer foreign debts and have produced much more for export to pay for those debts which would still have been incurred for justifiable foreign aid projects. Of perhaps greatest significance in the long run, the alternative pattern of development expenditure would not have been so regressive in effect. As it is, there is ample evidence to suggest that the limited effects of the development programme to date have made the rich richer and the poor poorer, as shown in Chapter III.

Given the lessons learnt and partially recorded from the past, does it look as though this accumulated experience will be used in the design of new projects in the future? The short answer is: No. Part of the explanation for this lies in the high turnover rate of local as well as foreign experts. As the Deputy Chief of the United States Mission to Afghanistan wrote towards the end of 1351 (1973) about the 1335 (1956)

Tudor Engineering Company report [T6] to which he had been referred by the Economic Counsellor because it had predicted in detail many of the problems which had occurred since then:

> A good report from all appearances. But probably hasn't been looked at in last 10 years. Good example of our lack of any institutional memory. [L3]

Another part of the explanation again lies in the high proportion of future expenditure which will go to finance carry-over projects. Finally, a brief glance through the proposed list of development projects of the Ministry of Agriculture and Irrigation for the Fourth Plan clearly indicates that dam building is still favoured [M18, Table 16, pp. 269-73]. Under new projects are listed three new dams, naturally absorbing almost all the funds allocated to new projects [M18, Table 16, p. 271]. In other sectors, large scale infrastructure projects also predominate. Despite only 40 per cent use of existing capacity [N3, p. 47], Afs $2\frac{1}{4}$ billion or $7\frac{1}{2}$ per cent of total development expenditure has been allocated to investments in electricity over the period of the Fourth Plan [M18, Table 20, pp. 282-84]. This can be compared with the road building and maintenance budget for the period of only Afs $1\frac{3}{4}$ billion of which nearly one-half was to be spent under the Kampsax improvement and maintenance programme on which an average return of 33 per cent was forecast. The Fourth Plan also illustrates the observation made in Chapter IV that a critical constraint in the planning process lies in the absence of expertise in project preparation. Unfortunately, as several observers have suggested, economic planning has deteriorated.

vii. *Variance in Rates of Return to Investment*

A glance at proposed investment expenditure for the Fourth Plan suggests that the variance in the expected returns from the different projects listed therein must be high. Why is it that funds for ancillary investment in such things as minor road improvement and maintenance are short when there is planned investment of considerable magnitude in electricity which is likely to yield low returns? The simple answer is that rate of return was not the sole criterion used for allocating development expenditure in Afghanistan. One must suspect that this criterion has in fact been given negligible weight in the decision making process despite verbal claims that investment is to be directed to high yielding projects. No cost-benefit analysis has ever been carried out by the Government, nor has reference to expected returns from projects listed in the plans been based on realistic analysis. Indeed, donors themselves seem to give low weighting to economic return when preparing and executing new projects (e.g. [B11, pp. 5-7]). The importance of the rates of return on investment was stressed by Edward Shaw during a visit to Afghanistan in 1352 (1973). He pointed out that part of a project to promote industrialisation through a protective tariff structure was misdirected in that it would not result in efficient resource allocation and high returns to investment. He suggested that *efficient* industrialisation might be fostered through the establishment of a Productivity Centre, reform of the commercial law and rapid financial development.

A simplistic interpretation of the low weight attached to the expected rate of return on the donors' part might run as follows. In the early years of the post-war period, Afghanistan was so poor and so obviously short of capital that it was inconceivable that any assistance would not be of great value. Twenty-five years later, the pendulum had swung to the extreme pessimistic view: Afghanistan is still so poor and has so little potential for development that few projects can be expected to be successful. Nevertheless, the unequal struggle must continue for humanitarian and/or political reasons. The latter view seems to have been responsible, in part, for the relatively high proportion of grant to loan funds still available to Afghanistan from the United States Agency for International Development. Few projects with expected returns high enough to justify loan finance have been forthcoming. Thus, the majority of projects have been grant financed on the implicit admission that returns are likely to be low.

It would appear that the economic lessons expensively learnt over the past quarter of a century throughout the Third World have been lost on Afghanistan. Lack of expertise amongst donors and the Government is one explanation. It is surprising that the donor agencies themselves have had such small or non-existent economic intelligence staffs. The lack of library facilities and the lack of interest in their provision have been another impediment to benefiting from mistakes of other countries. This is particularly unfortunate in a country like Afghanistan which because of its position still at the early stages of the course has most other countries as examples out in front. However, in one of the most important respects, namely in the pursuit of policies which increase rather than reduce fragmentation, Afghanistan appears to have gone down the same path as so many other countries and seems likely to continue down it. The following passage is an apt description:

> .... the strategy of interventionism with fixed nominal prices and rationing on some critical markets seems to be a deliberate choice. "Market forces"

> are mistrusted on the grounds that elasticities of response to relative
> prices are thought to be too high or too low for desired outcomes, that
> markets are vulnerable to exploitation or that "this country is different."
> Although markets are mistrusted, there is faith in the capacity of the civil
> service—especially if it includes a planning commission—to identify and
> establish the economy's appropriate growth path. [S8, p. 14]

The introduction of price lists drawn up by the Government, minimum
wage legislation, and the promise of exchange controls under the new
Republican Regime is one more illustration of this phenomenon.

Underlying the lack of concern for the rate of return on investment is
an information system so designed that it provides planners with the
message that capital is not scarce, that therefore returns do not matter.
Interest charges on both foreign and domestic institutional credit are low
in Afghanistan and domestic rates have remained static. This is not
atypical of capital-scarce underdeveloped countries:

> Despite this revealed scarcity and productivity of unsophisticated rural
> investment, the standard nominal lending rate to protected manufacturing
> activity, and real estate promotion (such as hotel building) is 8 or 9 percent
> in Ethiopia's few urban areas. Importers borrow at rates closer to 6
> percent. Together with the government, these borrowers absorb virtually
> all of the banks' lending resources. The legal interest rate ceiling on bank
> loans is 12 percent, although little lending takes place at that rate; and
> the maximum interest rate on two-year time deposits is 7 percent a year,
> the average nominal interest rate on deposits being much lower than this.
> These huge interest differentials between organized banking and informal
> "rural" credit in Ethiopia are not unusually great relative to those in other
> LDCs [Less Developed Countries]. Inflation is moderate, and thus
> Ethiopian interest rates are at least significantly positive in real terms,
> unlike the rates in many Latin American countries. Nevertheless, the
> disparity between rates charged in urban enclaves and those in rural
> areas—the latter containing 80 to 90 percent of the population—is startling
> if not uncommon. [M7, p. 71]

> Statute, custom, and moral law against interest rates that rise "too high"
> are widespread in the lagging economies—and elsewhere, too. [S8, p. 93]

In Afghanistan this is nowhere truer than in rates of interest charged
to the public sector on its two-thirds share of domestic credit and on its
official loans from abroad. The distortion in the price of capital has
inevitably resulted not only in capital intensive development expenditure
but, given capital's low cost, a lack of concern over the degree of capital
utilisation. It is therefore predictable that a situation in which shift work
is almost non-existent, University classrooms are used for an average of

five hours a day for only nine months of the year and excess capacity exists in the majority of larger industrial plants can be found.

Since the start of the First Plan in 1335 (1956) the public sector has increased its share of institutional domestic credit from one-third to two-thirds of the total. This has created a credit squeeze in the bazaar economy and the modern private sector. High yielding small scale investments have not been undertaken because of lack of relatively small amounts of credit. This situation, again far from atypical, has become increasingly serious in Afghanistan as possibilities for the Green Revolution are opened up. The poor farmer finds it virtually impossible to finance

> .... from his current savings the whole of the balanced investment needed to adopt the new technology. Access to external financial resources is likely to be necessary over the one or two years when the change takes place. Without this access, the constraint of self-finance sharply biases investment strategy toward marginal variations within the traditional technology. [M7, p. 13]

The potential gain from almost every agricultural innovation recommended by the army of advisors in Afghanistan is qualified to the extent that the farmer adopts "recommended practices." That the Afghan farmer is capable of making changes and following rational economic incentive is no longer disputed:

> The major problems of Afghan agriculture do not lie in the psyches of the individual farmers, but in simple practical problems of the physical environment, of supplies, credit and markets. [B10, p. 97]

And yet, the Agricultural Development Bank (AgBank), itself only established in 1348 (1970), had domestic loans outstanding at the end of 1351 (March 1973) of Afs 384 million. Most of this tiny sum has been lent for tractor purchases. The median expected return on these investments as a whole calculated by the author from AgBank loan records lies in the range 50-70 per cent. With a down-payment of 25 per cent and an 8 per cent interest rate charged by the Bank, the return on the farmer's own outlay is three times the return on the investment as a whole. Yet, because of the absence of an adequate commercial law, default rates on these loans are critically high.

The criticism of low interest rates leading to inefficient investment in the public sector is supported by Johnson:

> Governments now often enjoy the privilege of paying a rate of interest of $2\frac{1}{2}$ or 3 per cent; this encourages them to think, and to plan, as if capital were easily available. There seems no reason why Governments should

enjoy low rates of interest when capital is scarce; on the contrary, it promotes wasteful investment and also, for reasons explained below, tends in the long run to promote inequality of income distribution .... It may be preferable to stimulate private saving by offering high interest rates, rather than by forcing savings into the hands of the state by taxation or inflation. One argument against a policy of low interest rates and forced saving is that it may in the long run contribute to the inequality of income distribution. The reason is that the poor or small savers are mainly confined to low-yielding fixed-interest investments, directly or indirectly in Government debt, because these are safe and easily available, whereas the larger savers can invest their money in higher-yielding stocks and shares or directly in profitable enterprises. There is, therefore, an opportunity here for Government both to stimulate saving for development and to improve the distribution of income. [J2, pp. 160-61]

The effects of the increase in low cost public sector borrowing in Afghanistan combined with an average annual rate of inflation of about 5 per cent since the start of the First Plan has been twofold. First, financial savings have remained low as witnessed by the apparent absence of any reduction in velocity. Second, this has compounded the effects of heavy public sector borrowing and its rapid increase in total domestic credit in creating a credit squeeze in the private sector. The resulting higher non-institutional interest rates in the private sector increase the misallocation effects of low interest rates to the public sector.

Deposit rates are low in part because of low public sector interest rates. Uncertain real deposit rates fluctuating around zero are a deterrent to financial saving. This leads to socially wasteful hoarding. McKinnon illustrates this as follows:

If the real return on holding money is low or negative, a significant proportion of the physical capital of the economy will be embodied in inventories of finished and semi-finished goods that are not used directly for production or consumption. A small farmer may keep unduly large rice inventories as the embodiment of his savings—a portion of which the rats eat every year. Alternatively, a wealthy member of some urban enclave may build an unusually elaborate house, which he hopes will also maintain its value under inflation. A businessman might deliberately "over-invest" in plant capacity or in certain stocks of raw materials, relative to his current operating needs. [M7, p. 63]

The few examples of returns to small scale investments in the private sector have served to illustrate the effects of the absorption of a slowly expanding supply of domestic credit by the public sector and highlight the great variance of returns to investment in Afghanistan. McKinnon suggests, in fact, that development can be viewed as a process of reducing this variance and by so doing raising the average return to capital:

> The accumulation of capital per se means little in the underdeveloped economy, where rates of return on some physical and financial assets are negative while extremely remunerative investment opportunities are forgone. One farmer may save by hoarding rice inventories, part of which is eaten by mice so that the return on his saving is negative. Another may foresee an annual return of over 60 percent in drilling a new tube well for irrigation, but the local moneylender wants 100 percent interest on any loan he provides. The operator of a small domestic machine shop may find it impossible to get bank credit to finance his inventories of finished goods and accounts receivable, whereas an exclusively licensed importer of competitive machine parts has easy access to foreign trade credit at a subsidized rate of 6 percent.
>
> In the face of great discrepancies in rates of return, it is a serious mistake to consider development as simply the accumulation of homogeneous capital of uniform productivity. This simplistic view has been held explicitly by economic growth theorists and econometricians who incorporate homogeneous capital of uniform productivity into production functions. It is held implicitly by policy-makers in less developed countries (LCDs), who all too often have followed a strategy of maximizing short-run gross investment in virtually any form. It has been abetted by official international agencies that calculate the "need" for foreign aid on the assumption that output-capital ratios in recipient countries are fixed.
>
> It seems important to develop a distinct alternative view of the role of capital. To focus the analysis still more narrowly, let us define "economic development" as the reduction of the great dispersion in social rates of return to existing and new investments under domestic entrepreneurial control. The capital market in a "developed" economy successfully monitors the efficiency with which the existing capital stock is deployed by pushing returns on physical and financial assets toward equality, thereby significantly increasing the average return. Economic development so defined is necessary and sufficient to generate high rates of saving and investment (accurately reflecting social and private time preference), the adoption of best-practice technologies, and learning-by-doing. [M7, pp. 8-9]

This process has not yet begun in Afghanistan.

viii. *Conclusion*

Domestic resource mobilisation through the fiscal system has exhibited as poor a record as mobilisation through the financial sector. The former has exacerbated the latter situation because deficit finance has been inflationary. Not only has this adversely affected the budgetary position but has also repressed financial development. Inflation has weakened the budgetary position as a result of lower revenue than expenditure price elasticity. It has repressed financial development by making the real return on the liabilities of the financial institutions negative. This in turn has depressed the demand for money. A further undesirable effect of excessive deficit finance on the financial system has been the rapid increase in the proportion of domestic credit allocated to the public sector. This has caused a serious credit squeeze in the private sector.

The fiscal system barely able to meet ordinary expenditure has been inadequate as the vehicle for underwriting development programmes. Inadequacies spring from a tax structure which has placed far too much reliance on foreign trade taxes, has failed to create an internal tax base and has been inefficiently administered. Despite considerable technical assistance to remedy the latter problem and much advice on the subject of tax reform, particularly in relation to the land tax, changes have been minimal. Again, a parallel between the fiscal system and the financial sector can be drawn. Actions necessary to mobilise domestic resources through both channels have generally been understood but have not been implemented.

Domestic resource mobilisation has not held great attractions because benefits from development expenditure have been small. Too little emphasis has been attached to the expected rate of return criterion, too much on completing projects at any cost. Where feasibility studies conducted by the donor agencies have indicated high rates of return, these were in the main based on over-optimistic assumptions. Uncertainty in many areas is so high in Afghanistan that such studies cannot be expected to provide clear guidelines to decision makers. It is also evident, however, that projects have generally not been well conceived and outcomes far less satisfactory than could have been achieved even given many of the unconducive attributes of the environment.

The conclusion is reached that reform, if it is to take place, must be directed simultaneously along two fronts. Both revenue and expenditure need to be encompassed in such a programme. The former should concentrate on raising revenue from sources other than the foreign trade sector, the latter on improving the planning process, in general, and project preparation and implementation, in particular. Without increasing the effectiveness of development expenditure, its expansion cannot be justified. Without tax reform the finance for vital ancillary investment will not be available and an over-reliance on foreign aid and deficit finance will again occur. Neither source is a satisfactory substitute for increased tax revenue from greater tax effort.

The material provided in this chapter amply attests to the proposition put forward in Chapter IV that the mode of development finance in Afghanistan with heavy reliance on foreign aid suggests the existence of two of the Adelman-Morris critical constraints. Both the weak tax effort and the nature of the development programme have indicated a lack of commitment on the part of leadership to economic development and the absence of general support for development efforts. Both have seriously limited Afghanistan's capacity for development.

CHAPTER SEVEN

THE FOREIGN TRADE SECTOR

i. *Introduction*

The removal of the critical constraints to economic development discussed in the previous chapters will raise Afghanistan's development potential. The realisation of this greater potential must be achieved in large part through the rapid expansion of exports. Therefore, this chapter describes the foreign trade and exchange systems that have existed to date and analyses the determinants of exchange rate movements.

The importance of foreign trade not only over the past forty years but also as the sole viable path to economic growth in the future has been recognised for some time:

> .... trade provided the earliest access road to the riches of the world without which no Afghan King or private investor could hope to increase the country's productive capacity. Because trade has been the traditional and most natural way of adding to the meager resources, it has assumed increasing importance as development efforts have become more intensive. Benefits from trade preceded any direct forms of international assistance from advanced countries. [F18, p. 16]

> .... only by intensive efforts to increase the production of exportable raw materials and by solving the problems related to marketing agricultural products can a high rate of growth in economic development of the country be maintained. [P10, p. 5]

Exchange control measures introduced immediately after the establishment of the Republic, presumably designed to prevent capital flight, threw the foreign trade sector into confusion. Although it is still not clear what the position is at the time of writing, mid-1352 (December 1973), exchange controls have been relaxed and traders seem more optimistic than they were some months ago. Their previous concern and uncertainty resulted in postponement of import orders in the hope that the situation would become clearer. The effect of this was an appreciation of the Afghani which in turn deterred exporters. What is referred to below as the present position is generally that which existed prior to the coup. A gradual return to that situation in the loosening of the exchange controls imposed informally immediately after the coup seems to have been occurring. The possibility of drastic changes in the foreign exchange and trade system in the future cannot, however, be discounted.

Table 7.1

Afghanistan's Foreign Trade 1309-1351

(Millions of Dollars)

Date	Exports (f.o.b.)	Imports (c.i.f.)	
		Total	Loan and Grant Component
1309	4.6	8.8	
1310	5.1	10.8	
1311	5.7	11.6	
1312	7.4	15.4	
1313	8.4	13.0	
1314	10.8	16.2	
1315	11.3	18.3	
1316	11.4	24.2	
1317	7.7	14.4	
1318	12.3	13.8	
1319	12.6	12.7	
1320	11.3	13.3	
1321	4.7	6.6	
1322	21.8	6.0	
1323	30.0	6.6	
1324	37.2	16.6	
1325	28.3	25.0	
1326	28.7	16.0	
1327	17.9	13.5	
1328	13.2	15.6	
1329	18.9	13.7	
1330	20.9	18.5	
1331	21.8	19.6	
1332	25.6	27.9	
1333	34.2	24.4	
1334	29.9	27.8	
1335	51.3	46.2	1.7
1336	58.9	57.5	10.3
1337	46.4	72.8	20.7
1338	60.4	80.9	35.9
1339	49.9	86.8	37.6
1340	53.4	99.1	50.0
1341	58.9	115.9	56.5
1342	69.0	125.7	63.8
1343	70.7	141.4	74.5
1344	70.0	131.0	74.5
1345	64.7	150.8	84.1
1346	66.4	138.5	75.4
1347	71.8	124.4	58.9
1348	81.9	124.7	52.2
1349	85.6	110.8	19.3
1350	99.6	167.4	52.6
1351	90.2	n.a.	n.a.

Source: 1309-1334 from *Da Afghanistan Bank Economic Bulletin*, (in Dari), 5 (1), August 1961, Table 18.

1335-1342 from Ministry of Commerce, *Afghanistan's Foreign Trade 1335 through 1342* (Kabul: Ministry of Commerce, 1343), Table 1, p. 1.

1343-1348 from Ministry of Commerce, *A Summary of Afghanistan's Foreign Trade from 1343 to 1348* (Kabul: Ministry of Commerce, Qaus 1350).

1349-1350 from Ministry of Commerce, *Exports of Merchandise from Afghanistan, 1349 and 1350* (Kabul: Ministry of Commerce, 1352), Table 1 and Ministry of Commerce, *Imports of Merchandise into Afghanistan, 1349 and 1350* (Kabul: Ministry of Commerce, 1352), Table 1.

1351 from *International Financial Statistics*, 26 (10), October 1973, p. 40.

ii. *Foreign Trade*

A Quantitative View of Foreign Trade Developments

Afghanistan's foreign trade sector has never been large. However, with a floating exchange rate and no quota system, foreign trade has generally grown at a faster rate than Gross National Product (GNP) under what has been essentially a liberal foreign trade policy. Although the official statistics seriously understate the volume of trade, these are presented in Table 7.1. Table 7.2 provides a rough GNP series for comparative purposes. From this it can be seen that recorded exports have never exceeded 10 per cent of GNP, a relatively low percentage for a small country.

The peak in imports as a percentage of GNP in the first half of the 1340s (1960s) reflects the heyday of competitive foreign aid donations. The trough in exports as a percentage of GNP in 1345 (1966) coincides with the highest export taxes over the period on karakul which in turn was a result of rapid depreciation over the preceding two years, thus widening the gap between the fixed surrender rate and the free market exchange rate. The depreciating free market exchange rate was caused by domestic inflation. Two studies on the determinants of karakul exports indicate a strong negative relationship between the value of exports and the effective tax rate [G8; K7].

Tables 7.3 and 7.4 provide a somewhat more disaggregated picture of the direction of Afghanistan's foreign trade and composition of exports for the period 1331 to 1350 (1952-1971).

Fluctuations in the proportion of exports to "other countries" is closely correlated to karakul exports which go solely to convertible currency countries. Afghanistan auctions its karakul on the London market where the main buyers have been from Germany. The trends in total exports have shown a slight increase to the barter countries, reflecting increases in cotton, natural gas and wool exports to the U.S.S.R., fluctuations in trade with India and Pakistan, an effect of political

Table 7.2

Foreign Trade in Relation to Gross National Product 1314-1351

(Millions of Afghanis)

Date	Gross National Product (GNP)	Exports (f.o.b.)	Exports as a Percentage of GNP	Imports (c.i.f.)	Imports as a Percentage of GNP
1314	2,493	108	4.3	162	6.5
1315	2,558	110	4.3	178	7.0
1316	2,740	111	4.1	235	8.6
1317	2,909	87	3.0	162	5.6
1318	3,084	148	4.8	166	5.4
1319	3,399	165	4.9	166	4.9
1320	3,726	148	4.0	174	4.7
1321	4,683	61	1.3	86	1.8
1322	6,038	285	4.7	78	1.3
1323	7,659	391	5.1	86	1.1
1324	9,596	486	5.1	216	2.3
1325	12,135	388	3.2	342	2.8
1326	13,432	494	3.7	275	2.0
1327	13,963	482	3.5	364	2.6
1328	16,040	436	2.7	515	3.2
1329	17,306	739	4.3	533	3.1
1330	18,015	731	4.1	646	3.6
1331	19,053	806	4.2	727	3.8
1332	19,449	950	4.9	1,036	5.3
1333	21,778	1,440	6.6	1,027	4.7
1334	24,491	1,352	5.5	1,255	5.1
1335	31,320	2,775	8.9	2,501	8.0
1336	34,262	3,156	9.2	3,082	9.0
1337	34,856	2,486	7.1	3,898	11.2
1338	30,999	2,722	8.8	3,650	11.8
1339	29,211	1,950	6.7	3,392	11.6
1340	31,120	2,222	7.1	4,124	13.3
1341	37,151	2,968	8.0	5,841	15.7
1342	40,121	3,459	8.6	6,303	15.7
1343	50,789	4,152	8.2	8,304	16.3
1344	62,652	5,025	8.0	9,407	15.0
1345	68,814	4,835	7.0	11,271	16.4
1346	69,877	5,018	7.2	10,454	15.0
1347	69,151	5,348	7.7	9,267	13.4
1348	72,391	6,180	8.5	9,410	13.0
1349	84,363	7,160	8.5	9,271	11.0
1350	91,146	8,427	9.2	14,155	15.5
1351	93,554	7,162	7.7	n.a.	n.a.

Source: Gross National Product—Table 2.14 above.
Foreign Trade—1314-1334 from *Da Afghanistan Bank Economic Bulletin*, (in Dari), 5 (1), August 1961, Table 18; 1335-1342 from Ministry of Commerce, *Afghanistan's Foreign Trade 1335 through 1342* (Kabul: Ministry of Commerce, 1343), Table 1-A, p. 75; 1343-1348 from Ministry of Commerce, *A Summary of Afghanistan's Foreign*

Trade from 1343 to 1348 (Kabul: Ministry of Commerce, Qaus 1350); 1349-1350 from Ministry of Commerce, Exports of Merchandise from Afghanistan, 1349 and 1350 (Kabul: Ministry of Commerce, 1352), Table 1 and Ministry of Commerce, Imports of Merchandise into Afghanistan, 1349 and 1350 (Kabul: Ministry of Commerce, 1352), Table 1; 1351 from International Financial Statistics, 26 (10), October 1973, p. 40.

Table 7.3

Direction of Trade, 1331-1350

(Percentages)

	EXPORTS			IMPORTS (Excluding Loan and Grant Imports)		
Date	Barter Countries	India and Pakistan	Other Countries	Barter Countries	India and Pakistan	Other Countries
1331	31.9	26.3	41.8	n.a.	n.a.	n.a.
1332	12.6	39.1	48.3	n.a.	n.a.	n.a.
1333	18.8	36.7	44.5	25.2	41.4	33.4
1334	13.7	40.8	45.5	29.2	42.2	28.6
1335	34.9	24.4	40.7	36.6	35.2	28.2
1336	35.8	24.2	40.0	30.6	25.8	43.6
1337	28.8	29.9	41.3	32.5	20.4	47.1
1338	30.0	24.3	45.7	37.9	23.1	39.0
1339	28.0	23.3	48.7	33.9	24.0	42.1
1340	36.1	12.3	51.6	42.6	20.6	36.8
1341	44.5	13.5	42.0	45.8	15.1	39.1
1342	40.8	18.8	40.4	35.3	19.9	44.8
1343	37.9	25.0	37.1	35.1	19.4	45.5
1344	27.5	20.8	51.7	42.0	15.9	42.1
1345	38.3	21.4	40.3	42.0	17.0	41.0
1346	37.4	24.6	38.0	34.7	15.2	50.1
1347	39.3	29.9	30.8	26.3	21.8	51.9
1348	40.2	26.1	33.7	21.7	20.5	57.8
1349	41.0	23.0	36.0	31.4	17.7	50.9
1350	41.1	10.0	48.9	23.2	13.0	63.8

Source: 1331-1334 from P. G. Franck, The Economics of Competitive Coexistence: Afghanistan Between East and West (Washington, D.C.: National Planning Association, 1960), Tables II-4 and II-6, pp. 19-20.
1335-1350 Same as Tables 7.1 and 7.2

disputes with Pakistan, but a slight increase over the period, resulting from increased exports of dried and fresh fruits and nuts.

On the import side, there has been a significant increase in the proportion of commercial imports from "other countries," created by a large increase in manufactured imports from them, particularly from Japan, and a decrease in textile imports from the other two groups of countries. Additionally, sugar and tea imports have not risen as rapidly as total imports. In general, the barter countries, India and Pakistan have lost

Table 7.4

Composition of Exports, 1331-1350

(Percentages)

Date	Cotton	Karakul	Wool	Natural Gas	Other
1331	29.0	15.9	18.0	0	37.1
1332	17.8	17.5	15.7	0	49.0
1333	17.2	21.4	13.0	0	48.4
1334	10.4	21.6	10.9	0	57.1
1335	17.1	27.6	14.3	0	41.0
1336	21.5	26.1	12.6	0	39.8
1337	12.4	26.8	15.2	0	45.6
1338	12.7	28.8	16.1	0	42.4
1339	9.7	27.8	14.1	0	48.4
1340	15.6	28.6	11.4	0	44.4
1341	14.3	20.3	12.9	0	52.5
1342	18.3	24.4	10.7	0	46.6
1343	21.1	17.6	8.7	0	52.6
1344	15.9	23.0	2.8	0	58.3
1345	18.4	18.1	7.7	0	55.8
1346	11.8	21.2	7.3	4.4	55.3
1347	8.2	11.6	9.7	12.6	57.9
1348	6.8	15.9	8.2	14.8	54.3
1349	9.9	11.8	8.8	16.9	52.6
1350	12.5	17.3	8.0	14.6	47.6

Source: Same as Tables 7.1, 7.2 and 7.3.

ground because their exports (apart from petrol from Russia) have tended to be those with low income elasticities, whereas manufactured goods from the West have high income elasticities of demand.

Two attempts have been made to decompose imports into capital

Table 7.5

Composition of Imports, 1347-1348

(Percentages)

	1347		1348	
	All Imports	Commercial Imports only	All Imports	Commercial Imports only
Consumer Goods	34.4	61.9	55.7	77.4
Intermediate Goods	27.3	22.7	20.6	15.6
Capital Goods	38.4	15.4	23.7	7.0

Source: 1347 from United Nations, *Statistical Yearbook for Asia and the Far East 1970* (Bangkok: United Nations, 1971), p. 15.

1348 prepared by R. Manly for this study from Ministry of Commerce, *Imports of Merchandise 1348* (Kabul: Ministry of Commerce, 1349).

goods, raw materials and consumer goods. Unfortunately, these are
frustrated by the fact that no details on the composition of loan and grant
imports are available. On the assumption, however, that two-thirds of
these unspecified imports are capital goods and one-third consists of raw
materials the estimates in Table 7.5 have been derived. It should be stressed
that the estimates are not comparable since arbitrary definitions were used

Table 7.6

Export Distribution of Ten Selected Commodities, 1345-1348

(Thousands of Dollars)

Commodity		1345		1346		1347		1348	
			%		%		%		%
Dried Fruit	M	1,796	(12)	2,709	(15)	4,336	(23)	1,967	(10)
and Nuts	B	7,869	(51)	7,922	(44)	3,707	(20)	6,792	(35)
	C	5,597	(37)	7,378	(41)	10,917	(57)	10,697	(55)
Karakul	M	11,713	(100)	14,058	(100)	8,323	(100)	13,051	(100)
Skins	B	—		—		4	(–)	—	
	C	—		—		—		—	
Natural	M	—		—		—		—	
Gas	B	—		2,928	(100)	9,034	(100)	12,142	(100)
	C	—		—		—		—	
Fresh	M	—		—		26	(–)	7	(–)
Fruit	B	16	(–)	52	(1)	153	(2)	220	(2)
	C	6,537	(100)	8,097	(99)	7,834	(98)	8,709	(98)
Wool	M	346	(7)	573	(12)	580	(8)	507	(8)
	B	4,630	(93)	4,243	(87)	6,408	(92)	6,215	(92)
	C	1	(–)	42	(1)	3	(–)	—	
Carpets and	M	7,996	(100)	5,173	(100)	4,522	(100)	6,238	(100)
Rugs	B	—		1	(–)	—		—	
	C	—		—		—		—	
Raw	M	990	(8)	—		—		984	(18)
Cotton	B	10,910	(92)	7,857	(100)	5,882	(100)	4,623	(82)
	C	—		3	(–)	—		—	
Oil	M	20	(2)	68	(8)	399	(14)	832	(32)
Seed	B	400	(39)	505	(56)	1,663	(60)	1,570	(61)
	C	603	(59)	326	(36)	738	(26)	179	(7)
Hides and	M	1,457	(61)	1,198	(50)	1,001	(44)	1,609	(55)
Skins	B	908	(38)	1,179	(50)	1,206	(53)	1,316	(45)
	C	13	(1)	5	(–)	61	(3)	—	
Casings	M	1,412	(97)	1,232	(96)	1,025	(93)	932	(95)
	B	40	(3)	48	(4)	82	(7)	46	(5)
	C	—		—		—		—	

Note: M—Multilateral; B—Barter; C—India and Pakistan.

Source: Ministry of Commerce, *A Summary of Afghanistan's Foreign Trade from
1343 to 1348* (Kabul: Ministry of Commerce, Qaus 1350).

in both cases to classify individual items into one of the three categories. Nevertheless, the very substantial decline in foreign aid financed imports between 1347 and 1348 (1968 and 1969) does support the direction of change in the composition of imports over these years indicating a substantial decline in capital goods and raw material imports. Classification inconsistencies, however, probably account for a sizable part of the

Table 7.7

Import Distribution of Ten Selected Commodities, 1345-1348

(Thousands of Dollars)

Commodity		1345	%	1346	%	1347	%	1348	%
Wheat	M	13,129	(100)	8,852	(62)	3	(–)	6,710	(100)
	B	—		5,456	(38)	3,460	(100)	—	
	C	—		—		—		—	
Sugar	M	9	(–)	7	(–)	16	(2)	23	(1)
	B	8,816	(100)	5,319	(100)	929	(98)	3,839	(99)
	C	28	(–)	5	( )	—		—	
Tea	M	128	(2)	51	(1)	29	(–)	210	(2)
	B	2,155	(35)	915	(19)	869	(9)	1,045	(11)
	C	3,799	(63)	3,866	(80)	8,585	(91)	8,091	(87)
Petroleum	M	682	(12)	559	(10)	1,290	(20)	969	(13)
Products	B	4,773	(86)	4,654	(87)	4,773	(75)	6,113	(82)
	C	85	(2)	140	(3)	344	(5)	387	(5)
Pharma-	M	2,258	(99)	2,504	(99)	2,462	(98)	3,423	(99)
ceutical	B	26	(1)	36	(1)	37	(2)	33	(1)
Products	C	2	(–)	1	(–)	2	(–)	1	(–)
Rubber Tyres	M	2,785	(91)	3,600	(94)	2,623	(93)	2,735	(90)
and Tubes	B	203	(7)	203	(5)	208	(7)	260	(8)
	C	51	(2)	14	(1)	5	(–)	57	(2)
Textile	M	4,246	(48)	4,599	(53)	5,340	(58)	4,934	(53)
Fabrics	B	1,714	(20)	1,904	(22)	2,163	(24)	2,515	(27)
	C	2,792	(32)	2,163	(25)	1,684	(18)	1,929	(20)
Machinery	M	3,114	(81)	3,012	(87)	3,348	(83)	3,405	(81)
	B	525	(14)	311	(9)	339	(8)	330	(8)
	C	211	(5)	156	(4)	341	(9)	442	(11)
Motor	M	1,919	(63)	1,117	(44)	362	(17)	2,135	(63)
Vehicles	B	1,151	(37)	1,401	(56)	1,727	(83)	1,248	(37)
	C	—		—		8	(–)	—	
Other	M	3,735	(57)	4,217	(60)	5,562	(62)	9,721	(69)
Manufactured	B	1,886	(29)	1,961	(28)	2,451	(27)	3,072	(22)
Goods	C	912	(14)	801	(12)	996	(11)	1,343	(9)

Note: M—Multilateral; B—Barter; C—India and Pakistan.
Source: Same as Table 7.6.

reduction in the share of capital goods imports in commercial imports. A more detailed picture of composition and direction of trade for the period 1345-1348 (1966-1969) is provided by the figures given in Tables 7.6 and 7.7.

The amount of smuggling obviously cannot be estimated with any accuracy. However, it is known that many items are officially imported into Afghanistan for unofficial re-export to Pakistan. In return, wheat has been smuggled into Afghanistan from Pakistan. From the west of the country, large numbers of sheep have been smuggled into Iran. The value of smuggled goods has been estimated at about one-fifth of the value of total commercial trade [R9, p. 95; S13, pp. 328-29]. As shown later, this is probably an underestimate.

B The Foreign Trade System

The basis of Afghanistan's foreign trade system is a floating exchange rate for most items and a fixed rate for a small group of commodities. There have been a number of transfers of items between one group and the other, the most important being in 1342 (1963) and 1344 (1965) when items were transferred from the fixed exchange rate group to the floating rate group. In 1345 (1966), the Government Monopoly and public and

Table 7.8
Official International Reserves, 1335-1351
(Millions of Dollars)

1335	59.0
1336	65.0
1337	60.0
1338	55.0
1339	50.0
1340	42.3
1341	40.5
1342	45.5
1343	44.5
1344	45.3
1345	46.9
1346	38.3
1347	39.1
1348	41.2
1349	45.7
1350	60.6
1351	56.2

Source: *International Financial Statistics*, 26 (10), October 1973, p. 40; *International Financial Statistics: 1972 Supplement*, pp. 228-29.

private industry were no longer able to obtain foreign exchange at the fixed official rate. The reverse process had been taking place for several years prior to 1342 (1963). As an attempt to limit the extent of depreciation caused by inflationary levels of deficit finance in the 1330s (1950s), large losses of official foreign exchange reserves occurred, a list of prohibited imports was drawn up and a number of exports transferred to the fixed exchange group, whose earnings have to be surrendered to Da Afghanistan Bank, with the objective of providing cheaper foreign exchange for essential and Government imports. The fixed rates have always been below the floating rate except for a short time towards the end of 1351 (1973) when the fixed rate for karakul remained at Afs 70 to the Dollar for a few weeks after the devaluation of the Dollar; the Afghani appreciated to Afs 68 to the Dollar at that time.

Table 7.8 above presents estimates of official international reserves. The drain in reserves between 1345 (1966) and 1346 (1967) is noticeable, although in relation to the value of foreign trade they have always been ample. In fact, in the previous chapter it was suggested that they have considerably exceeded the level which might be regarded as optimal.

Table 7.9

Average Duties by Sector in 1352 Based on 1348 Imports

(Percentages)

	All dutiable goods	Goods for which there are no local producers	Goods for which there are local producers
All Dutiable Goods	37.0	38.9	34.1
Capital Goods	22.4	18.5	45.3
Intermediate Goods	33.1	35.3	20.5
Consumer Goods	39.2	43.0	34.9
Essential	(38.4)	(51.7)	(24.2)
Less Essential	(40.1)	(33.8)	(47.4)

Source: R. Manly, *Afghanistan: Report and Tables to Accompany Recommended Revised Customs Tariff Based on SITC Codes* (Kabul: Checchi and Company, mimeo, April 1973), Table III, p. 28.

The par value of Afs 45 to the SDR was agreed with the International Monetary Fund in 1341 (1963). Prior to then, there had been two official rates, one at Afs 20 to the Dollar, the other at Afs 28 to the Dollar, since 1335 (1956) [13, pp. 228-29]. The second rate was known as the industrial rate.

Tariffs range from zero to 100 per cent. The average import duty rate on all dutiable imports in 1352 (1973) was 37 per cent. A recent detailed study on the tariff structure brings to light several anomalies: a high average duty on essential goods for which there is no local production [M3, pp. 27-28], and a bias against local industry:

> Private industry pays the same average duty (35.3%) on imported intermediate goods and where such industry produces essential personal goods, it must compete with traders who pay only a 24.2 percent average duty on such goods. In this case, there is an unfavourable spread of minus 11 percent on the imports involved. [M3, p. 32]

This phenomenon can be clearly seen from the figures in Table 7.9. For a detailed analysis of the tariff structure the interested reader is referred to this study [M3]. At present, in 1352 (1973) twenty unimportant items (see Appendix C) are banned from importation. These include wood furniture, "soft" dyes and certain items prohibited for religious reasons.

Table 7.10

Effective Export Taxes on Cotton, Karakul and Wool, 1335-1350

(Percentages)

Date	Cotton	Karakul	Wool
1335		55.0	
1336		55.2	
1337		48.3	
1338		41.2	
1339		41.8	
1340		48.3	
1341		50.4	
1342		40.5	
1343		57.8	
1344	51.8	43.4	50.9
1345	53.2	41.9	51.0
1346	45.5	40.6	49.9
1347	15.4	27.3	38.0
1348	13.5	12.1	25.7
1349	13.7	19.9	32.2
1350	19.8	25.6	37.0

Source: 1335-1343 from A. H. Kayoumy, "Monopoly Pricing of Afghan Karakul in International Markets," *Journal of Political Economy*, 77 (2), March/April 1969, Table 1, p. 221.

1344-1350 from Research Department, Da Afghanistan Bank.

Earnings from the export of cotton, karakul and wool must be surrendered to Da Afghanistan Bank. Prior to 1352 (1973), the surrender was made at fixed rates. The effective tax which this requirement has levied on exports to convertible currency countries is shown in Table 7.10 above. In 1352 (1973), the system was modified so that the surrender of earnings on cotton and karakul was made at the free market rate unless that rate rose above Afs 70 and Afs 75 to the Dollar, respectively, in which case these fixed rates would apply. Wool was still to be surrendered at Afs 65 to the Dollar. Cotton and wool are also exported to the barter countries at a fixed surrender rate of Afs 60 to the clearing Dollar. Since data on the bazaar rates for clearing currencies are unavailable, effective export tax rates cannot be calculated. However, virtually all wool and a large proportion of cotton has in the past been exported to the barter countries, suggesting that effective export duties have not been so high here. Indeed, during the balance of payments crisis in the first half of the 1340s (1960s) exporters of cotton were actually required to export at least 20 per cent of their cotton to convertible currency countries. This restriction was lifted in 1346 (1967).

Much advice has been given to the Government by foreign advisory groups to abolish the discriminatory export taxes in the form of the fixed rate surrender requirements. However, this did not take place until 1352 (1973) since alternative revenue sources could not be found. The Government has also been advised to abandon the non-discriminatory export taxes but less has been heard on this since the equivalence of non-discriminatory import and export taxation, discovered so long ago [L2] and restated forcefully more recently [M6; M7, pp. 133-34], was brought to the attention to those dispensing advice on such matters.

Private capital transfers are in principle controlled since exporters are obliged by law to sell their foreign exchange earnings to Da Afghanistan Bank or one of its authorised agents (i.e. Bank Millie or Pashtany Tejaraty Bank) or to use it to import an equivalent value of goods. In fact, exporters are even required to sign an undertaking to this effect when goods are brought to the customs house. However, in practice there has been no control over capital movements. It is known that considerable capital has left Afghanistan for Europe and North America.

The banks have been unfavourably affected by the foreign exchange controls. Since 1343 (1964) payments for imports through the banking system could only be made under letters of credit for which 100 per cent pre-payment in Afghanis had to be made. As the exchange controls were relaxed banks began providing loans against these letters of credit. They now freely sell cheques and make payments by telegraphic transfers, as do the foreign exchange dealers. However, they are not permitted to accept bills for collection.

Liberalisation has also taken place with a reduction in the Government's direct involvement in foreign trade. Until 1348 (1969) the Monopoly Department was responsible for a wide range of imports. In this year, however, it was split into three departments, namely, petrol, sugar and liquidation. The monopoly privileges are now sold for a 10 per cent licence fee for all but petrol and sugar imports which are the only items still imported by the Monopoly.

So far, the major elements of the foreign trade system have been covered. To complete this general picture, a short description of the particular systems of trade with the barter countries and India and Pakistan is necessary.

By far the most important barter trading partner is the U.S.S.R. China and Czechoslovakia follow with Bulgaria, Hungary, Poland and Yugoslavia as minor trading partners. Annual protocols are negotiated with each barter country in which the quantities of the goods to be bartered are set out. Prices of cotton, wool and various other commodities are also established. Trade is initiated in the main by private enterprise in Afghanistan. Traders negotiate export/import packages within the protocol agreement with the Soviet Trade Mission in Afghanistan. Letters of credit for Afghan exports are opened through the Bank for Foreign Trade of the U.S.S.R. and the trader's clearing account (denominated in Sterling for China, Dollars for all the other barter countries) with Da Afghanistan Bank is credited. Theoretically, the trader then imports an equivalent value under similar financial arrangements and his balance is debited. In the case of cotton and wool exports the trader receives an Afghani sum converted at the particular fixed rate existing at the time for the commodity and the clearing currency is made available for Government imports of petrol, sugar and other items actually required by the public sector. The main use to which this exchange is put, however, is debt service.

Swing balances have been created with each barter trading partner. These enable excess export or import within the maximum set by the swing to take place without any interest charges. For example, the swing balance with the U.S.S.R. enables Afghanistan to have imported up to $C1 million more than she has exported without penalty and *vice versa*. Net imports in excess of this are subject to a 2 per cent overdraft charge on the outstanding balance. The other barter countries charge 3 per cent on the excess. The bilateral trade balances are presented in Table 7.11.

In 1349 (1970) the swing balance with the U.S.S.R. fell from $C0.48 million to —$C4.37 million. This was the result of a fairly complicated set of circumstances. There was an unforeseen shortfall in cotton exports. Government purchases from the U.S.S.R. had already been made before

Table 7.11

Bilateral Trade Balances, 1335-1350

(Millions of Clearing Dollars, End of Year Figures)

Date	U.S.S.R.	Czecho-slovakia	Poland	China	Total
1335	−2.87	−0.42	—	—	−3.29
1336	+0.73	−2.30	+0.08	—	−1.49
1337	−0.36	−1.54	+0.02	—	−1.88
1338	−0.07	−2.35	+0.16	+0.14	−2.12
1339	−3.53	−3.11	+0.04	+0.07	−6.53
1340	−4.26	−3.58	+0.10	+0.20	−7.54
1341	−4.92	−3.05	+0.02	+0.12	−7.82
1342	−1.90	−0.86	+0.59	+0.13	−2.04
1343	−2.34	+1.25	+0.62	+0.05	−0.42
1344	+1.88	—	+0.50	−0.05	+2.34
1345	+1.33	−0.40	+0.31	−0.06	+1.20
1346	−1.83	+0.61	−0.02	+0.07	−1.18
1347	+0.19	+0.43	−0.31	−0.10	+0.18
1348	+0.48	+0.72	−0.43	+0.40	+1.04
1349	−4.37	+0.35	−0.51	−0.12	4.79
1350	−5.74	+0.75	−0.19	+0.23	−5.11

Source: Research Department, Da Afghanistan Bank.

it was realised that revenue from cotton sales would not be forthcoming
to pay for them. Government enterprises increased their imports from the
U.S.S.R. in this particular year and certain non-trade items moved
unfavourably.

Trade with the U.S.S.R. has been generally more attractive to Afghan
traders than trade with the convertible currency countries [F18, pp. 26-27].
Indeed, in Jauza 1352 (June 1973), the clearing Dollar sold for Afs 72 per
Dollar in the money bazaar compared to Afs 61 for the United States
Dollar. In the latest agreement, the price established for cotton was $C800
per ton at an official exchange rate of Afs 70 to the clearing Dollar, with
the world price lying around $600 per ton at that time. The world price
has subsequently risen to over $2,000 per ton. Wool was sold to the
U.S.S.R. at $C1,300 per ton; the quality is so poor that there was not
much of a market for it in the West. However, the price was raised
substantially recently as world prices rose and wool began to be smuggled
out of Afghanistan to the West towards the end of 1351 (1973). Whether
the price paid for natural gas is generous has been subject to considerable
dispute. It has been suggested that the projects for which the gas earnings
are paying have been so unsatisfactory that the bargain is a very poor one.

On the import side, prices are generally favourable. The average price for sugar over the past four years has been $C95 per ton compared with a world price of $135 to $200 per ton. But recently supplies have been reduced because of the high world market price. Green tea, vehicles, books and petrol have also been imported at below world prices.

Da Afghanistan Bank's exchange rates used with the barter countries were Afs 70 to the clearing Dollar with the U.S.S.R., Afs 220 to the clearing pound Sterling with China and Afs 65 to the clearing Dollar with the other barter countries in 1352 (1973). These rates form the basis for the effective export tax on the export of cotton and wool to these countries through the fixed rate surrender requirements. Although changed several times, these rates have also indicated Da Afghanistan Bank's buying rates since it began dealing in clearing currencies in 1343 (1964). However, bazaar rates are also quoted for each clearing currency which have often differed considerably from Da Afghanistan Bank's fixed rates. The sales of clearing currencies in the money bazaars are mainly limited to the proceeds of consumer loan funds from China and the U.S.S.R.

Trade with India and Pakistan is conducted in inconvertible Rupees. In 1336 (1957) India began restricting its imports from Afghanistan and three methods of payment were instigated in 1344 (1965), namely, payment in inconvertible Rupees, payment through a special self-balancing account maintained by Da Afghanistan Bank with the State Bank of India and payment through letters of credit in convertible Dollars or Sterling. The second method is used for proceeds from Afghanistan's exports of hides and skins and India's exports of a range of specified commodities. The third method is used for exports of Afghan cotton and wool and Indian capital and durable consumer goods. In 1347 (1968) value limits previously set by India were abandoned in favour of quantity controls. The majority of trade with India and Pakistan is conducted in Rupees, the export and import of which are theoretically prohibited. Nevertheless, large values of Rupees are traded daily on the money bazaars of Kabul and Kandahar.

Under the latest agreement exports of fresh and dried fruits and nuts are valued at Indian customs houses. This agreement also sets a limit to Afghan/Indian trade with a maximum percentage of this being set aside for tea imports into Afghanistan. This limit is designed to prevent tea re-exports to Pakistan. In fact, lower quality tea has to be paid for in convertible currency since this is the type most commonly re-exported.

Official trade with Pakistan has become freer since the introduction of self-balancing accounts in Da Afghanistan Bank and the State Bank of Pakistan [F10, p. 10].

A discussion of Afghanistan's foreign trade would be incomplete without reference to the problems of transit trade arising from the fact that Afghanistan is a land locked country. A large part of the trade has taken place through Pakistan, which the continuing dispute over Pushtunistan has at times seriously jeopardised. Both Dupree and Fletcher provide excellent histories of the Pushtunistan issue [D10, Chapters 22-24; F9, Chapter 17]. The dispute has resulted in the disruption of transit trade or border closure in 1326 (1947), 1330 (1951), 1334 (1955) and 1340-1342 (1961-1963) [D10, Chapters 22-24; F9, pp. 275-76; F18, p. 24]. Because of this, trade through the U.S.S.R. has expanded. For both routes, however, costs are high and the time taken for shipment long and unpredictable. With overcrowding in the port of Karachi becoming increasingly serious, the agreement over transit trade through Iran to the Persian Gulf reached in 1353 (1974) bodes well. For rapid expansion of foreign trade, improvement in transit trade facilities by one means or another is essential.

iii. *Financing Foreign Trade*

Since their establishment, a major function of Bank Millie, Da Afghanistan Bank and Pashtany Tejaraty Bank has been export finance. Indeed, the absence of security and efficient court procedures discussed in Chapter V strongly deters these banks from lending for other purposes. All three banks compete to furnish loans for karakul exports. Because of the exchange surrender requirements and karakul valuation and grading conducted by the Karakul Institute, these export loans are the safest.

Cotton loans consist of money actually provided by Da Afghanistan Bank but distributed by Pashtany Tejaraty Bank on its behalf. Export loans are also made for carpets and dried fruit and nuts. The banks have been aided by the Carpet Institute with respect to carpet valuation, although Pashtany Tejaraty Bank still uses its own staff with apparently unfortunate consequences. Loans several times the value of the carpets have been given, thus providing no incentive on the part of the exporter to realise a sale. Pashtany Tejaraty Bank has apparently been faced with many defaults on the excuse that the carpet market has slumped and sales cannot be made. Since the establishment of the Institute, this has not been the experience of the other banks. Nevertheless, non-sale of exports provides the main risk to the lending institution.

Export loans against exports to barter countries are generally quite safe since earnings have to pass through Da Afghanistan Bank. However, occasional problems arise when the exports are not sold immediately and

payments pass through the Bank in instalments. Administrative inefficiencies can then lead to a failure to inform the lending institution of the
repatriation of funds.

Da Afghanistan Bank theoretically accepts bills of exchange for
discount to finance exports but the relevant department in the Bank is
now moribund. Security was provided by the fact that the Bank could
ensure that the trader lost his licence, thus preventing him from making
any more exports, in the event of default. The only major risk here lay
in the possibility of bankruptcy. Bills were generally discounted for three
to six months at an annual interest rate of $7\frac{1}{4}$ per cent and could be
extended for additional periods at double that rate.

Karakul is sold at auctions and thus requires financing until the time
of auction. Carpets are also exported for direct sale abroad. Sales of most
other exports, however, are negotiated before shipment. In these cases,
payment is normally made at the time goods pass through customs.
Thus, export finance is generally only required for local procurement
and processing prior to shipment. Cotton companies receive credit from
Da Afghanistan Bank for this purpose and the AgBank has made loans
to agro-business by lending against letters of credit placed with them by
foreign companies in advance of delivery.

On the import side, the variety of financing methods is considerably
greater. The banks do extend import loans but finance is also provided by
foreign exchange dealers, trade agencies and the suppliers themselves.
Payments are made through letters of credit, telegraphic transfers and
cheques to the convertible currency countries, letters of credit to the
barter countries and cash, cheques, letters of credit and *hundis* to India
and Pakistan.

The banks generally prefer to extend import loans against letters of
credit opened by them. In the case of barter countries, all letters of
credit are opened by Da Afghanistan Bank. After communication with
the Bank to confirm the existence of the letters of credit, the other banks
will make loans against them. Letters of credit are relatively expensive
in that a one per cent commission is charged and an annual interest rate
of 10 per cent is levied on any credit extended against the letter. Furthermore, the foreign exchange often costs Afs 1 to Afs 1.50 per Dollar more
in the bank than in the bazaar.

Import credit from the money bazaars generally takes the form of loans
against *hawalas* or *hundis*. These are simple drafts drawn on corresponding
traders in India, Iran and Pakistan by Afghan traders and foreign
exchange dealers. This is the usual method of making payments between

these countries. The banking system is hardly used at all for Rupee transactions. The purchase of such a draft normally includes a one per cent commission. Deferred payment naturally includes an interest charge which ranges from one per cent a month for first class risk borrowers through rates of two or three per cent to much higher figures for small scale operators. Foreign exchange dealers often have facilities for opening letters of credit and some have sufficiently good credit standing that their foreign bankers will open letters against a 30 per cent deposit. This is important for trade with Japan as Japanese suppliers insist on full payment in advance. Thus, credit is sometimes obtained from foreign banks to finance imports.

There are a number of trade agencies in Kabul acting on behalf of suppliers from their own country. Since 1344 (1965), foreign trade agencies have only been permitted to import from their own country, a special exception being made in the case of Indamer which is permitted to import Landrovers from Britain. Afghan trade agencies, on the other hand, are permitted to import from any country. The foreign trade agencies generally play an important role in the financing of imports from their country and do provide certain banking services. The demand for these arises from the prohibition on banks from accepting bills for collection. The credit standing of the foreign trade agency usually allows it to obtain supplier credit on a 25 per cent down payment with the balance on receipt, or three months after shipment, basis. Similarly, the Afghan-International Trade Agency recently obtained a guarantee from its Swiss bank which enables it to import on these terms. Thus, trade agencies import on commission for other traders who cannot obtain such favourable financing arrangements, because of the banks' inability to accept bills for collection. Indeed, the intention of this prohibition was precisely to prevent traders obtaining supplier credit. Trade agencies tend to prefer making payment by cheque since this is cheaper and more flexible than payment through letters of credit.

Trade agencies acting on commission are, of course, completely secured in that full payment is always insisted upon before the imported goods are actually released to the trader. Since the agencies also act on their own accounts, few problems are created in the rare event of a trader not producing the balance for his consignment. As most trade agencies export as well as import, they generally accept payments for imports on commission in domestic currency converted at the prevailing free market rate. Interestingly, trade agencies will not act on commission for the public sector without full payment in advance. The public sector has a notoriously bad record for settling accounts both with the trade agencies and foreign suppliers.

Capital imports sometimes receive medium term supplier credit. However, Afghanistan does not rank as a sufficiently important market to generate much competition in this respect. Nevertheless, good terms are reported for capital imports from China and the U.S.S.R. There are no "mixed credit" arrangements [H7] although, of course, a considerable volume of capital imports is financed by foreign aid.

iv. *Kabul and Kandahar Money Bazaars*

The history of foreign exchange dealing in Afghanistan can be traced back many centuries to the time when the great overland trade routes passed through the country. Despite steady decline since then, it has been only within the past fifty years that a series of events seriously disrupted the foreign exchange markets to a point of near extinction. In the past seven years, however, the markets of Kabul and Kandahar have experienced a period of rapid development and had regained the dominant position they held in foreign trade finance prior to 1309 (1930) by 1352 (1973):

> Prior to 1930, there were no banks in the country. All foreign exchange transactions were handled by private exchange dealers set up in the market places (bazaars) of Kabul and Qandahar. It is estimated that in 1930 there were about 30 to 40 such dealers in Kabul and from about 10 to 15 in Qandahar. Even the Government's requirements were bought from these dealers. [M21, p. 182]

With the establishment of the Shirkat-i-Sahami-i-Afghan, the predecessor of Bank Millie, in 1309 (1930) came repression. Not only was a large part of Afghanistan's foreign trade immediately acquired by this company, but three years later when reorganisation produced Bank Millie it was granted a monopoly over all foreign exchange dealings [G15, pp. 314-15]. Initially, the number of foreign exchange dealers was simply reduced [M21, p. 182]. However, in 1314 (1935) a fixed exchange rate system was adopted, free market dealings were prohibited and Bank Millie exercised its monopoly rights in foreign exchange [B6, p. 7; M21, p. 182]. It opened exchange departments in Kabul and Kandahar to replace the foreign exchange bazaars [M21, p. 182].

That the repression of the money bazaars was not altogether successful is evinced by the fact that by 1317 (1938) Bank Millie was forced to recognise and even place its own dealers in the bazaars [M21, p. 182]. This, however, was to be a short lived respite; after the assumption of its

foreign exchange responsibilities in 1322 (1943), Da Afghanistan Bank
which had been established in 1318 (1939) instigated new measures of
exchange control:

> The transfer was in recognition of the exigencies of the war and the desire
> of the Government to exercise complete control over trade and payments
> through its central bank. The new system of centralised control over all
> exchange receipts remained in effect until 1947 when new rules were
> introduced. [M21, p. 182]

It is clear that "centralised control" again failed to be effective since
free market exchange rates have been recorded throughout this period
showing severe depreciation for the first two years after the war [K7,
Table 1, p. 221] caused apparently by "a sudden and substantial increase
in imports . . . . . to meet unsatisfied demand during the war" [M21,
p. 182]. The changes in 1326 (1947) were in effect a return to the system
established in 1317 (1938), Da Afghanistan Bank presumably recognising,
as Bank Millie had before it, that the free market system could not be
eliminated [M21, p. 183].

The foreign exchange system now theoretically operates under Decree
No. 2632 promulgated in 1329 (1951) which is presented in Appendix A.
It represents a codification of the system introduced in 1326 (1947) [M21,
p. 183], which was a return to the 1317 (1938) system [I4].

That foreign exchange regulations have not changed since 1329 (1951)
does not imply that the foreign exchange system has not undergone any
changes over the past 20 years. Rather, the fact is that the Decree has
been a dead letter most of the time. The basic requirement for the
surrender of foreign exchange earnings at below free market rates from
exports of cotton, karakul and wool has remained throughout this
period, despite a continual stream of advice from foreign advisors to the
Government to abandon it. The surrender requirement formed the basis
for the multiple exchange rate system which has also survived with
modifications.

The complexity of the system increased until 1342 (1963), when the
majority of multiple exchange rate practices were eliminated. However, the
watershed in recent foreign exchange history came in 1344 (1965) when
Da Afghanistan Bank, under a stand-by agreement with the International
Monetary Fund, started its present policy of maintaining its free rate
within Afs 2 of that quoted in the Kabul money bazaar. At the same time,
the scope of the official rate was reduced, some export items removed
from the exchange surrender list, export taxes lowered and import
control liberalised. The details of the exchange system existing before the

establishment of the Republic are presented in Appendix B. No formal changes have been made since then.

The beginning of 1344 (1965) also marks the beginning of the renaissance of the money bazaars. Prior to that date foreign exchange dealers had been almost entirely Hindus and Jews. The position of the Jews, however, had been deteriorating since 1240 (1861) and "the fiercely competitive Hindu merchants gradually ousted the Jews from money-changing . . . . ." [G15, pp. 64-65]. The Arab-Israeli conflict of 1346 (1967) resulted in the withholding of trade licences from Jews; the last Jewish foreign exchange dealer emigrated a few years ago.

Although banking has not flourished in Afghanistan over the past decade, the money bazaars have undergone a period of rapid growth. The volume of business has increased substantially, specialisation has occurred and technical improvements such as the widespread installation of electronic calculators have taken place.

The present foreign exchange market in Kabul is situated near the river in Puli-Kheshti in a large courtyard known as Saray Shozda. Before this saray was constructed the money market was located in Saray Mohammad Qumi which lies behind the present market. The Saray Mohammad Qumi belonged to Shahzada Abdul Aziz but was demolished some twenty years ago for the site of the Puli-Kheshti mosque. Shahzada Abdul Aziz then bought the existing site and completed a two-storey courtyard in 1336 (1957). Eight years later a third storey was added.

When foreign exchange dealers moved into Saray Shozda there were apparently only three or four dealers, all Jews, who set up business. However, Hindus soon followed and by 1339 (1960) there were about fifteen dealers established in the courtyard. Religious scruples were finally overcome quite recently when the first Afghan Moslems set up business in Saray Shozda.

Dealers in the Kabul money bazaar appear to have accepted cheques drawn on foreign banks some time ago but this practice may have stopped during the Second World War, since present dealers believe that the first cheque was accepted in 1325 (1946) by a prominent dealer, Ibrahim Aranov. He emigrated to the U.S.A. ten years ago and there established a trading business. That cheques were accepted in the pre-war period is documented in the following extract from the British Legation's Office Manual of 1312 (1933):

> *Purchase of Afghanis*—When the balance of Afghanis in hand is less than Rs. 3,000 the Accountant will inform the Counsellor who will ascertain through the Oriental Secretary or Accountant the official rate of exchange

quoted for the day by the Shirkat Ashami Company, or the lowest exchange rate prevailing in the Kabul bazaar on that day. After approval of the rate by the Counsellor a cheque will be prepared on the Imperial Bank of India at Peshawar for an amount in Indian rupees equivalent to the sum required in Afghanis. The Accountant will then proceed to the bazaar accompanied by a Legation orderly and, after counting the money received from the banker, will bring it to the Legation in a suitable conveyance. The Accountant should obtain from the banker a statement in writing on the bank's official paper shewing the rate at which the exchange was effected. The money will immediately be brought to account in the cash book. In order to check the quotations made by the Shirkat Ashami Company or other Kabul Bankers, the Accountant will inform the Counsellor of the official rate quoted in the daily "Islah" newspaper for the day on which the purchase was made. [B33, p. 12]

In 1352 (1973) there were about 35 principal dealers together with 50 to 60 partners or agents operating on small commissions. Each principal rents one of the small shops in the courtyard, instals desk, safe, telephone and calculating machine and opens for business. He closes again if his turnover is insufficient, rates turn against currencies he is holding or personal or travellers' cheques which he has accepted are not honoured. Competition is keen and survival generally depends on cultivating business from large traders, specialisation and trading on one's own account.

Although foreign exchange transactions take place throughout the country, Kandahar is the only city besides Kabul in which there exists a physical marketplace for foreign exchange dealing. In Herat, for example, scattered tourist shops and traders act as foreign exchange dealers as a side line but there is no centralised location. The same situation exists in Jalalabad, Kunduz and Mazar-i-Sharif. In Kandahar, a courtyard similar to Saray Shozda exists in the Bazaar-e-Shekarpoor called Tara Singh in which foreign exchange transactions have reportedly been taking place for at least the past 70 years.

Most foreign exchange transactions in Kandahar were apparently conducted on the street until 1342 (1963) when three dealers opened shops in the newly re-built Saray Tara Singh. In 1348 (1969) another foreign exchange dealer moved into this courtyard and the complement of five found there in 1352 (1973) was completed in 1349 (1970). There are, however, several retailers in Kandahar who also engage in foreign exchange transactions as well as a dozen or more partners or agents operating at the entrance to Saray Tara Singh in the same way as they do in Saray Shozda.

Dealers in Kabul and Kandahar maintain close links with one another and with the foreign exchange markets in Beirut, Bombay, Delhi, Karachi, London, New York, Peshawar, Tehran, Zurich, etc. The Pakistani Rupee appeared to be the most important currency in Kandahar, while Dollars and Indian and Pakistani Rupees were the most common currencies in Kabul.

Despite the fact that Da Afghanistan Bank, as well as the other banks, has followed the exchange rates set in Saray Shozda in determining its own free market rate, the legality of these operations is still in some doubt. Indeed, the foreign exchange regulations reproduced as Appendix A hardly appear ambiguous on this matter. Furthermore, Bank Millie was itself not allowed to engage in any foreign exchange transactions between 1322 (1943), when Da Afghanistan Bank took over such activities from Bank Millie, and 1346 (1967) when it was recognised as an authorised dealer after submitting numerous applications to the Government on this matter. Prior to that date the only other authorised dealer apart from Da Afghanistan Bank had been Pashtany Tejaraty Bank.

In 1347 (1969), following several incidents of harassment, a police raid on Saray Shozda took place and dealers were marched off to the police station. After questioning, each dealer was obliged to show his trade permit, identity card and military service certificates, and to produce three photographs and a guarantee. It is also reported that baksheesh fines were imposed. For a while after this event, dealers discontinued their exchange operations and the Afghani depreciated substantially. At the same time, reports of a number of earlier incidents of police harassment came to light [F12]. However, after this report carried in Caravan Newspaper, no further incidents took place for some time. In 1351 (1972) there were rumours of dealers' mail being delayed and opened. Apparently, further repressive measures were feared. Under the new Republican Government, mail was again opened and dealers became reluctant to deal on anything other than a cash basis.

The main problem created by this dubious legal position concerning the activity of foreign exchange dealing lies in the fact that it prevents dealers from registering as businesses. Plans were in fact made by the Ministry of Finance several years ago to register dealers but were shelved before action was taken. This situation naturally greatly increases the difficulties of data collection. For example, no dealer will openly admit to the possession of foreign bank accounts to anyone who might be a Government official.

The increase in efficiency and scope of activities of both money bazaars over the past decade has been dramatic. Only ten years ago cross rates were reported to be inconsistent, turnover low, the spread between buying and selling rates high and fluctuations excessive [W5, p. 258]. Clearing currencies were not quoted and the market was miniscule. Ten years later, foreign missions were reporting that the market operated efficiently on fine margins between buying and selling rates. The fluctuations are no longer as violent as they used to be as can be seen from Figure 7.1 below.

The increase in efficiency springs from increased competition, particularly over the past five years. This, in turn, has led to specialisation within the bazaar. One indication of increasing competition is the movement in the rate of interest in the foreign trade sector over this period. Whereas interest rates have generally doubled over the past decade throughout Afghanistan, the rates in the bazaar for foreign trade finance have apparently declined. This can be attributed to increased competition in foreign trade itself which in turn has reduced profits. Thus, the opportunity cost of capital in this particular sector of the economy has declined and brought down interest rates from around 30 to around 20 per cent within five years. The possibility of declining rates in one sector and rising interest rates elsewhere is another illustration of economic fragmentation discussed in Chapter III.

Foreign exchange dealers can be divided into three groups of specialists, namely, those dealing in convertible currencies, those dealing in clearing currencies, and those dealing in Rupees. In fact, specialisation is not watertight and the first and third groups can only be distinguished in terms of their main emphasis. Thus, most dealers in convertible currencies can supply small quantities of Rupees and *vice versa*, although their own trading activities and main exchange business will be confined to a particular currency type.

Convertible currency dealers keep themselves informed by telephone of rate movements in the major international markets on a daily basis. For sums in excess of $5,000 it is usually worth shopping around the Delhi, Bombay, Beirut and Tehran markets for prices. Kandahar dealers keep in close touch with the Kabul market making several telephone calls a day. When Dollars are bought abroad the correspondent telegraphs New York to transfer funds and Afghanis are deposited in a Kabul account.

The clearing period is used for short term finance. Cheques for use outside the U.S.A., in particular Japan, can be sold 14 days or so prior to their reaching the U.S.A. Twelve days later the Dollars are bought and the transfer telegraphed to New York. Thus, the clearing period provides 12 days finance. Transactions can normally be conducted by cheque, telegraphic transfer or cash through a network of deposits. Most favoured centres for accounts are Hamburg, London and New York.

In 1351 (1972), a representative of one of the big American merchant banks visited Afghanistan to entertain traders from Kandahar who held large deposits with his institution and to solicit more accounts. Although a "wholesale" bank, this bank was keen to keep such personal accounts because its Afghan clients appear to have been content to hold demand deposits in excess of $100,000 each with few demands for services apart from easily undertaken credit standing enquiries. A charge of $3 per transaction is made to discourage small traders from opening accounts. It would seem, therefore, that dealers in the Kandahar bazaar also finance a substantial volume of trade from convertible currency countries.

In trade transactions, dealers operate on cash and credit and can also make use of their own credit standing to obtain supplier credit for customers in the same way as the trade agencies.

Four or five dealers in Kabul act as brokers in the market for clearing currencies. There are no clearing currency dealers in Kandahar. The market for clearing currencies is by no means as developed as that for convertible currencies; the margin fluctuates between Afs 1-5 per clearing Dollar, whereas it stays fairly uniformly at 50 Puls per United States Dollar. Although Afghan exporters to Russia negotiate an import list at the time of export, this can usually be modified or renegotiated by another trader who has bought clearing currency. The ability to modify or renegotiate an import list seems to depend on the individual trader's standing; there are first, second and third class traders. First class traders are almost entirely free to alter import lists whereas third class traders will be obliged to import a substantial proportion of the original list. Exporters can either use their clearing Dollars to pay for imports or can sell clearing currency from their clearing accounts to the brokers in the bazaar.

Dealers in Rupees have close links with India and Pakistan. The main method of payment is through the *hundi* or *hawala* which is a draft drawn on a trading associate. About fifteen large traders with Pakistan and ten with India possess first class credit standing with respect to the acceptance of *hundis*. There is usually a one per cent commission charged on the acceptance of a *hundi*. Smaller traders find it more expensive to sell their Rupee earnings in the form of *hundis*, but may nevertheless still find it provides a more attractive rate than selling cash. Because currency export from India and Pakistan is illegal, there is a considerable differen-

tial between currency and *hundi* exchange rates. *Hawalas* are also used extensively in trade with Iran as well as in domestic trade.

The existence of foreign exchange controls in both India and Pakistan means that all Rupees in Afghanistan have been taken out of India and Pakistan illegally. Given that exchange controls have naturally resulted in overvalued currencies at the official exchange rate, Rupees sell at a discount in Afghanistan as elsewhere. Because of the exchange controls, *hundis* and telegraphic transfers make use of code names for currencies and values.

There is reportedly a considerable trade in Roubles and gold. A Rouble rate and rates for gold coins are quoted in the bazaar. Apparently, Roubles are in greatest supply in Herat, i.e. near the section of the Afghan-U.S.S.R. border not on the Amu Darya (River Oxus). It is across this section of the border that sizable smuggling operations are reported to take place. However, Roubles also cross the river and can be found in Mazar-i-Sharif and Sherkhan Bandar, the largest river port.

Roubles finding their way into Afghanistan follow well established routes through Iran, Lebanon, Kuwait and Switzerland, where they are sold at about a 20 per cent profit back to the U.S.S.R. It can be assumed that they reach Afghanistan in payment for goods from the West smuggled into the U.S.S.R. and are eventually repatriated in return for gold or convertible currencies smuggled out of the U.S.S.R.

Gold in Afghanistan is generally in transit to India and Pakistan. There is little evidence of a large demand for gold in Afghanistan itself.

This brief survey provides an inadequate picture of the bazaar activities. The extra-legal position of the foreign exchange dealers makes them very reluctant to talk about their operations.

v. *Importance of the Money Bazaars in Foreign Trade*

It is impossible to make any accurate estimates of either balance sheet or turnover figures in the money bazaars. This difficulty is doubly compounded first by the questionable legal status of foreign exchange dealings and second by the high proportion of smuggled trade in total foreign trade. A number of observers [S13, p. 315; Z3, p. 71] have concurred with Wilber that "half of the lendable funds for the bazaar traders emanates from the bazaar moneylenders" [W3, p. 258].

A study in Herat and Kandahar found the relative importance of non-institutional finance significantly greater in the provinces than in Kabul for the simple reason that bank loans are extended only from the banks' head offices in Kabul. In Herat, a small survey at a meeting of the

Chamber of Commerce produced estimates that 50 per cent of agricultural production expenses, 40 to 50 per cent of trade and 30 per cent of construction investment was financed by non-institutional credit at annual interest rates of between 20 and 40 per cent [O2]. It was also reported in this study that interest rates had risen in recent years.

There is no doubt that in foreign trade the Kabul money bazaar is the dominant institution. Da Afghanistan Bank and the other two commercial banks not only keep closely in touch with activities in the bazaar but also have their own agents operating there. Da Afghanistan Bank is, however, the largest operator and has acted as a price setter while still keeping its own rates aligned to those in the bazaar.

Estimates of nine of the 35 or so dealers in the Kabul money bazaar for the total daily turnover in foreign exchange were collected by the author in 1352 (1973). Part of the high variance in these estimates is doubtless due to the increased use of cheques and telegraphic transfer for which value estimates would naturally be more difficult than for cash transactions. The main currencies dealt in the Kabul money bazaar were Dollars, Deutsche Mark, Sterling, Iranian Rials, and Indian and Pakistani Rupees.

There is a sizable business in clearing currencies, i.e. clearing Dollars for Czechoslovakia, Poland and Russia and clearing pounds Sterling for China. These transactions take the form of transfers of ownership of clearing accounts held by traders with the barter countries at Da Afghanistan Bank. There exist small quantities of many other currencies in the Saray Shozda primarily generated by tourists. The spread between buying and selling rates on these currencies is naturally greater than on commonly traded currencies. This results in certain discrepancies in cross rates.

The five dealers in the Saray Tara Singh in Kandahar provided estimates of their own average daily turnover. Apart from the evident difference in size between the two foreign exchange markets, only six currencies were traded in Kandahar, whereas a large number of currencies were traded in Kabul. In Kandahar there were only five brokers while in Kabul there were about 35. The Pakistani Rupee was the most important currency in the Kandahar market, the Dollar in Kabul. However, both bazaars operated in currency, *hundis*, cheques and telegraphic transfers.

One of the largest dealers in Kabul estimates that about 50 per cent of Afghanistan's foreign trade is financed through the bazaar. Foreign economic missions have also quoted this figure. Other estimates are even higher. A rough attempt has been made to provide some indication of the relative importance of the bazaar in Table 7.12. Averages for each

Table 7.12

Annual Turnover of Foreign Exchange, 1349-1351

(Millions of Dollars)

Institution	1349	1350	1351	
				Percentage
Kabul Money Bazaar	n.a.	n.a.	152	(60.3)
Kandahar Money Bazaar	n.a.	n.a.	3	(1.2)
Da Afghanistan Bank	49	75	71	(28.2)
Bank Millie	9	10	17	(6.7)
Pashtany Tejaraty Bank	9	9	n.a.	(3.6)
			(252)	(100)

Note: For the percentage calculations for 1351, the turnover of Pashtany Tejaraty Bank is assumed to be $ 9 million. Clearing currency transactions are excluded.

Source: Data provided by nine foreign exchange dealers in Kabul and five in Kandahar and by the three banks.

currency were calculated, added to figures obtained from the Kandahar dealers, converted at the average free market exchange rates for 1351 (1972) into Dollars and multiplied by 300 to obtain an annual estimate. Compared with a figure of $146 million for total foreign trade in 1350 (1971), excluding foreign aid financed imports and barter trade, the figures in Table 7.12 suggest an upper limit to smuggling of $106 million or 40 per cent of total recorded trade. This can be compared with estimates of 20 per cent produced by other observers [R9, p. 95; S13, pp. 328-29].

Virtually no payment connected with trade with India and Pakistan is transacted through the banks, much to the annoyance of the Indian authorities, who annually attempt to include such a requirement in the trade agreement with Afghanistan. This was a major point in the 1349 (1970) negotiations. India obtained one tiny concession in this connection last year when it was agreed that, as an experiment, payment for Afghan export of asafoetida would be made through banks. Otherwise almost all trade payments are made using *hundis*.

Table 7.13 presents the "bazaar rate" for the Dollar and Rupees. This is the average daily rate for drafts and cheques (buying rates for Dollars, selling rates for Rupees) in Saray Shozda obtained by the Research Department of Da Afghanistan Bank each day from a number of dealers. Figure 7.1 similarly presents monthly average rates of daily exchange rates for the Dollar, Indian and Pakistani Rupee, respectively.

The figures in Table 7.13 show a general trend in which the Afghani has depreciated against the Dollar. However, the extent of depreciation has been relatively modest in comparison to currency depreciation in

Table 7.13

Free Market Dollar and Rupee Exchange Rates "Bazaar Rates" 1329-1351

(Annual Average of Daily Rates for Drafts and Cheques.
Buying Rates for United States Dollars, Selling Rates for Rupees.)

Date	Afghanis to the Dollar	Afghanis to 10 Indian Rupees	Afghanis to 10 Pakistani Rupees
1329	39.0	73.2	78.4
1330	35.0	68.1	71.8
1331	37.0	71.2	70.2
1332	37.1	72.6	62.1
1333	42.1	82.2	64.3
1334	45.2	91.3	75.0
1335	53.8	106.0	76.2
1336	54.1	98.7	69.5
1337	54.7	101.5	71.3
1338	46.6	81.5	61.4
1339	40.8	66.1	54.6
1340	43.5	65.5	56.6
1341	52.8	74.9	67.0
1342	51.3	74.0	66.3
1343	63.6	78.3	72.3
1344	75.3	79.5	88.8
1345	76.4	69.1	89.5
1346	76.4	67.5	87.0
1347	74.8	71.4	84.0
1348	75.4	67.3	77.3
1349	84.8	64.7	78.3
1350	84.6	67.5	76.9
1351	79.4	74.2	69.0

Source: Research Department, Da Afghanistan Bank.

many underdeveloped countries. As in all cases, the exchange rate is primarily determined by relative prices which in turn are largely dependent on changes in the money stock.

Rates *vis-à-vis* the Indian and Pakistani Rupee are of some interest, particularly since 1344 (1965). The Afghani has appreciated substantially against both currencies. The modified purchasing power parity index for Afghanistan gives a 32.6 per cent price rise compared to 44.2 per cent in India and 34.2 per cent in Pakistan. Afghanistan's terms of trade have also improved substantially over this period. Furthermore, price controls in India and Pakistan have doubtless had a depressing effect on their indices.

A detailed investigation into the lagged response of the exchange rate to changes in the money stock has been conducted using the following relationships:

$$\Delta\log ER_t = a_0 + a_1 \Delta\log M_{t-n} \tag{7.1}$$

$$\Delta\log ER_t = a_1 \Delta\log M_{t-n} \tag{7.2}$$

$$\Delta\log ER_t = a_0 + a_1 \Delta\log M_{t-n} + a_2 \Delta\log L_{t-n} \tag{7.3}$$

$$\Delta\log ER_t = a_1 \Delta\log M_{t-n} + a_2 \Delta\log L_{t-n} \tag{7.4}$$

$$\Delta\log ER_t = a_0 + a_1 \Delta\log DC_{t-n} \tag{7.5}$$

$$\Delta\log ER_t = a_1 \Delta\log DC_{t-n} \tag{7.6}$$

$$\Delta\log ER_t = a_0 + a_1 \Delta\log DC_{t-n} + a_2 \Delta\log L_{t-n} \tag{7.7}$$

$$\Delta\log ER_t = a_1 \Delta\log DC_{t-n} + a_2 \Delta\log L_{t-n} \tag{7.8}$$

where ER is the Afghani/Dollar exchange rate, M the money stock, L international liquidity and DC domestic credit. "t" represents the date and "n" the number of months lag. The lagged response was tested for each month between 0 and 23. M, L and DC are mid-year estimates calculated by taking the average beginning and end of year figures. The exchange rate is the average over twelve month periods of the monthly averages of daily bazaar rates given in Appendix D. By taking the 12 alternative annual periods and a one year shift in the annual data, 24 possible lags were tested. Only Equations 7.1 and 7.2 gave good results. Domestic credit and international liquidity did not produce satisfactory results. Quite predictably, good results were not found using the Rupee rates in the same equations.

The average lag between changes in the money stock and changes in the Afghani/Dollar exchange rate has been investigated in some detail. Results of the regression analysis are presented in Tables 7.14 and 7.15. It can be seen that for one, two and three year moving averages the lag which produces the highest adjusted coefficient of determination, $\overline{R}^2$, is seven months, whether or not a constant is included in the regression. As the "t" value on the constant term was significant, its suppression in the equation used in Table 7.15 constrains the regression estimate. Theoretically this makes the coefficient of determination meaningless. However, as the value of the constant is so close to zero, no great damage is done in interpreting the results in the usual way. The omission of the constant is justified on theoretical grounds in that its inclusion in a regression of

Table 7.14

Lags between Changes in the Money Stock and the Exchange Rate 1332-1351

$$\Delta \log ER_t = a_0 + a_1 \Delta \log M_{t-n}$$

Lag in Months	Annual Average			Two Year Moving Average			Three Year Moving Average		
	a_0	a_1	$\overline{R}^2$	a_0	a_1	$\overline{R}^2$	a_0	a_1	$\overline{R}^2$
0	−0.03	0.66	0.23	−0.03	0.73	0.41	−0.04	0.88	0.58
1	−0.03	0.70	0.27	−0.03	0.77	0.46	−0.05	0.91	0.63
2	−0.03	0.73	0.31	−0.04	0.79	0.50	−0.05	0.93	0.68
3	−0.04	0.76	0.34	−0.04	0.83	0.54	−0.05	0.96	0.71
4	−0.04	0.78	0.39	−0.04	0.85	0.58	−0.06	0.97	0.75
5	−0.04	0.81	0.42	−0.05	0.87	0.61	−0.06	0.98	0.78
6	−0.05	0.83	0.43	−0.05	0.88	0.64	−0.06	0.98	0.80
7	*−0.05*	*0.84*	*0.44*	−0.05	0.89	0.65	−0.06	0.98	0.80
8	−0.05	0.84	0.43	−0.05	0.89	0.65	−0.06	0.97	0.80
9	−0.05	0.84	0.40	−0.05	0.89	0.63	−0.06	0.97	0.79
10	−0.05	0.82	0.37	−0.05	0.88	0.61	−0.06	0.96	0.78
11	−0.05	0.81	0.36	−0.05	0.87	0.59	−0.06	0.95	0.77
12	−0.03	0.72	0.29	−0.04	0.85	0.58	−0.06	0.96	0.77
13	−0.03	0.71	0.29	−0.04	0.84	0.57	−0.06	0.94	0.75
14	−0.03	0.70	0.29	−0.04	0.83	0.55	−0.05	0.92	0.73
15	−0.03	0.70	0.29	−0.04	0.81	0.52	−0.05	0.90	0.70
16	−0.03	0.68	0.29	−0.04	0.79	0.50	−0.05	0.87	0.66
17	−0.03	0.66	0.27	−0.04	0.76	0.46	−0.05	0.84	0.62
18	−0.03	0.65	0.25	−0.03	0.74	0.42	−0.04	0.80	0.57
19	−0.03	0.63	0.23	−0.03	0.71	0.39	−0.04	0.77	0.52
20	−0.02	0.61	0.20	−0.03	0.68	0.34	−0.04	0.73	0.46
21	−0.02	0.60	0.18	−0.03	0.65	0.31	−0.03	0.69	0.42
22	−0.02	0.58	0.15	−0.02	0.62	0.26	−0.03	0.66	0.37
23	−0.02	0.55	0.13	−0.02	0.58	0.22	−0.03	0.62	0.31

first differences is the equivalent of inserting a time trend variable in the equation relating the absolute levels of the same variables. Exclusion of such a time trend variable enables a better test of the particular behavioural relationship postulated. For forecasting purposes, its inclusion is justified if better results are thereby obtained.

The results indicate a highly significant relationship. For time series analysis conducted in central differences of the logarithmic values of the variables, the coefficients of determination, are relatively high for all cases using the seven month lag. Predictably, results are improved by taking two and three year moving averages thus dampening the effects of random factors such as border closures, agricultural fluctuations, etc. Thus, explanation of the variation in the rate of change of the exchange rate by changes in the money stock rises from 44 to 80 per cent by taking three year moving averages instead of simple annual data.

Table 7.15

Lags between Changes in the Money Stock and the Exchange Rate 1332-1351

$$\Delta\log ER_t = a_1 \Delta\log M_{t-n}$$

Lag in Months	Annual Average		Two Year Moving Average		Three Year Moving Average	
	a_1	$\overline{R}^2$	a_1	$\overline{R}^2$	a_1	$\overline{R}^2$
0	0.52	0.26	0.54	0.40	0.56	0.49
1	0.53	0.28	0.55	0.43	0.56	0.52
2	0.54	0.31	0.55	0.46	0.56	0.54
3	0.54	0.33	0.56	0.48	0.56	0.56
4	0.55	0.36	0.57	0.51	0.56	0.58
5	0.56	0.38	0.57	0.53	0.56	0.60
6	0.56	0.39	0.58	0.54	0.56	0.60
7	0.56	0.39	0.57	0.54	0.56	0.60
8	0.55	0.37	0.57	0.54	0.55	0.60
9	0.54	0.35	0.56	0.52	0.54	0.59
10	0.53	0.32	0.55	0.50	0.54	0.58
11	0.52	0.32	0.54	0.48	0.53	0.57
12	0.55	0.30	0.57	0.51	0.56	0.60
13	0.54	0.30	0.56	0.50	0.55	0.59
14	0.53	0.30	0.56	0.48	0.54	0.57
15	0.53	0.30	0.55	0.47	0.53	0.55
16	0.52	0.30	0.54	0.45	0.52	0.53
17	0.51	0.28	0.53	0.42	0.51	0.51
18	0.49	0.26	0.52	0.40	0.50	0.48
19	0.48	0.25	0.51	0.37	0.48	0.45
20	0.47	0.23	0.49	0.34	0.47	0.41
21	0.46	0.21	0.48	0.31	0.45	0.38
22	0.44	0.19	0.46	0.28	0.44	0.35
23	0.43	0.17	0.44	0.25	0.42	0.31

The results obtained from the three year moving average regression analysis warrant more attention. Therefore, the complete set of results from the seven month lag equation is shown below:

$$\Delta\log ER_t = -0.0579 + 0.9805 \, \Delta\log M_{t-7} \qquad \overline{R}^2 = 0.8031 \qquad (7.9)$$

"t"   (-4.0214)   (7.8864)   SEE = 0.0009

β 0   8.3253   DW = 1.0076

where $\overline{R}^2$ is the coefficient of determination, SEE the standard error of the estimate, DW the Durbin-Watson statistic and β the beta coefficient. The coefficient of determination gives a "t" value of 7.5575 which is significant well over the 99.9 per cent confidence level.

Equation 7.9 indicates that in the absence of any change in the money stock the exchange rate would appreciate by 5.79 per cent annually. An

increase in the money stock of 10 per cent depreciates the exchange rate
by 9.8 per cent. To have maintained a stable Afghani/Dollar exchange
rate over the period 1332-1351 (1953-1972), the money stock would have
had to have been increased annually by 5.91 per cent. This would, of
course, still have produced inflation roughly similar to that experienced
by the U.S.A.

Afghanistan's terms of trade improved dramatically during the 1340s
(1960s). Hansen has calculated that the income terms of trade improved
by about 85 per cent between 1338 (1959) and 1347 (1968) [U3, p. 37].
His figures are reproduced in Table 7.16 below.

Table 7.16
Commodity and Income Terms of Trade 1338-1347

Date	Commodity Terms of Trade	Income Terms of Trade
1338	94.1	103.8
1339	112.2	98.0
1340	100.0	100.0
1341	107.8	112.2
1342	116.6	137.0
1343	118.6	146.1
1344	143.0	166.4
1345	118.0	153.9
1346	165.2	177.1
1347	169.1	191.8

Source: United Nations, "Afghanistan," *Economic Bulletin for Asia and the Far
East*, 22 (3), December 1971, Table 14, p. 37.

If the elasticity of demand for imports were assumed to be 0.8 [H4,
p. 189], an improvement in the terms of trade, which makes imports
cheaper relative to exports, would result in currency appreciation. In
particular, an 85 per cent improvement in the income terms of trade
would increase the demand for imports by 68 per cent. To equate demand
and supply of foreign exchange, the Afghani would have to appreciate by
11 per cent. This is equivalent to an annual rate of appreciation of 1.2
per cent. This in part explains why the money stock could have been
expanded at a considerably faster rate than the real growth rate without
depreciating the Afghani over this period.

The broad trends in the exchange rate seem convincingly explained by
movements in the money stock. However, a number of observers have
analysed shorter run movements in the light of a number of other
factors. For example, the depreciation from Aqrab 1334 (1955) to Jauza

1335 (1956) has been explained both with reference to an excessive monetary expansion in 1333 (1954) and an embargo on trade through Pakistan in 1334 (1955). When this was lifted there was a rush to import.

A major fluctuation took place in the second half of 1341 (1962) when the Afghani appreciated from Afs 56 to Afs 46 to the Dollar. This was apparently the result of an expectation that an official devaluation would take place combined with an attempt to cause an appreciation of the bazaar rate to narrow the gap. The appreciation was caused by a temporary capital inflow [H1, p. VI-32]. The second measure was not taken and even before the devaluation from Afs 20 to Afs 45 to the Dollar in 1342 (1963) the bazaar rate had again depreciated to Afs 55 to the Dollar.

During the last quarter of 1344 (1966) the Afghani again underwent a considerable fluctuation. The depreciation of the Afghani from Afs 74 to Afs 82 to the Dollar was reportedly due to a large capital outflow to India. This outflow resulted from the National Defence Remittance Scheme of November 1965 which was designed to attract convertible currency held by Indians abroad. The Scheme was abolished in May 1966 and the capital flow was reversed. This contributed to the appreciation of the Afghani in 1345 (1966).

The depreciation in the second half of 1346 (1967) seems to have been the result of several factors, namely, poor karakul and rug earnings, large purchases of foreign exchange by Bank Millie and the provision of import facilities by Da Afghanistan Bank [P8].

Da Afghanistan Bank has at times played an important role in the exchange market. The Bank has followed the widely held belief that currency depreciation or devaluation is bad and should be avoided. The Bank supported the exchange rate by selling foreign exchange extensively during the period 1338-1340 (1959-1961) and continued to do so thereafter. However, since 1344 (1965), Da Afghanistan Bank has maintained its rate within Afs 2 of the bazaar rate, although as the largest dealer it can influence substantially the bazaar rate. Attempts to even out seasonal fluctuations were started in 1348 (1969) but a limit on reserve losses has been established.

Table 7.17 shows the differential between the selling rates for Dollars in the Saray Shozda and Da Afghanistan Bank for the last Tuesday of each month for the period 1344-1350 (1965-1971). Da Afghanistan Bank appears to have followed the bazaar rate with a slight lag. Hence, positive differentials are greatest when the Afghani is depreciating, negative differentials greatest when the Afghani is appreciating. If Da Afghanistan Bank were prepared to buy and sell unlimited quantities of foreign exchange (which, in fact, it is not) at its quoted rates, arbitrage would generally be profitable when the positive differential exceeded 50 Puls. When the rate is fluctuating erratically, the differential between buying and selling rates in the bazaar rises from the normal spread of 50 Puls to Afs 1. At these times, arbitrage would only be profitable when the positive differential exceeded Afs 1.

Table 7.17

Differential between Dollar Cash Selling Rates in the Kabul Money Bazaar and Da Afghanistan Bank for the Last Tuesday of Each Month, 1344-1350

(Afghanis—Positive figure implies bazaar rate is higher than Da Afghanistan Bank rate)

Month	1344	1345	1346	1347	1348	1349	1350
Hamal	11.00	1.75	1.00	−0.75	0.75	0.45	1.80
Saur	3.50	0.75	1.00	−0.25	−0.25	−1.50	1.50
Jauza	2.00	1.13	1.00	−0.25	0.25	0.50	2.00
Saratan	1.75	1.20	1.30	0.25	0.25	−1.00	2.00
Asad	0.50	1.80	−0.50	0.25	−0.75	−0.25	−1.00
Sunbula	1.25	2.00	−0.50	1.00	−1.50	−0.50	−0.50
Mizan	2.00	3.00	−1.50	0.70	0	0.50	2.60
Aqrab	2.00	2.05	1.00	−1.00	0	0.50	0.40
Qaus	2.00	1.30	0	0.75	0.50	1.50	−0.50
Jadi	2.50	1.75	1.50	−0.25	−0.75	2.50	1.50
Dalwa	3.50	2.00	0	−0.75	0	3.00	1.00
Hoot	1.75	1.25	1.25	0.25	0.50	2.00	−1.50

Source: Research Department, Da Afghanistan Bank.

Da Afghanistan Bank always maintains a differential of 50 Puls. Therefore, arbitrage would always be profitable when a negative differential exceeded 50 Puls. From Table 7.17 it can be seen that buying foreign exchange from Da Afghanistan Bank to sell in the bazaar is more frequently profitable than *vice versa*. However, since foreign exchange is not freely sold by Da Afghanistan Bank the more interesting case is when a negative differential implies that Da Afghanistan Bank is a buyer from the bazaar. This it is in the middle of the year when from Figure 7.1 it can be seen that the Afghani is usually at its most appreciated.

Having explained over three-quarters of the fluctuations in the annual average exchange rates by changes in the money supply, monthly fluctuations now require some attention. It generally appears that the Afghani is strongest in the third quarter of the year and weakest in the first, as is shown clearly in Figure 7.1.

The explanation for the seasonal fluctuations lies primarily in the seasonal pattern of exports. As an agriculturally based economy,

Afghanistan's exports naturally vary in accordance with the seasons. Road conditions are also important in this respect. However, this is partially dampened by the surrender requirements on foreign exchange earnings from cotton, karakul and wool. With the exception of carpets and gas, all major exports are agricultural products. Monthly export figures for 1344-1350 (1965-1971) are shown in Table 7.18 below. Their relationship with seasonal movements in the exchange rate is shown in Figure 7.2. Although monthly exports vary quite erratically a seasonal pattern mirroring the seasonal exchange rate movement can be detected.

Table 7.18
Afghanistan's Exports by Month, 1344-1350
(Thousands of Dollars)

Month	1344	1345	1346	1347	1348	1349	1350
Hamal	5,170	3,287	3,196	3,934	2,020	4,449	7,497
Saur	5,343	4,624	2,254	1,995	2,683	1,601	4,811
Jauza	3,847	5,939	1,637	2,506	2,358	2,527	5,248
Saratan	2,066	2,842	1,623	2,203	4,108	3,850	6,906
Asad	2,635	5,907	5,074	4,464	9,826	8,248	10,565
Sunbula	4,354	7,034	7,066	9,359	8,117	6,256	8,785
Mizan	7,233	8,996	10,422	12,856	13,529	10,441	10,278
Aqrab	10,445	6,177	12,063	5,928	10,321	6,170	6,410
Qaus	11,597	5,283	6,815	3,442	6,788	5,259	5,777
Jadi	6,774	4,612	3,090	3,819	3,163	10,574	6,047
Dalwa	4,310	5,587	7,398	5,403	3,025	6,517	2,695
Hoot	6,200	4,399	2,802	2,666	4,019	5,291	3,335
Total	69,974	64,687	63,440	58,575	69,957	71,183	78,354

Note: Earnings from gas exports to the U.S.S.R. have been excluded since they were recorded in the last month of the year.
Source: Ministry of Commerce, *Exports of Merchandise from Afghanistan* (Kabul: Ministry of Commerce, 1344-1348, monthly publication) and unpublished material from the Ministry of Commerce.

For clearing Dollars, there is also a seasonal swing caused by the fact that consumer loan funds are generally in largest supply at the beginning of the year. At that time the Afghani appreciates. Towards the end of 1351 (March 1973) the clearing Dollar rate for Russian trade stood at Afs 82 to the clearing Dollar. In the third month of 1352 (May 1973) it had appreciated to Afs 72 to the clearing Dollar.

The seasonal nature of Afghanistan's exports and the resulting effect on the exchange rate has been given some consideration by those who

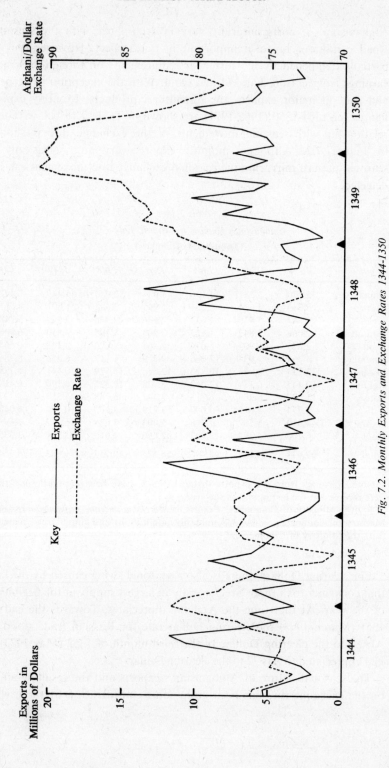

Fig. 7.2. Monthly Exports and Exchange Rates 1344-1350

would prefer a fixed exchange rate system which would hold the rate down at export time and up at other times of the year, thus favouring exporters:

> .... transfer possibilities for amounts resulting from selling in Pakistan are made on the basis of a kind of liberalised barter. The grapes are paid for in the wholesale market of Pakistan with Pakistan Rupees. The Rupees are bought by Afghan importers in Kabul from the grape exporter. During the table grape season the offers of Pakistan Rupees are considerable, because the grape export is very high compared with other produce exports and concentrated in September/October. These high offers in Rupees cause low exchange rates for Afghanis. During February/March, exchange rates for Rupees/Afghanis are generally 25% higher and it is thus worthwhile to sell the Rupees during February/March. The competing middlemen are taking advantage of this possibility and the cooperative should also have the possibility of credit to get the same advantages for the exports of its members. [P13, p. 42]

Table 7.19 presents the results of calculations of the return to holding foreign exchange over a four month period of each year during which seasonal depreciation is generally most pronounced. The average equivalent effective annual return ranges from 22 to 27 per cent depending on which currency is held over the period. It should be noted, however, that speculation of this kind is subject to considerable risk as shown by the relatively high standard deviations. Thus, these returns cannot be used as a proxy for the pure rate of interest or as a measure of social time preference. As mentioned above, returns from trade and interest rates for foreign trade finance appear to be considerably lower than these speculative returns. Nevertheless, a case can be made for intervention by Da Afghanistan Bank to smooth out seasonal fluctuations. If it is assumed that society's time preference is lower than individuals' time preference, intervention which effectively reduced returns from seasonal foreign exchange speculation to a level reflecting the society's time preference would be justified. Given the high risk element, however, this might only imply reducing fluctuations to provide an average effective annual return of around 15 per cent or so.

vi. *Conclusion*

The material presented in this chapter suggests that the foreign exchange dealers in the Kabul and Kandahar money bazaars have played an important role in Afghanistan's foreign trade. Although foreign exchange surrender requirements provide Da Afghanistan Bank with a monopoly over export earnings of about $40 million a year, as do the barter

Table 7.19

Returns from Seasonal Foreign Exchange Speculation, 1332-1351

(Percentage Returns from Holding Foreign Exchange from Mizan to Dalwa of Each Year, i.e. Returns over a Four Month Period)

Date	Dollar	Indian Rupee	Pakistani Rupee
1332	8.57	7.18	2.76
1333	6.10	12.07	19.11
1334	23.36	18.41	11.27
1335	5.12	8.70	5.84
1336	7.03	17.87	12.79
1337	1.32	6.21	11.53
1338	4.40	5.67	−0.17
1339	8.12	1.56	6.95
1340	9.55	1.08	8.96
1341	0.00	25.98	10.56
1342	11.29	7.83	8.28
1343	11.37	6.22	16.22
1344	3.91	−10.20	3.73
1345	7.98	3.59	4.34
1346	9.55	15.37	8.87
1347	7.65	10.98	2.74
1348	6.44	4.95	4.48
1349	7.59	11.31	6.55
1350	−2.80	4.81	1.61
1351	−0.13	5.89	0.45
Average Return	6.82	8.27	7.34
Standard Deviation	5.49	7.59	5.17
Equivalent Effective Annual Return	21.89	26.93	23.69

arrangements over a further $68 million, healthy competition has existed between banks and bazaar for all other foreign trade transactions. The liberalisation of foreign trade over the past seven years has increased this competition and reduced profits. This, in turn, has provided a small stimulus to industrialisation, since some funds have been transferred into this sector of the economy from trade.

An appreciating currency and indications of a number of new export possibilities (in particular cotton fabric and wheat) provide an ideal opportunity to permit banks to engage in all forms of foreign exchange transactions and to establish clearly the legal position of the foreign exchange dealers. In fact, the recent Cabinet policy statement on the banking law, carried in the Kabul Times, 6 June 1973, made provision for both [C1]. This, together with tariff reform and direct export promotion measures such as the provision of a market intelligence service, demonstration of quality control, standardisation and packaging techniques, are the essential ingredients of an export promotion programme which will be required if any increase in Afghanistan's development potential is to be realised.

Appendix A

Foreign Exchange Regulations in Afghanistan
Decree No. 2632
1329 (1951)

In order to regulate and balance the exports and imports of the country and fix the rate of afghani against foreign currencies, the following rules are approved:

Article 1

Buying and selling of foreign currencies, transfer of foreign currencies to other countries, together with all transactions related thereto, are strictly prohibited in Afghanistan except in accordance with the following rules and regulations.

Article 2

All foreign currencies earned through the export of goods shall be surrendered after deducting all expenses to Da Afghanistan Bank and sold against afghanis according to the following rules.
  a. The Council of Ministers shall fix, according to proposals made by the Supreme Council of Da Afghanistan Bank, the percentage of all foreign currencies earned through the export of merchandise to be surrendered to the Bank.
  b. Fixing and altering the afghani rates for buying and selling of foreign currencies is the prerogative of the Council of Ministers which shall act according to the country's economic and monetary needs.

Article 3

The foreign exchange needed by the Government, according to the budget, prepared by the Ministry of Finance and approved by the Council of Ministers and other lawful bodies, shall be provided by Da Afghanistan Bank.

Article 4

Economic projects needing foreign exchange proposed by national institutions or Government departments shall first be submitted to the

Ministry of National Economy (functions of this Ministry were assumed in 1956 by the Ministries of Planning and Commerce) and then to the Currency Commission for investigation. The Currency Commission shall be constituted according to Article 6 below. Proposals shall then be submitted, after approval by the Foreign Currency Commission and the Supreme Council of Da Afghanistan Bank, to the Council of Ministers for final decision.

Note: Government budgetary needs shall have first priority claim over the country's foreign exchange holdings. The next priority shall be for projects under approved development plans.

Article 5

The foreign exchange needs of productive institutions shall be referred first to the Ministry of National Economy. After approval of the Foreign Currency Commission and the Supreme Council of Da Afghanistan Bank, the sums assigned shall be paid to the designated institutions.

Note: The foreign exchange needs of projects approved before this Act shall be payable after the consent of the Currency Commission and of the Supreme Council of Da Afghanistan Bank have been obtained.

Article 6

The Foreign Currency Commission shall be composed of five members, three of whom shall be appointed by the Finance Ministry, the Ministry of National Economy and the Bank Milli respectively and the other two by Da Afghanistan Bank. The rank of the representatives of the Ministries shall not be less than Deputy Minister and that of the Banks not less than Assistant President.

Article 7

Any surplus or deficit in foreign currencies referred to in Article 2, both the total at the end of the year and amounts for individual projects, shall be reported by Da Afghanistan Bank to the Ministry of National Economy. The said Ministry shall be empowered to investigate the matter through the authorities concerned.

Article 8

The balance between the foreign exchange earned through the export of merchandise and amounts surrendered to the Bank shall be put freely at the disposal of merchants and firms earning it. Such balances shall be used for importing needed goods into the country. In this case a guarantee shall be given to Da Afghanistan Bank that goods equal in value to the balance shall be imported.

Note: The manner in which these guarantees shall be given, the mode of transfer and the way in which the accounting shall be made shall be set out in detailed regulations prepared specifically for the purpose by Da Afghanistan Bank.

Article 9

Every exporter shall be required either to import goods equal in value to a fixed percentage of the exported merchandise or to sell any excess foreign currency at a specified rate to Da Afghanistan Bank.

The percentage shall be fixed in accordance with Article 2 of this Decree after deducting real business expenses from the sale price of the merchandise.

Article 10

Each merchant's sale prices of exported merchandise and purchase prices of imported merchandise shall be calculated after deducting the real business expenses incurred.

Bills and invoices for exported and imported merchandise shall be subject to investigation by Da Afghanistan Bank. They shall be certified by the Bank's representatives according to the currency regulations in force.

Article 11

Merchants or other individuals earning foreign exchange in ways other than through exports shall be free to import goods to the amount of the exchange earned or sell it to the Bank or merchants guaranteeing to import goods to the same amount.

Article 12

Persons who travel to foreign countries for recreational, medical or other necessary purposes shall be permitted to export goods to the value of one thousand afghanis without guaranteeing to import goods for that amount.

Article 13

Export of gold and silver shall be strictly prohibited without the written consent of the Council of Ministers issued to the Customs through the Ministry of National Economy and subject to the formalities of the Customs.

Article 14

Travellers to or from Afghanistan shall be permitted to take out or bring in not more than five hundred afghanis in bank-notes.

Note: Notes permitted to be taken out or brought in (up to the five hundred afghanis allowed) shall be in two and five afghani bank-notes only.

Article 15

Foreign subjects entering Afghanistan shall declare the foreign currency in their possession to the Customs Officers at the Afghan border and such amount shall be certified in their passports. Foreigners wishing to leave Afghanistan shall approach Da Afghanistan Bank to authorise deduction of the amount they have spent (according to their mode of living). They shall be allowed to take the rest of the above-mentioned currency out of the country with written permission.

Note: Those living in Afghanistan as guests or earning their living expenses in the country shall be allowed to take with them the total they had imported.

Article 16

Foreigners having come to Afghanistan as employees shall be required to exchange at least 30% of their foreign currency income into afghanis at the fixed rate of exchange in Da Afghanistan Bank.

Article 17

Afghan nationals having to go to foreign countries for medical treatment shall be permitted to buy foreign currency needed in conformity with approved regulations provided the necessity for their treatment abroad is advised by the Ministry of Health.

Article 18

Da Afghanistan Bank shall sell foreign currency at the Bank rate when such currency is required for Afghan students studying abroad at their own or national institutions' expense, provided such expenses shall be certified by the Ministry of Education and provided that such expenses shall not exceed the expenses incurred by government students abroad.

Article 19

Da Afghanistan Bank shall sell foreign currency as needed to the Pilgrims of Haj and other Holy places after the approval of the Ministry of Interior, the Ministry of National Economy and the Currency Commission.

Note: The Currency Commission shall determine the amounts of foreign exchange needed for each pilgrim.

Article 20

Da Afghanistan Bank shall sell foreign currency at a fixed rate of exchange to those buying professional and scientific books or magazines, with the consent of the Currency Commission.

Article 21

As an exception to the foregoing articles Da Afghanistan Bank shall be empowered to export in bank-notes any foreign currency to be credited to its accounts abroad through any of its foreign dealers.

Travellers shall be permitted to export their foreign currency requirements in foreign bank-notes, provided the said bank-notes are provided to them by Da Afghanistan Bank according to its rules and regulations.

Article 22

The publication of these rules shall automatically render all previous rules and regulations regarding exchange invalid and abrogated.

Article 23

Da Afghanistan Bank shall be hereby authorised to apply these rules and made responsible for their application.

Da Afghanistan Bank shall formulate its own internal regulations to carry out these rules and put them into force.

Appendix B

Afghanistan's Foreign Trade System

[From International Monetary Fund, *23rd Annual Report on Exchange Restrictions 1972*, pp. 21-22]

A. Exchange Rate System

The par value is 0.0197482 gram of fine gold per Afghani. The Afghanistan Bank (the central bank) charges commissions ranging from $\frac{1}{10}$ of 1 per cent to $\frac{1}{2}$ of 1 per cent on exchange transactions. The Bank's official buying and selling rates for the U.S. dollar are Af 44.70 and Af 45.30, respectively. The official selling rate applies to certain foreign exchange payments by the Central Government. The official buying rate applies to the proceeds of exports of karakul (which is exported only to the convertible currency area), wool (except cashmere wool exported to the convertible currency area), cotton, and natural gas (which is exported only to the U.S.S.R.); to 30 per cent of the foreign currency salaries of foreign employees of the Government, government enterprises, and domestic companies; and to purchases of bilateral agreement currencies for maintenance in Afghanistan of embassies and state trading organizations by the respective bilateral partner countries. Exchange subsidies are applied to the official buying rate as follows: Af 3 per US$1 for export proceeds from cotton when payment is received under a bilateral payments agreement; Af 10 per US$1 for proceeds in convertible currencies from exports of wool; Af 25 per US$1 for proceeds in convertible currencies from exports of cotton; and Af 20 per US$1 for proceeds from exports of karakul.

All other transactions take place at free market rates through either the banks or the bazaar; proceeds from the export of walnuts received over bilateral payments accounts are subject to an exchange tax of 9.5 per cent. The Afghanistan Bank maintains its operational free market selling rate for the U.S. dollar within Af 2.0 per US$1 of the daily free market rate quoted in the bazaar. On December 30, 1971, the free market rate of the Afghanistan Bank was Af 78.00 buying, and Af 78.50 selling, per US$1, and the free market rate in the bazaar was Af 77.45 buying, and Af 77.95 selling, per US$1. The Afghanistan Bank also posts free market rates for deutsche mark, French francs, pounds sterling, and Swiss francs, which reflect their relative values to the U.S. dollar in international markets, and free market rates for the Indian rupee and Pakistan rupee that are determined by demand and supply for the currencies concerned. The Afghanistan Bank from time to time buys and sells in the free market bilateral agreement dollars and bilateral agreement sterling resulting partly from loans for consumer goods under certain of Afghanistan's bilateral payments agreements; most of this exchange sold by the Bank is purchased by government commercial and industrial enterprises for their imports from the countries concerned. The selling rate for U.S.S.R. clearing dollars was Af 60.50 per US$1 on December 30, 1971, and that for mainland China clearing sterling was Af 206.20 per £stg.1. On the same date, the selling rate for clearing dollars under the payments agreements with Bulgaria, Czechoslovakia, Poland and Yugoslavia was Af 55.50 per US$1.

B. Administration of Control

Foreign exchange is controlled by the Government through the Afghanistan Bank. The control is facilitated by the existence of relatively large companies, some of them government owned or government controlled, specializing in the export of such commodities as karakul, cotton, wool, and carpets. However, these companies do not exercise a monopoly over the export of such commodities.

C. Prescription of Currency

Settlements with countries with which Afghanistan has bilateral payments agreements (Bulgaria, mainland China, Czechoslovakia, Poland, U.S.S.R. and Yugoslavia. There is also a bilateral payments arrangement with India under which the bulk of trade is settled through a special account maintained in inconvertible Indian rupees with the Reserve Bank of India.) must be made in the foreign currencies specified in the agreements. The proceeds from exports of karakul, wool and cotton to other countries must be obtained in convertible currencies. There are no other prescription of currency requirements.

D. Imports and Import Payments

Imports are not subject to license. Imports of a few items (e.g. some drugs, liquor, arms, and ammunition) are prohibited on public policy grounds or for security reasons; in some instances, however, special permission to import these goods may be granted. The importation of certain other goods (e.g. a few textiles and selected non-essential consumer goods) also is prohibited. There are no quantitative restrictions on other imports. Most bilateral agreements, however, specify quotas (and sometimes prices) for commodities to be traded, and the Government facilitates the fulfillment of the commitments undertaken in the agreements. On the whole, trade with bilateral agreement countries is carried out on a compensation basis and usually both imports and exports are arranged by the same trader; imports against exports of cotton and wool are carried out by the Government and government agencies, or the proceeds of exports are allocated for the Government's external debt servicing.

Exchange is provided at the official rate for imports by the Government. Payments for imports through the banking system may be made only under letters of credit, against which a deposit of 100 per cent of the value of the imports in afghanis calculated at the prevailing free market rate, or in foreign exchange, is required upon establishment of the letter of credit. Such deposits may be used as collateral to obtain loans from commercial banks. The Afghanistan Bank is authorized to refuse to sell foreign exchange for the importation of a group of consumer goods that are regarded as non-essential. However, exchange for these items may be purchased either from the commercial banks or in the bazaar.

E. Payments for Invisibles

Central government payments for foreign debt service and other invisibles are made at the official rate. All other payments are settled at free market rates. Travelers leaving Afghanistan may take out no more than Af 500 in Afghan banknotes.

F. Exports and Export Proceeds

Exports are not subject to license. Exports of a few commodities (e.g. opium and museum pieces) are prohibited. Otherwise, control is exercised only over exports to bilateral agreement countries (see section on Imports and Import Payments, above). However, exporters of cotton are required to sell at least 20 per cent of their total exports to countries from which payments will be received in convertible currencies. Karakul is not exported to payments agreement countries.

Exchange receipts from exports of karakul, wool, and cotton must be surrendered at the official rate, irrespective of destination. The net proceeds of all exports other than karakul, wool and cotton, irrespective of the currency in which they accrue, must either be sold at free market rates to a domestic bank or be used by the exporter or a third party to pay for imports.

Export receipts from cotton are subject to an exchange subsidy at the rate of Af 25 per US$1 for convertible currency receipts and Af 3 per US $1 for exports settled under bilateral payments agreements. Convertible currency receipts from wool exports are paid an exchange subsidy at the rate of Af 10 per US$1 and those from karakul exports are paid an exchange subsidy of Af 20 per US$1.

Proceeds from the export of walnuts received over bilateral payments accounts are subject to an exchange tax of 9.5 per cent.

G. Proceeds from Invisibles

Thirty per cent of the foreign currency salaries of foreign employees of the Afghan public and private sectors must be converted into afghanis at the official rate, but the remaining 70 per cent may be remitted abroad or exchanged at the free market rate. Except in the case of India, receipts over bilateral payments agreement accounts from the embassies and state trading organizations of the countries concerned for their local expenses in Afghanistan are converted at the official rate. All other receipts from invisibles are sold at free market rates through either the banks or the bazaar. Travelers entering Afghanistan may bring in Afghan banknotes not exceeding Af 500.

H. Capital

Foreign investment in Afghanistan requires prior approval and is administered, as is domestic private investment, by an Investment Committee composed of five cabinet ministers. The Foreign and Domestic Private Investment Law (February 10, 1967) provides for a number of benefits, which include (1) income tax exemption for five years, beginning from the date of the first sales of products resulting from the new investment; (2) exemption from import duties on essential imports for five consecutive years after approval of the investment; (3) exemption from taxes on dividends for five years after the first distribution of dividends, but not more than eight years after the approval of the investment; (4) exemption from personal income tax and corporate tax on interest on foreign loans which constitute part of an approved investment; (5) exemption from export duties for ten years after the approval of the investment; and (6) mandatory purchases by government agencies and departments of their requirements from enterprises established under the law where such products are substantially competitive with imports in price and quality. The law also establishes that an investment approved by the Investment Committee shall require no further license to operate in Afghanistan.

Principal and interest installments on loans from abroad may be remitted freely to the extent of the legal obligation involved. Profits may be repatriated freely, and capital may be repatriated after five years at an annual rate not exceeding 25 per cent of the total registered capital. All the foregoing transfers are made through the free market. Joint ventures of foreign and Afghan capital are encouraged, but no specific percentages of domestic participation are prescribed and 100 per cent foreign-owned investments are not precluded by law.

I. Gold

Residents may freely import and purchase, hold, and sell domestically gold in any form. Exports of gold and silver in any form other than jewelry require licenses issued by the Council of Ministers; such licenses are not normally granted except for exports by or on behalf of the monetary authorities and industrial users. Commercial exports of gold and silver jewelry and of other articles containing minor quantities of gold or silver do not require a license and may be made freely. Customs duties are payable on imports and exports of silver in any form, unless the import or export is made by or on behalf of the monetary authorities. The import duty on gold is 1 per cent.

Appendix C. Prohibited Trade

Imports

Seditious or pornographic material

Poisons and drugs except by authorised pharmacists, etc.

Firearms and weapons of war

Television

Castor-oil

Iranian rugs and carpets

Silk turbans and cotton clothes

Sesame and other oil seeds

Silk cocoons excluding silk worms

Building stones

Various skins, e.g. marten

Various blankets and sheets made of cotton and rayon excluding woollen
    blankets

Various rugs, pillows, sheets (woollen or cotton pieces and prayer rugs)

Alcoholic beverages except under special licence by representatives of
    friendly countries

Appendix D. Free Market Dol.
"Bazaar Rate

Table 7.20

Free Market Dollar Exchange Rates "Bazaar Rates" 1332-1352

(Monthly Averages of Daily Buying Rates for Drafts and Cheques)

Month	1332	1333	1334	1335	1336	1337	1338	1339	1340	1341
Hamal	36.0	39.8	41.3	51.8	53.3	56.2	51.1	43.4	43.1	47.7
Saur	36.0	41.8	42.2	56.0	53.9	58.6	50.6	43.3	42.2	51.8
Jauza	39.0	41.8	42.4	57.6	55.3	60.0	53.9	40.1	42.0	51.8
Saratan	40.0	42.0	43.8	56.2	54.0	58.9	46.0	38.6	42.3	53.6
Asad	38.0	42.9	43.2	55.9	53.5	56.1	44.6	40.0	42.0	53.2
Sunbula	37.0	42.9	42.6	52.0	52.6	55.2	43.7	40.1	41.5	53.9
Mizan	35.0	41.0	42.8	50.8	52.6	52.9	43.2	38.2	41.9	53.1
Aqrab	35.0	41.5	43.5	52.0	52.7	52.1	43.1	38.6	41.8	54.1
Qaus	35.0	42.3	45.8	53.0	53.7	52.2	46.7	39.7	45.1	55.7
Jadi	37.0	44.3	49.1	54.5	54.8	50.5	49.2	43.5	46.6	55.2
Dalwa	38.0	43.5	52.8	53.4	56.3	53.6	45.1	41.3	45.9	53.1
Hoot	38.0	41.9	53.3	52.5	56.4	50.1	41.9	42.5	47.2	50.2
Annual Average	37.1	42.1	45.2	53.8	54.1	54.7	46.6	40.8	43.5	52.8

Source: Research Department, Da Afghanistan Bank.

Metal furniture excluding safes and drawers

Spring-metal beds rubber coated excluding rubber foam which is used for car seats

Dried peas

Straw products

Floor covering made of cotton

Stone utensils (marble)

Wooden furniture

Coloured rayon

Burlap

Cotton thread

Exports

Gold and silver

Afghanis in excess of Afs 500 per individual

Opium

Antique articles

Livestock

Grain

d Rupee Exchange Rates

32-1352

Table 7.20

Free Market Dollar Exchange Rates "Bazaar Rates" 1332-1352

(Monthly Averages of Daily Buying Rates for Drafts and Cheques)

1342	1343	1344	1345	1346	1347	1348	1349	1350	1351	1352
50.5	56.0	76.2	81.6	76.5	79.5	75.7	80.0	90.4	84.1	69.5
51.6	57.2	76.0	80.9	77.3	79.1	75.0	81.3	89.9	82.9	66.6
50.6	59.0	74.1	78.4	77.3	76.6	75.1	81.6	89.6	82.9	62.8
50.1	61.7	73.3	77.7	76.3	74.5	74.8	83.7	89.7	83.2	58.5
50.0	61.2	74.9	76.2	75.9	73.0	74.5	83.2	87.8	81.8	60.0
50.0	62.2	74.3	75.3	74.8	72.5	72.8	83.5	84.6	77.9	58.4
49.6	63.3	74.2	71.4	73.3	70.6	73.0	84.3	82.0	78.2	54.5
49.6	66.4	74.1	70.6	72.9	72.5	73.9	84.7	81.1	77.4	53.3
50.6	65.8	73.9	74.2	75.0	73.7	75.8	85.2	79.3	77.9	57.4
52.2	68.1	76.1	76.7	77.9	74.2	77.8	89.2	78.3	78.3	59.9
55.2	70.5	77.1	77.1	80.3	76.0	77.7	90.7	79.7	78.1	63.6
55.5	72.2	79.8	76.8	79.0	75.1	78.8	90.1	82.7	70.1	59.8
51.3	63.6	75.3	76.4	76.4	74.8	75.4	84.8	84.6	79.4	60.4

　　　　　THE FOREIGN TRADE SECTOR

Table 7.21

Free Market Indian Rupee Exchange Rates "Bazaar Rates" 1332-1352

(Monthly Averages of Daily Selling Rates for 100 Rupees in Drafts and Cheques)

Month	1332	1333	1334	1335	1336	1337	1338	1339	1340	134_
Hamal	717	755	888	1,058	1,000	1,099	1,009	728	675	65?
Saur	720	777	898	1,138	1,037	1,102	929	720	663	66¢
Jauza	752	808	885	1,135	1,020	1,119	889	655	663	71?
Saratan	760	811	858	1,103	988	1,064	790	630	650	70?
Asad	751	816	848	1,065	944	1,002	770	658	637	71▪
Sunbula	718	815	858	1,025	940	978	768	663	643	70¢
Mizan	682	787	853	989	912	934	741	640	648	68¢
Aqrab	705	822	894	1,013	913	925	732	606	632	76€
Qaus	708	853	942	1,020	937	970	820	628	660	87?
Jadi	713	858	985	1,073	1,005	978	819	675	674	82(
Dalwa	731	882	1,010	1,075	1,075	992	783	650	655	868
Hoot	752	878	1,040	1,028	1,074	1,011	727	684	659	81¢
Annual Average	726	822	913	1,060	987	1,015	815	661	655	74¢

Source: Research Department, Da Afghanistan Bank.

Table 7.22

Free Market Pakistani Rupee Exchange Rates "Bazaar Rates" 1332-1352

(Monthly Averages of Daily Selling Rates for 100 Rupees in Drafts and Cheques)

Month	1332	1333	1334	1335	1336	1337	1338	1339	1340	134_
Hamal	662	604	726	786	720	727	700	570	560	61(
Saur	645	618	733	786	720	728	674	565	557	62▪
Jauza	663	614	724	795	714	716	643	545	548	63▪
Saratan	660	617	735	797	695	701	601	528	534	64¢
Asad	640	620	728	760	622	673	591	538	542	65(
Sunbula	606	612	733	727	660	671	596	525	551	66(
Mizan	580	607	719	719	657	659	589	518	558	66?
Aqrab	603	638	734	743	665	722	588	530	562	67▪
Qaus	603	654	761	761	685	748	614	550	573	70¢
Jadi	596	677	796	772	715	762	616	558	588	72¢
Dalwa	596	723	800	761	741	735	588	554	608	73?
Hoot	598	731	811	733	741	720	565	568	613	72?
Annual Average	621	643	750	762	695	713	614	546	566	67(

Source: Research Department, Da Afghanistan Bank.

Table 7.21

Free Market Indian Rupee Exchange Rates "Bazaar Rates" 1332-1352

(Monthly Averages of Daily Selling Rates for 100 Rupees in Drafts and Cheques)

1342	1343	1344	1345	1346	1347	1348	1349	1350	1351	1352
799	735	853	738	680	756	727	642	692	720	760
773	735	839	726	663	743	683	628	669	725	701
743	763	846	742	672	735	675	624	706	740	697
749	803	853	690	681	744	690	634	710	778	687
753	795	860	669	671	692	667	619	681	790	685
719	784	790	670	660	676	636	609	664	720	653
690	772	804	669	644	665	646	628	645	713	608
699	790	757	647	638	681	670	649	671	736	542
728	791	739	672	644	709	675	644	645	725	
738	804	746	704	680	722	685	683	644	728	
744	820	722	693	743	738	678	699	676	755	
747	807	729	676	731	716	641	706	701	775	
740	783	795	691	675	714	673	647	675	742	

Table 7.22

Free Market Pakistani Rupee Exchange Rates "Bazaar Rates" 1332-1352

(Monthly Averages of Daily Selling Rates for 100 Rupees in Drafts and Cheques)

1342	1343	1344	1345	1346	1347	1348	1349	1350	1351	1352
706	656	835	932	889	891	799	750	805	748	652
701	653	868	924	890	896	791	745	839	762	617
678	663	898	881	887	883	788	773	812	724	589
655	678	906	884	884	868	791	773	738	685	566
660	681	896	883	842	843	763	770	748	687	551
643	689	876	874	826	821	734	754	746	662	530
628	709	885	875	823	802	737	763	746	667	485
634	738	883	876	843	803	764	793	772	675	487
644	767	882	888	884	812	785	819	763	672	
652	808	894	908	899	827	794	836	751	673	
680	824	918	913	896	824	770	813	758	670	
669	812	922	910	885	818	760	800	754	660	
663	723	888	895	870	840	773	783	769	690	

CHAPTER EIGHT

FINANCIAL AND FISCAL REFORM

i. *Introduction*

The five critical constraints to economic development in Afghanistan have been analysed in some detail in the previous chapters. In the final chapter, some essential elements in a programme of financial reform are discussed. An hypothetical exercise is then presented to show what might have been achieved during the Fourth Plan period in terms of domestic resource mobilisation had an aggressive programme of financial and fiscal reform been initiated at the outset, i.e. in 1351 (1972).

The inter-dependence of the two channels through which domestic resources can be mobilised, namely the financial sector and the fiscal system, was stressed in Chapter IV. The inadequacies of both were considered in Chapters V and VI. Because of the linkages between the two, any efforts at reform must take place simultaneously on both fronts [M7; S8]. The concentration in this chapter on financial development should not, therefore, be interpreted to imply that fiscal reform is less important. It only reflects the facts that numerous recommendations for the latter already exist and that the important constituents of a programme of fiscal reform are relatively simple, as shown in Chapter VI. Furthermore, the training requirements for this are virtually identical with those outlined in the programme of financial development.

Available empirical evidence, in addition to the Adelman-Morris results presented in Chapter I [A2], suggests that financial development has had overwhelming effects on the pace of economic growth in the countries where it has taken place. Germany and Japan since 1953, Taiwan and Iran since 1960, and South Korea since 1965 have all exhibited extraordinary real expansion in their banking sectors. These have also been countries in which the rate of economic growth has been spectacular. Some basic data on these five countries are provided in Table 8.1. Here the rate of decrease in velocity of circulation is used to measure the rate of financial development. Velocity is a useful indicator of the relative size of the financial sector in countries lacking sophisticated capital markets, particularly when the broad definition of money, M2, is used. The lower velocity, the higher the ratio of money to Gross National Product (GNP) and hence, *ceteris paribus*, the larger the supply of domestic credit and the relative size of the financial system.

Conversely, cases of declining financial sectors, i.e. rising velocities, and declining rates of economic growth have also been recorded. For example, industrial growth in Brazil declined from 9.8 per cent per annum in the 1950s to 3 per cent over the period 1963-1966. The real money supply contracted as a result of the increased inflation which had occurred between these two periods and the real volume of bank credit fell. The latter severely retarded industrial expansion [M34, p. 184]. Incidentally, Brazil reversed this trend and has provided another example of successful development over the past five years [I2, pp. 66-68].

Table 8.1

Annual Average Percentage Rates of Change in Real Money Stock, Per Capita Gross National Product and Velocities of Circulation in Six Countries

(Percentages)

Country	Average Annual Growth in Real Money Stock (M2/P)	Average Annual Growth in Real Per Capita GNP	Average Annual Change in Velocity of Circulation (GNP/M2)
Afghanistan 1340-1350	2.3	0.7	0.0
Germany 1953-1970	13.5	5.0	−4.3
Iran 1961-1970	15.0	6.2	−5.5
Japan 1954-1970	17.4	9.2	−3.0
South Korea 1965-1970	46.1	9.6	−20.1
Taiwan 1960-1970	20.7	6.6	−7.9

Note: Money supply data are centred annual averages, except in the case of Iran where centred monthly averages are used. Money supply for Germany includes bank bonds. Growth rates are annually compounded.

Source: *International Financial Statistics*, 25 (9), September 1972; *International Financial Statistics: 1971 Supplement; United Nations Statistical Yearbook 1971; United Nations Yearbook of National Accounts Statistics 1966; United Nations Monthly Bulletin of Statistics*, 26 (3), March 1972; Bank Markazi Iran, *Annual Report and Balance Sheet 1350* (Tehran: Bank Markazi Iran, 1972); *Bank Markazi Iran Bulletins*, 1-10, 1960-1971.

The importance of financial development has been stressed by a number of eminent economists. Friedman recently concluded:

.... in developing countries a major source of future development is an improved financial structure. In every country which is developed the financial institutions have played a major role in assuring a wide distribution of capital funds, in assuring the efficient utilization of capital, in assuring the availability of capital to people who do not themselves have the wealth. [F22, p. 709]

The two men who pioneered the theoretical work in this branch of economics, Gurley and Shaw, have produced a mass of material to support their contention that:

> Development involves finance as well as goods. [G25, p. 515]

Using the Gurley-Shaw theoretical framework, Patrick has extended this approach:

> There are three major ways in which the financial system can influence the capital stock for growth purposes. First, financial institutions can encourage a more efficient allocation of a given total amount of tangible wealth (capital in a broad sense), by bringing about changes in its users and in its composition, through intermediation among various types of asset-holders. Second, financial institutions can encourage a more efficient allocation of new investment—additions to capital stock—from relatively less to relatively more productive uses, by intermediation between savers and entrepreneurial investors. Third, they can induce an increase in the rate of accumulation of capital, by providing increased incentives to save, invest and work. [P9, p. 177]

From this, policy implications are derived:

> .... the basic objectives of financial policy for economic growth are to encourage savers (asset-holders) to hold their savings (assets) in the form of financial rather than unproductive tangible assets; to ensure that investment (capital stock) is allocated efficiently to the socially most productive uses; and to provide incentives to increase saving, investment and production. To achieve these objectives, policy-makers must encourage the proper foundation and expansion of financial institutions. [P9, p. 186]

McKinnon has recently developed a theory of money and capital in economic development, again based on the Gurley-Shaw approach, in which financial development plays a crucial role. The impetus for his work was provided by "the remarkable financial transformation that occurred in 1965-66 in Korea—where Shaw was an influential advisor" [M7, p. 2]. McKinnon's main propositions were outlined in Chapter VI.

McKinnon tests his theory extensively on a selection of both successful and unsuccessful underdeveloped countries. In every case, financial development is strongly correlated with the rate of economic growth and the causal relationship runs from financial development to economic growth, the key policy variable in each case being relatively high real rates of interest to attract time and savings deposits.

Ali [A14], Brimmer [B32], Chandavarkar [C11], Emery [E4] and many other monetary and development economists have produced evidence attesting to the importance of financial development in the process of economic growth. Perhaps one of the most significant collections of material is that of Brown [B35], Gurley, Patrick and Shaw [G24], Kanesa-Thasan [K5] and McKinnon [M7] on the Korean experience. This was undoubtedly a unique case. Of particular importance is the fact that both financial and fiscal reform took place simultaneously there [M7, p. 107].

On the essential role of the fiscal system in domestic resource mobilisation, material from Hart [H5] and Kaldor [K3], among others, was cited in Chapter VI. The discussion in Chapter IV also led to the conclusion that a successful development strategy had to be based on domestic resource mobilisation to a far higher degree than has to date been the case in Afghanistan.

Many reports have stressed the need for both financial and fiscal reform. On the latter, most recommendations agree that the two primary targets should be administration and agricultural taxation. Administrative shortcomings were considered in Chapter VI and the basic prerequisites for improvement suggested. The need for higher agricultural taxation was also stressed. It should be added here, however, that such taxes should be non-discriminatory and should not deter production. Various forms of land tax can be found which meet both criteria. Applied elsewhere, they have been generally simple to administer, a third essential criterion for taxation in Afghanistan. One hopes that administrative reform within the Ministry of Finance and the introduction of a new land tax are high on the list of priorities of the new Republican Government.

ii. *Outline of a Programme of Financial Development*

A Legislation and Legal Practices

Before financial development can take place in Afghanistan, legislation and improved legal practices are needed. It appears that this prerequisite has already been recognised by the Government. Three fundamental legislative measures have been generally recognised: lending and borrowing legislation providing for legal negotiable instruments, mortgage, expropriation of collateral on default, speedy debt collection procedures, credit standing enquiries, penalties for issuing cheques against insufficient funds, etc.; legislation for the establishment and operations of financial intermediaries such as commercial and development banks, insurance companies, credit cooperatives and any other institutions which transfer funds from savers to investors by the acts of accepting deposits and lending; central banking legislation establishing control mechanisms for the normal operation of monetary policy and the supervision of the financial sector.

By far the most urgent requirement consists of measures under the general heading of lending and borrowing. Although the *sine qua non* for the rapid expansion of banking activities, relatively little attention has so far been focused on this particular legislative requirement.

The two other groups of legislative measures are simpler. Many draft central and commercial banking laws have already been prepared, the best being those prepared by the Financial Development Committee with the assistance of a team from the International Monetary Fund in 1352 (1973). As well as central and commercial banking laws, the Committee also drafted a Deposit Insurance Act.

There is a critical need for improved legal practices along with new legislation. As mentioned in Chapter V, there is little knowledge of the existing Commercial Law and court procedures have not been adequate for the protection of banks as lenders. The Government must also show willingness to protect the banks in their lending activities by providing support for debt collection, etc.

B Revitalising the Existing Financial Institutions

Before the establishment of any new institutions, the existing financial institutions, with the possible exception of the Agricultural Development Bank, require help and support in increasing their efficiency and expanding their operations. It would seem that a programme of technical assistance in the form of experts in central, commercial and specialised banking is an essential concomitant to the implementation of the proposed legislation and improved legal practices. One cannot, for example, expect Da Afghanistan Bank to become a full central bank overnight simply by enacting a central bank law.

In conjunction with the provision of technical assistance a training programme is needed. In fact, the existing banks all have their own small programmes and one of their legitimate fears of competition from new or foreign banks is the loss of expensively trained staff. Given that the leakages of bank personnel who have been trained might be considerable, it would be reasonable to assume that the social benefits from training bankers are greater than the private benefits. From this, economic analysis suggests that the existing provision of training is socially sub-optimal and a clear case exists for state subsidy of such activities. Serious consideration might be given to the establishment of either a Bankers' College or a Banking Faculty within the Kabul Commercial College.

As well as technical assistance, the existing institutions, particularly Da Afghanistan Bank, are in considerable need of modern equipment such as electronic calculating machines. Here it is a matter of providing not labour saving devices but machines which eliminate the element of human error. The latter is in such abundance at present that even the accuracy of aggregate monetary statistics is seriously jeopardised. Inaccurate book keeping is a strong deterrent to potential depositors.

The unfavourable external environment faced by the banks was discussed in Chapter V. The enactment of banking and commercial legislation together with steps to ensure prompt and efficient court action should do much to improve this.

Although training is the critical requirement for improving the internal environment in which Afghanistan's financial institutions operate, there are two prerequisites to the success of large scale training efforts within the financial sector. The first is competent management to use trained personnel effectively, the second an efficient set of procedures in which to train.

The existing training needs can be separated into six distinct groups which can be illustrated as follows:

Existing Training Requirements

New Entrants   Existing Staff
High Level or Administrative Grade
Medium Level or Executive Grade
Elementary Level or Clerical Grade

Within the high level or administrative grade, it is generally recognised that the training of personnel already working in the banking system can only aim at the improvement of the execution of existing functions. Indeed, this is generally the case with all those presently working in the financial sector. Hence, the need here is solely for on-the-job training at all levels or grades for existing staff.

On the other hand, within the next five years it might be hoped that all banks, particularly Da Afghanistan Bank, will expand their range of activities and for this will recruit new staff at all levels. In Da Afghanistan Bank, new research, inspection and audit, and credit departments should be established for which personnel must be recruited. At the high level or administrative grade perhaps 10 to 15 new graduates a year might be hired by Da Afghanistan Bank for the eventual staffing of these departments. These graduates might be given one or two years' training in the form of both on-the-job instruction and academic courses in Kabul and then be sent abroad for one or two years' additional training. Those intending to enter research departments would receive academic training abroad in subjects such as monetary and international economics, while those planning to work in the fields of inspection, audit and credit would be sent to work in foreign commercial and central banks and accountancy firms for vocational training and on-the-job instruction. Although experienced employees drawn from existing staff would naturally head such departments at the outset, the aim should be to produce well trained young men and women who would soon gain sufficient experience to assume managerial responsibility over work in these departments.

At the second level or executive grade, the main thrust should be to train the existing personnel to carry out their duties more efficiently. Within this category fall directors and sub-directors and those at present in more junior positions who possess the capacity to gain promotion to higher positions when vacancies occur. Given that rapid expansion of the banking system is unlikely to take place within the next few years, only a small number of new recruits to replace retiring personnel will be accepted. Nevertheless, by offering suitable training facilities for all the banks it should be possible to provide new recruits with special training in banking procedures.

Within the medium level or executive grade there exist 100 to 150 people within Afghanistan's banking system, most of whom could benefit from on-the-job training programmes. For example, there is an urgent need to train people at this level to write business letters in Dari and English. Some of the better people (10 or 20) might also benefit from short periods (six months) of additional on-the-job training in Iran.

At the elementary level or clerical grade, there are over 1,000 employees within the banking system who require training to enable them to follow the banks' procedures with accuracy and efficiency. The length of time required to achieve this modest aim is fairly short, provided the fundamental prerequisite that procedures to be taught are clear, simple and efficient is met.

On-the-job training basically consists of part time classroom instruction (two or three hours a day) combined with supervision of the trainees' work during the training period by managerial and teaching staff. Again stressing the relatively modest aim of the training programmes at the medium and elementary levels, it is essential that all instruction be given in Dari rather than in English. Nevertheless, for teaching the teachers there is a need for a number of foreign advisors. The latter would also be used for direct teaching at the high level or administrative grade. A schematic picture of the present training needs and staff is shown below.

Training Needs and Staffing

Level	New Entrants	Existing Staff	Teaching Staff Afghan	Foreign
High or Administrative	10-15 a year	—	1	2
Medium or Executive	20-30 a year	100-150	2-3	1-2
Elementary or Clerical	30-50 a year	1000 +	8-10	1-2

Funds will be required for the provision of foreign experts and scholarships to send new recruits to the high level or administrative grade abroad. In conjunction with this, however, is a futher need for one or two foreign experts to work directly in the research departments and assist management in various ways in all three banks.

The United Nations recently announced that it is providing an additional grant of $2 million to Afghanistan. It might be suggested that one-tenth of this, i.e. $200,000, be allocated to the financial sector. In particular, this could finance the redrafting of procedures manuals, the first few years of the training programme and the provision of some equipment. It would seem that other sources of finance might be needed for the management assistance and organisational restructuring.

C Rapid Expansion in Real Volume of Domestic Credit

Concentration on the primary goal of financial development, namely a rapid expansion in the real volume of domestic credit, can be seen as the essential element of the next stage, after legal and educational problems have been tackled. Thought should then be given to the possibility of channelling more loan aid through the financial sector. Donors have not so far been noted for their ability to find and support productive projects. The necessary concentration on small scale investments, on-farm assistance, etc., to raise agricultural productivity in particular, requires a much larger field staff for evaluating and supervising profitable investment opportunities than the donor agencies can provide themselves. A modern, efficient financial sector should provide such a staff and administer these loans, as the Agricultural and Industrial Development Banks do at present with World Bank funds. The increased volume of domestic credit in real terms which financial development would generate should be directed primarily into the agricultural sector for small scale on-farm investments. It is difficult to envisage any viable alternative for raising agricultural productivity, seen in Chapter I to be one of the critical constraints to economic development at present.

Two elements in the programme of financial development outlined above require more detailed consideration. The first is the crucial role which a central bank must play in developing the financial sector. The second is the interest rate policy it pursues, since as pointed out above it is the interest rate, that most pervasive of prices, which is the key to both effective and efficient domestic resource mobilisation.

iii. *Central Banking for Development*

The primary function of a central bank is traditionally "to regulate the flow of money and credit in the economy" [L5, p. 556] through its role as banker to commercial banks and the government, the objective being the maintenance of full employment without inflation. In the main, this is achieved by the central bank's control over the supply of credit to its customers. During the past decade, however, several central banks have become involved in specific problems of economic development almost as much as in this traditional function of central banking.

There are many examples of measures taken by central banks which directly or indirectly have contributed to economic development. On the other hand, there are a number of measures designed for the same purpose which have invariably failed to make any such contribution. This section outlines some of the central banking activities which have been successful, as well as some which have not, in promoting economic growth.

The basic aim of financial development is to mobilise domestic savings into productive investment. This involves, on the one hand, increasing both the level of savings and the proportion of savings held in the form of financial assets. In a country like Afghanistan, the latter consists almost entirely of currency and bank deposits. On the other hand, it involves ensuring that the financial sector channels funds into the most profitable investment opportunities. Thus, in an underdeveloped country lacking a capital market the basic objectives are:

A. To increase the demand for money at every level of GNP;
B. To facilitate lending by the financial institutions to those who can use the resources in the most productive investments.

Central banking activities should therefore be analysed with these fundamental aims in view. If the demand for money can be shifted at every level of income as illustrated in Figure 8.1, the money supply can be expanded by that magnitude without causing inflationary pressures. Increasing the demand for money implies persuading the private sector to free voluntarily resources for use by those who provide the counterpart claims

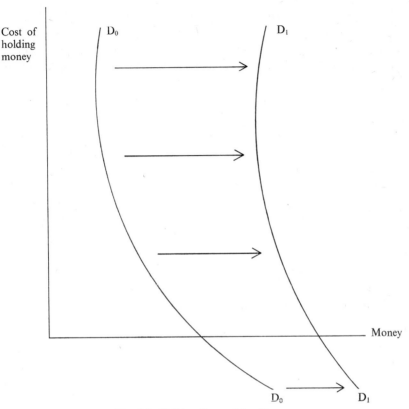

Fig. 8.1. Shifting Demand for Money

to the increase in the money supply. In other words, an increase in the demand for money enables, *ceteris paribus*, an equal non-inflationary expansion in the level of domestic credit. The importance of this has been expressed clearly by McKinnon:

> Whether authorities decided to nourish and expand the "real" stock of money (that is, the stock of money measured by its value in relation to the prices of goods and services) or allowed it to remain shrunken and heavily taxed, has critically affected the relation between saving and income and the efficiency of investment in a number of countries .... [M7, p. 3]

Money is a commodity supplied by the central bank in the form of currency and by the commercial banks in the form of deposits. Increasing the demand for money involves the same factors as increasing the demand for any other commodities, the two most important being price competitiveness and marketing.

The price competitiveness of Afghanistan's money supply can be measured by two inter-related variables, namely, the price of an Afghani in terms of the commodities for which it can be exchanged and the price of an Afghani in terms of foreign currencies. More precisely, price competitiveness of the Afghani is determined by the level of inflation (the *change* in the rate at which commodities can be exchanged for Afghanis) and the speed of depreciation (the *change* in the rate at which foreign currencies can be exchanged for Afghanis). The lower the level of inflation and the speed of depreciation, the greater the price competitiveness of Afghanistan's money and hence, *ceteris paribus*, the greater the demand for it. For the savings deposit component of the money stock, the rate of interest is a third variable determining price competitiveness.

When an individual increases his stock of money in an economy such as Afghanistan's where virtually no other financial assets exist, he automatically performs an act of saving. By increasing his money stock he abstains from spending. Where on balance people in a country are adding more to their stocks of money than they are drawing upon them, financial saving occurs in the economy. This saving can be mobilised, i.e. channelled, into productive investments by the institutions providing the additional money. An increased demand for currency, for example, enables the central bank to increase its lending in the form of new currency without creating inflation. The new currency put into circulation in this process is voluntarily added to currency holdings. The increased spending by those who receive new loans in this form from the central bank is matched by the increased saving of those wanting to hold the new currency which has been issued. Similarly, an increased demand for bank deposits enables increased lending to the same extent by commercial banks, the new spending being matched by new saving. This process is again non-inflationary, provided that the demand for currency has not concomitantly decreased. Thus, stimulating demand for money and allowing financial institutions to increase their loans for investment purposes without causing inflation is the most important objective of central banking for development.

The predominant factors involved in stimulating demand for money are security and return. When there is rapid inflation no one wants to hold money because the return is negative. The longer the money is held the less it is worth. Friedman has shown that with realistic demand for money parameters and a positive rate of economic growth, the level of domestic credit expansion in real terms is maximised in the long run when prices are falling [F23]. This result springs from the generally estimated high cost elasticities of demand for money. Hence, when even the return on holding currency is actually positive, as is the case when the price level is falling, the demand for money increases and so enables a larger level of domestic credit expansion. In practice, deflation has disadvantages; an optimal policy might, therefore, be to aim for a stable price level, thus gaining a demand for domestic currency both from those who previously preferred to hold tangible assets whose prices were rising and from those who previously held foreign currency. In both cases the substitution frees resources for investment.

The holders of foreign currency free resources for use by the country which supplies the currency, the holders of an increased supply of domestic currency free resources for domestic investment. The simplest way of making domestic currency more attractive is to cause it to appreciate *vis-à-vis* foreign currencies. A minimum condition for this is holding the rate of domestic inflation below that of the rest of the world. It has already been argued that this would also increase the demand for money by those who previously held tangible assets. Furthermore, it would stimulate savings from those who previously had not saved and increase savings of those who were already savers by providing positive returns to deposit holding.

The aim of financial development is to persuade people both to increase their saving and to hold their assets in financial claims rather than in unproductive tangible assets, such as gold and jewellery. Resources are thereby freed to finance expenditure by those whose liabilities constitute the assets of the financial system.

One of the striking visual differences between the cities of Afghanistan and those of neighbouring Iran, Pakistan and Turkey is the total absence of bank advertisements in the former. The Afghan financial system is completely passive in outlook; there is no active competition whatsoever amongst the banks for deposits. Perhaps the most important device open to Da Afghanistan Bank for increasing demand for money is the instigation of a positive policy for the encouragement of banking and the banking habit. This must involve furthering competition within the financial sector.

Another aspect of the security attribute of money is the protection of depositors from the risks of bank failure. The central bank is therefore usually given the responsibility for maintaining the "soundness" of the banking system. As controls for this purpose have a different objective from controls to regulate the total volume of credit for monetary policy, there is an advantage in keeping the two sets of regulatory devices distinct and separate from one another. Furthermore, regulation to ensure "sound" banking may well be linked to a deposit insurance scheme. The rationale behind this is twofold: first, the insurer, i.e. the central bank, can insist that certain conditions be met before it will issue a policy to a bank; second, the central bank will generally be obliged in any event to rescue banks which find themselves in difficulties in order that confidence in the banking system be maintained. Therefore, it might as well collect insurance premiums and run the operation on something approximating an actuarial basis. All commercial banks would be required to insure their deposits and the insurance department of the central bank would prescribe the conditions, like any other insurance agency, which had to be met before policies would be issued. Such conditions would be those of "sound" banking. The insurance department must be empowered to inspect banks to ensure that the conditions of the insurance, e.g. minimum capital, organisational structure, minimum liquid reserve requirements, acceptable lending practices, etc., were being observed. Such a department could also ensure that any monetary policy directives, e.g. special deposits, overall limitation of credit expansion, etc., were also being observed. In this way, the second element of security so important to money holders is provided.

The insurance premiums might form the basic source of funds for special central bank lending operations to help, where necessary, the establishment and activities of new financial institutions. This can take the form of subscriptions to part of the initial capital or special loans during the first few years of a new institution's operations.

Setting aside non-inflationary sources of funds to be used to help the development of financial institutions in the country is not a new idea. As Patrick states:

> The monetary authorities have an important institution-building role in encouraging the establishment of a wide array of financial markets (and financial institutions to operate in these markets) which allocate saving competitively to the most productive investors. One important approach is to encourage the private development of the financial system, in response to the demand for its services, by clearing away impeding institutional and other obstacles of a legal or customary nature. The financial authorities can create an environment which is conducive to growth both of the real economy and of the financial system .... [P9, p. 186]

It has already been suggested that a special fund based on deposit insurance premiums might be established to assist new institutions in the financial sector. Where this has been done, Tamagna found successful results:

In various cases their special funds have provided the capital, organization and techniques for autonomous institutions, which could enter the financial system on the basis of their own experience, complementing other institutions and without requiring any further special support and assistance from the central bank. [T1, p. 80]

One set of financial institutions which needs special consideration in this regard are the development banks. Frequently, such institutions remain too small for fully effective operation because of lack of funds. Where deposits are not accepted these institutions must rely on other ways of raising funds most of which are difficult in underdeveloped countries lacking developed capital markets. The central bank can play a role here by providing capital in the first instance, but much more important, purchasing their bonds as they expand and in this way help to create a market for their securities. Guaranteeing the bond issues of development banks can also be a valuable central banking service to these institutions [B32, pp. 784-86]. As suggested above, credit to the agricultural sector through the Agricultural Development Bank must be expanded as rapidly as possible to increase agricultural productivity. Da Afghanistan Bank can help here in the way described above.

The encouragement of new financial institutions and assets can be important in increasing financial saving:

.... the expansion of the banking system and nonbank financial institutions and a change in people's preference from money to other types of liquid assets, in addition to broadening the domain of monetary policy, will exert a downward pressure on interest rates and will increase the availability of credit throughout the economy. The central banks can also play an important role in mobilizing savings by helping to develop a market in government securities. [R2, p. 144]

Of equal importance is the encouragement of the regional spread of branches into the provinces. It may well be unprofitable for a bank to open a branch in a new location outside the main urban centres, as the banking habit takes time to develop. Nevertheless, it may be socially both productive and desirable from the income equality viewpoint. The central bank can encourage the spread of branches through positive incentives such as grants, tax reductions related to number of branches, etc.

Where private enterprise is seriously lacking for the establishment of a banking network, state banks may be founded. Not only can they be used to establish a network of branches throughout the country but they may also be indirectly beneficial in providing credit to sectors, particularly the agricultural sector, traditionally starved of institutional finance. The policy of spreading bank branches throughout the provinces will be accompanied, provided the branch managers have the authority to dispense loans, by an increase in the provision of credit to those living in these areas. In fact, the eventual profitability of rural branches is likely only if every branch grants loans. The provision of loans acts as the best potential advertisement the banking system can use: the wider the reach of the advertisement, the larger the number of depositors.

The main difficulties faced by banks in underdeveloped countries in giving branch managers authority to grant loans are first the lack of sufficiently well trained personnel and second the absence of strong accounting systems. The latter is, of course, intimately connected with the former. The central bank can play a major role in the provision of adequate management training and development programmes as well as direct assistance in the development of accounting systems. At the apex of the financial sector, the central bank is in the best possible position to assess educational requirements and provide technical assistance either from its own staff or by requesting it from foreign donor agencies. Foreign correspondent banks are also often willing to provide small training programmes. Such links can be fostered and developed with the aid of central bank initiative.

The central bank can develop the financial sector in a number of ways. Through judicious use of a development fund, new institutions can be started. Various incentives can be provided for the spread of branch bank networks. Training and technical assistance can be made available to enable these branches to carry out a full range of banking activities. The central bank should take on the responsibility for the development of its sector of the economy. This sector is not traditionally considered in the same light as, for example, the agricultural, industrial or transportation sector. Development plans do not set targets for, or assess achievement in, the financial sector. Regulation rather than development is the usual emphasis. Because the financial sector is not defined as a sector in this sense, there is no minister or ministry responsible for its development. In essence, this is why central bank initiative and responsibility for the financial sector's development is of such critical importance in almost all underdeveloped countries.

To undertake the development role sketched in the preceding sections, it has implicitly been assumed that the central bank possesses a well trained, competent staff. Where this is not the case, training and technical assistance must be channelled first into the central bank before it can carry out these important roles in the development process for which it is so well placed. Fortunately, in most underdeveloped countries, this prerequisite is met. Thus, an additional role as government advisor can be played:

> As a rule, the central bank is likely to be a well-equipped institution, with respect to staff and financial resources, to undertake the research and analysis on which a well conceived development plan must rest. [B32, p. 790]

The obvious field of development planning in which the central bank is best equipped to advise the government is the financial side of the plan. However, policies affecting the investment climate and private sector activities in general may also usefully be prepared by the central bank. It is, after all, in a position to know more about the private sector than most government ministries. In a general survey of the role of central banking in the planning process, Tamagna makes the following comment:

> It is in most cases the central bank that formulates the "financial framework of the program" according to flow of funds or related financial accounts at its disposal; such financial framework outlines the present and prospective savings formation, the availability of foreign capital, both from private and public and international sources, and the domestic credit expansion that the central banks regard as consistent with monetary stability. [T1, p. 79]

The central bank can further estimate the maximum possible overall investment target and indicate the monetary and fiscal measures needed to achieve it.

In several underdeveloped countries, central banks have succeeded in establishing themselves as important sources of advice and information. In a survey of the role of central banks as government advisors, Brimmer concludes:

> In general, where the central bank has been allowed to maintain a reasonable degree of detachment, its advice has tended to be objective and, even if not always received with enthusiasm, respected .... on the whole, the evidence suggests that in many countries the central bank is a senior partner in the development enterprise. [B32, pp. 789-90]

It would be somewhat unrealistic to assume that Da Afghanistan Bank is at present in a position to assume the role of impartial, expert advisor to the Government. Part of the problem lies in the lack of expertise and the lowly role assigned to the Research Department. Recruitment and training can do much to rectify this. However, a major part of the problem lies in the relationship between Da Afghanistan Bank and the

Government. At present, a multitude of Cabinet decrees ordering the Bank to make specific loans virtually eliminates the possibility of any independent policy design.

Da Afghanistan Bank is unlikely to develop into a prestigious institution attracting well qualified recruits so long as it remains in its present subservient position *vis-à-vis* the Government. It is therefore essential to discontinue the present practice of arbitrary interference in the Bank's activities so frequently engaged in by the Government. The obvious solution lies in the establishment of a Money and Credit Committee consisting of representatives from both the Government and Da Afghanistan Bank, as well as representatives of private sector interests, to determine the broad issues of monetary policy. This should then be the only source of Government influence over the Bank's activities. Precise rules governing the nature of such influence through representation on this Committee need to be drawn up. Da Afghanistan Bank would then attain the autonomy so crucial for its own development.

The potential which a central bank possesses to perform various development activities can be considerable. The realisation of this potential, however, requires certain conditions, the most important being a clearly defined relationship between government and central bank, providing the latter with exclusive authority over the implementation of monetary policy and sufficient autonomy to generate a useful position as external advisor to the former. Effective control over the supply of money and dynamic action in relation to all the other aspects of financial development discussed above require, on the one hand, that the government provides sufficient authority to the central bank and, on the other, that the central bank accepts willingly its responsibilities. There are many other details which must be given careful attention but the essential prerequisites for effective central banking for development, the importance of which can hardly be over-emphasised, are the establishment of a conducive working relationship between government and central bank and the acceptance of development responsibilities by the latter.

iv. *An Interest Rate Policy*

Interest rate policies have several dimensions. In the words of Chandavarkar:

> .... interest rates can be viewed as instruments for more effective mobilisation of savings (as deposit rates) through the offer of realistic rates on monetary savings, such as time and savings deposits, claims on financial institutions, and government securities. Similarly, interest rates can be

viewed as a social rate of discount to determine the optimum allocation of savings between consumption and investment and as a rationing device for efficient allocation among alternative forms of investment. [C11, pp. 49-50]

Thus, with the interest rate performing not just one but three functions, any policy must take all into consideration. In fact, these three functions can be simultaneously satisfied in a perfectly competitive economy without institutional constraints of any kind by allowing interest rates to find their own market levels at which supply equals demand. In most under-developed countries there are a number of existing constraints which militate against this passive policy. Afghanistan provides striking examples of two such constraints, namely, the lack of bankable projects on which loans can be made and artificially low interest rates to the public sector.

Interest rates on deposits are relatively low in a country such as Afghanistan, in which *a priori* one would expect high returns to savings and generally high rates of interest as a result of the scarcity of capital, because the effective demand for bank loans is small. The banks cannot lend as much as they would like to and even the small volume of deposits is, at present, sufficient for their operations. Thus, without additional measures, raising deposit rates would merely provide the banks with an excess supply of funds under most conditions.

The paradox of low equilibrium interest rates of Afghanistan's financial institutions and capital scarcity is explained by the existence of legal and management constraints. Where *de facto* the only security is shares in the few reliable joint stock companies, the effective demand for bank loans by the private sector is bound to be minute. Furthermore, the lack of any management expertise in project appraisal ensures that unsecured loans are not made on any economic criteria but only on the basis of personal acquaintance.

If it is accepted that relatively high interest rates should be a con-comitant to capital scarcity, for which there is evidence in Afghanistan in the form of both non-institutional interest rates and returns on small scale investments, then effective demand for bank loans must be increased. This can be achieved by legal reforms to increase the range of effective securities available to the banks in the form of chattel and real estate mortgages, liens, negotiable instruments, hire-purchases and guarantees, and speedy facilities for expropriation on default, as well as improved legal practices discussed above. Management expertise can also be developed through technical assistance and training programmes.

Once a central bank in an underdeveloped country has taken measures to facilitate banks' lending operations, interest rates will rise provided controls are not imposed. In many countries, maximum rates have been established by the central bank or agreed upon in some cartel arrangement between the commercial banks. The argument tends to be that loan rates must be kept down if investment is to be encouraged. Where such ceilings are effective, resources are misallocated. In fact, in the vast majority of countries where they exist they are not effective. It is in the interests of both the banks and prospective clients who might otherwise not receive a loan at all to agree on a higher rate. This is most easily accomplished by an undertaking on the part of the borrower to keep a specified proportion of the loan in an account with the bank. In this way, the effective interest rate is made infinitely variable. For example, a 25 per cent deposit agreement raises the effective interest rate to the borrower by one-third, a 50 per cent deposit doubles the rate and a 75 per cent deposit raises the effective interest rate by a factor of four.

Accepting the undesirability of trying to enforce maximum interest rates for whatever misguided purpose, and assuming no such controls exist, the central bank's actions to facilitate bank lending will result in a rise in interest rates on loans. Demand increases, hence price, i.e. in this case the rate of interest, goes up. Provided the banking system is competitive, a rise in loan rates will cause a rise in deposit rates, each bank now wanting more funds for profitable lending operations and thus raising deposit rates to attract more deposits. The desired result is achieved.

Unfortunately, banking systems in both developed and underdeveloped countries are notoriously uncompetitive (e.g. for Britain see [J4, Chapter IV]). Cartel agreements, often with the approval of the central bank, purportedly to ensure a "sound" banking system, abound. Where fixed interest rates on deposits have been agreed upon to prevent cut throat competition, rising loan rates simply make banking more profitable. There are no other effects. Given that this will often be the case, the central bank can be given the authority to establish minimum interest rates on deposits to considerable advantage. Then, where cartel arrangements are clearly resulting in monopolistic profits, banks can be obliged to raise their deposit rates. The minimum deposit interest rate requirement is, in fact, the only interest rate control which can be justified.

The final aspect of interest rate policies concerns the common practice of differential rates not reflecting differential risk and duration for activities in selected economic sectors. The almost universal case is differential interest rates between public and private sectors. Afghanistan is no exception, with a rate of 2 per cent being charged by Da Afghanistan Bank on Government loans while rates from the banks to the private sector range from 8 to 11 per cent. In many countries economic sectors such as agriculture and industry are also provided with loans at lower rates. Various forms of incentive are provided to the commercial banks, such as differential rediscount facilities, lower reserve requirements for a more preferred portfolio, etc., for this purpose.

Evidence suggests that differential interest rate policies have not been successful [B32, pp. 786-89]. Furthermore, there is no economic justification for this practice. Where particular economic sectors are to be encouraged, direct subsidy has considerable advantages. First, with a direct subsidy it is easier to ensure that the benefit actually accrues to the sector to be encouraged. With differential interest rates, borrowers in the favoured sector can re-lend their loans to those outside the sector. There is much evidence that this practice occurs in Turkey where differential interest rate policies have been pursued most unsuccessfully [F25, Chapter 6]. More important, where a policy of this kind is successfully enforced it results in a greater subsidy to capital intensive than to labour intensive methods of production within the favoured sectors. Given general capital scarcity, the net result is over-capital intensive production in the favoured sectors and even greater capital scarcity elsewhere. Illustrations of this were given in Chapter VI. By substituting an overall subsidy for differential interest rates, correct allocation of resources between capital and labour can be maintained, the subsidy can be tied to the particular activities for which it is meant, and a more effective boost given to selected sectors.

This argument is as equally applicable, of course, to subsidies to public versus private sector activities as it is to agricultural versus trade sectors. As Chandavarkar points out:

> The very enjoyment of monopsonist borrowing powers makes it all the more incumbent on governments in the less developed countries to borrow at more competitive rates in keeping with the real cost of capital in the economy, rather than to continue to borrow at artificially low rates in the organized sector. Neither the capacity of governments to borrow at low rates nor the existence of a captive market for private savings can be regarded as a decisive argument against more realistic interest rates. To continue to offer unattractive interest rates to one class of savers, when effective rates in the rest of the economy are much higher, amounts to subsidizing one category of borrowers (public sector) merely because the lenders (private sector) have no alternative. But this argument is based not merely on grounds of equity to the savers but even more importantly on criteria of economic efficacy in allocating scarce investible funds, which

are clearly vitiated by permitting excessive diversion of funds to the public sector through the captive market. To the extent that these conditions prevail, the economic rationale of low and stable rates on government borrowing in some of the less developed countries is not well founded, since it disregards the opportunity cost of public borrowing and investment. This issue is of vital importance for developing countries, as the organized sector (public and private), although small in relation to the total economy, accounts for the major share of new investment under development plans. [C11, pp. 108-109]

McKinnon argues in favour of high interest rates as follows:

Paradoxically, cheap credit in a populist sense may not benefit the little man at all. Quite the contrary. It may effectively prevent him from competing for long-term finance from the organized banking system, and as a result he is confined to getting month-to-month credit from the village storekeeper. [M7, p. 73]

In conclusion, therefore, the case has been presented for an interest rate policy which aims at equating supply and demand for funds in a competitive market environment. In Afghanistan this must start with action to facilitate bank lending and raise public sector interest rates. With all sectors of the economy competing on an equal basis for loans, the following benefits should accrue:

A. Scarce capital is allocated more efficiently;
B. Saving is increased as is the proportion held in financial form;
C. Income is more equally distributed because small savers receive a positive return and small borrowers have a greater opportunity to borrow from financial institutions.

Two advantages of the higher interest rates expected from financial development deserve consideration. The one relates to hoarding, the other to greater equality of income distribution.

Not all hoarding is anti-social. People who hoard money actually allow a larger quantity of money to be issued without inflationary effects. This money can initially be lent by the central bank to finance investment which benefits everyone. People who hoard gold and silver can create additional employment opportunities and so raise wages of the workers, if by so doing gold and silver mining industries flourish. If there is no gold and silver to be mined then hoarding simply raises, or at least maintains, prices of such precious metals to no one's evident detriment. Only where such hoarding results in large inflows of precious metals into a country in return for exports is there a social loss to the inhabitants of the country. It would be much more beneficial if, instead of unproductive precious metals, productive machinery, etc., were imported. This is an acute problem in countries like India but fortunately is of little significance in Afghanistan, except to the extent that official international reserves are held above the optimum level.

In the case of grain, hoarders buy at harvest time when prices are low and sell before the harvest when prices are high. The increased demand generated by the hoarders at harvest time actually keeps prices higher than they would be otherwise, thus giving farmers a better return. Conversely, the increased supply before harvest keeps prices lower, to the benefit of the bread eating public. If no one stored grain, there would be two months of gluttony followed by ten months of starvation. Similarly, extra purchases in years of good harvest for sale in years of drought dampen price fluctuations to the benefit of both farmer and consumer.

When grain is hoarded for long periods for non-commercial purposes, a phenomenon which certainly exists in Afghanistan, it can be argued that there is no social benefit; prices are not evened out by the process and no one profits. It can also be argued that were all unproductive assets such as gold, silver, grain stocks, etc., converted into productive assets, such as machinery for a new factory, everyone, including the hoarder, would benefit.

Thus, it can be concluded that those forms of hoarding which are anti-social are generally those which are also unprofitable. The question which must now be examined is: Why does anyone hoard if it is unprofitable? Having answered that, it may then be possible to suggest a better remedy to this problem than the enactment of anti-hoarding legislation which hits at the symptoms rather than at the causes.

Anyone wanting to save in a country like Afghanistan faces difficulties. In the industrial countries of the West, there are myriads of savings outlets—time deposits, savings and loans accounts, government bonds, equities, etc. In most areas of Afghanistan there is not even a bank within easy reach. If a saving account is eventually opened, the meagre 6 per cent interest is soon eroded through inflation. There are virtually no other forms of financial assets available here apart from a few shares in joint stock companies for which no organised market exists.

The result is that for most people the only way of saving is to hold tangible assets such as gold, jewellery, grain, etc. Even if such assets yield no positive return, they do have the advantages of easy procurement and liquidity, i.e. they can also easily be sold. Furthermore, they may maintain their value better than money. Thus, rather then viewing the hoarder with disdain, his activities can better be understood as a natural reaction to the deficiencies of his environment. He, as well as society, loses by holding unproductive tangible assets.

Saving is in fact critically important in the process of economic development. It needs to be encouraged as much as possible in Afghanistan. However, it does no one much good if it is immediately invested in unproductive inventories of grain, etc. As important as savings, therefore, is their direction into productive investments. This is where a well developed financial system plays a crucial role.

Economic development can be achieved only from the mobilisation of resources into productive uses. In the present technological era, this often necessitates the concentration of capital into large units of production. In a mixed economy, the most important way in which this can be done is through the voluntary pooling of resources.

It is only through the financial system that this can be achieved. On the one hand, the business enterprise needs resources for five, ten, maybe fifty years to use in what at the outset will be an uncertain, risky venture. On the other hand, individuals generally wish to keep the majority of their savings in liquid, risk free forms. By drawing together large numbers of savers, who will not all want to withdraw their savings at the same time, and financing large numbers of enterprises, thereby spreading and reducing risk, a developed financial system can meet not only business medium and long term financial needs but also depositors' requirements of liquidity and security.

Savers all over the world are found to be highly susceptible to the real return, i.e. the rate of interest minus the expected rate of inflation, received on their savings. Where financial assets such as savings deposits yield a fluctuating real return averaging zero, savers are not attracted. Instead, they prefer to hold tangible assets whose return, although zero, does not tend to fluctuate. Hence, the answer to the problem of anti-social hoarding lies in both the availability of and real return on financial assets. In conclusion, the remedy for eliminating anti-social hoarding lies not in legislation but in the rate of interest.

Raising interest rates on deposits benefits the small saver to a greater extent than the large saver for the simple reason that the latter has a much wider range of opportunities open to him for using his savings productively. On the other hand, the small saver is unable to invest in any indivisible investment which exceeds his savings and is usually less well informed and less sophisticated than the large saver in locating other assets in which to hold his savings. A deposit is a simple financial claim with two attributes particularly desirable to small savers, namely, liquidity and convenience.

Small scale business benefits from both higher deposit and, paradoxically, higher loan rates. Higher deposit rates which result in increased resources in the financial system mean that the small scale businessman is more likely to be able to borrow from the system. Similarly, higher loan rates curb the demand of big business, which normally receives priority, and rations credit on a price rather than a non-price basis. Non-price rationing invariably eliminates small borrowers first and simply rations credit to the large ones. The small businessman then has to borrow from non-institutional sources at far higher rates. Hence, he actually benefits from higher institutional rates provided that this enables him then to borrow from the financial institutions.

Raising interest rates hits hardest those whose returns are lowest and dissuades them from borrowing, thus allowing scarce resources to flow into investments which are now on average yielding higher returns. Furthermore, higher interest rates promote labour as opposed to capital intensive investments. It appears that Afghanistan may soon, if it does not already, suffer from an unemployment problem. Hence, there is an added urgency for producing more employment opportunities through given amounts of investment. This higher interest rates should do.

Of equal importance is the fact that higher institutional interest rates will narrow the gap between institutional and non-institutional rates. This in itself should increase the efficiency of resource allocation not only through its effect on the behaviour of existing institutional borrowers in terms of deterring low yielding and capital intensive investments but also through attracting additional funds into the financial institutions which can be lent to new borrowers with high yielding investment projects who previously were excluded from these sources of finance.

This happy picture will of course only be realised to the extent that new banking legislation and improved legal practices enable such new borrowers to be brought into the orbit of the institutional system. In essence this is a matter of reducing costs and risks of lending to small scale businesses which in Afghanistan tend to be those with potentially very high returns.

In the absence of exchange controls, for which there is sound economic justification for not imposing, Afghanistan's financial institutions must compete with the international market for funds. It is well known that capital has left Afghanistan and that considerable amounts are now invested abroad. With international markets offering 10 per cent and more on relatively short term, safe financial assets, there has been increasing incentive to remove funds from Afghanistan to take advantage of this differential. Until two years ago, the depreciating domestic currency enhanced the incentive provided by this differential. A rise in deposit rates would realign institutional interest rates in Afghanistan with increased rates throughout the rest of the world.

There is always a delayed reaction to a change in the economic environment. People in Afghanistan are probably just now beginning to realise that the Afghani is no longer depreciating. Hence, this is an ideal time to try to attract capital back by offering competitive returns on short term, safe financial assets, which in the present context implies higher returns on deposits. At this time rates do not have to provide additional compensation for expected currency depreciation. However, this is still needed for loss of convenience and will continue to be the case until the efficiency of Afghanistan's banking system in respect to international transactions is increased. The introduction of exchange controls would effectively ensure that no capital returned when financial development occurred and the investment climate improved.

The scope for an interest rate policy in Afghanistan is limited by the absence of reserve requirements for commercial banks and a central bank to act as lender of last resort to these banks, the relatively small effective demand for bank loans, the exceedingly undeveloped nature of the financial sector and the small volume of deposits held and credit extended by it.

On the other hand, Da Afghanistan Bank does engage in commercial banking activities and so can act as a price leader in an oligopolistic market. By changing its own commercial interest rates on deposits and loans not only would it affect directly a sizable portion of the market (31 per cent for deposits, 24 per cent for loans to the private sector) but it would almost certainly force the other banks to change their rates in step.

However, an important consideration here is: Why, when interest rates all around them have been rising, have Afghanistan's financial institutions not already raised their rates? The answer seems to be that there has been little desire to increase resources, since the opportunities for using them profitably are so limited, and no desire whatsoever to foster competition. This being the case, raising deposit rates to attract a larger proportion of domestic savings into the financial system will not by itself produce the desired result of raising the average productivity of investment by allocating resources more efficiently. In fact, under existing conditions precisely the reverse might occur. Banks would attract more resources which could only be used to finance the relatively inefficient large scale private and public enterprises while leaving productive small scale business even more starved of funds.

Thus, the success of an interest rate policy designed to attract a larger proportion of domestic savings into the financial system, which under normal circumstances could be expected to increase the efficiency of resource allocation and the productivity of investment, is not guaranteed in Afghanistan. Additional measures are required in conjunction with such a policy for the latter to achieve the desired results.

The key to a policy of raising interest rates within the financial institutions appears to lie with the ability of these institutions to increase rapidly their range and volume of lending. Given that there is ample evidence of many highly profitable investment opportunities in Afghanistan, to be expected of course in a country in which capital is scarce, the necessary measures consist of those which can facilitate bank lending. These have already been outlined in Section ii above.

v. *Domestic Resource Mobilisation*

Velocity in the neighbouring countries of Iran and Pakistan was 3.6 in 1970. Assuming an income elasticity of demand for money of 2.0, an initial velocity of 3.6 and an annual growth in real income of 4.4 per cent, the non-inflationary increase in the money supply and, on the assumption that foreign exchange reserves remain unchanged, domestic credit would be 2.44 per cent of GNP. The GNP estimate in Afghanistan for 1350 (1971) of Afs 91,146 million given in Table 2.14 would allow a "safe" expansion in domestic credit of Afs 2,228 million, a sum equal to 27 per cent of total investment in 1350 (1971) given in Table 4.5.

The example presented above is quite unrealistic in the actual circumstances now existing in Afghanistan. It simply illustrates the potential level of domestic credit expansion to which Afghanistan might aspire. Afghanistan's velocity lies around 10 which, even with an income elasticity of demand of 2, would allow a "safe" annual level of domestic credit expansion of Afs 802 million. There is, however, no evidence to suggest that income elasticity is as high as 2 in Afghanistan, although elasticity in Iran, Pakistan and Turkey appears to lie within this range. If income elasticity in Afghanistan under the existing institutional constraints were more realistically estimated at 1.1, the "safe" annual level of domestic credit expansion falls still further to Afs 441 million, still assuming a 4.4 per cent rate of real economic growth.

Table 8.2 presents estimates of currency/deposit ratios and velocities of

Table 8.2

Currency/Deposit Ratios and Velocities of Circulation
in 45 Underdeveloped Countries, 1969

Country	Currency/Deposit Ratio (Demand and Time Deposits)	Velocity
Afghanistan	3.439	10.312
Argentina	0.446	3.442
Bolivia	1.673	6.807
Brazil	0.201	4.646
Ceylon	0.649	4.268
Chile	0.278	6.580
China (Taiwan)	0.190	2.974
Colombia	0.397	5.010
Costa Rica	0.361	4.409
Cyprus	0.191	2.066
Ecuador	0.370	4.772
Egypt	0.846	2.542
El Salvador	0.292	4.277
Ethiopia	1.191	7.368
Greece	0.392	2.062
Guatemala	0.397	5.347
Guyana	0.320	2.955
Honduras	0.357	5.043
India	0.737	4.381
Indonesia	1.105	14.282
Iran	0.220	3.970
Iraq	1.407	3.754
Israel	0.200	2.413
Jamaica	0.129	2.976
Jordan	1.453	2.034
Korea (South)	0.217	3.780
Kuwait	0.134	2.581
Lebanon	0.311	1.270
Libya	0.592	4.487
Malawi	0.433	5.945
Malaysia	0.343	3.255
Mauritius	0.345	2.852
Morocco	0.589	2.999
Nicaragua	0.379	6.527
Pakistan	0.618	4.073
Paraguay	0.463	6.434
Philippines	0.298	3.744
Portugal	0.169	1.214
Saudi Arabia	1.094	4.356
Spain	0.166	1.246
Sudan	0.986	5.408
Syria	4.371	3.579
Thailand	0.392	2.999
Tunisia	0.392	2.448
Turkey	0.333	3.786

Note: 1349 (1970) data are used for Afghanistan.
Source: Afghanistan—Tables 2.12 and 2.14 above.
All other countries—*International Financial Statistics*, 25 (9), September 1972 and
International Financial Statistics: 1971 Supplement.

circulation for 45 underdeveloped countries. Afghanistan has both the highest velocity, with the exception of Indonesia which experienced an increase in the level of prices of 27,510 per cent between 1343 (1964) and 1348 (1969) and the highest currency/deposit ratio, with the exception of Syria.

In a recent 47 country comparative study [P12], Perlman found the following two relationships:

$$\log M = 0.337 + 0.396 \log Y - 0.923 \dot{P} \qquad (8.1)$$
$$R^2 = 0.53 \qquad (0.045) \qquad (0.272)$$

$$\log C/D = 1.05 - 0.56 \log Y \qquad (8.2)$$
$$R^2 = 0.59 \qquad (0.05)$$

where logM is the logarithm to base 10 of the money stock broadly defined (M2) expressed in terms of the number of weeks of income held, logY is the logarithm to base 10 of per capita real income in Dollars, adjusted for distortions introduced by fixed exchange rate systems, $\dot{P}$ is the expected rate of inflation expressed as a proportion, which is approximated by the slope of the logarithmic trend fitted to the cost-of-living index over preceding eight year periods, and C/D is the ratio of currency to bank demand and time deposits. Standard errors are given in brackets.

Taking a per capita income in Afghanistan of $88 [U16, Table A.1, p. 177] and expected inflation of 5.75 per cent from Table 2.13, the velocity predicted for Afghanistan from Equation 8.1 is 4.591 and the currency/deposit ratio from Equation 8.2, 0.914. In 1349 (1970), actual velocity was 10.312 and the currency/deposit ratio 3.439. These two figures are both predicted by Perlman's equations if, instead of taking a per capita income of $88, an income of $10 is used. One might conclude, therefore, that measured velocity and currency/deposit ratios for Afghanistan are consistent with one another, and hence that money supply and GNP estimates are also consistent, but that the financial system is so undeveloped that it should only be found in an economy in which per capita income was $10. Since per capita income in Afghanistan is at least eight times greater, the financial system lags behind other parts of the economy to an alarming degree.

A 60 per cent allocation of additional bank credit to the public sector during the Fourth Plan might be accepted as a first approximation. A total of Afs 27.7 billion was to be spent by the public sector on economic development during this period [M18, Table 6, p. 256]. It will be suggested here that deficit finance could have covered 34 per cent of the planned public sector development expenditure under favourable conditions of active financial development. It is assumed that under a programme of financial reform, Afghanistan could achieve a falling velocity such that the velocity predicted above for a country with a per capita income of $88 would be achieved by the end of the Plan period. That other countries have experienced rapidly falling velocities is illustrated by the figures provided in Table 8.3.

Table 8.3

*Changes in Currency/Money Ratios and Velocities
of Circulation in 10 Countries, 1964-1969*

	Currency Money Stock		Gross National Product Money Stock		Average Annual Percentage. Change in Velocity,
	1964	1969	1964	1969	1964-1969
South Korea	0.365	0.178	11.771	3.780	−20.32
Jordan	0.428	0.592	3.161	2.034	−8.44
Honduras	0.365	0.263	7.629	5.043	−7.95
Paraguay	0.421	0.316	9.050	6.434	−6.60
Israel	0.205	0.166	3.326	2.413	−6.22
Taiwan	0.180	0.160	3.936	2.974	−5.45
Turkey	0.357	0.250	4.993	3.786	−5.38
Jamaica	0.141	0.114	3.920	2.976	−5.36
Sudan	0.492	0.496	7.059	5.408	−5.19
Thailand	0.370	0.282	3.898	2.999	−5.11

Note: An annually compounded growth rate is used in the final column.
Source: *International Financial Statistics*, 25 (9), September 1972 and *International Financial Statistics: 1971 Supplement.*

The implications of these assumptions for "safe" levels of deficit finance for the period of Afghanistan's Fourth Plan can now be calculated. The results are presented in Table 8.4. Case A uses the draft Plan figures for deficit finance and calculates the implied fluctuations in velocity. Case B assumes no financial development but that the existing financial conditions are maintained, i.e. constant velocity. Case C uses a 15 per cent annual fall in velocity which would bring it down to the predicted 4.591 by 1355 (1976).

One of the simplifying assumptions which has been used is highly

Table 8.4

Velocity and Deficit Finance during the Fourth Five Year Plan, 1351-1355

(Millions of Afghanis)

		1350	1351	1352	1353	1354	1355
	Gross National Product	91,146	95,165	99,361	103,741	108,316	113,091
A.	*Plan Estimates*						
	Velocity	10.406	10.015	9.899	9.855	10.012	9.717
	Money Stock	8,759	9,502	10,037	10,527	10,819	11,639
	Increase in Money Stock		743	535	490	292	820
	Deficit Finance		446	321	294	175	492
B.	*No Financial Development*						
	Velocity	10.406	10.406	10.406	10.406	10.406	10.406
	Money Stock	8,759	9,145	9,548	9,969	10,409	10,868
	Increase in Money Stock		386	403	421	440	459
	"Safe" Level of Deficit						
	Finance		232	242	253	264	275
C.	*Active Financial Development*						
	Velocity	10.406	8.835	7.501	6.369	5.407	4.591
	Money Stock	8,759	10,771	13,246	16,288	20,033	24,633
	Increase in Money Stock		2,012	2,475	3,042	3,745	4,600
	"Safe" Level of Deficit						
	Finance		1,207	1,485	1,825	2,247	2,760

Note: Figures derived by method described in the text.

Source: Ministry of Planning, *Draft Fourth Five Year Plan: National Development Plan for Afghanistan, 1351-1355 (1972/73-1976/77)* (Kabul: United Nations Development Programme, mimeo, July 1973), Table 1, p. 249 and Table 7, p. 257; and Table 2.14 above.

misleading. It is that GNP will grow at the same rate regardless of the degree of financial development. All the available empirical evidence refutes this and it can be expected that the achievable growth rate under active financial development, where more resources are available for development expenditure, will be considerably higher than would be possible under Case A or B financial conditions. In fact, the 4.4 per cent annual average growth target might be considered unrealistically optimistic under existing financial conditions. If the incremental capital/output ratio (ICOR) for the Fourth Plan period were assumed to be 2.5, a low figure, the planned total investment of Afs 30.9 billion would achieve a growth rate of under 2.6 per cent per annum. If the resources made available from aggressive financial development were added to those already allocated, the growth rate would increase under these assumptions to 3.6 per cent.

Another important assumption made was that Afghanistan is a closed economy. Balance of payments disequilibria disturb the results produced above. However, so long as there is no attempt to increase foreign exchange reserves, the "safe" levels of domestic credit expansion and deficit finance will if anything be under rather than overestimated. Similarly with "other items" in the monetary survey accounts, a continuation of its trend over the past five years would allow a greater "safe" level of deficit finance than estimated.

A deliberate policy of financial development in Afghanistan could be expected to accelerate the rate of economic growth and provide much needed additional funds for development expenditure. If financial development slightly more than halved velocity of circulation, i.e. more than doubled the demand for money at every level of income, over the next five years, and if the rate of economic growth were partly thereby raised to the target of 4.4 per cent per annum, the "safe" annual levels of deficit finance would be those given in Case C in Table 8.4. Thus a total of Afs 15,874 million would be made available over the period of the Fourth Five Year Plan which would finance over 50 per cent of planned total investment. The "safe" level of deficit finance would provide funds for 34 per cent of planned public sector investment.

Some forms of investment are likely to accelerate monetisation, i.e. increase demand for money, more rapidly than others. For example, the better communications are, the faster monetisation will occur. Investment in roads can be particularly effective in causing the demand for money to increase. To the extent that they cause an increase in the demand for money, such investments can be regarded as self-financing and, therefore, particularly attractive.

Without an active policy of financial development the total "safe" level of deficit finance would be Afs 1,266 million on the assumptions used in calculating figures in Table 8.4. It could be argued that the growth rate would not be the same in both cases and therefore that the difference in the "safe" levels of deficit finance under active financial development and under the *status quo* would be considerably greater.

The potential for increased domestic resource mobilisation from greater fiscal effort can be examined in the same manner as that from financial development. Here, it is assumed that fiscal effort is to reach the average level, i.e. $E = 1$, by 1355 (1976). It is also assumed that the Government's ordinary expenditure increases annually at the planned rate of 7.26 per cent [M18, Table 1, p. 245], and that the approach to average fiscal effort takes place gradually. Figures in Table 8.5 are derived on the basis of these assumptions. For average fiscal effort, it has been assumed that domestic revenue would equal 11.31 per cent of GNP

Table 8.5

Current Account Balance during the Fourth Five Year Plan, 1351-1355
(Millions of Afghanis)

		1350	1351	1352	1353	1354	1355
	Gross National Product	91,146	95,165	99,361	103,741	108,316	113,091
A.	*Plan Estimates*						
	Domestic Revenue	5,823	6,200	7,170	7,957	9,191	9,837
	Ordinary Expenditure	5,504	5,608	6,238	6,721	7,339	7,881
	Current Account Balance	319	592	932	1,236	1,852	1,956
B.	*No Increase in Fiscal Effort*						
	Domestic Revenue	5,823	6,080	6,348	6,628	6,920	7,225
	Ordinary Expenditure	5,504	5,608	6,238	6,721	7,339	7,881
	Current Account Balance	319	472	110	−93	−419	−656
C.	*Approach to Average Fiscal Effort*						
	Domestic Revenue	5,823	6,816	7,977	9,337	10,928	12,791
	Ordinary Expenditure	5,504	5,608	6,238	6,721	7,339	7,881
	Current Account Balance	319	1,208	1,739	2,616	3,589	4,910

Note: Figures derived by method described in the text.

Source: Ministry of Planning, *Draft Fourth Five Year Plan: National Development Plan for Afghanistan, 1351-1355 (1972/73-1976/77)* (Kabul: United Nations Development Programme, mimeo, July 1973), Table 6, p. 256; and Tables 2.14 and 6.3 above.

in 1355 (1976). The current account surplus produced by a gradual approach to average fiscal effort equals Afs 14,062 million or over 50 per cent of planned public sector investment during the Fourth Plan.

If the resources from aggressive financial development and fiscal reform were added to those already allocated, total development expenditure would rise to Afs 51,069 million which with an ICOR of 2.5 would enable a 4.1 per cent average annual growth rate. However, if there were to be no increase in fiscal effort total resources for development expenditure would fall from the projected Afs 30.9 billion to Afs 23.7 billion even if the donors' contributions remained unchanged. This would yield a growth rate of only 2.0 per cent, provided that the ICOR remained at 2.5.

vi. *Conclusion*

It has been argued in this book that Afghanistan's development potential during the post-war period has been low. Two of the factors contributing to this low potential, namely the inadequate financial system and the apparent lack of commitment on the part of the country's leaders to development, were analysed in detail. The lack of commitment was examined in respect to both the planning and budgetary processes in

Chapters IV and VI, respectively. The absence of financial development was discussed at length in Chapter V.

It was suggested in Chapter III that the critical constraints to economic development have been closely related to economic fragmentation which in turn has greatly inhibited the results of development efforts. Economic integration must be viewed as an intermediate objective in removing the five critical constraints to economic development presented in Chapter I. Financial development can be designed in the first instance to remove fragmentation in the capital market, feeder road construction to reduce geographic fragmentation. The latter would in turn do much to remove fragmentation in product markets. In pursuit of economic integration, much more attention should also be focused on effective agricultural credit, demonstration, extension and supplies programmes. For this and for the feeder road programme greater fiscal effort is imperative. This is also required for the much needed reform of civil service pay scales and the introduction of financial incentives for improved performance.

A substantial improvement in the levels of domestic resource mobilisation through the financial sector and the fiscal system of the order illustrated in the hypothetical examples given in the previous section would do far more than just double the growth rate. Such changes would be clear indications of a rapidly improving financial system and strong commitment to economic development on the part of the country's leadership. The increased resources could be used to maximum effectiveness to improve agricultural productivity and the country's feeder road network. For neither is foreign aid likely to be forthcoming in sufficient volumes to make the necessary impact.

Thus, four of the Adelman-Morris [A2] indicators of development potential could be directly manipulated by reform programmes in the financial and fiscal areas. The result in the form of rapid economic growth through an active export promotion programme which an increase in Afghanistan's development potential would enable could be dramatic. Indeed, the widespread benefits which should accrue could well secure the support of a substantial proportion of the community for development efforts. This, it may be remembered, is the fifth determinant of development potential [A2].

BIBLIOGRAPHY

No references have been made in either the text or the bibliography to the excellent reports prepared regularly by the Asian Development Bank, the International Bank for Reconstruction and Development (World Bank) and the International Monetary Fund, since their distribution and use are restricted. The interested reader will not, however, encounter much difficulty in consulting these reports.

The mimeographed material referred to in the bibliography has been placed in the library of the United States Agency for International Development Mission to Afghanistan. Sets of the 41 Financial Development Committee reports have been deposited as follows:

In Kabul — Da Afghanistan Bank Library
Kabul Public Library
Kabul University Library
Ministry of Finance Library
Ministry of Planning Library
Research Department, Da Afghanistan Bank
Resident Representative of the International Monetary Fund
United Nations Development Programme Library
United States Agency for International Development Library

In Britain — Documentation Centre, Middle East Centre, University of Durham, Durham

In U.S.A. — Afghanistan Studies and Research Program,
University of Nebraska at Omaha, Omaha, Nebraska

A1 I. Adelman and C. T. Morris, *Society, Politics, and Economic Development: A Quantitative Approach* (Baltimore: Johns Hopkins Press, 1967)
A2 I. Adelman and C. T. Morris, "Performance Criteria for Evaluating Economic Development Potential: An Operational Approach," *Quarterly Journal of Economics*, 82 (2), May 1968, pp. 260-80
A3 Afghan Embassy, *Afghan Progress in the Third Year of the Plan* (London: Afghan Embassy, September 1959)
A4 J. P. Agarwal, "Optimal Monetary Reserves for Developing Countries," *Weltwirtschaftliches Archiv*, 107 (1), 1971, pp. 76-91
A5 Agricultural Development Bank, *Charter of the Agricultural Development Bank of Afghanistan* (Kabul: Agricultural Development Bank, 1970)
A6 Agricultural Development Bank, *Loan Regulations* (Kabul: Agricultural Development Bank, October 1970)
A7 Agricultural Development Bank and Helmand-Arghandab Agricultural Finance Agency, *Annual Report for the Year 1350 Ended on 20th March 1972* (Kabul: Agricultural Development Bank, 1972)
A8 Agricultural Development Bank and Helmand-Arghandab Agricultural Finance Agency, *Annual Report for the Year 1351 Ended on 20th March 1973* (Kabul: Agricultural Development Bank, 1973)
A9 Agricultural Development Bank, *Agricultural Lending Activities* (Kabul: Agricultural Development Bank, mimeo, May 1973)
A10 Agricultural Development Bank, *Agricultural Credit: Existing Problems and*

Recommended Solutions (Kabul: Ministry of Finance, Financial Development Committee, Report No. R/024, mimeo, 22 May 1973)

A11 J-ud-D. Ahmad and M. A. Aziz, *Afghanistan: A Brief Survey* (Kabul: Dar-ut-Talif, 1313)

A12 S. S. Ahmady, *A Glance at Afghanistan's Trade* (in Dari) (Kabul: Chamber of Commerce, Extra Publication of Iqtisad Journal for the 45th Anniversary of Independence, 1343)

A13 R. T. Akhramovich, *Outline History of Afghanistan after the Second World War* (Moscow: Nauka Publishing House, 1966)

A14 A. Ali, "Banking in the Middle East," *International Monetary Fund Staff Papers*, 6 (1), November 1957, pp. 51-79

A15 M. Ali, *Progressive Afghanistan* (Lahore: Punjab Educational Electric Press, 1933)

A16 M. Ali, *Commercial Afghanistan* (Delhi: Mohammed Ali, 1946)

A17 M. Ali, *Afghanistan: The National Awakening* (Lahore: Punjab Educational Press, 1958)

A18 M. Ali, *Afghanistan: The Mohammedzai Period* (Kabul: Mohammed Ali, 1959)

A19 R. G. D. Allen, *Macro-Economic Theory: A Mathematical Treatment* (London: Macmillan, 1968)

A20 American Embassy, *Afghanistan: Economic Trends Report* (Kabul: American Embassy, September 1972)

A21 American International Investment Corporation, *World Currency Charts 1970* (San Francisco: American International Investment Corporation, June 1970)

A22 P. Anciaux, A. Forgeur and Y. Farjot, *Advisory Mission on Industrial Planning in Afghanistan—Final Report* (Two volumes) (Kabul and Brussels: Research and Development Consulting Engineers, mimeo, October 1971)

A23 C. J. Anderson, *A Banking and Credit System for the Economic Development of Afghanistan* (Washington, D.C.: Robert R. Nathan Associates, mimeo, 1967)

A24 C. J. Anderson, *Afghanistan: The Banking Act 1967, Preliminary Draft* (Kabul: Robert R. Nathan Associates, mimeo, 1967)

A25 L. C. Andersen, "Federal Reserve Defensive Operations and Short-Run Control of the Money Stock," *Journal of Political Economy*, 76 (2), March/April 1968, pp. 275-88

A26 S. van Atta, "A Note on Usury Legislation in the Philippines," *Philippine Economic Journal*, 10 (1), First Semester 1971, pp. 48-62

B1 R. W. Bahl, "A Regression Approach to Tax Effort and Tax Ratio Analysis," *International Monetary Fund Staff Papers*, 18 (3), November 1971, pp. 570-612

B2 R. W. Bahl, "A Representative Tax System Approach to Measuring Tax Effort in Developing Countries," *International Monetary Fund Staff Papers*, 19 (1), March 1972, pp. 87-124

B3 G. B. Baldwin, *Planning and Development in Iran* (Baltimore: Johns Hopkins Press, 1967)

B4 E. Baltensperger, "Economies of Scale, Firm Size, and Concentration in Banking," *Journal of Money, Credit and Banking*, 4 (3), August 1972, pp. 467-88

B5 Bank Millie, *Report of Bank Millie's Activities in 1330* (in Dari) (Kabul: Bank Bank Millie, 1331)

B6 Bank Millie, *Report of the Board of Directors and Balance Sheet for the Year Ended 30th Hoot 1336* (Kabul: Bank Millie, 1958)

B7 Bank Millie, *Report of Bank Millie's Activities in 1344* (in Dari) (Kabul: Bank Millie, 1345)

B8 Bank Millie, *Report of Bank Millie's Activities in 1350* (in Dari) (Kabul: Bank Millie, 1351)

B9 A. P. Barnabas, *Farmer Characteristics in the Baghlan Pilot Area* (Kabul: United

Nations Food and Agriculture Organisation, Technical Report No. 8, mimeo, 1972)

B10   L. Baron, *Sector Analysis: Helmand-Arghandab Valley Region* (Kabul: United States Agency for International Development, mimeo, February 1973)

B11   L. Baron, *A Critique of the Proposed Helmand-Arghandab Valley Project (1971)* (Montreal: McGill University, mimeo, July 1973)

B12   L. Baron, *The Paktia Development Project, Afghanistan: A History, Analysis, and Summary of Project Proposals* (Montreal: McGill University, mimeo, July 1973)

B13   L. Baron, *Post War Development Experience in Afghanistan* (Montreal: McGill University, mimeo, July 1973)

B14   L. Baron, *The Traditional Agricultural Sector* (Montreal: McGill University, mimeo, July 1973)

B15   L. Baron, *Agricultural Development Projects in Afghanistan* (Montreal: McGill University, Ph. D. thesis, 1974)

B16   R. U. Battles, *Sectoral Planning Study of Afghan Agriculture: The Agricultural Credit Situation in Afghanistan* (Manila: Asian Development Bank, mimeo, 1971)

B17   R. W. Beck and Associates, *Electric Power Survey Report: Helmand and Arghandab Valleys Afghanistan* (Denver: R. W. Beck and Associates, mimeo, November 1964)

B18   G. L. Bell and L. S. Berman, "Changes in the Money Supply in the United Kindom, 1954 to 1964," *Economica*, 33(130), May 1966, pp. 148-65

B19   M. J. Bell (Ed.), *An American Engineer in Afghanistan: From the Letters and Notes of A. C. Jewett* (Minneapolis: Minnesota University Press, 1948)

B20   M. Beloff, *The Foreign Policy of Soviet Russia 1929-1941*, Volume II 1936-1941 (London: Oxford University Press, 1949)

B21   R. E. Benedick, *Industrial Finance in Iran* (Cambridge, Mass.: Harvard University, Graduate School of Business, 1964)

B22   G. J. Benston, "Economies of Scale of Financial Institutions," *Journal of Money, Credit and Banking*, 4 (2), May 1972, pp. 312-41

B23   J. S. Benz and E. N. Holmgreen, *The Helmand Valley: An Overall Review* (Kabul: United States Agency for International Development, mimeo, November 1962)

B24   J. Bhagwati and B. Hansen, "A Theoretical Analysis of Smuggling," *Quarterly Journal of Economics*, 87 (2), May 1973, pp. 172-87

B25   J. Bharier, "Afghanistan II: Growth Prospects Remain Bleak," *Financial Times*, 17 August 1971, p. 9

B26   J. Bharier, *Vicious Circles of Poverty* (Durham: University of Durham, Department of Economics, typescript, 1972)

B27   J. S. Blacklock, *Report on PACCA to the Financial Development Committee* (Kabul: United Nations Food and Agriculture Organisation, mimeo, 4 March 1973)

B28   Board of Trade, *Hints to Businessmen Visiting Afghanistan* (Edinburgh: H. M. Stationery Office Press, 1969)

B29   L. Bogdanov, "The Afghan Weights and Measures," *Journal of the Asiatic Society of Bengal*, N.S., 24, 1928, pp. 419-35

B30   A. Bonné, *State and Economics in the Middle East: A Society in Transition* (London: Kegan Paul, 1948)

B31   M. R. Brant, "Recent Economic Development in Afghanistan" in *Afghanistan in the Seventies* edited by L. Dupree and L. Albert (New York: Praeger, 1974), pp. 144-86

B32   A. F. Brimmer, "Central Banking and Economic Development: The Record of Innovation," *Journal of Money, Credit and Banking*, 3 (4), November 1971, pp. 780-92

B33   British Legation, *Office Manual* (Kabul: British Legation, 1933)

B34   J. R. Brooks, *Recommendations for a Bank for Industrial Development of Afghan-istan* (Washington, D.C.: International Cooperation Administration, Office of Private Enterprise, mimeo, 1960)

B35   G. T. Brown, *Economic Policy and Development: A Case Study of Korea in the 1960s* (Washington, D.C.: United States Agency for International Development, mimeo, 1970)

B36   K. Brunner and A. H. Meltzer, "Predicting Velocity: Implications for Theory and Policy," *Journal of Finance*, 18 (2), May 1963, pp. 319-54

C1   "Cabinet Policy Statement on the Banking Law," *Kabul Times*, 16 Jauza 1352 (6 June 1973), p. 3

C2   P. Cagan, *Determinants and Effects of Changes in the Stock of Money, 1875-1960* (New York: National Bureau of Economic Research and distributed by Columbia University Press, 1965)

C3   R. Cameron (Ed.), *Banking and Economic Development: Some Lessons of History* (New York: Oxford University Press, 1972)

C4   C. D. Campbell, "The Velocity of Money and the Rate of Inflation: Recent Experiences in South Korea and Brazil" in *Varieties of Monetary Experiences* edited by D. Meiselman (Chicago: University of Chicago Press, 1970), pp. 339-86

C5   J. Carr and L. B. Smith, "Money Supply, Interest Rates, and the Yield Curve," *Journal of Money, Credit and Banking*, 4 (3), August 1972, pp. 582-94

C6   E. Caspani and E. Cagnacci, *Afghanistan: Crocevia Dell'Asia* (Milan: Antonio Vallardi, 1951)

C7   Central Statistics Office, *Revised National Price Indexes for Afghanistan for the Years 1348-1350* (Kabul: Central Statistics Office, mimeo, 1972)

C8   Central Statistics Office, *Weekly Prices: Foods* (Kabul: Central Statistics Office, Report 009.059, mimeo, 18 Saratan 1352 (9 July 1973))

C9   V. Cervin, "Problems in the Integration of the Afghan Nation," *Middle East Journal*, 6 (4), Autumn 1952, pp. 400-16

C10   V. Cervinka, *Afghanistan: Structure Économique et Sociale; Commerce Ex-térieure* (Lausanne: Office Suisse d'Expansion Commerciale, 1950)

C11   A. G. Chandavarkar, "Some Aspects of Interest Rate Policies in Less Developed Economies: The Experience of Selected Asian Countries," *International Monetary Fund Staff Papers*, 18 (1), March 1971, pp. 48-110

C12   Checchi and Company, *The Demand for Debt Financing in Afghanistan's Private Industry Sector* (Kabul: Checchi and Company, mimeo, September 1971)

C13   Checchi and Company, *A Discussion of the Market Available to the Industrial Development Bank of Afghanistan* (Kabul: Checchi and Company, mimeo, November 1971)

C14   Checchi and Company, *Financial Projections: Industrial Development Bank of Afghanistan* (Kabul: Checchi and Company, mimeo, January 1972)

C15   Checchi and Company, *Fourth Semi-Annual Report, January-June 1973* (Kabul: Checchi and Company, mimeo, June 1973)

C16   H. B. Chenery and A. MacEwan, "Optimal Patterns of Growth and Aid: The Case of Pakistan," *Pakistan Development Review*, 6 (2), Summer 1966, pp. 209-42

C17   B. I. Cohen, "Relative Effects of Foreign Capital and Exports on Economic Development," *Review of Economics and Statistics*, 50 (2), May 1968, pp. 281-84

C18   *Constitution of Afghanistan*, 9 Mizan 1343 (1 October 1964)

C19   J. S. Costa, *Tax Revenues Sources of the Royal Government of Afghanistan* (Kabul: United States Agency for International Development, mimeo, October 1967)

C20   G. H. Craig, *Industrial Development Bank* (Kabul: Robert R. Nathan Associates, typescript, November 1965)

C21 G. H. Craig, *Banking System in the Third Five-Year Plan* (Kabul: Robert R. Nathan Associates, mimeo, 13 August 1968)

D1   Da Afghanistan Bank, *Statutes of Da Afghanistan Bank, Kabul* (Kabul: Da Afghanistan Bank, 1942)
D2   M. Daoud, "Proclamation of the First Republic of Afghanistan," *Kabul Times*, 27 Saratan 1352 (18 July 1973), p. 1
D3   M. Daoud, "Address to the Nation," *Kabul Times*, 4 Sunbula 1352 (26 August 1973), pp. 1-4
D4   Department of Press and Information, *Fortieth Anniversary of the Independence of Afghanistan* (Kabul: Department of Press and Information, 1959)
D5   Department of Trade and Industry, *Afghanistan—Hints to Business Men* (London: Department of Trade and Industry, 1972)
D6   Development Assistance Directorate, *Performance Compendium—Consolidated Results of Analytical Work on Economic and Social Performance of Developing Countries* (Paris: Organisation for Economic Co-operation and Development, Development Assistance Directorate, 1973)
D7   G. S. Dorrance, "The Instruments of Monetary Policy in Countries Without Highly Developed Capital Markets," *International Monetary Fund Staff Papers*, 12 (2), July 1965, pp. 272-79
D8   J. W. Duggar, "An Examination of the Feasibility of Using Monetary Data for National Income Estimates," *Review of Income and Wealth*, 14 (4), December 1968, pp. 311-39
D9   L. Dupree, "Afghanistan and the Unpaved Road to Democracy," *Royal Central Asian Journal*, 56 (3), October 1969, pp. 272-78
D10 L. Dupree, *Afghanistan* (Princeton: Princeton University Press, 1973)
D11 L. Dupree, "Afghanistan: Problems of a Peasant-Tribal Society" in *Afghanistan in the Seventies* edited by L. Dupree and L. Albert (New York: Praeger, 1974), pp. 1-23

E1   Economist, "Cinderella of the City: Insurance 1973—A Survey," *The Economist*, 9 June 1973
E2   Z. A. Eltezam, "Afghanistan's Foreign Trade," *Middle East Journal*, 20 (1), Winter 1966, pp. 95-103
E3   W. V. Emanuel, "Some Impressions of Swat and Afghanistan," *Journal of the Royal Central Asian Society*, 26 (2), April 1939, pp. 195-213
E4   R. F. Emery, *The Financial Institutions of Southeast Asia: A Country-by-Country Study* (New York: Praeger, 1970)
E5   G. Étienne, *L'Afghanistan ou Les Aléas de la Coopération* (Paris: Presses Universitaires de France, 1972)
E6   H. Ezekiel, "Monetary Expansion and Economic Development," *International Monetary Fund Staff Papers*, 14 (1), March 1967, pp. 80-88
E7   H. Ezekiel and J. O. Adekunle, "The Secular Behavior of Income Velocity: An International Cross-Section Study," *International Monetary Fund Staff Papers*, 16 (2), July 1969, pp. 224-37

F1   L-S Fan, "Some Observations on Central Banking in Asia," *Philippine Economic Journal*, 9 (1), First Semester 1970, pp. 125-41
F2   D. I. Fand, "Some Issues in Monetary Economics," *Banca Nazionale del Lavoro Quarterly Bulletin*, 90, September 1969, pp. 215-47
F3   K. Ferdinand, "Nomad Expansion and Commerce in Central Afghanistan: A Sketch of Some Modern Trends," *Folk* (Copenhagen), 4, 1962, pp. 123-59

F4   M. E. Fieser, *Memorandum on Meeting on Possible Improvement in the Afghan Financial System* (Kabul: Robert R. Nathan Associates, mimeo, 1 April 1967)

F5   M. E. Fieser, *Memorandum to the Committee on Banking and Finance* (Kabul: Robert R. Nathan Associates, mimeo, 14 May 1967)

F6   M. E. Fieser, *The Forthcoming Issue of Bonds by the Government of Afghanistan* (Kabul: Robert R. Nathan Associates, mimeo, 17 May 1967)

F7   Financial Times, "Afghanistan: Financial Times Survey," *Financial Times*, 17 August 1971

F8   I. Fisher, *The Rate of Interest* (New York: Macmillan, 1930)

F9   A. Fletcher, *Afghanistan: Highway of Conquest* (Ithaca: Cornell University Press, 1965)

F10   G. Flores, *Afghanistan's Foreign Trade* (Kabul: United States Agency for International Development, mimeo, February 1972)

F11   R. Floto, *First Draft of Proposals for Banking Security Law* (Kabul: Agricultural Development Bank, typescript, November 1970)

F12   Z. Fojan, "The Adventure of the Police and the Brokers—The Foreign Exchange Rate Has Risen—Is Brokerage Legal?" (in Dari), *Caravan Newspaper*, 9 Dalwa 1347 (29 January 1969)

F13   P. Fooks, *Report on the Findings of a Study of the Problems of Industrial Enterprises in Afghanistan and a Proposed Solution to these Problems* (Kabul: Ministry of Mines and Industries, mimeo, November 1972)

F14   P. G. Franck, "Problems of Economic Development in Afghanistan—I," *Middle East Journal*, 3 (3), July 1949, pp. 293-314

F15   P. G. Franck, "Problems of Economic Development in Afghanistan—II," *Middle East Journal*, 3 (4), October 1949, pp. 421-40

F16   P. G. Franck, "Technical Assistance through the United Nations: The UN Mission in Afghanistan, 1950-53" in *Hands Across Frontiers: Case Studies in Technical Cooperation* edited by H. M. Teaf and P. G. Franck (Leiden: Sijthoff's Uitgeversmaatschappij for Netherlands Universities Foundation for International Cooperation, 1955), pp. 13-61

F17   P. G. Franck, "Economic Progress in an Encircled Land," *Middle East Journal*, 10 (1), Winter 1956, pp. 43-59

F18   P. G. Franck, *The Economics of Competitive Coexistence: Afghanistan Between East and West* (Washington, D.C.: National Planning Association, 1960)

F19   W. K. Fraser-Tytler, *Afghanistan: A Study of Political Developments in Central and Southern Asia*, Third Edition (London: Oxford University Press, 1967)

F20   J. G. French, "Changes Under Nadir Shah," *The Times* (London), 11 November 1933, p. 11

F21   M. Friedman, "Monetary Data and National Income Estimates," *Economic Development and Cultural Change*, 9 (3), April 1961, pp. 267-86

F22   M. Friedman, "Monetary Policy for a Developing Society," *Bank Markazi Iran Bulletin*, 9 (54), March-April 1971, pp. 700-12

F23   M. Friedman, "Government Revenue from Inflation," *Journal of Political Economy*, 79 (4), July/August 1971, pp. 846-56

F24   M. Friedman and A. J. Schwartz, *A Monetary History of the United States, 1867-1960* (Princeton: Princeton University Press. A study by the National Bureau of Economic Research, 1963)

F25   M. J. Fry, *Finance and Development Planning in Turkey* (Leiden: Brill, 1972)

F26   M. J. Fry, "Manipulating Demand for Money" in *Essays in Modern Economics* edited by J. M. Parkin (London: Longman, 1973), pp. 371-85

F27   M. J. Fry, *Financial Reform: Draft Legislation and Recommendations for Afghanistan* (Kabul: Ministry of Finance, Financial Development Committee, Report No. R/015, mimeo, 27 March 1973)

F28 M. J. Fry, *Problems of Bank Lending in Afghanistan* (Kabul: Ministry of Finance,
     Financial Development Committee, Report No. R/017, mimeo, 3 April 1973)
F29 M. J. Fry, *Government Bonds* (Kabul: Ministry of Finance, Financial Develop-
     ment Committee, Report No. R/018, mimeo, 4 April 1973)
F30 M. J. Fry, *Financing the Wheat Price Support Programme* (Kabul: Ministry of
     Finance, Financial Development Committee, Report No. R/020, mimeo, 9 May
     1973)
F31 M. J. Fry, *An Interest Rate Policy for Afghanistan* (Kabul: Ministry of Finance,
     Financial Development Committee, Report No. R/032, mimeo, 1 July 1973)
F32 M. J. Fry, *Relevant Laws in Afghanistan* (Kabul: Ministry of Finance, Financial
     Development Committee, Report No. R/035, mimeo, 17 July 1973)

G1   H. J. Galliot, "Purchasing Power Parity as an Explanation of Long-Term
     Changes in Exchange Rates," *Journal of Money, Credit and Banking*, 2 (3),
     August 1970, pp. 348-57
G2   German Economic Advisory Group, *Industrial Survey, 1345-1348* (Kabul: Royal
     Government of Afghanistan, Ministry of Mines and Industry, mimeo, Sep-
     tember 1971)
G3   German Economic Advisory Group, *Memorandum for the Fourth Five-Year
     Plan Sector Program for "Money and Banking"* (Kabul: German Economic
     Advisory Group, mimeo, September 1971)
G4   German Economic Advisory Group, *Measures to Promote Socio-Economic
     Progress in Afghanistan* (Kabul: German Economic Advisory Group, mimeo,
     March 1972)
G5   German Economic Advisory Group, *Afghanistan's Foreign Trade 1336-1348
     and Prospective Development during the Fourth Five-Year Plan 1351-1355* (Kabul:
     German Economic Advisory Group, mimeo, Hamal 1351 (April 1972))
G6   German Economic Advisory Group, *Memorandum: Economic Growth and
     Employment through Modernization of Government Economic Activities* (Kabul:
     German Economic Advisory Group, mimeo, October 1972)
G7   A. Gerschenkron, *Continuity in History and Other Essays* (Cambridge, Mass.:
     Harvard University Press, 1968)
G8   T. T. Gibson, *Factors Influencing the Variability of Karakul Exports* (Kabul:
     United States Agency for International Development, typescript, May 1968)
G9   W. E. Gibson, "Interest Rates and Inflationary Expectations: New Evidence,"
     American Economic Review, 62 (5), December 1972, pp. 854-65
G10 R. V. Gilbert, *Note on Afghanistan's Development Program* (Kabul: United
     States Agency for International Development, mimeo, March 1971)
G11 M. Gillett, "Afghanistan," *Royal Central Asian Journal*, 53 (3), October 1966,
     pp. 238-44
G12 T. S. Gochenour, "A New Try for Afghanistan," *Middle East Journal*, 19 (1),
     Winter 1965, pp. 1-19
G13 R. W. Goldsmith, *Financial Structure and Development* (New Haven and London:
     Yale University Press, 1969)
G14 S. I. Greenbaum and C. F. Haywood, "Secular Change in the Financial Services
     Industry," *Journal of Money, Credit and Banking*, 3 (2, ii), May 1971, pp. 571-89
G15 V. Gregorian, *The Emergence of Modern Afghanistan: Politics of Reform and
     Modernization, 1880-1946* (Stanford: Stanford University Press, 1969)
G16 K. Griffin, "Foreign Capital, Domestic Savings and Economic Development,"
     Bulletin of Oxford University Institute of Economics and Statistics, 32 (2), May
     1970, pp. 99-112
G17 B. Griffiths, *Competition in Banking* (London: Institute of Economic Affairs,
     Hobart Paper 51, 1970)

G18 B. Griffiths, "The Welfare Cost of the U.K. Clearing Banks' Cartel," *Journal of Money, Credit and Banking*, 4 (2), May 1972, pp. 227-44

G19 B. Griffiths, "Resource Efficiency, Monetary Policy and the Reform of the U.K. Banking System," *Journal of Money, Credit and Banking*, 5 (1, i), February 1973, pp. 61-77

G20 J. C. Griffiths, *Afghanistan* (New York: Praeger, 1967)

G21 A. Guha, "Economic Development of Afghanistan, 1929-1961," *Journal of International Studies*, 6 (4), April 1965, pp. 421-39

G22 A. Guha, "The Economy of Afghanistan during Amanullah's Reign, 1919-1929," *Journal of International Studies*, 9 (2), October 1967, pp. 161-82

G23 M. C. Gupta, "Differential Effects of Tight Money: An Economic Rationale," *Journal of Finance*, 27 (4), September 1972, pp. 825-38

G24 J. G. Gurley, H. T. Patrick and E. S. Shaw, *The Financial Structure of Korea* (Seoul: United States Operations Mission to Korea, mimeo, July 1965)

G25 J. G. Gurley and E. S. Shaw, "Financial Aspects of Economic Development," *American Economic Review*, 45 (4), September 1955, pp. 515-38

G26 J. G. Gurley and E. S. Shaw, *Money in a Theory of Finance* (Washington, D.C.: The Brookings Institution, 1960)

G27 J. G. Gurley and E. S. Shaw, *The Impact of Economic Development on Financial Structures: A Cross-Section Study* (Stanford: Stanford University, photocopy, undated)

H1   B. Hansen, *An Appraisal of Economic Development in Afghanistan—1960 to 1970* (Berkeley: Institute of International Studies at the University of California at Berkeley, mimeo, July 1971)

H2   B. Hansen and K. Tourk, "Three Papers on Price and Trade Indices for Afghanistan," *Economic Bulletin for Asia and the Far East*, 22 (1-2), June/September 1971, pp. 13-24

H3   J. S. Hanson and R. C. Vogel, "Inflation and Monetary Velocity in Latin America," *Review of Economics and Statistics*, 55 (3), August 1973, pp. 365-70

H4   A. C. Harberger, "Some Evidence on the International Price Level" in *International Finance: Selected Readings* edited by R. N. Cooper (Harmondsworth: Penguin Books, 1969), pp. 165-90

H5   A. G. Hart, "Fiscal Policy in Latin America," *Journal of Political Economy*, 78 (4, ii), July/August 1970, pp. 857-89

H6   M. M. Hassanein, *Agricultural Credit under the Second Plan* (Kabul: Ministry of Planning, mimeo, undated)

H7   J. Hawley, *Responses for Mixed Credit Working Group: Afghanistan* (Kabul: American Embassy, mimeo, October 1972)

H8   A. C. Hess, "An Explanation of Short-Run Fluctuations in the Ratio of Currency to Demand Deposits," *Journal of Money, Credit and Banking*, 3 (3), August 1971, pp. 666-79

H9   H. H. Hinrichs, *The Role of Public Finance in Economic Development in Afghanistan* (Washington, D.C.: Robert R. Nathan Associates, mimeo, May 1967)

H10 S. Huddleston, "Europe and Afghanistan," *The New Statesman*, 28 January 1928, pp. 485-86

H11 A. E. Hudson and E. Bacon, "Inside Afghanistan Today," *Asia*, 40 (3), March 1940, pp. 119-22

I1   Institut für Entwicklungsforschung und Entwicklungspolitik, *Proposals for Possible Improvement of the System of Governmental Revenues in Afghanistan* (Bochum: Ruhr Universität, mimeo, 1973)

I2   *International Financial Statistics*, 26 (10), October 1973

I3 *International Financial Statistics: 1972 Supplement*

I4 International Monetary Fund, *Annual Report on Exchange Restrictions* (Washington, D.C.: International Monetary Fund, 1950-1973)

I5 Investment Advisory Center, *Investment Opportunity List: Basic Projects which May Be Feasible for Afghanistan* (Kabul: Ministry of Commerce, Investment Advisory Center, Publication No. 2, 1972)

I6 Investment Advisory Center, *A Survey of Projects Operating under the Foreign and Domestic Private Investment Law (1st Hoot 1345)* (Kabul: Ministry of Commerce, Investment Advisory Center, mimeo, March 1972)

I7 Investment Committee of Afghanistan, *Foreign and Domestic Private Investment Law of Afghanistan 1st Hoot 1345* (Kabul: Investment Committee of Afghanistan, 1969)

I8 *Iqtisad Journal* (Journal of the Chamber of Commerce published from 1310 (1931) in Dari)

I9 *Islah Newspaper*, 4 Qaus 1319 (25 November 1940)

J1 W. Jensch, *Die afghanischen Entwicklungspläne vom ersten bis zum dritten Plan* (Meisenheim am Glan: Verlag Anton Hain, 1973)

J2 H. G. Johnson, *Money, Trade and Economic Growth* (Cambridge, Mass.: Harvard University Press, 1962)

J3 H. G. Johnson, "Notes on the Economic Theory of Smuggling," *Malayan Economic Review*, 17 (1), April 1972, pp. 1-7

J4 H. G. Johnson and Associates, *Readings in British Monetary Economics* (Oxford: Clarendon Press, 1972)

K1 M. A. Kabiri, *Financial Survey of Construction and Transport Sectors* (Kabul: United States Agency for International Development, mimeo, November 1973)

K2 *Kabul Times Newspaper*, 4 Mizan 1352 (26 September 1973)

K3 N. Kaldor, "The Role of Taxation in Economic Development" in *Problems in Economic Development* edited by E. A. G. Robinson (London: Macmillan, 1965), pp. 170-89

K4 Kampsax, *Highway Maintenance Programme—Stage II, 1973-1977: Draft Final Report* (Kabul: Kampsax, mimeo, August 1972)

K5 S. Kanesa-Thasan, "Stabilizing an Economy—A Study of the Republic of Korea," *International Monetary Fund Staff Papers*, 16 (1), March 1969, pp. 1-26

K6 G. C. Kaufman, "Bank Employment: A Cross-Section Analysis of the World's Largest Banks," *Journal of Money, Credit and Banking*, 2 (1), February 1970, pp. 101-11

K7 A. H. Kayoumy, "Monopoly Pricing of Afghan Karakul in International Markets," *Journal of Political Economy*, 77 (2), March/April 1969, pp. 219-36

K8 R. A. Kessel and A. A. Alchian, "Effects of Inflation," *Journal of Political Economy*, 70 (6), December 1962, pp. 521-37

K9 D. R. Khatkhate, "Analytic Basis of the Working of Monetary Policy in Less Developed Countries," *International Monetary Fund Staff Papers*, 19 (3), November 1972, pp. 533-58

K10 J. D. Khazzoom, "Covariations in the Currency Ratio and the Velocity of Money in Underdeveloped Countries," *Journal of Development Studies*, 3 (3), April 1967, pp. 293-306

K11 N. Koenig and H. V. Hunter, *A Wheat Stabilization Program for Afghanistan* (Kabul: United States Agency for International Development, mimeo, September 1973)

K12 D. and F. Kuhn, *Borderlands* (New York: Knopf, 1962)

L1   D. Lal, "When is Foreign Borrowing Desirable?" *Bulletin of Oxford University Institute of Economics and Statistics*, 33 (3), August 1971, pp. 197-206

L2   A. P. Lerner, "The Symmetry Between Import and Export Taxes," *Economica*, 3 (11), August 1936, pp. 306-13

L3   S. Lewis, *Inter-Office Memorandum from Deputy Chief of Mission to Economic Counsellor* (Kabul: American Embassy, handwritten, February 1973)

L4   W. Lewis, *Revenue Requirements for the Third Five-Year Plan* (Kabul: Robert R. Nathan Associates, mimeo, April 1968)

L5   R. G. Lipsey, *An Introduction to Positive Economics*, Third Edition (London: Weidenfeld and Nicolson, 1971)

L6   I. Little, T. Scitovsky and M. Scott, *Industry and Trade in Some Developing Countries: A Comparative Study* (London: Oxford University Press, 1970)

L7   A. Lösch, *The Economics of Location* (New Haven and London: Yale University Press, 1954)

M1   E. Maillart, "Afghanistan's Rebirth: An Interview with H. R. H. Hashim Khan in 1937," *Journal of the Royal Central Asian Society*, 27 (2), April 1940, pp. 224-28

M2   R. P. Manly, *Survey of Fertilizer Warehouse and Transport Requirements in Afghanistan* (Kabul: Checchi and Company, 1972)

M3   R. P. Manly, *Afghanistan: Report and Tables to Accompany Recommended Revised Customs Tariff Based on SITC Codes* (Kabul: Checchi and Company, mimeo, April 1973)

M4   R. H. Marshall, "The Underdeveloped Economy: Some Implications for Central Banking," *Rivista Internazionale di Scienze Economiche e Commerciali*, 18 (3), March 1971, pp. 269-77

M5   E. M. Martin, *Development Co-operation: Efforts and Policies of the Members of the Development Assistance Committee, 1972 Review* (Paris: Organisation for Economic Co-operation and Development, December 1972)

M6   R. I. McKinnon, "Intermediate Products and Differential Tariffs: A Generalization of Lerner's Symmetry Theorem," *Quarterly Journal of Economics*, 80 (4), November 1966, pp. 584-615

M7   R. I. McKinnon, *Money and Capital in Economic Development* (Washington, D.C.: The Brookings Institution, 1973)

M8   A. H. Meltzer, "The Behaviour of the French Money Supply: 1938-54," *Journal of Political Economy*, 67 (3), June 1959, pp. 275-95

M9   A. A. Michel, "Foreign Trade and Foreign Policy in Afghanistan," *Middle Eastern Affairs*, 12 (1), January 1961, pp. 7-15

M10 R. F. Mikesell and J. E. Zinser, "The Nature of the Savings Function in Developing Countries: A Survey of the Theoretical and Empirical Literature," *Journal of Economic Literature*, 11 (1), March 1973, pp. 1-26

M11 Ministry of Commerce, *Afghanistan's Foreign Trade, 1335 through 1342* (Kabul: Ministry of Commerce, Statistical Department, mimeo, March 1965)

M12 Ministry of Commerce, *Afghanistan's Trade Development over 50 Years, 1297-1347* (in Dari) (Kabul: Ministry of Commerce, Special Publication for the Fiftieth Anniversary of Independence, 1347)

M13 Ministry of Education, *Education in Afghanistan* (Kabul: Ministry of Education, 1956)

M14 Ministry of Planning, *First Five Year Plan, 1956/57-1961/62* (Kabul: Ministry of Planning, mimeo, 1956)

M15 Ministry of Planning, *Second Five Year Plan, 1341-45* (Kabul: Ministry of Planning, 1342)

M16 Ministry of Planning, *The Third Five Year Economic and Social Plan of Afghanistan, 1967-1971* (Kabul: Ministry of Planning, 1967)

M17 Ministry of Planning, *Revised Third Five-Year Plan Presented to the Jirga* (Kabul: Ministry of Planning, mimeo, 1968)

M18 Ministry of Planning, *Draft Fourth Five-Year Plan: National Development Plan for Afghanistan, 1351-1355 (1972/73-1976/77)* (Kabul: United Nations Development Programme, mimeo, July 1973)

M19 Ministry of Planning, *A Survey of Progress 1958*, Volumes I and II (Kabul: Ministry of Planning, 1958)

M20 Ministry of Planning, *Survey of Progress 1959*, Volumes I-IV (Kabul: Ministry of Planning, 1959)

M21 Ministry of Planning, *Survey of Progress 1960* (Kabul: Ministry of Planning, 1960)

M22 Ministry of Planning, *Survey of Progress 1961-62* (Kabul: Ministry of Planning, 1963)

M23 Ministry of Planning, *Survey of Progress 1962-64* (Kabul: Ministry of Planning, 1964)

M24 Ministry of Planning, *Survey of Progress 1964-65* (Kabul: Ministry of Planning, 1965)

M25 Ministry of Planning, *Survey of Progress 1965-66* (Kabul: Ministry of Planning, 1966)

M26 Ministry of Planning, *Survey of Progress 1966-1967* (Kabul: Ministry of Planning, 1967)

M27 Ministry of Planning, *Survey of Progress 1967-1968* (Kabul: Ministry of Planning, 1968)

M28 Ministry of Planning, *Survey of Progress 1968-1969* (Kabul: Ministry of Planning, 1969)

M29 Ministry of Planning, *Survey of Progress 1969-1970* (Kabul: Ministry of Planning, 1970)

M30 Ministry of Planning, *Survey of Progress 1970-1971* (Kabul: Ministry of Planning, 1971)

M31 Ministry of Planning, *Survey of Progress 1971-1972* (Kabul: Ministry of Planning, 1972)

M32 Ministry of Planning, *Statistical Pocket-Book of Afghanistan 1350* (Kabul: Ministry of Planning, Department of Statistics, 1972)

M33 A. Mohamed (Khan), "Progress in Afghanistan," *Asiatic Review*, 32 (112), October 1936, pp. 863-66

M34 S. A. Morley, "Inflation and Stagnation in Brazil," *Economic Development and Cultural Change*, 19 (2), January 1971, pp. 184-203

M35 R. M. S. Morrison, "H. M. King Mohammed Nadir Shah-i-Ghazi of Afghanistan," *Journal of the Royal Central Asian Society*, 21 (1), January 1934, pp. 170-75

M36 Mortgage and Construction Bank, *The Executive Committee's Report to the Annual General Assembly on Activities of 1348* (in Dari) (Kabul: Mortgage and Construction Bank, 1349)

M37 Mortgage and Construction Bank, *The Executive Committee's Report to the Annual General Assembly on Activities of 1349* (in Dari) (Kabul: Mortgage and Construction Bank, 1350)

M38 Mortgage and Construction Bank, *The Executive Committee's Report to the Annual General Assembly on Activities of 1350* (in Dari) (Kabul: Mortgage and Construction Bank, 1351)

M39 G. Myrdal, *Asian Drama: An Inquiry into the Poverty of Nations* (New York: Pantheon, 1968)

N1 H. Nägler, *Privatinitiative beim Industrieaufbau in Afghanistan* (Düsseldorf: Verlagsgruppe Bertelsmann GmbH/Bertelsmann Universitätsverlag, 1971)

N2   Nathan Associates, *Planning Study of the Agricultural Sector of Afghanistan*, Volumes I-III (Washington, D.C.: Robert R. Nathan Associates, mimeo, December 1971)

N3   Nathan Associates, *Economic Advisory Services Provided to the Ministry of Planning, Royal Government of Afghanistan, September 1961 to June 1972: Final Report* (Washington, D.C.: Robert R. Nathan Associates, mimeo, July 1972)

N4   R. S. Newell, "Afghanistan: The Dangers of Cold War Generosity," *Middle East Journal*, 23 (2), Spring 1969, pp. 168-76

N5   R. S. Newell, *The Politics of Afghanistan* (Ithaca and London: Cornell University Press, 1972)

N6   W. T. Newlyn, *Theory of Money*, Second Edition (Oxford: Clarendon Press, 1971)

N7   D. G. Norvell, *A Rural Bazaar in Afghanistan* (Kabul: United States Agency for International Development, mimeo, January 1972)

N8   D. G. Norvell, *Agricultural Credit in Afghanistan: A Review of Progress and Problems from 1954 until 1972* (Kabul: United States Agency for International Development, mimeo, November 1972)

N9   D. G. Norvell, *Cost and Returns of Applying Fertiliser to Improved Wheat in Afghanistan* (Kabul: United States Agency for International Development, mimeo, February 1973)

N10   D. G. Norvell, *Markets and Men in Afghanistan* (Kabul: United States Agency for International Development, mimeo, July 1973)

N11   D. G. Norvell and M. Y. Hakimi, *Azim Khan and Associates: A Family of Agricultural Entrepreneurs in Afghanistan* (Kabul: United States Agency for International Development, mimeo, November 1972)

O1   N. Oblensky, *Draft Status of the Da Afghanistan Bank* (Kabul: Ministry of Planning, mimeo, 8 May 1968)

O2   N. Oblensky, *Suggestions to Extend and Attract a Credit System—Long-term Deposits in Afghanistan and Getting Advantages from these Financial Means for the Country's Economic Growth and Development* (Kabul: Ministry of Planning, mimeo, 1970)

O3   B. Olsen, *Background Paper for UNDP Country Programme 1972-76 — Afghanistan* (Kabul: United Nations, mimeo, May 1971)

O4   "Organisation of Bank Millie," (in Dari), *Kabul Almanac 1317*, pp. 123-33

P1   G. F. Papanek, "Aid, Foreign Private Investment, Savings, and Growth in Less Developed Countries," *Journal of Political Economy*, 81 (1), January/February 1973, pp. 120-30

P2   Y. C. Park, "The Variability of Velocity: An International Comparison," *International Monetary Fund Staff Papers*, 17 (3), November 1970, pp. 620-37

P3   Y. C. Park, "Some Current Issues on the Transmission Process of Monetary Policy," *International Monetary Fund Staff Papers*, 19 (1), March 1972, pp. 1-45

P4   G. L. Parker, *The Status of the Industrial Development Bank of Afghanistan* (Kabul: Robert R. Nathan Associates, typescript, February 1966)

P5   G. L. Parker, *Background and Present Status of the Industrial Development Bank of Afghanistan* (Kabul: Robert R. Nathan Associates, mimeo, March 1967)

P6   G. L. Parker, *Central Bank Law Draft* (Kabul: Robert R. Nathan Associates, mimeo, June 1967)

P7   G. L. Parker, *Notes on Meetings with Palmer, December 12, 1967* (Kabul: Robert R. Nathan Associates, mimeo, December 1967)

P8 G. L. Parker, *Factors Affecting Recent Movements of Foreign Exchange Rates on the Kabul Bazaar* (Kabul: Robert R. Nathan Associates, mimeo, February 1968)

P9 H. T. Patrick, "Financial Development and Economic Growth in Underdeveloped Countries," *Economic Development and Cultural Change*, 14 (2), January 1966, pp. 174-89

P10 A. Paul, "Role of Trade in Afghanistan's Development," *Asia Foundation Program Bulletin*, December 1963, pp. 1-5

P11 A. Paul, "Constraints on Afghanistan's Economic Development and Prospects for Future Progress," *Asia*, 29, Spring 1973, pp. 1-15

P12 M. Perlman, "International Differences in Liquid Assets Portfolios" in *Varieties of Monetary Experiences* edited by D. Meiselman (Chicago: University of Chicago Press, 1970), pp. 297-337

P13 T. F. Petersen, *Report to the Government of Afghanistan on the Improvement and Development of Marketing of Table Grapes and Raisins in Afghanistan* (Rome: United Nations Food and Agriculture Organisation, 1972)

P14 L. B. Poullada, *Interview with Abdul Majid Zabuli* (Kabul: American Embassy, typescript, 4 September 1968)

P15 Press Department, *Afghanistan at a Glance* (Kabul: Government Printing House, 1957)

P16 A. R. Prest, "On the Distinction between Direct and Indirect Taxation" in *Public Finance, Planning and Economic Development: Essays in Honour of Ursula Hicks* edited by W. L. David (London: Macmillan, 1973), pp. 44-56

P17 Princeton University Conference, *Current Problems in Afghanistan* (Princeton: Princeton University Conference, 1961)

P18 Public Administration Service, *Ministry of Finance Pay Schedule and Related Problems* (Kabul: Public Administration Service, Report No. 95, mimeo, January 1963)

P19 Public Administration Service, *Government Bonds Manual* (Kabul: Public Administration Service, Report No. 130, mimeo, June 1967)

Q1 A. Qadir (Khan), "Afghanistan Since the Revolution," *Journal of the Royal Central Asian Society*, 17 (3), July 1930, pp. 331-33

Q2 A. Qadir (Khan), "Afghanistan in 1934," *Journal of the Royal Central Asian Society*, 22 (2), April 1935, pp. 211-20

R1 G. N. Rahimi, *Studies on Agricultural Loan Securities* (Kabul: Agricultural Development Bank, typescript, November 1970)

R2 H. Y. Rahmatabadi, "Importance of the Central Bank and State-Owned Banks in the Conduct of Monetary Policy" in *CENTO Symposium on Central Banking, Monetary Policy and Economic Development Held in Izmir, Turkey, April 5 to 12, 1971* (Ankara: Office of United States Economic Coordinator for CENTO Affairs, February 1972), pp. 142-44

R3 J. Raj and J. Filippi, *Industrial Financing in Afghanistan* (Washington, D.C.: International Bank for Reconstruction and Development, Report No. C-37, mimeo, November 1963)

R4 V. K. R. V. Rao, "Investment, Income and the Multiplier in Underdeveloped Countries," *Indian Economic Review*, 1 (1), February 1952, pp. 55-67

R5 V. K. R. V. Rao, "Deficit Financing for Capital Formation and Price Behaviour in an Underdeveloped Economy" in *Essays in Economic Development* by V. K. R. V. Rao (London: Asia Publishing House, 1964), pp. 105-41

R6 P. J. Reardon, "Modernization and Reform: The Contemporary Endeavor" in *Afghanistan: Some New Approaches* edited by G. Grassmuck and L. W. Adamec (Ann Arbor: University of Michigan, 1969), pp. 149-203

R7   Regional Cooperation for Development Secretariat, *Regional Cooperation and
      Development among Iran, Pakistan and Turkey: Establishment of Aims; Progress
      of Activities* (Tehran: Regional Cooperation for Development Secretariat,
      1969)
R8   *Report of the President's Commission on Financial Structure and Regulation,*
      Hunt Report (Washington, D.C.: United States Government Printing Office,
      1971)
R9   E. Rhein and A. G. Ghaussy, *Die wirtschaftliche Entwicklung Afghanistans
      1880-1965* (Bielefeld: C. W. Leske Verlag Opladen, 1966)

S1   B. A. Schiro, *The Statistical System of Afghanistan: A General Overview with
      Guidelines for Improvement* (Kabul: United States Agency for International
      Development, mimeo, 1970)
S2   R. B. Scott, *The North Shamalan: A Survey of Land and People, Helmand Valley,
      Afghanistan* (Kabul: United States Agency for International Development,
      mimeo, August 1971)
S3   R. B. Scott, *Khalaj Market*, Paper No. 1 (Kabul: United States Agency for Inter-
      national Development, mimeo, July 1972)
S4   C. Sérignan, "Le Plan Quinquennal Afghan," *Orient*, 4, 1960, pp. 77-96
S5   I. A. Shah, *Afghanistan of the Afghans* (London: Diamond Press, 1928)
S6   I. A. Shah, "Nadir Shah and After," *Contemporary Review*, 145, March 1934,
      pp. 337-42
S7   I. A. Shah, *Modern Afghanistan* (London: Sampson Low, 1939)
S8   E. S. Shaw, *Financial Deepening in Economic Development* (New York: Oxford
      University Press, 1973)
S9   E. S. Shaw, *Interest-Rate Reform: Impact Effects, Indicators and Smoothing
      Techniques* (Kabul: Ministry of Finance, Financial Development Committee,
      Report No. R/036, mimeo, 10 July 1973)
S10   E. S. Shaw, *Notes on the Development Savings Certificate* (Kabul: Ministry of
      Finance, Financial Development Committee, Report No. R/037, mimeo, 17
      July 1973)
S11   E. S. Shaw, *Resource Mobilization in Afghanistan* (Kabul: Ministry of Finance,
      Financial Development Committee, Report No. R/038, mimeo, 31 July 1973)
S12   T. Singh, "Enlarging the Economic Base for Domestic Savings" in *Public
      Finance, Planning and Economic Development: Essays in Honour of Ursula Hicks*
      edited by W. L. David (London: Macmillan, 1973), pp. 181-88
S13   H. H. Smith *et al.*, *Area Handbook for Afghanistan* (Washington, D.C.: United
      States Government Printing Office, 1969)
S14   J. L. Soerensen, *Planning Highway Maintenance and Improvement* (Kabul:
      Kampsax, mimeo, October 1972)
S15   G. Squire, "Recent Progress in Afghanistan," *Journal of the Royal Central Asian
      Society*, 37 (1), January 1950, pp. 6-18
S16   *Statesman's Yearbook 1932*
S17   *Statesman's Yearbook 1934*
S18   A. A. Strauss, *Industrial Development in Afghanistan: A Forward Look* (Kabul:
      Robert R. Nathan Associates, mimeo, September 1965)
S19   C. F. Strickland, "The Economic Development of Afghanistan," *Contemporary
      Review*, 143, June 1933, pp. 714-22
S20   P. Sykes, *A History of Afghanistan* (London: Macmillan, 1940)
S21   P. Sykes, "Afghanistan: The Present Position," *Journal of the Royal Central
      Asian Society*, 27 (2), April 1940, pp. 141-71
S22   P. Sykes, "Afghanistan" in *Islam Today* edited by A. J. Arberry and R. Landau
      (London: Faber and Faber, 1953), pp. 178-97

T1 F. M. Tamagna, "Central Banking in Development Planning" in *CENTO Symposium on Central Banking, Monetary Policy and Economic Development Held in Izmir, Turkey, April 5 to 12, 1971* (Ankara: Office of United States Economic Coordinator for CENTO Affairs, February 1972), pp. 73-81

T2 G. Thaiss, "The Bazaar as a Case Study of Religion and Social Change" in *Iran Faces the Seventies* edited by E. Yar-Shater (New York: Praeger, 1971), pp. 189-216

T3 The Times, "Afghanistan Today," *The Times* (London), 16 April 1932, p. 11

T4 H. Toepfer, "The Bazar Centres of the Capitals of Three Afghan Provinces," *Geographical Review of Afghanistan*, 10 (1-2), 1971, pp. 17-23

T5 J. F. Trosper, *The Status of Insurance in Afghanistan* (Indianapolis: Indiana University, Division of Business Administration, mimeo, 1972)

T6 Tudor Engineering Company, *Report on Development of Helmand Valley, Afghanistan* (Washington, D.C.: Tudor Engineering Company, November 1956)

U1 United Nations, *Some Considerations for Planning and Management Assistance to Afghanistan during the Fourth Five Year Plan 1972-76* (Kabul: United Nations, photocopy, 31 October 1972)

U2 United Nations, *Afghanistan: Country Programme Proposal for United Nations Development Programme Assistance 1972-1976* (Kabul: United Nations, mimeo, December 1972)

U3 United Nations, "Afghanistan," *Economic Bulletin for Asia and the Far East*, 22 (3), December 1971, pp. 24-53

U4 United Nations, "Deficit Financing for Economic Development with Special Reference to ECAFE Countries," *Economic Bulletin for Asia and the Far East*, 5 (1), November 1954, pp. 1-18

U5 United Nations, *Economic Survey of Asia and the Far East 1954* (Bangkok: United Nations Economic Commission for Asia and the Far East, 1955)

U6 United Nations, *Economic Survey of Asia and the Far East 1955* (Bangkok: United Nations Economic Commission for Asia and the Far East, 1956)

U7 United Nations, *Economic Survey of Asia and the Far East 1956* (Bangkok: United Nations Economic Commission for Asia and the Far East, 1957)

U8 United Nations, *Economic Survey of Asia and the Far East 1957* (Bangkok: United Nations Economic Commission for Asia and the Far East, 1958)

U9 United Nations, *Economic Survey of Asia and the Far East 1960* (Bangkok: United Nations Economic Commission for Asia and the Far East, 1961)

U10 United Nations, *Economic Survey of Asia and the Far East 1966* (Bangkok: United Nations Economic Commission for Asia and the Far East, 1967)

U11 United Nations, *Economic Survey of Asia and the Far East 1967* (Bangkok: United Nations Economic Commission for Asia and the Far East, 1968)

U12 United Nations, *Economic Survey of Asia and the Far East 1969* (Bangkok: United Nations Economic Commission for Asia and the Far East, 1970)

U13 United Nations, *Economic Survey of Asia and the Far East 1970* (Bangkok: United Nations Economic Commission for Asia and the Far East, 1971)

U14 United Nations, *Economic Survey of Asia and the Far East 1971* (Bangkok: United Nations Economic Commission for Asia and the Far East, 1972)

U15 United Nations, *World Economic Survey, 1967—Part I, The Problems and Policies of Economic Development: An Appraisal of Recent Experience* (New York: United Nations, 1968)

U16 United Nations, *World Economic Survey, 1969-1970—The Developing Countries in the 1960s: The Problem of Appraising Progress* (New York: United Nations, 1971)

U17 United Nations Educational, Scientific and Cultural Organisation, *Educational*

Missions—IV: Report of the Mission to Afghanistan (Paris: United Nations Educational, Scientific and Cultural Organisation, 1952)

U18 United States Agency for International Development, *Non-Capital Project Paper: Financial Administration Improvement (Revenues)* (Kabul: United States Agency for International Development, mimeo, September 1970)

U19 United States Agency for International Development, *Near East and South Asia: Economic Growth Trends* (Washington, D.C.: United States Agency for International Development, Bureau for Program and Policy Coordination, May 1972)

U20 United States Agency for International Development, *The Private Enterprise Program, Afghanistan* (Kabul: United States Agency for International Development, mimeo, November 1972)

U21 United States Agency for International Development, *Issues Paper: Afghanistan's Development Program (Reconsidered)* (Kabul: United States Agency for International Development, mimeo, December 1972)

V1   A. Vasudevan, *Deficit Financing, Controls and Movements of Prices in India since 1947* (Bombay: Allied Publishers Private, 1967)

V2   M. G. de Vries, "Exchange Depreciation in Developing Countries," *International Monetary Fund Staff Papers*, 15 (3), November 1968, pp. 560-77

W1   R. J. C. Wait, *Preliminary Draft of a Central Bank of Afghanistan Act* (Kabul: Ministry of Finance, mimeo, 10 July 1968)

W2   G. C. Whiting and R. B. Hughes, *The Afghan Farmer: Report of a Survey* (Washington, D.C.: Robert R. Nathan Associates, mimeo, October 1971)

W3   D. N. Wilber (Ed.), *Afghanistan* (New Haven: Human Relations Area Files, 1956)

W4   D. N. Wilber, *Bibliography of Afghanistan*, Second Edition (New Haven: Human Relations Area Files, 1962)

W5   D. N. Wilber *et al.*, *Afghanistan: Its People, Its Society, Its Culture* (New Haven: Human Relations Area Files, 1962)

W6   A. Wilson, "Inside Afghanistan—A Background to Recent Troubles," *Royal Central Asian Journal*, 47 (3 and 4), July-October 1960, pp. 286-95

W7   W. E. Winebrenner, *Insurance in Afghanistan*, Supplementary Report (Kabul: Ministry of Commerce, mimeo, April 1960)

Z1   M. H. K. Zia, "From Brokerage to National Bank," (in Dari), *Iqtisad Journal*, 220, Saratan 1319, pp. 321-28

Z2   C. H. Zondag, *Afghan Legislation* (Kabul: United States Agency for International Development, mimeo, April 1971)

Z3   C. H. Zondag, *Private Industrial Investment in Afghanistan* (Kabul: United States Agency for International Development, mimeo, 1971)

INDEX

Compiled by Sheena E. Will, A.L.A. and Leonard D. Will

Authors of items in the bibliography are included in the index if the items are cited in the text; page numbers containing such citations are printed in *italic type*. Items given only as sources in notes to tables are not indexed. The letter *t* after an index entry indicates that additional information on the subject appears in one or more tables included on the page or pages referred to. Dates in the index have been given in the Afghan *Shamsi* form; the relationship of these to Gregorian dates is explained in the note on page [xii].

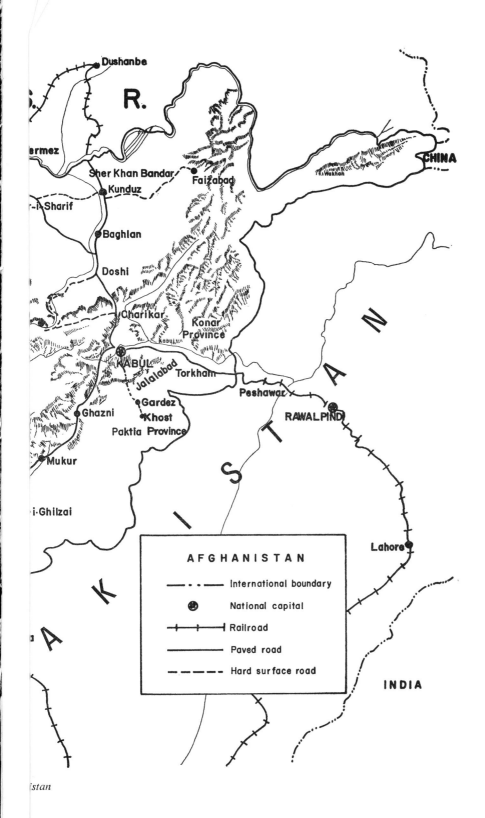

Dushanbe

R.

ermez

Sher Khan Bandar

Faizabad

Kunduz

r-i-Sharif

Baghlan

CHINA

Wakhan

Doshi

Charikar

Konar
Province

KABUL

Jalalabad

Torkham

Gardez

Khost

Paktia Province

Peshawar

RAWALPINDI

Ghazni

Mukur

i-Ghilzai

A
F
G
H
A
N
I
S
T
A
N

P
A
K
I
S
T
A
N

Lahore

AFGHANISTAN

—·—·— International boundary

◉ National capital

|—+—+—| Railroad

——— Paved road

— — — Hard surface road

INDIA

istan